Kurt Weill

By the same author:

The Romantic Tradition in Germany
E. T. A. Hoffmann
The Art of the Minnesinger
The Intellectual Tradition of Modern Germany
Richard Wagner: His Life, Art and Thought
Literature and Society in Germany 1918–1945
Robert Schumann: His Life and Work
Franz Liszt: The Man and the Musician

For Brigitte

KURT WEILL

Composer in a
Divided World

RONALD TAYLOR

SIMON & SCHUSTER

LONDON·SYDNEY·NEW YORK·TOKYO·SINGAPORE·TORONTO

First published in Great Britain by
Simon & Schuster Ltd in 1991
A Paramount Communications Company

Copyright © Ronald Taylor, 1991
The quotations from Weill's music are reproduced
by kind permission of Universal Edition
and the Chappell Music Company.

Simon & Schuster Ltd
West Garden Place
Kendal Street
London W2 2AQ

Simon & Schuster of Australia Pty Ltd
Sydney

A CIP catalogue record for this book is
available from the British Library
ISBN 0–671–71070–2

Typeset in Sabon 11/13 by Selectmove Ltd, London
Printed and bound in Great Britain by
Butler & Tanner Ltd, Frome

Contents

List of Illustrations

Nos 17, 18 and 24 are in the possession of the author; No 14 is in the Lenbach Haus, Munich. The remainder are reproduced with the kind co-operation of the Kurt Weill Foundation.

Preface

'Will the real Weill please stand up?'

Many are still uncertain which way to turn when the name of Kurt Weill comes into the conversation. Do we look to the European composer of 'Mack the Knife' and the *Dreigroschenoper*, Brecht's partner in the *Rise and Fall of the City of Mahagonny* and *The Seven Deadly Sins*? Or to the American composer of *Lady in the Dark*, *Street Scene* and Broadway musicals? And what about Weill the young modernist, writer of highly intellectual operatic and orchestral music we rarely get to hear? Surveying his restless wanderings after leaving Germany in 1933, Brecht described himself as 'having changed countries more often than shoes'. Weill seemed to change styles more often than countries.

These different Weills stand in a chronology but it is not a chronological question we ask. There is a linear continuum within which we accommodate without difficulty the Beethoven of the Opus 2 piano sonatas, the Eroica Symphony and the C sharp minor quartet; or the Schoenberg of *Verklärte Nacht*, *Pierrot Lunaire* and *Moses and Aaron*. We do not play one off against the other. With Weill, it seems to become an 'either-or' situation. People perceive a split in his musical personality which fatally divides the European from the American, the former brilliant and sparklingly original, the latter a sad regression and capitulation to inferior values.

The American composer and critic Virgil Thomson spoke for many:

> It has long been the opinion of this reviewer that Kurt Weill's contributions to the German theatre were more original than anything he wrote here [*i.e.* in America]. His American work was viable but not striking, thoroughly competent but essentially conformist. His German works, on the other hand, made musical history.

This is a judgement of musical quality. But it cannot be understood, let alone accepted or rejected, independently of the successive contexts of time and place out of which this apparently discrepant music emerged – the pressures and conflicts, personal, political, social, aesthetic, to which this remarkable man was exposed over the years of his short creative life.

And what years! Having narrowly escaped military service in the war of 1914–18, he lived through the post-war inflation nightmare in Berlin, rose on the swelling wave of cultural excitement through the decade of the Weimar Republic, fled from the Nazis in 1933 to Paris, then to New York, becoming an American citizen during the Second World War, adapting to each new environment in turn, and ever bobbing to the surface like the proverbial cork. His is a story of survival, a paradigm of the fate of thousands of German Jews who shared with him the first fifty years of the twentieth century, half a century of troubled, tragic history with its own corporate claim on our minds and emotions.

This is the background against which I have set out to describe the course of Kurt Weill's life, to chart his intellectual development in terms of his private and public statements on music, on society, on art and the community and on the social responsibility of the artist, and to examine the substance of his compositions.

He was the very opposite of the flamboyant, extrovert character on whom biography feasts. Reserved and modest in manner, a workaholic, he subjected everything to his art. When, in the early years of their marriage, Lotte Lenya complained of feeling neglected, he was aggrieved. 'But Lenya,' he protested, 'you know you come right after my music.' Nor did music mean only composition. He was a highly conscious musician, conscious not only of what he saw as the context of his music but also of what he held to be the role of art in society and the artist's obligations to that society. Throughout his life – as a young modernist in Berlin, as the sensationally successful composer of the *Dreigroschenoper* and, at the end, seeking to establish an 'American opera' on Broadway – he was at pains to make his socio-aesthetic positions clear.

This inseparability of Weill's career from the society into which it was woven sets the terms of any biography. Tracing his personal fate involves pursuing movements in the political and social climate in general, and taking the discussion into wider contexts which have a life of their own.

Conceived in this spirit of broad relevance, this book is not addressed to specialists. A minimum of technical description is unavoidable and I have included a handful of scattered musical examples that make the point in a way that no amount of descriptive prose can. But I have not been concerned with analysis of technique, or with the investigation of musico-historical issues. Readers who seek a detailed reference book to his oeuvre will find themselves admirably served by David Drew's *Kurt Weill: A Handbook* (London and Berkeley 1987). Rather, I have had in mind those who have whistled 'Mack the Knife', 'Surabaya-Johnny' and the 'Alabama Song' for years and would like to know more about the man who composed them, his life, the people he knew, the things that mattered to him, the works he wrote. I have therefore tried to strike a balance between the description of a life and an assessment of that life's achievements, between an account of physical and psychological events and a discussion of musical works, along with issues raised by these works.

I have drawn as extensively as possible on Weill's own utterances in letters, published articles and interviews, and on the personal testimony, sometimes anecdotal, sometimes critical, of contemporaries who watched him at work – witnesses both of his life and of his times. In this I have been in the privileged position of being able to incorporate a body of valuable material – family letters and early compositions – which unexpectedly turned up in the early 1980s and became accessible only in the last few years.

Every writer assumes that he has something to say which others before him have not. At the same time he is indebted, in whatever measure, to all the predecessors whose work he knows. My bibliography makes explicit the main secondary sources which I have gratefully consulted and to which the interested reader can turn.

First and foremost among the individuals and institutions to whom I wish to express my sincere thanks is David Farneth, Director of the Kurt Weill Foundation for Music in New York. He placed the resources of the Foundation at my disposal, helped me to pursue points of detail and provided the most pleasant of ambiences for the weeks that my wife and I worked in the Weill-Lenya Research Center. Sharing in this congenial atmosphere was Lys Symonette, Musical Executive of the Foundation, whom I should like to thank cordially for her personal insights and reminiscences of Weill and Lenya. And I would not like to leave the realm of personal retrospects without saying a particular thank-you to Mrs Anneliese von Molnár, née Jolowiecz, who sang Jenny in the Kassel performance of the *Mahagonny* opera in 1930, and to the evergreen Maurice Abravanel, from whose mouth it was a joy to hear the vivacious memories of a lifetime's friendship with both Weill and Lenya. Berthold Goldschmidt too was kind enough to give me his personal reminiscences.

The house in East Berlin (Chausseestrasse 125) where Brecht died, and where the Brecht Archive is located, has long been open to the public. But it was an unexpected delight to be invited by the present owner, Herr Kurt Poralla, to visit the private lakeside villa in Grünheide, east of Berlin, where Georg Kaiser lived in the 1920s. Here he and Weill discussed their works for the musical stage, and here Weill first came together with Lenya. A similar pleasure was a visit to Weill's house in Kleinmachnow, in the south-west of Berlin, which was made possible by a chance encounter with Herr Kurt Jordan, resident in one of the two apartments into which the house has since been divided. I am obliged to both these gentlemen for allowing me that special little *frisson* which comes from standing in a place which has made history.

Of the collections and libraries I have used, I wish to extend my gratitude in particular to the Deutsche Staatsbibliothek in East Berlin (Frau Dr Jutta Theurich, Herr Thüringer), to the Music Library of the University of London (Dr M. Baird), to the British Library (especially its Music Library), to the Institut für Theater-, Film- und Fernsehwissenschaft der Universität zu Köln (Dr Roswitha Flatz), and to the Yale University Music Library (Helen Bartlett, Ken Crilly). As always in matters German, the Institute of German Studies of the University of London – with its most helpful librarian William Abbey – and the German Historical Institute in London have been invaluable sources of background material. And for helping me to locate elusive sources of information on Dessau, I wish to offer a special word of thanks to my brother-in-law Wolf-Dietrich Kürschner.

It is also a pleasure to acknowledge the valuable comments on my manuscript, benevolently encouraging and critically salutary, made by my friend Frederic Reynold Q.C.; to record my appreciation of the sympathetic support I have had from my agent John Richard Parker; and to thank my friend David Harman for again having been willing to read the proofs of a book of mine with such care and despatch.

Excerpts from Kurt Weill's letters in the possession of the Kurt Weill Foundation for Music are reproduced by kind permission of the Foundation. Quotations from the correspondence between Weill and Universal Edition are given by permission of Universal and the Kurt Weill Foundation.

Finally a big thank-you to my wife Brigitte, who not only typed the manuscript and prepared the index but also spent many hours with me in the Yale University Music Library and the Weill-Lenya Research Center, poring over letters and documents, sorting illustrations, and drawing my attention to details I might have overlooked or underestimated. I could not have fulfilled my task without her help.

R. T.

CHAPTER I

A Jewish Childhood

Seventy miles south-west of Berlin, a road turns off Hitler's autobahn and heads west towards the confluence of the Elbe and the Mulde. The road is tree-lined and straight but seems in no hurry to arrive anywhere in particular. Copses punctuate the meadowy landscape and marshy vegetation takes over as the sand flats left by the meandering river emerge. In the distance, combine harvesters, tired old war-horses of socialist agriculture, grind their way up and down the patient fields. The scene is tranquil – subdued rather than relaxed.

A crude concrete bridge spans the eighty-yard-wide River Mulde. A sharp turn north towards the town centre and the first brutal confrontation with history: an immense, desolate sandy waste, carpeted with a stubble of mangy grass and scrub. On one side the remains of a stone gateway and a cobblestone courtyard, on the other a battered tower, bricked up and unsafe. Then, in sullen resentment, appears the single surviving wing of a once huge complex, sixteenth century, its roof now open to the elements, gaping wounds in its peeling walls, the grimy ground littered with the detritus of the consumer society – bottle tops, cigarette ends, condom packets, left by a generation for whom such an unreal place has an irresistible romantic attraction. Who, after all, can build such exciting ruins today?

Dessau, 1990, population 100,000. More intimately, all that remains of the great palace of the Dukes of Anhalt-Dessau. On a single day in March 1945 eighty per cent of the town surrendered its life in an air raid. The pock-scarred terrain they left has been made only the more savage by stark new housing estates and office blocks in the preferred style of the New Brutalism.

But it once knew happier days. As capital of the Duchy of Anhalt, it could trace a powerful intellectual tradition back to the seventeenth century. It had excellent theatre and opera. Industrialisation had brought prosperity without destroying its leisurely pace, and it was in the vanguard of progressive German states pledged to the emancipation of the Jews. It is a far cry from the dismal, browbeaten dilapidation of today to the enlightened, self-assured, comfortable Dessau where, a few months into the twentieth century, Kurt Weill was born.

Entry No. 292 in the municipal register of births for the year 1900 reads:

> Today appeared before the undersigned, his identity confirmed by his marriage certificate, the cantor and teacher of religious knowledge Albert Weill, resident in Dessau, Leipziger Strasse 59, of the Hebrew faith, and stated that his wife Emma Weill, née Ackermann, of the Hebrew faith, resident with him, had on the 2nd of March 1900, at four-thirty in the afternoon, given birth to a boy, and that the child had received the names Curt Julian.

The Weills had a long unbroken history to their name, and were proud of the fact. In 1957 an American descendant by the name of Ernest B. Weill published a genealogy that stretched back without interruption to one Judah, born in 1360 in the village of Weil der Stadt, near Stuttgart. When Judah's son Jacob left his birthplace, he added its name to his own, and in time this became regarded as his 'family' name. In itself Weil means simply 'settlement, hamlet', and, like the suffix '-weiler', is a common element in place-names in south-west Germany, where the earliest references to the family name Weil, or Weill, occur.

Albert Weill, Kurt's father, did full credit to the family's long cultural and intellectual heritage. Born in 1867 in Kippenheim, in Baden – the heart of Weill country throughout the centuries – he had been appointed in his early twenties as cantor to the synagogue at Eichstätt in Bavaria. In 1893 he published a collection of chants for cantor and *a cappella* male voice choir. Intended for liturgical use, these are undistinguished pieces, contrapuntally sometimes gauche and harmonically conventional, products of the synthetic fusion of the Jewish melodic ductus with the idiom of the German Protestant chorale. But to have one's compositions published at all, with the blessing of one's ecclesiastical employers, represents in itself a kind of vote of confidence, and the young Kurt grew up in the knowledge that his father not only had a fine voice but could also compose music.

Albert Weill had married Emma Ackermann in 1897, when he was thirty and she twenty-five. They had four children in successive years – three sons and a daughter – all of whom made sound careers for themselves: Nathan, born in 1898, became a doctor; Hanns Jakob, born in 1899, went into the metal business; Kurt arrived in 1900, and Ruth, who became a private schoolteacher, in 1901.

Emma Weill came from a family as pious and intellectual as her husband's. In particular, her brother Rabbi Aaron Ackermann, also a composer of synagogue songs, had become by the turn of the century a leading authority on the music of the Jewish rite, ascribing to this music, and indeed to all art, a metaphysical essence which led to the heart of religion itself. This belief in the power of art, especially of music, to raise the level of man's spiritual awareness and complement the force of religion found its place in Emma Weill's scheme of things, and had its part in the spiritual and moral atmosphere which she helped to create around her children. She was also a woman of firm conviction and principle. Years later, Nathan Weill's wife characterised her mother-in-law as 'seeing things as she wants to, and of course what she thinks and does is always perfect and right'.

In 1898, the year after his marriage, Albert Weill was appointed cantor and schoolteacher to the Jewish community at Dessau. Situated in flat pasture land on a bend of the River Mulde, just before it joins the Elbe, Dessau could trace its origins back to a time between 600 and 900 A.D., when Slavs settled the area from the east. But its substantive history from the modern point of view begins in the seventeenth century when the Dukes of Anhalt made it their capital, building a splendid palace, laying out fine streets and parks, and promoting the interests of culture and education. Moses Mendelssohn, founder of the Enlightenment in Germany, immortalised as the hero of Lessing's drama *Nathan the Wise* was born here in 1729; so too was the Romantic poet Wilhelm Müller in 1794, affectionately remembered today as the poet of Schubert's *Winterreise* and *Die schöne Müllerin*.

Favoured as the town was by its position on the railway line from Berlin to Leipzig and by the proximity of the Elbe, one of the great waterways of Europe, the nineteenth century brought steadily-accelerating industrialisation, from textiles and rolling stock, to breweries and a sugar refinery. Hand-in-hand with industrialisation went a dramatic rise in population – 14,000 in 1850, 27,000 in 1880, 50,000 in 1900, by faith overwhelmingly Protestant – and a blossoming cultural life.

On their arrival in Dessau, the Weills moved into an apartment in a three-storey house at Leipziger Strasse 59. The Leipziger Strasse lay in the south of the Jewish quarter and led in one direction to the Jewish cemetery at the southern end of the town and, in the other towards the synagogue, the Jewish school and the main concentration of the Jewish population. Unlike Prague, Frankfurt, Mainz and many other German cities, Dessau had no ghetto, but over the centuries the Jews had collected in this part of the town with the consent, and under the direct protection, of the ruling Dukes, who, by the standards of the time, ranked among the more progressive of rulers.

Leipziger Strasse 59 is no more. Like its neighbours it survived the bombs of the Second World War but not the dogged determination of post-war planners to flatten all the buildings in the area and erect soulless, prefabricated housing in their place. Indeed, the whole once-proud thoroughfare that was the Leipziger Strasse, designed by Duke Leopold I in the seventeenth century, has been reduced to a few pointless yards of cobblestones leading from nowhere to nowhere – more precisely, from the middle of a housing estate to the backyard of an engineering works.

At the turn of the century, the time when Albert Weill took up his new post in Dessau and his third son, Kurt, was born, the town had a Jewish population of some five hundred. The Jews had first been admitted to the town in 1672, and in 1687 they received permission to build a synagogue and establish their own cemetery. The Age of Enlightenment brought Jew and Gentile closer together through a shared spirit of rational enquiry and the common pursuit of humanistic values. However, it was not until 1848, the year of European revolutions, that the Jews of Anhalt-Dessau received their full political, social and educational rights as 'emancipated' citizens. No longer under pressure to defend their embattled minorities, wealthy Jews showed their willingness to contribute to the welfare of the community in general. The criticism from conservative quarters that this compromised traditional Jewish values was countered by the predication of Judaism as a rationalist religion compatible with the moral precepts of Christianity.

In the inevitable dichotomy between the custodians of orthodoxy and the forces of reform Dessau was in the vanguard of the movement towards secularisation and assimilation. In 1808 its synagogue had been the first in Germany where sermons were delivered in the vernacular. After 1848 the Jewish children who had hitherto followed their own educational path now took their place on the school benches alongside their Gentile fellows. By the end of the nineteenth century the liberalism of the Dukes and the reform-conscious development of the Jewish community had brought about a happy *modus vivendi*, and the new thirty-year-old Cantor Albert Weill, with his young wife and the first of his children, found himself in settled circumstances. A triumphant occasion to celebrate this sense of well-being was the dedication a few years later of a magnificent new synagogue, with an adjoining building to house administrative offices, educational facilities and accommodation for the cantor and his family.

The money for this cultural centre came from a five-million-mark legacy to the Jewish community from Baroness Julie von Cohn-Oppenheim, daughter of Baron Moritz von Cohn – court banker to Kaiser Wilhelm I – and heir to the family banking firm in Dessau. The Baroness died in 1903, having stipulated in her will that the legacy be used for the furtherance of religious activities and education and for the foundation of charitable institutions to benefit not only the Jewish congregation but also the people of Dessau as a whole.

Standing on a prominent thoroughfare, close to its predecessor and to the Jewish school where Albert Weill taught, the new synagogue was built in an eclectic Romanesque style, with a great central dome and an opulent interior which included a large organ. Its ceremonial dedication in February 1908 was led by Duke Friedrich II of Anhalt and brought all the local dignitaries to its doors – civic pride was openly shown to transcend religious differences. Cantor Weill, a neat, stocky figure with a clipped, dark beard, led the first part of the service, singing the antiphonal responses with the choir, while his wife, with the seven-year-old Kurt, his two brothers and his sister, watched from their pew in the gallery.

Like synagogues and Jewish property all over Germany, the building was set on fire and plundered in the orgy of persecution and destruction unleashed by the Nazis in the night of November 9, 1938, the so-called *Reichskristallnacht*. It was struck by bombs in the air-raid of March 7, 1945, the darkest hour in Dessau's seven-hundred-year history, and the ruins were removed in the 1960s. A grassy area now covers the site, marked by a stone column in memory of the murdered Jews of the town and the place where they worshipped. One house nearby, close to the site of the old nineteenth-century synagogue, miraculously survived the Second World War and bears commemorative plaques to the town's two most famous Jewish sons – Moses Mendelssohn and Kurt Weill. But today there is no Jewish community left.

The Weills were a closely-knit family, united by the commands of their religion, though no less by open affection and a grateful sense of security. The outward forms of orthodoxy were observed with the natural strictness of Albert Weill the schoolteacher and servant of his faith, and although he had inherited in Dessau a community on the reformed, liberal wing of the Judaic observance, he retained a tendency to revert to earlier, more conservative values. A pride in the durability of the family tree, and in the intellectual achievements and services of successive generations of Weills, strengthened his trust in tradition. The more keenly, therefore, was he to feel this loss when his son Kurt, under the pernicious spell of Berlin in the 1920s, later drifted further and further away from the family religion to marry eventually outside the faith.

Music played an important role in home life. Albert Weill rehearsed his chants and played through the hymns prescribed for the services. Emma too, perhaps more emotional and more liberal than her husband, in cultural as in personal matters, also played the piano and was a sufficiently skilled versifier to have a religious poem published which was designed to be sung to a well-known chorale melody. From early on Kurt was her favourite. Not that her other children were unaffectionate, unintelligent or in any other way a source of disappointment to her – just that she felt Kurt had something special about him, though special in what way, she could not yet tell.

Many years later, as an old lady of eighty-two, she was asked by her daughter-in-law, Lotte Lenya, to answer a few questions about Kurt's childhood. Weill had died four years earlier, and Lenya, with the intention of writing his biography, had prepared a questionnaire in order to collect information about his life in the period before she had known him. Instead of replying directly to the questions she was asked, Emma Weill launched into pages and pages of ecstatic praise, written in a bold, confident hand, of young Kurt's qualities – how well-behaved he had always been, how popular at school, how consistently hard he worked (not true), how he always got top marks in his examinations (not true either), and so on.

Kurt received his first piano lessons from his father at the age of six. After three years, however, Albert Weill realised that a more expert, perhaps more secular, hand was needed, and a Parisian lady, Madame Margarète Evelyn-Schapiro, was engaged to carry his musical education further. In his Berlin heyday, in the 1920s, Weill had the reputation of being an indifferent pianist, barely capable of doing justice to his own works when he introduced them at the keyboard. Yet we find him as a teenager accompanying singers from the Dessau opera and playing Chopin and Liszt in public, which suggests a firm technical foundation as well as sound musicianship. His brother Nathan remembered that 'while still a boy Kurt used to compose little pieces and was always willing to play to musical people'.

This was music in the personal, private realm. But perhaps of greater impact on Kurt in his childhood years was the all-enveloping experience, visual and dramatic as well as musical, of the world of the synagogue.

Music had a history of fluctuating fortunes in its association with the rituals of the synagogue, from the traditional Biblical chants, eastern in provenance and monodic in essence, sung by the chazzanim, to the polyphonic antiphons, mixed choirs, harmonic conventions and other elements of the modern western tradition. Indeed, the confrontation of the rival worlds reveals itself as starkly in music as in ideology and mores. 'The musician,' as James Frazer put it in *The Golden Bough*, 'has done his part as well as the prophet and the thinker in the making of religion. Every faith has its appropriate music, and the difference between the creeds could almost be expressed in musical notation.'

The secularisation of the music of the synagogue spread steadily through the seventeenth and eighteenth centuries, with the growth of choral singing and the introduction – re-introduction, looking as far back as Biblical times – of instruments, including the organ. The growing penetration of harmony drove out the remaining oriental features in Jewish music, and by the early nineteenth century hymnals for synagogue use had been openly infiltrated by Protestant chorales, including some of the most familiar found in Bach's St Matthew Passion and Christmas Oratorio. An almost bizarre exercise in assimilation was the publication in the early nineteenth century of a macaronic hymn book in which Protestant chorale tunes were provided with Hebrew words, the music being written from right to left to conform to the text.

From the hymnals and compendia of melodies in the family possession the young Kurt, impressionable and quick on the uptake, absorbed the elements of these different traditions in the natural course of his musical education, which drew him more and more firmly into the cultural tradition of Christian Europe. Like Mendelssohn, Mahler and Schoenberg, he was a European composer who was a Jew, not a Jewish composer. But the Hebrew melodies that surrounded him in childhood and youth, like the culture which they expressed, remained a latent, inalienable power in his experience and his memory.

Anti-Semitism in Germany during the half-century of Kurt Weill's lifetime – indeed, since long before that – had never been far beneath the surface of public life. During the years of the Weimar Republic, when the championship of liberal values in culture and politics often lay in the hands of Jewish intellectuals, Jewish interests merged with common European interests, and his Jewishness became effortlessly assimilated into the larger unity. At other times the vicious pressure of political events threw up the image of the Jew as outcast, the Jewish people as homeless wanderers, and his Jewish consciousness reasserted itself. This was to happen on a number of occasions during his years in America, especially in the aftermath of the holocaust, and when passions ran high over the Zionist crusade for the establishment of the state of Israel.

Inseparable, finally, from the substance of this Hebrew music was the ambience in which it was experienced. The synagogue shrouded its worship in a ritual of symbol, drama and music – a kind of Jewish *Parsifal* – which, through its intensity, compelled the allegiance of mind and soul, an allegiance claimed by instinctual response, not by intellectual persuasion. Kurt had a highly developed sense of the theatrical. In his later school years, during the First World War, he put on impromptu performances of Weber's *Freischütz* and other operas as domestic entertainment at a time when public functions were being severely curtailed, and planned to write his own opera on Theodor Körner's high-flown patriotic tragedy *Zriny*. Musical theatre was to become his life. His experience of the *Gesamtkunstwerk* of the synagogue service, during the years he spent in his parents' home, played its own part in heightening his susceptibility to the power of drama.

During the years of his primary school education Kurt attended the synagogue school run by Dr Isidor Walter, chief rabbi of the town, at which his father also taught. Here, in two or three hours' instruction a week, he learned the history of the Scriptures, the tenets of the Jewish faith, the meaning of the synagogue rites, and to read and write Hebrew. At the age of ten, he moved up into the boys' *Oberrealschule* (secondary school) where he studied English and French, together with Mathematics, Latin, History and the natural sciences, in the broad sweep of subjects prescribed by the Prussian educational reform of 1892.

Shortly after the inauguration of the new synagogue in 1908 Albert Weill and his family moved into the ground-floor apartment provided for the cantor in the Jewish community centre that adjoined the synagogue. Emma Weill, on whom fell the practical problems of raising the four children, was delighted to find herself in surroundings so much more spacious than the Leipziger Strasse. Many years later, after settling with her husband in Israel, she could still recall the joy with which she first set eyes on the new apartment. In particular she remembered her pleasure when they bought a grand piano and how her favourite son had impressed their visitors with his playing.

At peace with each other and with the world, the family was held together by bonds of natural affection. The paths along the river banks and the expanse of green fields beyond were a ready source of delight, and Kurt, in particular, loved to go swimming. They also enjoyed chess, a pastime willingly resorted to at times when children were required to be seen and not heard. For all the musical powers at work within him, Kurt had no pretension to behaving differently from any other normal boy of his age, and took no interest in the adult conversation going on around him. But there was no secret about what mattered most to him. As Nathan said, looking back over their childhood, 'Kurt lived only for music.'

As he worked his way through school, doing enough – just – to move up from one class to the next at the end of the year, Kurt found the focus of his external musical interests changing from the religious to the secular, from the synagogue to the theatre. At the centre of the theatrical and musical life of Dessau stood the Court Theatre of the dukes, and it was this theatre that now brought startling new dimensions into his experience of the arts.

Performances of music, opera and drama had been given in the rooms of the palace and in the hall of the Duke's riding school from the days of

Duke Leopold Friedrich Franz – 'Father Franz', as he was affectionately known. But such limited facilities quickly proved inadequate to cope with the flood of works which surged on to the stage from the 1770s onwards, and at the end of the century, one of the day's largest and finest theatres was built across the street from the palace. In 1855 it caught fire and was gutted, but within a year it had been rebuilt on the same foundations. This house survived for almost seventy years and was the one in which the young Kurt Weill had his earliest experiences of opera. In 1922 this theatre too went up in flames, and its successor was destroyed in an air raid in 1944. After the Second World War the Communist inheritors of the town chose to regard this as the *coup de grâce* and made no move to rebuild it. Today a department store and public walkways stand on the site, and only the older generation of Dessauers remember the theatres which once stood here.

Although it put on productions of Shakespeare and the German classics, the Dessau theatre, unlike most others, had always favoured opera rather than drama. In a court such as that of the Grand Dukes of Weimar, home of the German classical dramatists, Liszt was constantly embroiled in squabbles to extract more money for opera and concerts from a management convinced of the artistic superiority of drama. In contrast, by the end of the century, *Figaro*, *Don Giovanni* and *The Magic Flute* were in repertory in Dessau; *Fidelio*, Gluck's *Iphigenia in Tauris*, Weber's *Freischütz* and *Oberon*, and various Italian operas followed, and in the new house, built after the fire of 1855, *Tannhäuser*, *Lohengrin*, *The Mastersingers of Nuremberg* and other works of Wagner were enthusiastically received. In 1872 the Master himself came to the town at the invitation of the director to see Gluck's *Orfeo*, and wrote afterwards: 'Let me state categorically that I have never enjoyed a nobler and more perfect performance in an opera house than this.' The Dessauers basked in this praise for years to come and turned their town into what came to be called, to their no small gratification, 'a North German Bayreuth'.

From the beginning, the excellence of the Dessau opera had owed much to the active interest of successive Dukes, an interest founded not, as in many principalities and duchies, on the ruler's calculated aggrandisement of his cultural reputation but on a genuine desire to be involved in the artistic proceedings. Kurt retained a clear memory of watching from the window of his school, across the street from the colonnaded entrance to the theatre, as Duke Friedrich II regularly drove up from his palace between eleven and twelve in the morning to attend rehearsals.

But he was to come to know the Duke and his theatre far more intimately than from looking through a school window or watching the stage from a seat in the auditorium. It had been clear for some time that Madame Evelyn-Schapiro had taught him as much as she could. Sight-reading, keyboard technique and similar matters of practice and discipline had their value, but his horizons were widening: he was looking to extend his general musical knowledge, to probe the mysteries of musical theory and above all, to acquaint himself with the rudiments of composition. In the earliest published essay on Weill and his works, written in 1925 and evidently based to a large extent on information from Weill himself, Rudolf Kastner refers to his having 'filled many pages of manuscript paper with compositions from the age of ten onwards, without any instruction'. 'He tried,' said Kastner, 'to write down anything and everything that was buzzing around in his head.'

So at fifteen he persuaded his father to let him take lessons with Albert Bing, a Jewish musician who had recently arrived in Dessau as Kapellmeister at the court theatre. Bing, born in Berlin in 1884 to a well-to-do family of coffee importers, had studied composition at the Stern Conservatoire under Pfitzner and conducting under Arthur Nikisch, director of the Berlin Philharmonic Orchestra. His wife, Edith, was the youngest sister of the expressionist dramatist Carl Sternheim, and added her own intellectual background and cultural interests to her husband's gifts as composer and conductor. The Bings were to make a considerable contribution to the cultural life of Dessau and became close friends of the Weill family. As Kurt now began his serious musical studies with Albert Bing, so later, back in Berlin, the Bings' son Peter was to return the compliment and become Kurt's first pupil in theory and harmony.

During the two to three years that he spent under Albert Bing's tutelage Kurt developed at a remarkable pace, not only in the specifically instructional respect that had led him to Bing in the first place but also intellectually and as a person. Through his official position at court, and given the Duke's personal interest in the affairs of his theatre, the new Kapellmeister had a direct line of approach to the ducal family and their entourage and so was able to introduce his young protégé to the musical life of the palace. At a pre-Christmas charity concert in 1915 given in the Great Hall of his school Kurt played a Chopin Prelude and the third of Liszt's *Liebesträume*, and was engaged in the following year to give piano lessons to the Duke's niece and two nephews.

So rapidly had his powers of musical perception and skill in sight-reading developed that Bing invited him to work in his spare time as a rehearsal coach at the court theatre. True, it was an opportunity that would hardly have come the way of a schoolboy in normal times. Europe was entering its third year of war, and the army had already claimed many of the young men, musicians and technical staff alike, without whom the theatre could barely survive. But any public occasion, however humble, implies a level below which no performance can fall without reducing the whole undertaking to a travesty, and if Bing had the confidence to entrust his young pupil with certain tasks, the fact speaks for itself. Sometimes, having attended a concert together, the two would go back to the Bings' apartment, where they would be joined by three other string players; with Kurt at the piano, they played for their own enjoyment, and in their own terms, some of the music they had just come from hearing.

Not surprisingly, within the framework of its music lessons, the school had little to offer to so precocious a talent. 'The singing lessons were rotten', he replied to a questioner many years later. But there were compensations:

> The headmaster of my *Gymnasium* in Dessau and the master in charge of
> the senior classes took a tremendous interest in music and did a great deal
> to encourage my activities. I composed pieces for the school orchestra and
> – something I can barely credit today – even wrote patriotic war songs.

Of the pieces for the school orchestra nothing is known. The two Dessau secondary schools, the *Oberrealschule* and the *Gymnasium*, were housed in the same building and shared certain areas, such as the assembly hall, so that the combined forces of the two schools were available for plays, concerts and the like. With a total of over five hundred boys, ranging in age from ten to nineteen, there was no difficulty gathering a complement of performers for choral and orchestral concerts. In the early decades of the nineteenth century, the school choir was even pressed into service to augment the chorus at opera performances in the court theatre, with boys being taken out of their lessons to rehearse, much to the displeasure of the teachers but to the undisguised delight of the budding stars.

One of Kurt's 'patriotic war songs', a setting for four-part male voice choir of a typical piece of pre-1914 sentimental bombast, '*Ich weiss wofür*' ('I Know Why') has survived. The intrinsic value of the conventional, hymn-like music is scant, although it is always interesting to trace a composer's first steps. But '*Ich weiss wofür*' has another claim on our attention. As one of the very earliest pieces of Kurt Weill's music that we know, it belongs to a group of early manuscripts which only surfaced in 1983; up till then we had been able to do nothing with tantalising references by Weill himself and by others to pieces he wrote while still at school. One of the items in this collection is an harmonically interesting song-setting of Richard Dehmel's '*Die stille Stadt*' ('The Silent City'); another is an even more adventurous Intermezzo for piano, Brahms-like in pianistic manner and full of chromatic experimentation.

In some ways more interesting than the internal musical evidence of these juvenilia is the way they reflect the German-Jewish world in which Kurt was brought up. One is a Hebrew wedding song, another a cycle of settings (in German translation) of poems by the medieval Hebrew poet Judah Halevi, called *Ofrah's Lieder*. He wrote two soprano duets, thickly Straussian in idiom, to poems by Otto Julius Bierbaum, a popular *fin de siècle* poet of the pseudo-folksong. Hebrew rite and Christian poetry are then brought directly and symbolically together in a piece for his sister Ruth inscribed '*Gebet* ('Prayer'). Von Em. Geibel. Zu Ruths Confirmation. Kurt Julian Weill'.

Music may, as Nathan later said of his brother, have been the only thing which Kurt lived for. Sport certainly did not appeal to him. But this did not mean that he denied himself the discoveries and pleasures of adolescence. A photograph of him at fifteen, taken with him sitting at the grand piano in his parents' apartment, shows a trim figure, his full head of dark hair neat and closely-cropped, his lively, wide-eyed gaze absorbed in the music before him. At five-thirty each afternoon, his school homework done, this young man would spruce himself up and set out with his brother Hanns, similarly dressed to kill, in the direction of the theatre.

Here the daily ritual of the *Bummel* took place. In the appropriately-named Cavalierstrasse outside the neo-classical court theatre, the local teenagers would promenade up and down in twos and threes, eyeing each other, giggling among themselves, the boys looking to engage the attention of the young ladies from the *Töchterschule*, the girls playing hard to get or letting slip a sly, properly embarrassed titter of encouragement. It was a game of growing up. Some of his remarks to his sister Ruth, in whom he particularly confided during these years, suggest that his quiet, reserved nature made him more hesitant, more self-doubting than his less inhibited fellows to pursue the company of the opposite sex, but his thoughts strayed in that direction as naturally as those of any young man.

By 1916 the war was striking deep into family life as more and more of the nation's manhood were pitched into the trenches. At the end of that year those who had escaped the clutches of the army by some means or another found themselves caught in the meshes of the Emergency National Service Law which virtually placed the entire male population between the ages of seventeen and sixty at the disposal of the war machine. Those not sent to the front formed a labour pool for direction to armaments, engineering and any other factories. This was total war of a protracted kind to which the Germans, accustomed in their recent conflicts to rapid and decisive victory, were unprepared – politically, economically and psychologically. The public mood, and in particular public morale, now bore painful witness to this.

In 1914 things had looked very different. Apart from motley pacifist and Communist voices crying in the wilderness, the Germans had greeted the outbreak of war with wild enthusiasm and an unyielding conviction of the righteousness of their cause. But when the Schlieffen Plan for the expected *Blitzkrieg* victory was seen to have failed, awkward questions began to be asked about war aims and the ultimate interests of the German nation. Food rationing was introduced early in 1915; the economy became increasingly militarised; the euphoria of 1914 evaporated, and the longer the war lasted, the deeper the cracks became in the pious conviction that the German cause was right, and that God would crown it with victory.

The Weills of Dessau suffered no more and no less than the next family. As vegetarians, they were not affected when shortages led to the imposition of two meatless days a week, but with little butter, and a monotonous reliance on turnip and barleycorn soup for the day's warm meal, the strain could not be disguised. Conditions varied considerably from one part of the country to another. On holiday in Wiesloch near Heidelberg; with their grandparents, the Ackermanns, Kurt and Ruth discovered that the shops had much more food in them than in North Germany. To their delight they even found chocolate – though this was small consolation when the time came for them to go back to Dessau. Their parents' pride made them keep their day-to-day difficulties to themselves as far as they could. They did not burden the children with tales of woe, and Kurt never lost his admiration for the way they preserved the equilibrium of the family.

Nathan was called up for the army in 1916 and sent to the western front as a medical orderly. In spring of the following year, Hanns was drafted too, but a deformity in one of his hands kept him from active service.

Only Kurt and Ruth were now left. Cultural events still offered some distraction from the increasing gloom, and as Kurt wrote to Hanns in his barracks, productions of *Fidelio*, *Rigoletto* and *Hamlet* (with the great Alexander Moissi playing the lead) were still being staged; in particular, he had been overwhelmed by a performance of Eugen d'Albert's opera *Tiefland*.

As to his own music-making, he was studying the Chopin Studies and the Brahms Intermezzi with Bing, and had started instrumentation and score-reading. His public career too was gathering pace. He regularly conducted the school orchestra and a male voice choir, and accompanied performances of vocal and choral music at school concerts, at one of which his two Bierbaum songs were performed. At a recital in Cöthen, as he wrote to his brother Hanns, he had accompanied the Dessau soprano Elisabeth Feuge in the 'Liebestod' from Wagner's *Tristan* and played pieces by Grieg, for which, to his delight, he had received a fee of forty marks and a huge bouquet of flowers. In a touching little P.S. he confides that he is writing his letter during school lessons and had nearly been caught more than once.

The predominant characteristic of school life, however, was tedium. He confessed to Hanns that in his last report he had received a Grade 2 in Mathematics, a Grade 3 in English and another Grade 3 for Conduct – which, on a five-degree scale with Grade 4 reserved for inveterate slackers and Grade 5 for juvenile delinquents, can hardly be called covering himself with glory. Sometimes Ruth would attach a page of her own to these letters, sometimes his mother would add a few lines. It was a family at one with itself – grateful, tolerant, supportive.

Helped by Bing, Kurt's musical education made great strides. As well as his regular piano lessons (he mentions Weber's First Sonata), he started orchestration, conducting (*The Mastersingers*) and score-reading (*Fidelio, Tristan* and *Lohengrin*), took up the organ and began work on a string quartet of his own. All this side by side with the daily school routine – which included Saturdays.

But hanging over him, as his eighteenth birthday approached and the war, though palpably lost, still dragged on, was the fear that he too would be called up. Most of his classmates had already gone. The Americans had entered the war, the winter of 1917–18 was even worse than its predecessor, mutterings of discontent were being heard from the soldiers at the front – there had been a naval mutiny in June 1917 – and civilian morale had reached its lowest ebb. Ruth remembered Kurt asking her plaintively: 'Why must there be a war? Why must they shoot? Why can't people be friends?' Gone were the days when he could be moved to write patriotic choruses like 'I Know Why'. Like most Germans in their sinking ship, he no longer knew why.

One stratagem he contemplated in order to avoid being drafted was to learn the trumpet, so that he could be posted to a military band unit. In the event he resorted to a more reckless ruse. Having been summoned to present himself for medical examination, he swallowed a large number of aspirin tablets the night before, so that when he appeared the following morning, he was sweating, his breathing was irregular and his pulse pounded at an alarming rate. Ruth, from whom the story comes, said that he had taken a hundred tablets and that she sat up with him throughout the night while he put himself through this ordeal.

Had he really taken a hundred aspirins, we would never have heard of Kurt Weill. But wherever the truth lies, the fact remains that, on no other discernible grounds, he was allowed to see out his school career without interruption, then go on to university. The end of the war found him at the Hochschule für Musik in Berlin, and he never saw military service.

Eighteen years old almost to the day, Kurt took his *Abitur* (school-leaving certificate) in March and immediately made plans to leave the town which had become too small for him. Albert Bing had brought a whiff of the metropolis to Dessau, and although there were many other places in Germany – Cologne, Hamburg, Munich, not to mention Vienna – which offered both a vigorous cultural life and the facilities of a large university and a conservatoire, none, at that moment, had the magnetism of Berlin. For Kurt himself it was music or nothing. His parents hesitated, conscious of the uncertainties of a life devoted to music, preferring a broad education in the humanities for their son from which he could embark on a career in law or teaching.

In the end they agreed to a compromise: he would apply for admission to the Hochschule für Musik but also enrol for the summer term at the University of Berlin as *stud. phil.*, an undergraduate in the Faculty of Arts. In April 1918, at a time of national deprivation and hardship, when many would have been happy to cling to the affection and reassurance of a cherished home, the fledgling musician left the warmth of the family nest for the dangers of life in the unfeeling, impersonal metropolis.

At the university he attended lectures by the philosopher Ernst Cassirer and the aesthetician Max Dessoir. Before leaving home, he told Hanns that, like many young men of their generation, he wanted to study the works of Schopenhauer and Nietzsche. But Cassirer's theory of 'symbolic forms' pointed to a totally different conception of philosophy, one hardly calculated to arouse the young Weill's interest. As he went out of the university building in the ponderous Prussian formality of Unter den Linden, however, and made his way through the Brandenburg Gate and the Tiergarten park to the conservatoire in the Hardenbergstrasse – where it still stands today – we may suspect that his step lightened. Once there, he knew why he had come to Berlin.

CHAPTER II

The Lure of Berlin

Germany was stumbling to the end of the Kaiser's war. As week followed despairing week, the only real question became: How could it best be stopped? And how was the little word 'best' to be construed? Did it mean stopping the fighting at all costs and bringing the pride of the nation's manhood back as fast as possible? Or did it imply the invocation of 'Peace with Honour', a noble-sounding, though often mockingly hollow slogan?

For many men in the street, and even more for the women, the peace mattered more than the honour. But the German General Staff had its own answer to the question, and since the moment in August 1916 when the Kaiser had appointed Field Marshal Hindenburg and General Ludendorff to control the affairs of the General Staff, the military had been the *de facto* government of the country. Far from protesting against being governed by army officers, many were relieved to see the destiny of the nation in strong hands. 'Hindenburg will take care of everything', they told themselves, with a strange mixture of pride and relief. The values embodied by the army – loyalty, honour, service, devotion to duty, the virtues encapsulated in the appellation 'Prussian' – held a potent attraction. Strength, unity, tradition, forces sustained by a Romantic idealism and nurtured by the nineteenth-century philosophy of *Geist*, found their communal expression in a highly-charged nationalism.

To those whose political position lay left of centre this nationalism stood for militarism and reaction, the assertion of those very qualities which had driven Germany and Europe into the Great War, and provoked the disasters which the people were now being made to endure. But to the rest – and they were in a vast majority – it represented a patriotism in which they could find a legitimate splendour and dignity. What is wrong, they said, with clinging to national honour and traditional national interests as a sheet anchor in an age of disintegrating values? If we can keep our heads while all about us are losing theirs . . .

And many were indeed losing theirs, looking desperately for something to hold on to, as what only a few years earlier had seemed indestructible lay in ruins around them. The younger generation in particular, resentful and inflamed by a sense of betrayal, was in rebellious mood, though just what their rebellion was set on achieving, apart from the destruction of the discredited past, only a few extremists had the confidence to proclaim.

When the eighteen-year-old Kurt Weill arrived in the imperial capital of this disintegration and confusion, the blood-letting of the war still had six months to run. Here everything was magnified – the doomed defiance of those who looked backwards, the revolutionary ardour of those impatiently determined to bring in a brave new world. Berlin was not just a city, it was a way of life – a larger-than-life way of life. The sky was the limit. But there was a long way to fall.

For the moment, however, he needed to turn his mind to the reason he was there. Finding a room at an affordable rent proved the first problem. Anything between twenty and forty marks a month was the going rate in these pre-inflationary days, and for some time he found himself having to sponge on relatives and family friends. It came as manna from Heaven when, through family influence, he was offered 250 marks a month to train and conduct a Jewish choir – money, he said, which he found absolutely necessary for survival.

Presenting himself in April at the Hochschule für Musik, he elected to study counterpoint, conducting and composition, a combination of subjects which left little doubt about the direction in which his thoughts were moving. His counterpoint teacher was Friedrich Ernst Koch, a fifty-six-year-old composer who had held master classes in composition at the Berlin Academy of Arts since 1901 and been appointed head of the Department of Music Theory at the Hochschule in 1917. Koch's popularity as a teacher rested on his lucidity of thought and an unreserved kindness towards his pupils. One of these, a few years later, was to be the composer Boris Blacher, himself Director of the Hochschule from 1953 to 1970.

For conducting Weill joined the class of Rudolf Krasselt, a younger man who had played violoncello in the Berlin Philharmonic Orchestra and in the orchestra of the Vienna Court Opera, and had been Kapellmeister at the Deutsches Opernhaus (today the Deutsche Oper) since 1912. The practical appeal to Weill of a knowledge of conducting was self-evident. In the first place there is no surer way of becoming intimately familiar with the masterpieces of music than by absorbing the minutiae of the score. The conductor has an overview of the music denied to any member of his orchestra, and thus stands closer to the creative moment in which the music was born.

But over and above this there is for the composer, or would-be composer, the special thrill of knowing that, with musical forces at his professional disposal, he can ensure the virtually immediate realisation of his creative vision. In political and social terms there had been a high price to pay in Germany for the continued division of the country into a mass of separate sovereign states in the nineteenth century, but culturally it presented posterity with an enviable wealth of autonomous theatres and opera houses, offering a ceaseless flow of opportunities to those in the performing arts. Those who desired nothing more than a quiet life in settled circumstances would be content to exercise their talents in a provincial backwater; the more ambitious would make for the excitement of the growing urban centres. What mattered was the availability of openings, at whatever level. And the conductor, with the prospect of preparing stage productions as well as concerts, and perhaps cherishing the secret ambition of eventually performing his own works, faced a particularly rich future.

How far and how clearly the young Weill saw his career in these terms is open to surmise. He later claimed that at this time conducting had attracted him more than composition, and it was to be only a matter of months before he returned to Dessau to embark on just such a career. He had around him the example of men like Mahler, Pfitzner and Richard Strauss, who had learned the craft of handling opera from the orchestra pit, but although in the course of the 1920s he insisted on involving himself in the preparations for the performance of his stage-works, he expressed no desire to conduct them.

In his third subject, composition, he worked under the genial eye of Engelbert Humperdinck, composer of the charming and ever-popular fairy-tale opera *Hänsel und Gretel*. Humperdinck stood firmly in the Wagnerian lineage, and from the moment when he had joined the Master's circle as a young man, he had pledged himself to the cause of Wagner's music. A custodian of tradition rather than a protagonist of reform, Humperdinck nevertheless held the respect and affection of his students, who, compared with their pre-war counterparts, were less in a mood to accept unchallenged the values and adhortations of their seniors.

The three semesters that Weill spent under Humperdinck can hardly be weighed against the three years he was soon to study with Busoni. Yet after leaving the Hochschule, he continued to write about his musical plans to the man who had looked so benignly on his early compositions, in particular a string quartet that Weill had begun shortly before leaving Dessau. And it was Humperdinck who would recommend the young Weill for the post of Kapellmeister in Lüdenscheid at the end of the following year.

In July, his first semester over, he returned home to his parents. Cassirer and Dessoir, he explained to them, were no doubt very enlightening but he did not envisage his future in philosophy. It must be music and nothing but music. With the help of Bing's persuasive pleading they accepted his case, and in September, after the summer vacation, he took the train to Berlin and re-enrolled with his three professors at the Hochschule für Musik.

Although the war was still not over, anxious thoughts were already turning to what the peace would bring. The political situation in the capital was growing vicious. Extremists of left and right were preparing their own battles, and in both camps there were elements openly urging pogroms against the Jews. Kurt watched these developments with alarm. 'When under pressure,' he wrote to Hanns, 'every party uses the Jews as an effective means of distracting attention . . . The mob is just waiting for the call to revolt and pillage, and their favourite target will be the Jews.' He attended revolutionary meetings addressed by the inflammatory Karl Liebknecht and excitedly described the parades of the rival political factions and the fighting that broke out in front of the Reichstag building.

For all that, the firm sense of values he had brought with him from his family environment protected him from falling prey to the intellectual fads of the moment. 'Remember Goethe,' he wrote to Hanns, whose faith in these traditional values seemed to be faltering, 'remember Shakespeare and Beethoven and Feuerbach, remember Faust and Hamlet and the Ninth Symphony and Iphigeneia – then you will feel fine, in spite of the philistines and petits-bourgeois all around.'

Politics also intruded into the otherwise sedate affairs of the Hochschule over the question of its directorship. Early in 1919 the seventy-year-old Hermann Kretzschmar finally announced his decision to retire. The students saw Humperdinck as his obvious successor. However, a cabal of senior staff members opposed to Humperdinck's appointment sent a malicious letter to the Prussian Minister of Culture containing various damaging allegations against him, which so enraged the students that, led by Weill, they took up cudgels on Humperdinck's behalf and lodged their own angry protest with the Minister:

> The letter from the professors and teachers at the Hochschule für Musik contains statements about our teacher, Herr Professor Humperdinck, to which we take the most vigorous exception. We look up to Professor Humperdinck with the respect due to a musician of his stature, a respect hardly merited by anyone else at the Hochschule. We do not know whether any of the authors of the letter has ever studied with our Master, but we have done so for a number of semesters and can assure you that the allegations testify only to the kind of hate and bigotry often directed by petty minds against a great man. Proof of the justification for

our protest is the fact that the entire student body has refused to give its support to the teachers' action.

(signed)
Humperdinck's composition class

The students did not get their way. At the suggestion of the music adviser to the Ministry, the formidable Leo Kestenberg, the Director's post was given to the Austrian composer Franz Schreker, and the authorities shabbily allowed Humperdinck's contract to lapse at the earliest possible moment.

That young Kurt Weill, from a middle-class Jewish background in the provinces, and only in his second term, should have been the one to lead this open protest at so prestigious an institution in the nation's capital has a ring of improbability. Quiet, withdrawn, reserved – such descriptions of him would be more readily recognised than extrovert, demonstrative, let alone aggressive or cantankerous, as the students' action must have appeared. Perhaps it was the first sign of the forthrightness that was to characterise the public expression of views on art and society which marked his early twenties.

Cultural life in Berlin outside the conservatoire made up for many of the dissatisfactions within it. The war had not closed the opera houses or theatres; museums and art galleries had remained accessible, and the Berlin Philharmonic Orchestra had played out its concert seasons. In a letter to Hanns in March 1919 Kurt wrote of a shattering performance of Beethoven's Fifth Symphony conducted by Arthur Nikisch, adding 'but nobody can conduct like that any more'. Schoenberg, Reger, Bruckner's Fourth Symphony and Mahler impressed him. After hearing the 'Resurrection' Symphony, he told Hanns: 'This, I believe, is the kind of orchestral work that offers the richest prospects for the future.' Hanns, who had wide cultural interests and was himself very musical, later invited his brother to give a lecture on Mahler to the Jewish cultural circle in Halberstadt, where he was living.

As to opera, the 1918–19 season in Berlin offered the classical German repertoire from Gluck and Mozart to Wagner and Richard Strauss, together with modern novelties like Pfitzner's *Palestrina* and works by Humperdinck and Franz Schreker. An unforgettable experience was a performance of *Salome* at the Staatsoper conducted by Strauss himself, for which he had managed to squeeze in as a standee in the gallery.

Among the works Kurt is known to have completed during his three semesters at the Hochschule are the four-movement string quartet in B minor, a remarkable display of contrapuntal facility, of which Humperdinck thought so highly; a Suite in E for full orchestra in six movements, dedicated to his father; a cycle of five songs to short poems by Lenau called *Schilflieder* ('Songs of the Reeds and Rushes');

a highly intellectual, modernistic Sonata for Cello and Piano; and, most adventurous of all, a symphonic poem based on Rilke's powerful little prose poem *Die Weise von Liebe und Tod des Cornets Christoph Rilke* ('The Lay of Love and Death of Cornet Christoph Rilke').

It is the list of a precocious talent. The volume of production alone, resting on a fluency that showed itself early in his life and never deserted him, is extraordinary in a nineteen-year-old student whose principal commitment lay in mastering the techniques of his chosen subjects, not in indulging the adolescent whims of an untrained imagination. Not only this, but the variety of genres in which he tries his hand reveals how far-reaching his interests were and how confident he was of finding adequate forms of expression. The firmness of the foundations that Albert Bing had laid could hardly be made more proudly manifest. Nor was the flesh less willing than the spirit. The 'strenuous but rewarding work' on his symphonic poem, he wrote to Hanns, took up fourteen hours of his day – from six in the morning till eight in the evening.

In the atmosphere of post-war Germany, Lenau and Rilke offered an overwhelming emotional experience to the young men of Weill's generation, trying to come to terms with the legacy of defeat and shame which their fathers had bequeathed to them. Nikolaus Lenau, Romantic poet of *Weltschmerz*, presented the world as a vale of sorrows where the only course open to man is that of renunciation and resignation. Rilke's Cornet, a young officer of Weill's own age, rides furiously into the battle after a night of love and, bearing the standard of his regiment, charges the ranks of the enemy in the joyful knowledge that he will not emerge alive. The heady language of this work carried a wartime generation along with it, and as British soldiers took Housman's *A Shropshire Lad* with them into the trenches, so their enemies carried Rilke's *Cornet* in their knapsacks. A few years later Weill returned to Rilke to set a group of poems from the *Stundenbuch*.

Nothing has survived of Weill's symphonic poem, and we know of no performance of it, whether at the Hochschule or elsewhere. The first and only known reference to its music comes in a survey of Weill's works by the critic Heinrich Strobel in the journal *Melos* in 1927. Strobel describes it as reminiscent of Schoenberg's early symphonic poem *Pelléas und Mélisande*, a comparison which probably goes back to an interview with Weill himself. That the *Cornet* is the earliest piece which Strobel mentions also suggests that it was the first of his juvenilia that Weill considered worth including in a survey of his output. As early as spring 1919 we find him telling Hanns that the decisive influence on his generation of composers was the axis from Mahler to Schoenberg, and that he saw in Schoenberg the beacon that was lighting the way for the music of the future. Also hovering on the fringes of this early music is the later Max Reger, in whom he found, still in a tonal context, a contrapuntal exuberance and harmonic versatility that stimulated his musical imagination.

Yet his approach has nothing of the eclectic about it. Indeed, even what we know of these earliest works reveals the highly personal handprint of the composer who was to emerge in the early 1920s with stage and orchestral works of unmistakeable individuality. From the beginning, his ever stricter and more uncompromising modernism, in firm line of descent from Schoenberg, with its points of contact with the surrounding, equally personal modernisms of his seniors such as Stravinsky, Alban Berg and Webern, and his contemporaries Hindemith and Křenek, had its own tone of voice. This makes his works no better and no worse. But it does make them distinctive.

Recognition of Weill's promise came during his last semester at the Hochschule, when he received a grant of 300 marks from the Felix-Mendelssohn-Bartholdy-Stiftung, a liberal Jewish foundation which awarded annual prizes 'for the training of talented and ambitious musicians, irrespective of age, sex, religion or nationality', as its constitution stated. As a beneficiary of the Foundation's bounty, Weill found himself in the company of contemporaries who were to make their own mark on the musical world in the 1920s, among them Artur Balsam, Berthold Goldschmidt and Wilhelm Kempff. But even such a gesture of confidence had not the power to influence the young Weill's view of the future. The Hochschule had helped him on his way, had extended his historical awareness and given him room to practice the techniques of the professional musician. But it had now served its purpose. Alone it could no longer hold him in Berlin, nor could a budding relationship with a certain Fräulein Gartenau, with whom, as he confided to his brother, he went rowing on the Berlin lakes and took for long walks in the Tiergarten. 'You would like her,' he assured him. Unfortunately, the Gartenaus made it clear that their daughter's association with a struggling music student did not, in their eyes, represent a desirable match.

A vision of what might have been led him to write wistfully to Hanns about a friend at the Hochschule on whom the gods had looked with greater favour: 'His example has shown me once again how wonderful it is, once one has found the right person, to get married as young as possible.' It is the desire to perpetuate the sense of security that his family life had given him. But security also needs passion, a passion he equates with the overpowering experience of great art: 'If only I could fall madly in love and forget everything else. I am sure that would do me good. There is only one force which has an effect on me equal to what I imagine love to be like – and that is Beethoven.'

Even his Jewishness sometimes seemed an unjust burden, thwarting his creative powers. 'We Jews,' he told his brother, 'are just not productive. Or when we are, the effect is subversive rather than constructive ... Never will a Jew write a work like the Moonlight Sonata.' Harsh, despairing words that would have shocked his parents, as though he were masochistically using the language of anti-Semitism – Jewish art as a parasitic growth with no national roots of its own, the accusation which Wagner had made in his infamous tract *Music and the Jews*.

So, mainly, no doubt, for reasons connected with the Hochschule and with his emotional uncertainties, but also in response to developments within his family, he broke off his studies at the end of the summer semester of 1919 and went back to Dessau in July to take up a full-time job as operatic coach under his old teacher and friend Albert Bing. It was a reluctant decision, taken only after prospective jobs in Munich, Cologne and Tilsit had fallen through, and after financial considerations had put an end to the idea of going to Vienna to study with Schoenberg. Hanns had offered to help tide him over in Berlin but he was always loath to accept hand-outs, generous though he himself was in helping others when he was in a position to do so.

The harmonious family in which Kurt had grown up had inevitably begun to disperse. Nathan had returned safely from the war and was studying medicine at the University of Leipzig. Hanns had gone into business in the historic town of Halberstadt, on the fringes of the Harz Mountains, fifty miles to the west. Only Ruth was still at home. And Cantor Weill himself was on the point of losing his position to the post-war financial pressures that forced the synagogue to dispense with his services. Kurt's return to Dessau, in certain respects a retrograde step at this moment in his career, would at least help his parents over a difficult period until his father found a new position, not that easy for a man turned fifty.

In retrospect, Weill's career as a composer seems to have emerged with an almost providential immediacy from the union of the three courses of study he had followed at the Hochschule in Berlin. From Humperdinck's classes in composition had come the joy of flowing melody and a grasp of what constituted dramatic effectiveness on the stage – popular appeal in the best sense – reinforcing the fascination that opera and stage music already held for him. The disciplines of counterpoint to which he was submitted by Koch, issuing in a sometimes forbidding intellectualism and a modern conquest of form, were to dominate the works that established his eminence among young avant-garde composers over the coming years. And finally Krasselt, with his years of experience at the Deutsches Opernhaus, turned his young pupil's mind to the practical realities that bore upon the problem of converting private ideas on paper into a public musical experience. It is as though Weill, the student, had faithfully preserved the thoughts that had been passed on to him by his teachers and brought them into play when the occasion called.

What the occasion now called for, as he found himself in the familiar circumstances he had left barely a year ago, was the application of his practical skills to the preparation of the operatic repertoire at the Friedrich-Theater, as the Duke's Court theatre was called in the new republican age.

He worked enthusiastically under Bing, rehearsing chorus and solo-ists, preparing them for their cues, acting as conductor's assistant and attending to the numerous small chores involved in the operatic productions. He also celebrated his return with a recital in the opera house, in which he accompanied Elisabeth Feuge in a mixed programme of operatic arias and Lieder, including two items of his own. A notice of the recital in a local paper reported enthusiastic applause from a large audience, although he himself remembered the occasion rather differently, telling Hanns that the 'severe modernity' of his songs (one of which was probably Dehmel's 'Die stille Stadt') had baffled his listeners.

Only a few weeks after Weill and Bing had started work together on the new season's repertoire, the peace was disturbed by the unexpected appointment of a new and ambitious Kapellmeister from Leipzig as music director. Hans Knappertsbusch was a man of thirty-one and had his sights set high as a conductor; in 1922 he succeeded Bruno Walter in Munich, spent the years of World War II at the Vienna Staatsoper, then returned to Munich after the war, where he reached the peak of his reputation, above all as a conductor of Wagner. By the 1950s, the time of his regular engagements at the Bayreuth Festival, he had evolved a ponderous view of Wagner's works which provoked the quip: 'Knappertsbusch doesn't beat time, he beats eternity.'

Whatever he beat in Dessau, Knappertsbusch stayed there less than three years. But where Bing seemed content to accept the situation under Knappertsbusch, the ambitious Weill felt cramped and unfulfilled. His parents and his sister Ruth had now left the family home adjoining the synagogue and moved to Leipzig, where Albert Weill had been appointed director of an orphanage run by B'nai B'rith, the Jewish fraternal society. So when in December, on the recommendation of Humperdinck, Kurt was offered the post of conductor of the orchestra at the theatre in Lüdenscheid, in Westphalia, he accepted without hesitation.

Lüdenscheid, a small industrial town south of Hagen, was barely half the size of Dessau. But its recently established municipal theatre offered the new Kapellmeister a variety and freedom of activity that more than compensated for the superior facilities of the Friedrich-Theater. And when the principal Kapellmeister left at the beginning of the New Year, Weill became responsible for the musical side of the whole range of productions that a town like Lüdenscheid was expected to mount, from Wagner's *Fliegender Holländer* through *Cavalleria Rusticana* and Flotow's *Martha* to operettas like Johann Strauss' *Zigeunerbaron*.

A young man thrown in at the deep end like this and expected to guide his players and singers through so varied a repertory, must needs possess a high order of musicianship, swiftness of perception and power of adaptability. And the more modest the musical forces at his disposal, the greater the need for these qualities in the conductor. In this sense, the baptism of fire in this undistinguished little town tempered Weill's mind and imagination as a man of the theatre. And although his engagement there came to an end in the summer of 1920, he later said, gratefully: 'That was where I learned everything I know about the stage.'

Nor was the relationship one-sided, for the inhabitants of Lüdenscheid gained as much from their young Kapellmeister as he from them. He conducted at least five performances a week, each week containing one new work. If, as not infrequently happened, certain members of the orchestra failed to turn up, he had to improvise the reallocation of the missing parts to other instruments, while treating his cantankerous troupe of singers with a firmness and tact characteristic of one twice his age. 'I can tell you without putting on airs,' he wrote to his sister Ruth, 'that I have really achieved something here. After every performance the director assures me that whatever operetta it was has never sounded better.' A special triumph was *Die Fledermaus* – 'by the unanimous verdict of critics, audience and management alike the best performance of the season so far', he proudly told his parents.

Such reassurances, he knew, were what they looked for. His letters to them have a warm, honest tone, the tone of a young man who loves and respects his parents but can never completely forget their disappointment, usually tactfully concealed, at his lapse from the faith of his forefathers. Albert Weill writes as the earnest Jewish paterfamilias, solicitous of his son's moral well-being while preserving a benevolent awareness of the generation gap; Emma is usually content to add a phrase or two of conventional greeting to her son at the end or in the margin.

To his sister Ruth, however, Kurt confided far more, both of his private thoughts and of his artistic hopes. He is contemplating, he writes to her from Lüdenscheid, a work dealing with some great human problem embodied by a Biblical figure such as Job or Ahasuerus, the Wandering Jew – a kind of gigantic *Gesamtkunstwerk* in which what cannot be expressed in words will be expressed in music. 'Let us allow life, in all its divine beauty, to flood our being,' he cries. 'Let us give thanks to our Creator every moment for the gift of life and rejoice over every little ray of light. Joy is all – so is creation and contemplation.'

And from this self-induced, trance-like state he drew for himself the consequences which he knew she would understand:

> I have been here all alone in my room the past few days. . . . It is a solitude that I have sought, for it alone brings me satisfaction, allowing me to savour the moment and listen as the rain of time slowly falls. Life is short, and one minute is more precious than a thousand dollars. There is so much to imbibe, so many problems to grapple with, where no book can provide the answers.

Not that he was heading for the self-denying life of a recluse. 'Have you not got among your pupils,' he slily asked Ruth, who was a schoolteacher, 'some girl who would make me a decent wife? My terms – extremely pretty, extremely stupid, unmusical, with a dowry of a million marks.' The daily *Bummel* after school had left its mark.

Although it was in Lüdenscheid that he discovered his bent for musical theatre, it irked him that his duties left him so little time for composing. 'If theatre life would only allow me more time and leisure for my own writing,' he told Ruth, 'I would be able to complete the one-act piece by Ernst Hardt' – a reference to a Romantic tragedy of passionate intrigue and incestuous love called *Ninon de Lenclos*. Weill waxed enthusiastic about the poetic language of Hardt, a contemporary dramatist, poet and novelist who had considerable success with reinterpretations of legendary and historical subjects, and who, he thought, could provide him with an ideal libretto. But nothing came of the idea, nor, it seems, of the plan for another opera, based on Hermann Sudermann's sentimental naturalistic novel, *Das hohe Lied* ('The Song of Songs').

There is no music to write about where *Ninon de Lenclos* and *Das hohe Lied* are concerned. There is not even a libretto. But plans, too, albeit never realised, can reveal an artist's interests and predilections, and unusual links can form. Who could have foreseen, for example, that Ernst Hardt, who in the course of the 1920s turned from Romantic symbolism to the promotion of left-wing social drama, would reappear in Weill's life as producer of the radio cantata *Der Lindberghflug* in 1929? And although *Das hohe Lied* never became an opera, its Old Testament Jewish context embraced the choral fantasia for soprano, women's voices and orchestra called *Sulamith*, which Weill composed in the autumn of 1920.

In his 1927 survey of Weill's career, Heinrich Strobel points to Debussy and early Schoenberg as influential forces in the background of Weill's early musical experience, and describes *Sulamith* as 'impressionistic', with broad, expressive melodic lines and a severe contrapuntal manner, breaking the mould of conventional tonality. Nothing survives of the piece today save parts of a draft in short score but they are sufficient to confirm the onward march of free tonality and dissonance in his music.

At the end of the summer of 1920, after conducting the Lüdenscheid opera in its summer season on the North Sea island of Norderney, Weill returned to his parents in Leipzig, uncertain of his future. He divided his time between conducting local choral societies, giving lectures, accompanying vocal and instrumental soloists, and composing – a typical patchwork of activities for a musician who, while by no means just marking time, had yet to make up his mind whether to spread his energies over a variety of fields or to commit himself to one, as yet unstated, all-consuming pursuit.

One of his public appearances at this time was at a recital in Halberstadt organised by his brother Hanns on behalf of the Behrend-Lehmann-Verein, the local Jewish cultural association. The entire evening consisted of twentieth-century music – songs sung by the Dessau soprano Elisabeth Feuge and piano pieces played by Weill, who was described on the handbill as 'Herr Kapellmeister Kurt Weill – Leipzig'. He played two pieces by Max Reger and two Preludes to operas by Franz Schreker and Pfitzner; Elisabeth Feuge sang works by Reger, Joseph Marx, Pfitzner and Weill himself, ending with Tove's love-song from Schoenberg's *Gurrelieder*. It was a programme of unashamedly strenuous music. So to prepare the audience for what awaited them, he opened the evening's proceedings with what the programme called 'Introductory Remarks'.

We have grown accustomed to the self-justifying programme note in which a composer – or a painter or a sculptor, for that matter – describes what was in his mind as he worked, and acts the role of tourist guide through his opus, drawing our attention now to this point of interest, now to that. The provision of an introductory commentary to a piece of music began in the age of Romanticism, when, for example, it was thought that the literary or pictorial 'programme' from which the work had issued – Schumann's *Carnaval*, say, or Liszt's symphonic poems – needed to be made explicit. And although any piece of music ultimately stands or falls on purely musical criteria, we readily accept the usefulness of knowing in advance who Till Eulenspiegel was, or what was associated with the castle of Tintagel. But when a work of 'abstract' or 'absolute' music, so called, is subjected to the same pre-performance treatment, it seems tantamount to an advance vote of no-confidence in the ability of the music to speak on its own behalf. A work of art cast in the form of notes is thought to require an accompanying explanation, or justification, in the form of words.

We do not know how deep Weill went into such analytical matters but we can imagine that, with his challenging programme of pieces before him, he directed his 'introductory words' towards describing the advance of chromaticism in the years since the death of Wagner and Liszt, and the consequent disintegration of the tonal system most radically exploited by Schoenberg. He might also have 'explained' the non-tonal nature of his own two songs in the programme by referring to his 'struggles to find new harmonic and melodic means of expression', as he later described these years. Perhaps he thought he could help the audience to avoid the disgruntled sense of alienation provoked by the 'severe modernity' of his songs, as he had called it when he and Elisabeth Feuge had performed them in Dessau six months earlier.

Although Weill was to claim years afterwards that his season in Lüdenscheid had fired his inner commitment to musical theatre as his true *métier*, his actions at the time took him elsewhere. For stronger than the attraction of the theatre at this moment was the feeling that the development of his musical consciousness and his creative personality demanded a challenge from without, the personal influence of a commanding figure who could both question his motives and stimulate his powers. It was a demand acknowledged by a whole generation, and Weill, looking back a few years later, felt entitled to speak in their name:

> After the defeat of Germany we young musicians too were filled with new ideals, aflame with new hopes. But we were not capable of giving shape to the new values which we so earnestly sought, or of finding the proper form for our content. We snapped the chains that bound us but did not know what to do with the freedom we had won. We broke new ground but forgot to glance back. So as a result of being cut off from the outside world for so long we suffered from paroxysms of emotional intemperance which descended on us like nightmares but which we nonetheless held so dear because they had brought us liberation.

Waiting in the wings, poised to bring order into this chaos, was one of the most curious, most enigmatic characters in the history of music, a powerful personality who changed the course of Weill's musical life as the young ex-Kapellmeister stood on the threshold of his fame.

CHAPTER III

Busoni and His World

If one only knows Busoni as a musician, one does not know him. (And who knows him as a musician?)

        – Alfred Einstein

It is a far from rhetorical question that the critic Alfred Einstein asks. That Busoni was a virtuoso pianist; that he made arrangements for piano of Bach's organ music as the well-known composer 'Bach-Busoni'; that he wrote a treatise on the aesthetics of music; that he composed a handful of large-scale works, so few in number as to be familiar by name to most concert- and opera-goers, whether or not they have actually heard them – this would seem to provide at least a basis for an answer. But who *knows* him?

Part of the enigma – for us, that is, not for him, for he never saw himself as other than a Tuscan – lies in his cosmopolitanism, a cosmopolitanism close to caricature. Born near Florence, his father an itinerant Italian clarinet player of Corsican origin, his mother a pianist, part Italian, part German, by the time he was twenty-four he had lived in Vienna, Graz, Bologna, Leipzig, Berlin, Helsinki and Moscow, where he married his Swedish wife. After three years in the United States he settled in Berlin, which after 1894 became the centre to which he generally returned from his wide-flung tours as a concert pianist, and where, after spending the war years in Switzerland, he made his home for the last years of his life.

The course of Busoni's professional life ran uncannily close to Liszt's – and he both recognised and cultivated the parallels. Both men founded their early fame on their careers as virtuoso pianists, and in technique and approach Busoni belonged to the Lisztian school. He had met Liszt in 1877 as an eleven-year-old schoolboy and later became a friend of Liszt's pupil Bernhard Stavenhagen, who took over the master classes in Weimar after Liszt's death and was succeeded in this role by Busoni in 1900. As Liszt abandoned the glamorous life of the international star in his thirties and devoted himself to composing, so Busoni, though, clinging to his performing career until within ten years of his death, also increasingly sought time to compose and to reflect on the nature of music – above all – on the music of the future. From their sense of the power of the keyboard sprang their magnificent piano transcriptions – Liszt's of Berlioz, Schubert, Wagner and others, Busoni's of Bach. And – to match Liszt's pursuit of the music of the Hungarian gypsies Busoni took up the folk-songs of the North American Indians.

But perhaps the most far-reaching affinity between the two men lay in their activity as teachers, in their urge, virtually their need, to communicate the principles, theoretical and practical, that they wished to see guide and enlighten the younger generation. Intensity and conviction sustained them, as did a sympathy and generosity, a liberality of spirit, linked to a critical personal involvement in the intellectual and emotional development of those they had agreed to accept into their circle. For their part, the disciples gathered at the feet of the master and took from the experience a set of ideals and values, a sense of direction, a self-confidence born of sharing the aura of inspiration which emanated from the master's presence.

Yet whereas Liszt produced an endless stream of compositions throughout his life – over-produced, many might say – Busoni seemed to have to wrench his works from his mind in a process of intense strain, almost agony. This leads to the heart of his creative personality, the essence of the impressive but less than fully convincing uniqueness that gives him his strangely equivocal position in the history of music. Critic after critic writes about the significance of *Arlecchino, Turandot* and *Doktor Faust* but an increased familiarity with these works does not appear to have made them more accessible, more welcoming, more evocative of an emotional response on our part.

And in a way this is almost as Busoni himself wished it. Like Schoenberg, Hindemith, Křenek and many others, including Weill, he put pen to paper in order to make explicit his answers, or partial answers, to the perennial questions: What is the nature of music? What are its aims? What is the relationship between creation and reception – i.e. How does the artist communicate with his public, and how is this public constituted – or maybe he does not see art as communication at all? And finally, How does he evolve a style, a language, which shall be the practical correlative of his responses to these aesthetic problems?

Busoni struggled for many years to give his aesthetic final form. The earliest substantial manifestation of that form came in the first, private edition of his *Entwurf einer neuen Ästhetik der Tonkunst* ('Outline of a New Aesthetics of Music'), published in 1907, but in his restless intellectual way he almost immediately set about revising and extending it, and it was not until 1916 that the second and definitive edition appeared. He dedicated it to Rilke, whom he apostrophised as 'the musician in words'.

In a spirit akin to that in which E.T.A. Hoffmann, Schopenhauer and other nineteenth-century Romantics saw music as the purest expression of the meaning of the world, Busoni seeks the absolute music 'which pervades the universe', rejecting as relativistic the historicist approach and all assessment of the achievements of the past. Not even Bach and Beethoven achieved this absoluteness, and since the historical perspective is false, nothing less than the creation of a new abstract totality, based on unconfined technique and a limitless range of harmonies, can fulfil our needs. 'Harmony as we know it today,' he proclaims, 'will not be with us much longer. Everything testifies to a transformation and a next step.'

And as the theorist, so the composer. What Busoni the pioneer meant to those who opened their minds to his influence was recalled by Weill in an article written two years after Busoni's death:

> Busoni sought the quality of wonder. His music needed to free itself from the confinement of Classical forms, from the stifling restrictions of tonality. So he moved steadily onwards along the laborious path followed by music in the first two decades of this century. As creator and performer, composer and interpreter, he was a proponent equally of impressionism as of the succeeding movement of complete detachment, finally achieving his supreme goal in the 'New Classicality' that he created – a synthesis of modern achievements with whatever can be profitably taken over from earlier generations.

The concept of synthesis, in terms of which Weill here characterises the work of the mature Busoni, can carry one a long way in a review of trends and fashions in European music in the early twentieth century, both before and after the Great War. It is also a concept, embracing many different kinds of novelty, from the far-reaching to the trivial, that has a constant relevance to the music of Kurt Weill himself.

Like many others from the arts – the cabaret balladeer and dramatist Frank Wedekind, novelists like Stefan Zweig, Franz Werfel and James Joyce, the poet Ivan Goll, the actress Tilla Durieux – Busoni had sought refuge from the war in Zurich. Among the many who, seeing him for the first time, could never forget the experience, was a nineteen-year-old girl from Vienna, a drama and ballet student at the Stadttheater, who was to find that the memory held more than passing interest. 'Busoni's attitude at the piano was very special,' she recalled. 'His long, beautiful hands seemed to belong more to the keyboard than to his body. He created a sort of stillness. I only remember one other pianist who made a similar impression on me, and that was Schnabel.' The girl called herself Lotte Lenya. Nine years later she became Mrs Kurt Weill.

Safe haven though it was, Switzerland had an alien sense of confinement about it which the Zurich Stadttheater and the Cabaret Voltaire, home of the then rampant Dadaists in the city, did not have the power to offset. So when in 1919 the prospect was put before him of a return to Berlin, Busoni needed little persuasion. Specifically, the prospect took the form of an invitation to conduct a small and exclusive master class in composition at the Prussian Akademie der Künste: the teaching term would cover six months, leaving the other half of the year free for him to travel at will, and classes would be held at his convenience in the lofty first-floor apartment above a wine restaurant at No. 11 Viktoria-Luise-Platz, in the Tiergarten district, which had been his Berlin home since 1913.

Busoni's contract provided for him to give two classes per week to a group of six students, whom he himself would select from those who approached him. The tuition was free, Busoni, as a public servant, receiving a stipend from the Prussian state. Three of the six – Luc Balmer from Bern, Robert Blum from Zurich and Walther Geiser from Basel – guaranteed their places by following in the Master's retinue from Zurich, where they had already been studying with him, and brought their inflation-proof Swiss currency with them. The fourth was Erwin Bodky, whom Busoni inherited from the master class of his predecessor Richard Strauss, and the fifth was the prolific Vladimir Vogel, who had arrived in Berlin from Moscow two years earlier, 'a headstrong Russian who always wants to be in the right but who accomplished little', as Busoni none too gently characterised him.

The last to join the group was described by Busoni as 'a very fine little Jew, who will certainly make his mark and has already become something of a factotum around the house'. This 'very fine little Jew', having read that Busoni was returning to Berlin, had left his parents' house in Leipzig towards the end of 1920 and taken up residence again in the capital in order to study with the Maestro. Busoni's caretaker had been instructed to turn all visitors away but Weill managed to leave a composition for his inspection, accompanied by a request to be admitted to the master class. Busoni was impressed, and for the next three years the development of Kurt Weill's musical personality owed its direction primarily to Busoni's guidance – 'the invisible leader of European musical life', Weill called him.

The critic Rudolf Kastner, also a member of the Busoni coterie, was struck by Weill's personality and by his special relationship to his teacher:

One afternoon Busoni introduced me to a quiet little man some twenty years of age. Behind his spectacles his eyes glistened like two twinkling stars. As we talked, he emerged as a remarkably serious person, purposeful and with a strong personality. After he had left us, Busoni spoke of him with great affection – indeed, he nurtured him as a gardener, like a loving father, shows his devotion to a blossom or a tree. It also fell to Weill to experience to the full the happiness and the grief of being with Busoni through the sad years of his suffering and at the moment when he departed this life. . . . When Busoni went from us, the closest disciples he left behind, in the musical and spiritual sense, were Jarnach and Weill.

In contrast to what the high intellectualism and aestheticism of many of Busoni's theoretical writings, matched by the earnestness of his young acolytes, would invite one to expect, his sessions at the Viktoria-Luise-Platz had a casual, mildly chaotic air about them. He did not 'teach' in the conservatoire sense. He held court, surrounded not only by those who had officially applied for the privilege but also by others, poets, painters and scholars among them, whom his magnetic personality attracted. One such 'outsider' was Dimitri Mitropoulos, at this time set on making his mark as a composer, later to become conductor of the Minneapolis Symphony and the New York Philharmonic. Another was Ernst Křenek, a precise contemporary of Weill's who, a few years later, was to score a scandalous hit with his jazz opera *Jonny spielt auf*. It was an odd scene that Křenek recalled:

> The composer sat between a fortune-telling mystic and, for good luck, like Verdi's Prince of Mantua, a hunchback. . . . This strange trinity was separated from the guests by a row of chairs. Busoni did all the talking and was never less than brilliant. Coffee was served regularly but once we were given *Sekt,* which had not been paid for; even as we were drinking it, the merchant [from the wine restaurant below] pounded on the door demanding his money.

The pianist Artur Schnabel painted a similarly bizarre picture, while assessing the participants with a more sceptical eye:

> Busoni had a great affection for freakish people; he felt a kind of sympathy for them. Every day after lunch he had his group for two or three hours – a strange collection, not very gifted either. He was very good to them. Yet with a kind of devilish glee he would tell them the most absurd things about music which he simply invented. They accepted blindly all these fantasies, and would afterwards spread them as the last word in music.

As Busoni affected the life of an aristocrat, despising money and squandering it when he had it, so he also saw art as the privileged domain of the few, a world which by its nature must remain inaccessible to the masses. 'In matters of art,' he wrote to his biographer Gisella

Selden-Goth, 'my feelings are those of an autocrat. I am convinced that there has to be a great barrier between the public and a great work of art.'

There was, of course, more practical substance to the sessions in Viktoria-Luise-Platz than the roguish accounts of Křenek and Schnabel suggest. In discussions of opera, for example, Busoni put forward his argument for a return to a pattern of closed numbers with self-contained musical values, as in Handel. Other class meetings were given over to orchestration, where one of his procedures was to take a piano reduction of, say, a section of a Mozart symphony and have his students score it without reference to the original, then compare the results. Or he would dictate a fugal subject and discuss the resulting compositions when the class next met. In the practice of counterpoint, austerity and openness of texture were cultivated, a polyphony of clarity and firm contours, not of luxuriance and self-indulgence.

To put flesh on to his arguments, so to speak, Busoni once took his entire class to Weimar, at his own expense, to attend a concert of the kind of contemporary music he considered beneficially stimulating for them. The concert, as Vogel recalled in his memoirs, consisted of Busoni's Five Short Polyphonic Pieces, played by his star piano pupil Egon Petri, Hindemith's song cycle *Das Marienleben* (to poems by Rilke), Křenek's Concerto grosso and Stravinsky's *L'Histoire du Soldat*.

But whatever knowledge and technical skills may have been acquired through such exercises, the profoundest value of the classes still lay in the unquantifiable realm of stimulus, of encouragement, of participation in the stream of consciousness of an inspiring mind, and in the process of artistic creation. It was not the 'what' that mattered but the 'how'. 'Today,' wrote Weill in 1925, 'composers of all classes are still under the spell of the principles which the dying Busoni set forth.'

In the same essay he describes Busoni's 'New Classicality' as 'a synthesis of all the styles of recent decades'. It is in the nature of a synthesis that, whereas the source and influence of individual elements – 'styles' in this context – may be readily identified, the synthesis itself cannot be reproduced in precisely the same form. Thus, although Busoni founded no 'school' with a recognisable and traceable accent, like Schoenberg, the presence of particular ingredients in his synthesis, whether original or not, can be located in the work of his followers. His partiality for an oscillation between major and minor forms of the same chord, for example, became a staple term in Weill's harmonic vocabulary.

The air of aristocratic elegance that issued from the Busoni apartment, and the rare intellectual stimulus, literary and philosophical as well as musical, that agitated the eager young minds who presented themselves for instruction, offered a harsh contrast to the humble circumstances of Weill's day-to-day life. An allowance of fifty marks a month from Leopold Weill, his father's elder brother in Mannheim, made it possible for him to rent a furnished room in Zehlendorf, a middle-class suburb in the south-west of the city. Leopold Weill had no children of his own and was both able and willing to support what was clearly a remarkable musical talent in the family.

Weill supplemented this with part-time jobs of almost bizarre disparity, on the one hand playing the organ for synagogue services, on the other, playing piano in a down-to-earth *Bierkeller* until late into the night. 'Here,' recalled the loquacious Hans Heinsheimer, who later became head of the opera division of Universal Edition and came to know Weill well,

> there was nothing of the silks-and-satins atmosphere that prevailed in the house of his master. What he earned depended on the generosity of the patrons, who would leave their donations on a plate that stood in a prominent position on the battered old piano. In order to encourage contributions he would invariably break out into a crescendo of tremolandos whenever he observed that a particularly prosperous-looking party of guests were preparing to leave.

Incongruous as the combination of synagogue and *Bierkeller* may seem, the two institutions provided public platforms for Weill to make manifest two areas of activity which held an unflagging fascination for him throughout his life. One was the tradition of Jewish culture, with a span stretching from the Jewish song-settings of his schooldays to his setting of the Hebrew Kiddush and his orchestral arrangement of 'Hatikvah', the Israeli National Anthem, in the last years of his life.

The other sphere was jazz, a popular source of stimulation to 'serious' composers in the post-war years and an idiom which, after its triumphant explosion in the *Mahagonny Songspiel* and *Die Dreigroschenoper,* carried Weill through to the world of his Broadway musicals. Interestingly, a manuscript draft of Weill's has survived of a cabaret number for voice and piano in foxtrot tempo, which he appears to have jotted down at this time, and which may well have been one of the items in his *Bierkeller* repertoire.

Outside the *Bierkeller*, the synagogue and the apartment in Viktoria -Luise-Platz an ugly world was developing. Ironically it was a world from which, in their own ways, these three establishments might have offered a refuge – an escape into alcohol and conviviality, into religion or into the private realm of the mind, of art. There was no such escape. The war had been over for two years but its economic consequences, given a deliberately cruel twist by the punitive conditions of the Treaty of Versailles, were only now beginning to corrode the structure of organised society. The basic element in that corrosive process has a name that has etched itself deeply into the collective historical consciousness of the Germans – inflation.

Inflation reaches to the heart of a nation in a way no purely political event can, and the fledgling German republic never recovered from it, politically or socially. It had started during the war itself, when, as in all wars, the volume of money increased as the supply of goods on which to spend it declined. Moreover the situation was cynically exacerbated by the central government itself, which, while printing ever more millions of valueless banknotes in order to pay off the reparations imposed on them, granted huge credits to industry to buy real estate and capital equipment with increasingly worthless money. The urban middle classes, traditional exemplars of thrift and custodians of family welfare, who regarded themselves as the most loyal and stable elements in society, had their savings wiped out. They were powerless victims of forces over which they had no control, and they knew it. Mark values were becoming increasingly meaningless, and only goods, property or foreign currency provided a basis for setting real prices and values. With inflation at its height, a day's work would earn a factory worker a pound of margarine, six weeks' wages would buy him a pair of boots, and twenty weeks' wages, a suit.

In his autobiography *Die Welt von Gestern* ('Yesterday's World'), the novelist Stefan Zweig remembered some details of what these incredible times were like in Berlin:

> There were days when a newspaper cost 50,000 marks in the morning and 100,000 marks in the evening. . . . I sent my publisher a manuscript on which I had been working for a year, thinking that I would be covering myself if I asked for an immediate advance on 10,000 copies. But by the time I received the cheque, it barely covered my postage on the manuscript a week earlier. . . . You could purchase whole rows of six- storey apartment blocks on the Kurfürstendamm for $100, and what used to buy a wheelbarrow now bought a factory. Some youths who had come across a crate of soap bars standing near a jetty lived like lords for months by selling one bar per day, while their parents, once well-to-do, hobbled about like beggars.

As Weill's friend Felix Joachimson recalled, public morality was among the early casualties of such conditions:

> The boys in their big suits walk by, coats down to their ankles, dirty sandals on their feet. And the girls in see-through blouses and black stockings, their skirts shoved up high to display their offerings. A whiff

of sweet perfume and sweat. And then the pimps with their caps aslant, their scarves draped round their necks, keeping their glacial eyes on their strolling wares.

At the top of the hit parade at the time was a song that began –

> *Warum denn weinen, wenn man auseinandergeht,*
> *Wenn an der nächsten Ecke schon ein andrer steht. . . .*
> ('What's the use of crying, if your love has been in vain?
> There's another round the corner who will pick you up again.')

Intellectuals underwent their own particular experience of betrayal and insecurity. Those of the older generation who had set their course by what they saw as the imperishable values of German *Geist* now found themselves in a no-man's-land of disillusion and impotence. They had put their faith in the tradition of nineteenth-century idealism, in the edifying values of the ordered life of the spirit, in a conviction of the God-given destiny of the German nation. Now, with their deities in disgrace and their nation in dishonour, they tried to salvage what they could from the wreckage, while their children turned their backs on them and on the ruins for which they were responsible. Even the generation gap itself had been a subject of literary attention for angry young writers since Walter Hasenclever's drama *Der Sohn* in 1914, receiving its most frightening representation in the nihilistic furore of Georg Kaiser's expressionist *Gas*-trilogy, produced in Berlin by Leopold Jessner in 1918–20.

Much of the bitterness of the age, and even more of the mockery, found its most pungent expression in the political cabarets which became so prominent a feature of Berlin life in the 1920s. Places like Max Reinhardt's 'Schall und Rauch', Rosa Valetti's establishment in the old Café des Westens in the Kurfürstendamm, the 'Wilde Bühne' in the basement of the Theater des Westens, run by Trude Hesterberg, rocked with the laughter that accompanied the barbed satirical sketches and verses of men like Walter Mehring, Erich Kästner, Kurt Tucholsky and Marcellus Schiffer. The music came from familiar names such as Friedrich Holländer (composer of the music for the Marlene Dietrich films *The Blue Angel* and *Destry Rides Again*), Theo Mackeben (music director of the original *Dreigroschenoper* in 1928) and Mischa Spolianski, who did the music for the revue *It's In The Air* and later for Kaiser's *Two Neckties* – composers who lived in the next room, so to speak, to the Kurt Weill of the *Dreigroschenoper*.

Together with operas and concerts, theatrical life in Berlin was restored remarkably quickly after the war. Enterprising impresarios like Carl Meinhard and Rudolf Bernauer put together repertories of classics ancient and modern, German and European. Max Reinhardt, who considered himself the creator of expressionist drama, used his Deutsches

Theater for works by Franz Werfel, Oskar Kokoschka, Arnold Zweig and others of the expressionist generation. At the same time he converted the barn-like Grosses Schauspielhaus into a theatre aimed at the masses, putting on *Hamlet, Julius Caesar,* the *Oresteia* and Büchner's *Danton's Tod* with Heinrich George, Werner Krauss and other leading actors of the day. Later on in the 1920s Karlheinz Martin took over at the Volksbühne and the revolutionary Erwin Piscator emerged with his politicised Proletarian Theatre.

Financing theatre has always been a speculative business, and although there was a lot of money to be made for the fortunate, there was also a lot for the casualties to lose. Nevertheless, whereas there had been thirty theatres in Berlin in 1914, after the war there were forty. The arts provided a distraction, a means of escape from the real-life miseries of the moment and a chance to rescue something of lasting value from the moral debris of defeat. For notwithstanding the relentless economic disintegration, Germany at the end of the Great War was not, as in 1945, a bombed and shattered ruin but physically intact, its buildings defiantly unharmed. The princes and kings departed, a Hoftheater was re-christened a Staatstheater, but cultural life surged on as before.

Berlin audiences, moreover, were sophisticated and recognised quality when they saw it, whether that quality lay in a production of Goethe or Shakespeare, or in a revolutionary drama of protest. The cultured and discerning public from the Grunewald and other fashionable western suburbs still found what it wanted, while the intellectual avant-garde was offered rival stimuli. Stanislavsky and his ensemble arrived in the early 1920s with plays by Tolstoy, Gogol and Gorky and dramatisations of Dostoevsky. Meyerhold and his troupe came too. There was even Yiddish theatre. It was a kaleidoscope, a time of fascinating contrasts, a reflection of the coruscating brilliance of the artistic and intellectual life of a city that was on the brink of becoming the most exciting capital in Europe.

CHAPTER IV

The Young Modernist

All this lay spread out at the feet of the young Weill as he set about the enjoyment of his precious privilege as a chosen student of Busoni's. Busoni was a master not easy to satisfy. His autocratic nature set a deliberate distance between him and his entourage, and however confident they may have felt of the Master's good will, he could pass scathing judgement on them to others.

Thus while appreciating Weill's talent, he could complain in a letter to his son Raffaello that Weill and his fellow-student Robert Blum were 'incapable of the simplest things, their forms are complex yet not sophisticated, and they exercise the right universally claimed by young people today to declare every crooked line a manifestation of individuality and freedom'. Though only in his fifties, Busoni was tired, strained, and a sick man for the last years of his life. This made such tensions the harder to bear – and to conceal.

According to Vladimir Vogel, Busoni sensed that it would be in the realm of musical theatre that Weill would make his mark. And apart from the few orchestral and chamber works written between 1919 and 1924 – with the much later Symphony No. 2 (1934) standing out like an erratic block in its musical landscape – it is indeed music for the stage, in one form or another, that filled his mind to the very end of his life. But with the single exception of the pantomime *Zaubernacht* (1922), not one of the works he is known to have composed during his three years with Busoni is for the theatre.

To practise in the forms of 'absolute' music was in large part a reaction against the Wagnerian line and against Romantic concepts of hybrid 'programme' music. That practice remained relevant, however, for the eventual discovery, or rediscovery, of a true tradition of musical theatre in a form matched to the contemporary situation. There is not one 'pure' and one 'applied' music. The unity of the musical experience is inviolable. There is no less drama in Beethoven's Fifth Symphony and C sharp minor quartet than in *Fidelio* – and it is the same drama.

For Weill the most triumphant proof of this lay in Mozart, his operatic composer *par excellence*. 'Mozart,' he wrote a few years later in an essay called 'Commitment to Opera',

> is the same in opera as in symphony or string quartet. He always maintains the momentum of dramatic action. Hence he remains an absolute composer even when he lets all hell break loose in *Don Giovanni*. By the same token his Allegro movements have the power to make us imagine events taking place on the stage. . . . For in the last analysis what stirs us in the theatre is the same as what moves us in all art, namely, the heightened experience, the pure expression of an emotion, humanity.

Weill knew, when he approached Busoni in 1920, that he was exposing himself to a régime of intellectual rigour. He could, after all, have chosen to return to the Hochschule and study with, say, the recently appointed and more easy-going Franz Schreker, also a composer of opera. But his mind was developing fast, and as he became exposed to influences which had no place in Busoni's world, so his creative urges led him in directions which could not have been foreseen and which Busoni could not help deploring. On the one hand, he felt himself drawn towards the socio-aesthetic activities of the so-called 'Novembergruppe', with its radical realignment of the focus of artistic activity. At the same time, in the space of a mere two months in the summer of 1921, he wrote his very un-Busonian First Symphony.

The Novembergruppe – the 'German Association of Radical Painters and Artists', as they defined themselves – took its name from the abortive revolution of November 1918. Originally a forum for painters and sculptors, founded at the suggestion of the expressionist painters Max Pechstein and César Klein, and later attracting the interest of Kandinsky, Feininger, Gropius, Mies van der Rohe and other famous names, it acquired sections for literature and music in 1920. First of the musicians to join were the conductor Heinz Tiessen and the composer Max Butting; they were followed by Hanns Eisler, a pupil of Schoenberg's, Philipp Jarnach, Busoni's factotum and closest musical associate, the American composer George Antheil, the critic Hans Heinz Stuckenschmidt, the conductor Hermann Scherchen, who had recently returned to Berlin from internment in Russia, and Kurt Weill.

Couched in a high-flown, expressionistic language, the declared aims of the Novembergruppe had an immediate appeal for those susceptible to a message of egalitarian idealism and anxious to find a new, meaningful context for their art. 'We are not a separate party or class but men. . . .' ran their manifesto. And as men they saw art as an activity directed towards the enlightenment of their fellow-men and the enrichment of their lives – an art for the many, not for the few. The needs of society, as projected by the movement, were paramount and demanded a personal and political commitment from each artist. But the decision how to fulfil these needs remained with the individual artist. Thus the early exhibitions sponsored by the Group could accommodate Impressionist, Expressionist, Cubist and Futurist paintings within the public political frame of reference and thereby reconcile artistic freedom with a common social purpose. The names that figure in the concerts organised by the music section in the 1920s – from Satie and Ravel to Schoenberg, Berg and Webern, from Bartók and Kodály to Hindemith and Weill, from Stravinsky to Křenek, Hába and Martinu – reveal a similar catholicity of taste, though here the interests of ideological engagement, as the Novembergruppe originally understood the term, have been partially eroded by purely musical demands.

No artistic movement dedicated to a social purpose can escape the tension that develops within any politicised activity – in this case the tension between the art and the politics – and it was not long before a predictable split developed in the Novembergruppe. On the one side stood those, predominantly of Marxist persuasion, who complained that the Group was not wholeheartedly engaged in promoting the advancement of the working class and the establishment of a classless society. To their rivals the preservation of their artistic integrity came before all else – a consideration as important, they argued, to their customers, i.e. the society they served, as to themselves, since unless the authenticity of the artistic product were assured, both art and society would be betrayed.

This was the view that prevailed, not surprisingly, among the musicians, whose art was less susceptible to direct politicisation than the representational arts like painting and sculpture, let alone literature. Weill, who had a keen social awareness but never pledged himself to a particular political party, was too absorbed in his developing artistic powers, and in savouring the cultural delights that Berlin had to offer, to think otherwise than the majority of his fellow-musicians. As he put it in a letter to Busoni in 1922: 'We must realise that, however complicated it may be, we must first discover the quintessence of our existence as human beings before we can create a true work of art.' Busoni would have recognised himself in this remark, which also stands in its own right as one of the many testimonies, in thought and in deed, to the fundamental humanism of Weill's personality.

To help finance their activities, the musicians of the Novembergruppe organised two large fancy-dress balls each year. These brought in a great deal of money, which they immediately changed into dollars, so as to avoid the inflation which was rapidly reducing German banknotes into so much worthless paper. When the first measure to stabilise the currency, the creation of the Rentenmark, was introduced in November 1923, the dollar stood at the mind-boggling rate of one trillion paper marks. Those who had converted their marks into foreign currency in the past few years, in spite of the irresistible deterioration of the situation, had ensured that at least something of value would be in their hands when a semblance of financial normality returned after the adoption of the Dawes Plan in 1924. The progressive young musical idealists saw no reason why they too should not salvage what they could for their cause from the ruins of a society to which they felt little loyalty.

Equally shrewd was the plan to hold their recitals in the small hall of the Vox-Haus – the Broadcasting House of Berlin radio – in the Potsdamer Strasse. Max Butting disarmingly described the tactic in his autobiography:

> It was a deliberate decision, for the little hall was always crowded, and all the papers had to emphasise this fact. Had we taken a hall of even medium size, with the same number of listeners, they would probably have reported that it was half-empty.

Weill was a keen participant in the discussion of aesthetic and technical issues that accompanied these performances. Stuckenschmidt recalled that, whereas many of the Group could not grasp what Busoni was about with his 'classicistic calls to order', as Stuckenschmidt called them, Weill had a broader outlook on the contemporary scene and frequently defended Busoni's position. In agitated exchanges over the situation of the arts in the Soviet Union at the time, Weill took a progressive line, whereas his Russian fellow-student Vladimir Vogel, who came from the school of Scriabin, had more reservations. Weill's own later contribution to the Novembergruppe's recitals was a String Quartet, Op. 8, which was played by the Roth Quartet in 1923.

But before this he had composed a far larger and more adventurous piece, a remarkable, even startling achievement, the earliest of his works to have its place in our overall perception of his mature creative life – his First Symphony.

The fate of the work, which was neither performed nor published during Weill's lifetime, relates like a novel. He composed it between April and June 1921, privately, even secretly, and independently of any supervision by Busoni who, when confronted with the work in a version for piano, four hands, found most of it highly distasteful. Whether from aesthetic reservations or for some other reason, Weill apparently kept the manuscript to himself and made no attempt to get the work performed. He even left it out of a list of his compositions which he made in 1925, choosing to make the pantomime *Zaubernacht* of 1922 the earliest item he quoted.

This state of oblivion lasted until the early 1930s, when he lent a number of his unpublished manuscripts, including that of the symphony, to one Herbert Fleischer, a Berlin music critic. Weill had been a name on everybody's lips since *Dreigroschenoper* and the *Mahagonny* opera, and Fleischer, after publishing a short article on him in 1932, then planned a monograph. Towards the end of that year, no doubt foreseeing the consequences of being found in possession of manuscripts of 'decadent' music by a Jewish composer, Fleischer took the material to Italy and worked on it for a while in a hospice attached to a convent. Some time in 1933, deciding that he no longer needed, or dared to keep, the manuscripts, he sent them in a parcel to Berlin – not to Weill personally but to Universal Edition, his publishers.

What happened to this parcel; what it contained; and why, if Fleischer feared it would be confiscated if he sent it direct to Weill, he did not send it to the safety of Universal's head office in Vienna, which had not yet been swallowed up into Hitler's *Grossdeutsches Reich*: these are questions we cannot answer. Not knowing where Weill then was, Fleischer may not unreasonably have assumed that Universal did, and that they would forward the parcel to him. At all events it has never been found. But, by an extraordinary chance, the score of the symphony was never enclosed. Instead it found its way into some of Fleischer's personal possessions which were left behind in the convent, intentionally or otherwise, when he went back to Germany.

Twenty years later Fleischer returned to the convent to find the score of the symphony still there. He took it back with him to Berlin, and when in 1955 he read an advertisement in the newspaper that Lotte Lenya, Weill's widow, was asking for information about lost or unpublished works of her husband's, he reported the existence of the precious manuscript and shortly after was able to return it to its rightful owner. It was heard for the first time, thirty-six years after its composition, in a concert given by the North-West German Radio Symphony Orchestra in 1957.

The roots of Weill's Symphony No. 1 lie in a work of literature, a passionate, strident, bombastic, inflammatory exercise in utopian expressionist drama with a title that says it all: *Arbeiter, Bauern, Soldaten: Aufbruch eines Volkes zu Gott* ('Workers, Peasants, Soldiers: A People Sally Forth to God'). Its author was Johannes R. Becher, an immensely productive and stimulating poet nine years Weill's senior, whom he had met in the famous Romanisches Café soon after his return to Berlin.

Carried along by the expressionist protest movement that had started before the war and roused so many young artists and intellectuals down into the early 1920s, Becher had a remarkable career. At the time Weill met him, he was riding a wave of exalted, Strindbergian religiosity, writing – or rather shouting – a poetry full of extravagant rhetoric and an often violently offensive imagery. The self-imposed task of this John the Baptist was to prepare the way, if not of the Lord, then of the expressionist New Man, to expose the decrepitude of a world doomed to destruction and proclaim the dawn of a new humanism. Very quickly, however, this apocalyptic claim turned into a quest for a quasi-metaphysical power which, like the Christian Church, brought promise of salvation and a form of authority that would preserve man from anarchy. The quest led Becher to Communism, an authoritarian creed which provided a materialist basis for the ideal socialism which before, like many others, he had perceived as a proper consequence of the doctrines of a humanistic Christianity. So in 1924, five years after its original appearance, Becher transformed the *Arbeiter, Bauern, Soldaten* which had captured Weill's imagination into a 'revolutionary drama of the class struggle', and from then on he devoted his energies to the cause of the proletarian revolution. After ten years in exile in Moscow from 1935 to 1945, he returned to East Germany, where he was Minister of Culture from 1954 until his death four years later.

'I have an invitation,' Weill had written to his brother Hanns back in November 1920, 'to write music for a piece by Johannes Becher. It is a huge undertaking, and the most prominent young composers are falling over each other in their eagerness to do it, since among young poets Becher is considered the one with the brightest future. So one of the others is sure to beat me to it.' In the event nobody beat him to it, for no music is known to have been written to Becher's play, and a proposal that Max Reinhardt might produce it came to naught.

But it remains, in Weill's words, 'a huge undertaking', and its fascination for him is not hard to understand. In what passes for the 'action' of the three-part play, The Man, i.e. The Poet – the characters are archetypes, with no personal names – assumes the mission of leading the masses to joy and salvation. The Woman – a Christ-figure who preaches peace and goodness, and is specifically described as a Jewess – persuades The Soldiers to lay down their arms and rebel against their oppressors but The Tyrant has her shot, only to be murdered himself by his angry Soldiers. The final part presents a vision of The Saint leading The Man and The People towards a world of liberation and peace, when The Tyrant shall renounce his power, the rich shall give away their wealth and a divine humanity shall prevail. 'Up and away to the Promised Land, to the Holy Land!' they cry triumphantly at the end, singing a joyful Gloria as, in the words of the title, they sally forth to meet their God.

Even as it stands, this is the text less of a drama than of an opera-cum-oratorio, with a great deal of musical imagery in the poetry, revolutionary marches, choirs and other features of a work conceived as much in musical as in literary terms. So although Weill's hopes for a commission foundered, the hold that Becher's drama had taken on his mind impelled him to convert the intellectual and literary experience into that musical equivalent which is his Symphony No. 1.

Cast in one continuous movement, less a symphony in character than a symphonic poem in the tradition of Liszt and Richard Strauss, it is divided into three broad sections corresponding to the three parts of Becher's play – Allegro vivace, Andante religioso, Larghetto – with a solemn Introduction and a ceremonial Coda. The highly-effective scoring is for double woodwind (one oboe), two horns, trumpet, trombone, timpani, percussion and strings. Mahler lurks in the background, so, in the pervasive fourth-chord harmony, does Debussy. There is also a relationship in form and tonal language to Schoenberg's Chamber Symphony Op.9, a work which Weill later described in an admiring survey of Schoenberg's development as heralding the iconoclastic atonality of the Three Piano Pieces Op. 11.

Chromaticism – in melody, in harmony, as a principle of formal construction – dominates the dissonant idiom of the work, creating freedoms and fluctuations of tonality so radical as to defy useful pursuit and analysis, and leaving only somewhat evasive, negative terms like 'non-tonal', 'free-tonal' and 'atonal' to characterise the result. Harmonically, great use is made of fourth-chords and fifth-chords and on progressions constructed from them, including the so-called 'semitonal slip', which is also part of the complex of extended chromaticism. Related features such as false relations and dissonant, agglomerated chords rich in added, or 'wrong' notes, as Constant Lambert called them, serve to sharpen still further the jagged edges of Weill's harmony.

As uncompromising as the harmonic idiom of the symphony is the steely relentlessness of the counterpoint, which makes few concessions to the comfortable world of diatonicism and stands in a middle ground between Schoenberg and Hindemith. To complement this Weill has put together a taut, complex rhythmic structure, while the overall principle of construction, running parallel to the action of Becher's drama, is rather that of an associative montage of separate thematic elements than of a unitarian master plan.

The result is a work of characteristic complexity and intensity, its texture almost oppressively dense at times, the product of an exuberant imagination stimulated by a wild, intoxicating piece of literature. At the same time it is remarkably assured and remarkably original, full of drama, with a power to command attention that makes it hard to understand why Weill virtually disowned it and why modern programme planners take so little notice of it.

Impressively accomplished through his First Symphony is, Weill felt, or was persuaded by Busoni to feel, that he would profit from further studies in counterpoint. Busoni himself did not stoop to such humdrum tasks as 'teaching' harmony and part-writing, so he suggested that Weill work for a while with Jarnach, in order to move towards the ideal of classicistic poise which lay at the heart of his doctrine.

Eight years Weill's senior, Philipp Jarnach had a cosmopolitan background that rivalled Busoni's. Of Spanish descent, he was born and educated in France, then went to Germany; he met Busoni in Zurich in 1915 and followed him to Berlin, making vocal scores of his operas and acting as his general assistant. Today he is remembered chiefly for his completion of Busoni's *Doktor Faust* but in his day his own music, neo-Classical in style, atonal in language, with antecedents in Bach and late Beethoven, was frequently performed in concerts of contemporary music. He was instrumental, with Heinz Tiessen of the Novembergruppe, in bringing about the first performance in Berlin of Stravinsky's *The Rite of Spring* in 1921, and developed a friendship with Schoenberg after the latter's appointment to the Akademie der Künste.

Little gain usually accrues from a simplistic determinism that would see conceptual or technical influence and ensuing creative activity as a syndrome of cause and effect. But it is hardly possible to view Weill's subsequent works of the early 1920s other than in the light of the 'New Classicality' of Busoni and his complementary studies with Jarnach. Two orchestral works followed each other in quick succession in 1922 – a Divertimento for small orchestra with male chorus, and a symphonic structure called Fantasia, Passacaglia und Hymnus, dedicated to Jarnach, which is sometimes catalogued as *Sinfonia Sacra*.

The chorale in the final movement of both these works points backwards to the Symphony No. 1 and forwards to the String Quartet of the following year, while the male chorus in the finale of the Divertimento, singing a hymn appealing to the mercy of God, in the spirit of the Becher-inspired chorale in the final section of the Symphony, brings Busoni's Piano Concerto to mind.

Both these pieces were publicly performed in the year after their completion – the Divertimento at a concert of music by Busoni's pupils, the Fantasia, Passacaglia und Hymnus in the Berlin Philharmonie. But they have never been published, and only manuscript sketches and fragments of drafts have survived. In his account of the latter work, Rudolf Kastner referred to 'an original technique of overlapping contrapuntal parts derived from late Busoni' but also to the brittle, unyielding character of the melodic line, a general atmosphere of gloom that hung over the work and the 'restricted range of colour' in the orchestration. A notice of the concert in the Philharmonie by Adolf Weissmann dug rather deeper:

Kurt Weill ... maintains the highest standards, but in so doing, he suppresses his best. His Passacaglia, which Alexander Selo conducted skilfully and with respect, is the product of a deep seriousness. But whether there is a sensuousness beyond this logic-propelled intellectuality we can scarcely judge. We should like to think so. Certainly, compared with Anton Webern, Kurt Weill is a musical sensualist.

With the sound of the 'Benares Song' or the 'Alabama Song' in our ears, we shall hardly ask whether there is a sensuous side to Weill's art. But in the post-war confusion of 1922, with young musicians looking in all directions for a foothold from which to launch their careers, and in an anti-Romantic world which affected to despise the display of emotion, the cult of intellectual ingenuity had many followers. Complexity was equated with profundity, and the more notes to the square centimetre, the greater the degree of alleged inventiveness and subtlety. The speed with which Weill could work, the sharpness of his musical mind and the abundance of his creative gifts made him at times prey to the temptation of over-facility, a kind of musical verbosity where too many notes were chasing too few substantial ideas. But he was too alert, too self-critical not to recognise the danger.

As the German economy ran amok after the war, so developments in the arts acquired their own bewildering momentum as one form of modernism followed another. In 1920 Mahler, Debussy and Richard Strauss were still regarded as 'new'; Stravinsky drove a coach and horses through what the establishment considered 'music', while the cultivation of Schoenberg and his atonal followers was left to the extreme avant-garde – the lunatic fringe, as the pre-war conservative public saw them. But as the new became older in one direction and still newer in the other, so Strauss came to be no longer seen as 'new', while the pursuit of novelty took on ever more challenging, at times outrageous forms. Some performers, like the Amar String Quartet, in which Hindemith played viola, and the Kolisch Quartet from Vienna, staked their honour on a commitment to contemporary music. Some ambitious young soloists took on the performance of new pieces, often 'difficult', both conceptually and technically, in the calculated knowledge that the critics would be present and that they would read their names in the paper the next day. Likewise although a few leading conductors – Scherchen, Klemperer, Erich Kleiber, Fritz Busch – performed contemporary works out of conviction, others sought the prestige of giving a first performance and then withdrew their interest. As Max Butting wrily observed, it was more difficult to get a second performance than a first.

While not exactly a *querelle des anciens et des modernes*, the polarisation of musical tastes did acquire, in a manner characteristically if displeasingly German, political overtones. Those prominently identified with the cause of contemporary music, whether as composers, performers, sponsors or in some less direct way, included a considerable number of Jews – Schoenberg, Egon Wellesz, Milhaud, Weill, Klemperer, Kleiber, Artur Schnabel, Leo Kestenberg and others less well-known. Reactionary and nationalistically-minded members of the concert-going public who were disposed to believe that Germany had not really lost the war but been 'stabbed in the back', as the phrase had it, principally by the Jews and the Communists, transferred their political antipathies to the arts and equated the new revolutionary music with subversive anti-German proclivities. Elements with no interest in the music but eager to politicise the situation joined in the action and instigated riots such as that witnessed at the first performance in Berlin of Schoenberg's *Pierrot Lunaire* in 1912. Fighting broke out between rival parties in the auditorium and anti-Semitic insults were hurled at the performers. The early concerts of the International Society for Contemporary Music, founded in the spirit of re-establishing the links between musicians whom the war had made enemies, were also disrupted by such outbursts.

At the same time, there emerged after 1918 a growing willingness to view music, indeed all art, not merely as a product for relaxed, 'culinary' consumption – to use Brecht's preferred term – but as an entity to be studied, to be comprehended, a path to education and the growth of historical awareness. The 'Classics', familiar and loved, a repository of tried and tested values, remained a source of comfort in troublous times to those who had no wish to see their assumptions or prejudices challenged. But curiosity, even a genuine, expanding open-mindedness, particularly among the younger generation, gradually infiltrated concert programmes and gave encouragement to the more adventurous promoters. A sober, more questioning attitude to art took root, mirroring the radical revaluation of values, above all moral and social values, on which progressive forces in the young Republic had already embarked. 'Concerts became music galleries', as Butting described the change.

The wealth of exhibits on display in these pre-radio, pre-gramophone galleries leaves no doubt about the liveliness of contemporary musical life, a liveliness in which no young musician like Weill could fail to revel. A glance at the publishers' announcements and the review pages of *Melos*, *Die Musik* and other journals of the day shows a range of recent works stretching from Janáček, Pfitzner and Richard Strauss through Medtner, Reger, Ravel and Scriabin to Busoni, Schoenberg (the Piano Pieces Op.11 and Op.19; the two Chamber Symphonies), Bartók, Stravinsky, Alban Berg (Piano Sonata Op.1; songs), Hindemith

(*Mörder, Hoffnung der Frauen*; Kammermusik No.1), Webern and many lesser names. Only a year or two later Weill too was to find himself in this company.

Indeed, his name was already being increasingly heard in Berlin musical circles. Always a quick learner and a quick worker, he had sharpened both his technical musical skill and his general intellectual perception, preparing the way for the variety of professional tasks that were to challenge him in the coming years. His contributions to the meetings of the Novembergruppe had earned him the respect of his fellow-progressives and made it clear that he was a force to be reckoned with. More important, Busoni, who saw Weill as his star pupil, made no secret of his willingness to use his prestige to help further Weill's career, which meant, at this moment, not only urging concert promoters to give his works a hearing but also encouraging him to build up a circle of pupils of his own.

And this he did, discovering that even in these inflationary times there were those, perhaps with funds in more stable currencies abroad, who were looking to widen their musical horizons in Germany. One who made his way to the room that Weill had found in the Winterfeldtplatz – in May 1922, by his own evidence – was Maurice de Abravanel, a Greek-born musician of Portuguese descent who had come to Berlin from Switzerland and who as a conductor, first in Europe, then in American exile, later became a staunch advocate of Weill's music. Another was the pianist Claudio Arrau, who had arrived in Germany from Chile in 1918 to study with Martin Krause, a pupil of Liszt's.

Arrau, who, like Abravanel, was only three years younger than Weill, came not in order to learn how to compose – Weill never taught composition – but to be coached in aspects of practical musicianship, such as transposition, and in the analysis of 'difficult' contemporary music, in particular that of Schoenberg and the atonalists. Arrau recalled that Weill had a boundless admiration of Mozart, especially of 'the transparency of his orchestration', contrasted with the 'messy' instrumentation of Brahms. He also admired the 'extraordinary craftsmanship' of Bach and the purity of Schubert: 'In Schubert's Lieder there is not one superfluous note'. The neo-Classical Stravinsky was to leave his mark on Weill's music, and later the two men struck up a cordial relationship that lasted into the 1940s, when they were both living in America, but Weill seems to have disliked Stravinsky's earlier music, going so far, according to Abravanel, as to call *The Rite of Spring* 'garbage' (*Dreck*).

As Claudio Arrau remembers him, Weill was an extremely intense and alert teacher, not only committed to music but much interested in painting, modern German architecture – these were the early years of the Bauhaus – and modern dance, a man scornful of anything sham or pretentious, someone with whom one knew where one stood. 'An extraordinarily bright and clear thinker – never vague,' said Arrau admiringly.

Abravanel recalled that Weill made his pupils buy Schoenberg's treatise on harmony – the *Harmonielehre* of 1911 – but never worked from it in the lessons themselves (Abravanel described Schoenberg a few years later as 'the most powerful intellectual force in contemporary musical life'). He also remembered that Weill's fee for each one-hour lesson was half-a-pound of butter. Not that butter actually changed hands on each occasion, but at a time when prices rose from one day to the next, a barter unit of currency like butter provided a firmer foundation for doing business than the tottering mark. A board outside the Schlossparktheater in Berlin in 1920 announced that admission prices for evening performances of *White Horse Inn* ranged from two eggs for the cheapest seats to one pound of butter for the most expensive.

Weill must have acquired quite a number of private pupils, for Abravanel reported that he used to take the tram to various parts of the city to give his lessons. In contrast to the appreciative Arrau, however, Abravanel put on record: 'Weill was a lousy teacher'. Maybe this tells us more about Abravanel than about Weill.

In the course of 1922 Kurt's brother Hanns became engaged to a lady called Rita Kisch. At the engagement party there appeared one Nelly Frank, née Weill, wife of a well-to-do cousin of Rita's. Kurt and Nelly, who was three years older, became emotionally involved and the following year they shared a holiday in Italy, after he had stayed at the Frank villa in Davos. In a letter to his sister Ruth from Florence during this trip he signs himself 'Kurt the Happy One'. When the couple got back to Berlin, Nelly asked her husband for a divorce. He refused and shortly afterwards took her with him on a visit to America, stopping the affair in its tracks.

This gives us a rare glimpse of a private life which its owner was concerned to keep private. In the shadow cast by the hopelessness of the emotional situation he composed his song cycle *Frauentanz* the following year, transmuting his suffering into the Platonic symbolism of medieval courtly love, the worship of an unattainable ideal of happiness fulfilled. But he never forgot Nelly Frank, and over twenty years later, on his way back to America from visiting his parents in Palestine, he stopped over in Switzerland to see her again and look back over the joys – and sorrows – of those distant days.

In that autumn of 1922, in the wake of Stanislavsky and Meyerhold, the Russian choreographer Vladimir Boritch came to Berlin with his ballet troupe. Among the projects he brought with him was a scenario he had written for a children's fairy-tale ballet called *Zaubernacht* ('Magic Night'), in which a fairy brings toys and storybook characters to life while the children sleep. Whether Busoni suggested to Boritch that Weill would be an ideal composer to write the music, or whether Weill made his own persuasive approach to Boritch, he was given the commission and conducted three matinée performances of his work at a double bill in the prestigious Theater am Kurfürstendamm. The distinguished occupant of the other half of the afternoon's programme, whose presence will have given Weill no little pleasure, not least for its benefit to the box office, was Stravinsky's *Petrushka*.

Zaubernacht brought two people to the Kurfürstendamm Theatre, each with a private purpose in mind, who were to give Weill good cause to remember the occasion. One was the extraordinary Georg Kaiser – extraordinary as a man and extraordinary as the doyen of contemporary expressionist dramatists. Kaiser had become attracted to the idea of doing a stage work with music and had come to see whether Weill might be his man.

The other was a young actress and dancer called Karoline Blamauer, who had recently arrived in Berlin from Zurich with her drama teacher and his family. 'One day after we arrived there,' she later recounted,

> he showed me a notice in a newspaper about auditions for young singers and dancers for a ballet called *Zaubernacht*. He took me along because he was hoping to get the job of director, and when I was called to the stage, the producer said: 'Miss Lenya, I would like to introduce you to our composer, Kurt Weill.' And I said: 'Where is he?' The producer indicated that he was sitting in the orchestra pit but I couldn't see him. I only heard a soft voice say: 'Very glad to meet you, Miss Lenya.' But I never actually met him. So that was our first meeting. And although I did get the job, I didn't take it, so I didn't see Kurt Weill again at that time.

Fräulein Blamauer had been calling herself Lotte Lenya for some time. A little more than three years later she became Frau Weill.

Weill's predilection for music theatre, whatever forms it might take, had long been no secret. He had embarked on his first opera while still at school; at nineteen he had planned the one-act *Ninon de Lenclos* and incidental music for Gerhart Hauptmann's *Die Weber*, while his First Symphony had started life as the musical representation of a poetic drama. Then came his practical experience in the theatres at Dessau and Lüdenscheid. All this over a mere five years.

But *Zaubernacht* was his first composition for the theatre actually to reach the stage, and has, as such, a special position. It was also his first commission. Weill was very conscious of the conditioning factors, as he wrote a few years later:

> Only when I sensed that my music had the tension proper to dramatic events did I turn to the stage, and write the pantomime *Zaubernacht* for a Russian ballet troupe at the Theater am Kurfürstendamm. The concentrated intensity of the Russian theatre taught me two things: that the stage has its own musical form, the laws of which emerge organically from the course of the action, and that in the theatre significant utterances can be made only by using the simplest, most unobtrusive means.

Externally the simplicity was imposed by the circumstance that this was a piece for children; internally it rests on the modesty of the performing forces – a nine-man orchestra (string quartet, flute, bassoon, harp, piano and percussion), a solo soprano, two ballerinas and a group of children – on the openness of the astute scoring and on its basically homophonic manner. Weill later referred to the work, mentioning Busoni – not fortuitously – in the same breath, as the first 'in which my simple style can be recognised'. Indeed, the music has a free-flowing lightness and melodiousness, accompanied by the springy ostinato rhythms that later became part of his unmistakeable stock-in-trade, and with the equally characteristic harmonic acerbity that also finds its way into the modern children's music of Bartók, Hindemith and others.

Zaubernacht was never published and the orchestral score, like Boritch's scenario, is lost. All that survives is an incomplete piano rehearsal score in manuscript. Six months later, however, he assembled a four-movement suite for full orchestra out of the *Zaubernacht* material and called it *Quodlibet*, dedicating it to his old friend and teacher Albert Bing, who conducted its first performance in the familiar haunts of the Friedrich-Theater in Dessau in June 1923.

The Russo-romantic extroversion and exuberance of *Petrushka* hardly represented the direction in which Weill's musical mind was moving at the time of *Zaubernacht*. But the following year a completely different Stravinsky hit Germany, with a cool, brittle, objective music that epitomised contemporary reaction against the subjectivity, the self-indulgence and the orchestral opulence of the Wagnerian and Straussian tradition. This was the music of *L'histoire du soldat*, the music of the non-pompous, popular, even vulgar situation, like that of the fairground in Satie's *Parade*, or Stravinsky's own burlesque ballet *Renard* and choreographic cantata *Les Noces*.

In particular the appearance of jazz in the part-dramatic, part-lyrical, part-verbal, part-musical stage world of *L'histoire du soldat* set intellectual audiences talking. 'Jazz meant a wholly new sound in my music,' wrote Stravinsky later. And not only in Stravinsky's, for the captivating rhythms of ragtime, tango and foxtrot, the melodic droop of the blues, and the brash woodwind and brass of the jazz band were to prove at least temporarily irresistible in the Twenties and

Thirties to composers of very different casts of mind, from Milhaud to Hindemith, from Honegger to Křenek, from Aaron Copland to Walton and Constant Lambert. Not to mention *Die Dreigroschenoper* and *Mahagonny*.

L'histoire du soldat had its first German performance in the Festival of Chamber Music held in Frankfurt in June 1923. A further performance in Weimar a few weeks later, part of the festival that accompanied the first Bauhaus exhibition, was attended by a number of celebrities, among them Busoni and Stravinsky himself. Weill was present both times. His judgement was shrewdly critical, implying that, for all his skill, Stravinsky was on the fringe of expending his energies on inferior tasks. 'The music is masterfully constructed,' he wrote to Busoni, 'to the extent that this sort of piece allows. And that he has one eye on the taste of the common man can be accepted because the subject matter lends itself to such treatment.' The tone is more reserved than one might have expected.

The Frankfurt occasion also had a very personal meaning for him. For alongside *L'histoire du soldat* and other such formidable works of contemporary music as Hindemith's song-cycle *Das Marienleben* and Schoenberg's *Buch der hängenden Gärten*, the Festival included the first performance of his own String Quartet Op. 8, given by the Amar Quartet.

Dedicated to Albert Weill, his father, the quartet is harmonically 'difficult' in that although individually the three movements work towards a triadic tonal conclusion, the body of the musical argument denies all that the triadic and diatonic principles stand for, with chromaticism dominating both the part-writing and the melodic line of the more homophonic sections.

Already in these early years Weill showed the characteristics of the musical squirrel, hoarding snippets of melody for future use and returning to dig them out when the moment seemed propitious – though when he came to do so, the contents of the cache did not always turn out to be as nutritious as he had hoped. The return in the third movement of the quartet, for instance, of the chorale melody that opens the Coda of the First Symphony is a pale reflection of its predecessor, not only because a string quartet cannot be made to sound like a fanfare of brass but also because the original context and its meaning have disappeared.

The classicistic and somewhat grim asceticism that hangs over the quartet – a piece at times close in spirit to the chamber works of Hindemith – met with Busoni's particular approval and led him to recommend to Universal Edition in Vienna that they should offer Weill a publishing contract. 'I know hardly any other contemporary work by a twenty-three-year-old composer that is so attractive and rewarding . . . a work of outstanding quality, full of power and imagination,' wrote Busoni to Dr Emil Hertzka, director of Universal. 'It is "modern" through and through, with no unwelcome characteristics.' With a nice personal touch he added: 'Moreover – and this is why the matter is so important – Weill is a thoughtful and well-read man, a man of the most upright character.'

While conceding Weill's earnestness of intent, the critics did not share Busoni's enthusiasm for his music. 'A not very significant attempt at writing a quartet', one unkindly described it, feeling that the composer was groping his way towards some uncertainly perceived formal mode of expression. Hindemith and his partners in the Amar Quartet also seemed less than enthusiastic. After attending a rehearsal a few days before the recital, Weill wrote to Busoni from Frankfurt: 'Today was the first time I heard my quartet, because the Hindemith people are very overworked. Strangely enough, it appears to have been the last movement, which was both for you and for me the most mature, that the four gentlemen found the least rewarding.' He then added, rather snidely: 'I'm afraid Hindemith has danced too far into the land of the foxtrot.' Hindemith, who was five years older than Weill, had already flirted casually with jazz. But at this moment the earnest young Weill found such behaviour unbecoming in a serious composer. No wonder people asked, after bouncing to the jazzy sounds of the *Dreigroschenoper* five years later: 'Is this the same man?'

As a form, the string quartet imposes a discipline which may stimulate one composer but inhibit another. For Weill this essay in the genre represented, in a personal sense, a genuflection towards Busoni and his ideals; in the broader context it reflects the penchant in the 'new music' of post-war Germany for smaller, more intimate forms – chamber music, piano pieces, songs, works for small orchestra.

From one point of view this trend expressed a conscious reaction against the expansive, large-scale works of the lingering pre-war Romantic tradition. From another, it represented an equally conscious calculation that, in a world where most impresarios fought shy of investing in unfamiliar and often forbidding music, recitals of chamber music were easier and cheaper to mount. Above all, the urge to pare down the musical utterance to its essentials and reveal its central objectivity, where its true validity resides, was well served by forms which restricted the scope for external display and forced a concentration on the substance.

Weill persisted in this spirit in the remaining two works he completed under Busoni's gaze, works which show his increasing assurance and stylistic independence. This assurance is the most striking feature of the music of this young and still comparatively unknown Kurt Weill. It owes a debt, conceptually more than technically, perhaps, to Busoni, but it is not just a Busonian derivate. In its free tonality it shares the legacy of Schoenberg, but it becomes quite unlike Schoenberg. At times it reminds one of Hindemith, of Alban Berg, of Hanns Eisler, even of Webern, but can never be confused with them. It is a clear, individual voice in a large and sometimes clamorous company, the voice of a subtle personality which, only a few years later, was to burst upon an unsuspecting world with an all-conquering, shockingly novel brand of musical originality.

The first of these two works of 1923, composed a few weeks after the première of his String Quartet at Frankfurt, was *Frauentanz* ('Dance of Women'), a set of seven Middle High German love poems, in modern versions, for soprano voice with accompaniments drawn from flute, viola, clarinet, bassoon and horn. The accompanimental instruments vary from song to song: in one the voice is joined only by the viola in a piece of two-part counterpoint.

The 'Frauen' of the title are the noble ladies of the medieval *Minnesang*, the venerated objects of the poetry of courtly love and the embodiment of ideal virtues. In its private meaning *Frauentanz* is Weill's obituary to his love for Nelly Frank – more accurately, to the hope of its consecration. It is dedicated to her – his response in music to a roundelay of poetic situations in which the object of a man's desire remains unattainable, leaving him to bear his suffering in silence yet also, in moments of fool-hardy passion, to cherish the blissful vision that his lady may requite his love.

Weill's musical correlative of this perception takes the form of a detached, objective reproduction of the poetic substance in conceptual, not formal terms, and without sentimentality – even without warmth, as though he were publicly denying any personal emotional reference. The voice part proceeds recitative-like from one phrase to the next in a nervous series of unequal, word-dictated segments which take no account of the symmetry of the poetic structure. In one sense, the music is true to the text by following it as the vehicle of an argument; in another sense, it creates a tension by cutting across the poetic form and conducting itself as though the starting-point of each song were a passage of prose. Rhythmic sophistication, sometimes rather patternised and predictable in execution, is endemic, and the vocal line is correspondingly chromatic, though less spiky than that of Schoenberg and closer to that of Hindemith's *Marienleben*. The accompaniment, by comparison, while exposing the desiccated Stravinsky-like texture expected of the chosen instrumentation, has a far more conventional character, with an ambiguous use of pseudo-diatonic harmony which anticipates the musical irony of which Weill later became such a master.

As *Frauentanz* expresses an autobiographical moment, so *Recordare: Klagelieder Jeremiae V. Kapitel* Op.11 returns to the literature of his forefathers in a mood of black despair. '*Recordare, Domine, quid acciderit nobis*', sings the doleful prophet in the final chapter of the Lamentations of Jeremiah – 'Remember, O Lord, what is come upon us: consider, and behold our reproach.' We have betrayed our divine heritage and corrupted our culture: would that God would lead us sinners back to Him. 'But thou hast utterly rejected us, thou art very wroth against us.' *Frauentanz*, whatever its challenging modernity, has an accessibility: it invites participation, and although the solo part makes considerable demands, singers were not reluctant to put themselves to the test. *Recordare*, faithful to the anguished message of lamentation which inspired it, seems to resent any move to approach it as an intrusion into an hermetic world of collective Jewish suffering. 'To my brother Hanns Weill', says the dedication – the earnest of a shared family destiny.

The twenty-two verses of the Lamentation are set as a continuous, sectionalised motet for unaccompanied mixed choir and two-part boys' choir, singing now with each other, now against each other. The words 'Recordare, Domine' recur time and again as a kind of dramatic *leitmotiv*, and individual phrases from different verses are set against each other in a verbal counterpoint that runs parallel to the polyphony of the musical texture. The unyielding dissonant austerity of this polyphony, overwhelmingly chromatic in idiom and with even a temporary tonal centre hard to find, makes for a confusing, problematical musical experience. Much of the part-writing, moreover – a feature of post-Schoenbergian atonal music in general – would be better suited to instruments than to voices. 'It does contain a number of difficulties,' Weill admitted to his publisher, 'but they offer no obstacle to a choirmaster who is prepared to take the trouble to rehearse the work properly.' When he showed it to Hermann Scherchen, no stranger to complex modern scores, Scherchen considered it virtually unsingable. For years nothing was heard of it, and it seemed to have vanished without trace until a manuscript copy – though not in Weill's own hand – turned up in a music shop in Paris in 1970. A score was finally published from this in 1983.

In an interview published in 1930 Weill described his works between *Zaubernacht* of 1922 and the *Mahagonny Songspiel* of 1927 as 'technical experiments which represent a grappling with new means of harmonic and melodic expression'. This detached, even dismissive view, which takes in the Violin Concerto and no fewer than four operas, provides a pertinent gloss on *Recordare*. The very word 'experiment' implies an adventurous uncertainty, a leap in the dark, and also, since an experiment must proceed without guarantee of success, a readiness to accept failure. Furthermore, unless an artist subsequently withdraws it, or public disinterest consigns it to oblivion, an 'experimental' work remains on display as an identifiable artefact, an end in itself, whether or not it be judged a success, whereas in the world of the natural sciences, from which the analogy comes, an experiment that fails, i.e. does not prove what it was designed to prove, loses its *raison d'être* the moment it has served its purpose. Scientific progress may be by linear advance, by the acquisition of more, and more refined, knowledge. The arts do not behave in this way. The whole concept of 'experiment' in the arts, in a sociological or other applied sense no less than in innate aesthetic and technical terms, needs to be approached very warily.

In December 1923 Weill came to the end of his three years in Busoni's master class. Only a little over a year earlier his ballet-pantomime *Zaubernacht* had been performed in Berlin, and 1923 had seen first performances of four works – the Divertimento, the Fantasia, Passacaglia und Hymnus, the String Quartet Op.8 and the *Quodlibet* orchestral suite. Busoni had expressed public confidence in his abilities and Universal Edition were on the point of welcoming him into their fold. Inflation had driven the cost of a private room beyond his reach, but he found friends willing to put him up and tide him over his worst moments – even when a ticket for a concert cost a billion marks. And although he had only just ceased to be *in statu pupillari*, he had already acquired highly talented pupils of his own. Above all, he could hardly fail to sense his ever-increasing mastery of his medium, the fluency and versatility which led him to seek ever new challenges.

But a constant succession of rises to such challenges cannot, in the long run, remain a way of life. The way ahead held too many choices, and he recognised the need for a single direction. Perhaps it was in part a personal problem. Quiet and modest in manner, though also both candid and punctilious, he was sociable and appreciative of friendship without, it seems, having a desperate need for intimate companionship. The unhappy memory of his affair with Nelly Frank was still fresh, and no one had taken her place. During these years in Berlin it was in letters to his family, especially to his sister Ruth, and to his spiritual mentor Busoni, that he conveyed the considered thoughts about life and art which he was most anxious to communicate to others.

As 1923 drew to a close, Weill was engrossed in the early poetry of Rainer Maria Rilke. A mystical sense of loneliness and isolation permeates the six poems from Rilke's *Stundenbuch* which he began to set at this time, images from the poet's struggle to express his concept of God. In his youth Weill had been among the thousands who were swept off their feet by Rilke's *Cornet*. Now he had become absorbed in the Rilke who, in the guise of a young monk, uttered the prayers in his *Book of Hours* which would bring him closer to understanding the nature of his God, of the life-force. It represented, in a different form, the same desire for a single path to follow. And that two of these Rilke songs come from the section of the *Stundenbuch* called 'The Book of the Monastic Life', with the other four belonging to 'The Book of Pilgrimage', adds its own note of relevance. Most of the actual musical material is missing, though four of the songs were given a public performance in Berlin in 1925.

It was to Rilke, 'the musician in words', that Busoni dedicated the second edition of his *Ästhetik der Tonkunst*. It is through the poetry of Rilke that we can watch Weill leave a stage of his life behind. So, properly and symmetrically, it is to Busoni that we may give the last word, as, in a letter to Jarnach in October 1923, he offers what amounts to an end-of-term report on the personality, the talents, the shortcomings and the prospects of his favourite pupil:

> Considering his cool, withdrawn personality and the complicated nature of his work, this young man's fecundity is remarkable. He has, as you say, a great number of 'ideas' but they are concealed, hinted at, so that only people like you and me can discover them and admire them. He does not seem to me to realise when he has reached the right place: instead, he strides past it, as though crossing an area of sand and stones with curiously attractive blossoms sticking up in the cracks. He does not trample on them but neither does he pick them or linger over them. He is richly endowed but at the moment his powers of discrimination are dormant. One feels envy and would like to help. But he will find the right path on his own. There remains the perpetual question – is he still developing or has he reached his peak?

Busoni did not live to hear the answer to his question.

CHAPTER V

'All the World's a Stage. . . .'

Weill's career in the 1920s pivots round three points – more precisely, round three individuals, each of whom offered him new stimuli, pointed him in new directions, and made him aware of new ways of exploiting his gifts. When he was twenty it had been Busoni. At twenty-seven it would be Bertolt Brecht. In between, at the beginning of 1924, a figure crossed his path whom time has relegated to the pages of literary history but who, in these post-war years, was one of the most popular German dramatists of the day – Georg Kaiser.

Born in Magdeburg in 1878, almost a generation older than Weill and then the poets, like Brecht, who had gone through the Great War, Kaiser led an unstable life, at times almost pathologically so. Breaking off his business studies, which were intended to set him on the same path as his father, he fled to Argentina in his early twenties, where he caught malaria. He returned to Germany in 1901, was confined for a while to a mental hospital, then bedridden for eight years, during which time he wrote his first plays. These preached, in Nietzschean vein, an unconditional affirmation of life and the regeneration of mankind through a new morality, out of which would emerge the expressionist 'New Man'. From these dizzy heights he then plunged to the depths of disillusionment and despair with a series of frenzied dramas, black statements of utter pessimism, heavily indebted to Strindberg, with which he overwhelmed the German stage in the latter half of the war and the early 1920s. The only realistic philosophy now became one of hopelessness, of *nirvana*. 'We expected Karl Marx,' commented one critic, 'but what we got was Schopenhauer.'

In his personal life Kaiser had no intention of pursuing the self-abnegation of Schopenhauer, and certainly had no sympathy for the dictatorship of the proletariat. He was also a complete egocentric, consumed with a desire to surround himself with the properties of luxury and success. 'He had a mania for boats. . .' Lotte Lenya told an interviewer many years later. 'One of the reasons why he was always in debt was that whenever there was any sign of money coming his way, he bought a new boat.' This mania led him to rent a superb villa in Grünheide, on the shores of Lake Peetz, in the woods to the east of Berlin, where in the 1920s he graciously received the deference of a succession of aspiring young *literati*. 'He was the most enigmatic and contradictory man I have ever known,' said Lenya. 'He dreamt of being an English country squire and master of an estate, and yet lived a life which swung like a pendulum between *gut bürgerlich* and Adlon elegance' [a reference to the famous Adlon Hotel in Berlin].

At the time of his encounter with Weill in January 1924 Kaiser was in a literary no-man's-land. The expressionist 'new man' had been forced to reveal his feet of clay but retained a limited usefulness as an inspiring fiction, an object for the exercise of one's powers of self-persuasion. In this ambivalent role man was half reality, half illusion. The problem, philosophically, lay in distinguishing the one from the other. For art, as Kaiser realised, and as Weill soon came to agree, there was capital to be made out of keeping them in a state of confusion.

Across this no-man's-land from the flamboyant pessimism and lurid despair of expression lay the newly fashionable *Neue Sachlichkeit*, a territory representing a return to realism via the brutal facts of everyday existence in a material world. *Neue Sachlichkeit* – 'New Objectivity', 'Neo-Realism' – was a vague, sometimes contradictory but useful term coined to denote the anti-idealist, anti-subjective, anti-aesthetic reaction of the mid-1920s to the self-centred indulgences of expressionism. Sobriety took the place of exaltation, theory gave way to practice, form to function, matter was preferred to spirit. In the socio-political dimension it coincides with the economic consolidation of the Weimar Republic, the brief span of years when Germany steadily worked her way back to prosperity after the post-war inflation.

The integration of art into the life of the community which the 'New Objectivity' implied left its most durable manifestations in the architecture and the applied arts associated with the institution of the Bauhaus, founded in 1919 by Walter Gropius. The role of art in society was seen to rest on a functional basis of aesthetic ideals and the techniques of practical craftsmanship, including those of modern industry.

Music too had its response to the new philosophy in its cultivation of *Gebrauchsmusik* – 'Utility Music' or 'Music for Use'. Again the starting point is social reality. And again the challenge is how to educate and enrich society, how to achieve the democratic cultivation of an art not only for the people, as listeners, but by the people, as performers, and to that extent as co-creators of the final musical experience. Weill was to have his own contribution to make to this movement – but this was not yet the moment.

Kaiser, who kept his ear to the ground where questions of public taste and fashion were concerned, had taken a passing interest in the potentialities of musical theatre for some time. In 1914 he had been fascinated to watch his war drama *Europa* being adapted as a *Singspiel* by his friend Fritz Stiedry, then principal conductor at the Staatsoper in Berlin. After the war the growing success of entertainment-with-music, ranging from the songs and sketches of cabaret to dance – like the expressionist ballets of Kurt Joos – light opera and the precursors of the modern musical, prompted the ever-acquisitive Kaiser to turn his eye again to the possibility of collaborating with a musician. It was probably such enlightened self-interest, rather than idle curiosity or pure chance, that had taken him to Weill's *Zaubernacht* a few years earlier.

Stiedry conducted the first performance of Weill's song-cycle *Frauentanz* in January 1924, and it may well have been he who introduced Weill to Kaiser. Weill's star was in the ascendant but his following was confined to the musical avant-garde, while the established and vastly popular Kaiser had his influential future already behind him. Also to play a catalytic role in this incipient collaboration was Fritz Busch, conductor of the Dresden opera and a long-standing friend of Kaiser's. Busch had met Weill the previous year at a performance of Busoni's *Arlecchino* in Dresden and, at Busoni's suggestion, now brought Weill to Kaiser's attention on his own account. Dresden, where Busch arrived in 1922, had a long tradition of first performances, going back to Wagner's *Rienzi, Der fliegende Holländer* and *Tannhäuser*, and taking in Richard Strauss' *Salome* and *Elektra*. Busch himself conducted the premières of Strauss' *Intermezzo*, Busoni's *Doktor Faust* and Hindemith's *Cardillac* during his time there, and kept a constant eye on the contemporary scene for suitable works through which to maintain the reputation of his house. Kaiser and Weill did not let him down.

When Kaiser approached Weill with the suggestion that they consider working together on a musico-dramatic project, Weill was highly gratified. In the programme book for the first performance of the work to which the cooperation eventually led, he describes how matters had worked out:

> I was delighted when Georg Kaiser offered to write for me a libretto for a full-length ballet. We set about the task together. After ten weeks the work was almost three-quarters finished. The score of the Introduction and of the first two acts was complete. There we came to a standstill. We had outgrown the material. It irritated us that the characters were mute: we had to break the shackles of the dumb-show – it had to turn into an opera. Georg Kaiser went back to one of his earlier plays, the one-act *Der Protagonist*, which he had once conceived of as an opera.

> This was what we were looking for – a natural, almost fortuitous blend
> of opera and mime-show.

The marriage of opera and mime-show produced its progeny in due
course. But it remains something of a mystery that Weill should have
got so far with the composition of the original pantomime to Kaiser's
scenario before realising that he would never be able to see it through to
the end. Only a fragment of the full score to which he refers has survived,
while Kaiser's scenario has disappeared without trace. We are thus denied
the pleasure even of speculating – usually to little practical effect in such
cases but always with considerable enjoyment – what point in the mimed
action Weill might have reached, why he could get no further, and why
the inventive Kaiser could not manipulate his storyline in order to help
his musical colleague over the obstacle and towards the final goal.

Like Kaiser with his scribbled notes on scraps of paper, so too Weill
had a mind that never rested. His fertile imagination constantly threw
up ideas and motifs for as yet indistinctly perceived works. There are
leaves of manuscript extant on which he has jotted down such motifs
for a number of different works which were in his mind, or at least on
the periphery of his thoughts, at a certain moment. And a motif noted
in the manuscript as being intended for one work might also, or instead,
find its way into another.

A few weeks after laying the foundations of his collaboration with
Kaiser, Weill permitted himself an extended vacation away from the
frenetic pressures of life in Berlin. He made first for the Villa Bergfried
in Davos, home of Nelly Frank, with whom he had been in love the
previous year. Any sense of embarrassment over that affair had vanished,
and he revelled in sled rides and mountain walks with her, sending Busoni
eloquent descriptions of the Alpine scenery and of the vacation guests he
watched in the town. The English contingent, he observed, cut a splendid
figure 'but were too keen on sports for my liking'.

From Switzerland he travelled via Milan, where he heard Toscanini
conduct Charpentier's *Louise* in La Scala, to Florence, then to Rome. A
perceptive observer, intoxicated by the works of Raphael – and also, on
occasion, by the wine of Tuscany – he rhapsodised to Busoni over the
artistic beauties that surrounded him. These were some of the happiest
days of his life, he wrote, though in Rome a jarring note was struck by
Mussolini's rampant Fascists, whose aggressive militarism was 'fully the
equal of anything found in Germany in 1914'.

In April, soon after his return to Berlin, Weill received an invitation
from Dr Emil Hertzka, head of the Universal Edition publishing house,
to visit Vienna to sign a contract. For months, sometimes writing two
or three times a week, he had implored them to offer him a publishing

agreement that would lay some kind of foundation for his career. Now at last, it seemed, they recognised his worth.

Universal was one of the two leading publishers of modern music in the German-speaking world (the other was Schott of Mainz) and had a policy of trying to attract promising young composers on to their list. To the aspiring but usually impecunious recipients the offer of such a contract came as an 'Open, Sesame'. In reality, to no outsider's particular surprise, the balance of advantage came down fairly and squarely on the publishers' side. On the one hand they gained credit for making new music available, on the other they were poised, once they had covered their production costs, to reap the profits from the successes of the occasional high-flier, who was obligated to give them an option on whatever he wrote over the following ten years. The composer, for his part, pocketed a regular if humble monthly advance on projected sales of his works. Committed to this regular outlay, the publishers were naturally concerned to avoid backing the wrong horse too often.

Hans Heinsheimer, a contemporary of Weill's who had just begun working in the opera division of Universal, described the situation in his characteristically irreverent manner: 'To us Kurt Weill was just another man who had drawn a ten-year sentence from Hertzka. He was prisoner No. 376, a man without a face but with a little asterisk to his name. The asterisk meant "Handle with Care. Pupil of Busoni. Dangerous high-brow."'

As to the personal impression Weill made, Heinsheimer remembered him as a 'small, balding young man,'

> squinting at the world through thick, professorial glasses with eager, burning, curious eyes, quiet and measured in his manner, deliberate and always soft-spoken, with a ready, mocking wit, dressed more like a candidate for a degree in divinity than a young composer in the flamboyant Germany of the time, sucking a conservative pipe with the absent-minded absorption of an instructor in higher mathematics.

'Who could have anticipated,' Heinsheimer concluded, 'that this son of a cantor in the provincial town of Dessau. . . . would one day be the juke-box king of the world with such hits as "Mack the Knife" and "September Song"?'

The first piece of Weill's that Universal published was *Frauentanz*, which had had its first performance at the beginning of the year. When he got back to Berlin from Vienna with his 'ten-year sentence' in his pocket, he set to work on a piece in the same vein – the Concerto for Violin and Wind Instruments, Op. 12. It was to be his last purely instrumental work for eight years – a work of consolidation rather than innovation. As such, it is his valedictory tribute to Busoni, who died only a few weeks after it was finished and never heard it played.

It is a forbiddingly modernist piece, complex in its non-tonal manner, often redolent of the midnight oil. Outwardly it has a kinship, through its scoring for ten wind and brass instruments, double bass and percussion, with the contemporary Stravinsky of *L'histoire du soldat*, the *Symphonies of Wind Instruments* and the Piano Concerto, as well as with Hindemith. It was a kinship observed at the time, leading Adorno to identify the Concerto as the work of 'a German Stravinsky, with a consummate classicistic clarity in the music and some effective wind writing'. Weill himself looked in a different direction. 'Before one can understand this music,' he said, 'one must have absorbed a goodly portion of Schoenberg.'

As soloist for his Concerto Weill had in mind Joseph Szigeti, who broke many lances for contemporary music and had given the first performance of Busoni's Concerto in Berlin in 1922 – a moving occasion at which Weill had been present. But after first accepting Weill's dedication with enthusiasm, Szigeti lost interest in the work and the première fell to Marcel Darrieux, who played it at a concert in Paris in June 1925. Here it was well received. At subsequent performances in Germany, however, and in particular after an ISCM concert in Zurich in 1926, critical voices were raised. In *The New York Times* Alfred Einstein complained that Weill 'had annoyed a lot of people with his violin concerto', while Aaron Copland, reviewing the same concert, sarcastically dismissed the piece out of hand:

> Last, and probably least, was a Concerto for violin and woodwind by Kurt Weill, a young German. The less said about this very dull work, the better, particularly since there seems to be a certain tendency to regard his more recent one-act opera *Der Protagonist* as quite important.

In his survey of Weill's works down to the year of the Violin Concerto, Rudolf Kastner wrote: 'There is now not a single superfluous note left in his music'. This is the Busonian predicament into which Weill's talent and industry had led him. In successive acts of self-discipline since leaving the expressionist world of the First Symphony behind him, he had taught himself to pare away more and more extraneous, non-germane elements from his works – one might even call them elements of natural, unplanned-for spontaneity. The work has become more athletic – fitter, so to speak, and stripped for action. Or, to change the metaphor, the world it inhabits has become self-sufficient, hermetic, generating and re-generating its own atmosphere.

In Thomas Mann's novel *Doktor Faustus* the hero Adrian Leverkühn describes to his friend Serenus Zeitblom a 'strict compositional principle' – in essence the serial technique of Schoenberg – according to which all thematic development is governed centrally from within: variation and diversity are achieved by obedience to the prime motivic substance embedded in the heart of the individual work, and by acceptance of the discipline, i.e. the voluntary denial of the arbitrary, unpredictable will, which Leverkühn defines as artistic freedom. 'In accordance with this principle,' Zeitblom recalled, 'this style, this technique permitted no note, not a single one, that did not fulfil its motivic function in the structure as a whole.' In sum: 'There was not a free note left.' Perhaps it is Weill, with 'not a single superfluous note' in his music, who comes closest to forging a link between the ideals of Busoni and the 'no-free-note' dodecaphony of Schoenberg.

The summer of 1924 found Georg Kaiser installed in the luxury of his lakeside villa. One Sunday morning he invited Weill to come out from the city and discuss with him how to pick up the threads of their collaboration. A young lady was staying with him and his wife Margarethe at the time. This young lady can take up the story for herself. 'Oh, Lenya,' she remembers Kaiser saying to her,

> 'I am expecting a young composer. Would you pick him up from the station?'
> 'Sure,' I said.
> There were two ways to get to the station. One was a long walk through the woods, the other was to take a row-boat across the lake.
> 'How will I recognise him?' I asked.
> 'All composers look alike,' he said. What he meant was that at that time most composers wore a certain style of black-brimmed hat which was very easy to recognise. So I rowed across to the little station. There was sun on the waves. At the station I saw a very short young man, just a little taller than I, with a blue suit and a little blue tie, very neat and correct, heavy, thick glasses, and of course, the black hat.
> 'Are you Herr Weill?' I asked, and he said: 'Yes.' Then I invited him to enter our 'transportation'. We sat down and I rowed – in typical German fashion the woman does all the work. While I was rowing, he was looking at me and after a while he said: 'I think we've met before.'
> I said: 'Oh, really? Where?'
> And he said: 'You didn't come back for the rehearsal of that ballet.'
> I said: 'Oh, yes.'
> He said: 'I am the composer.'
> We were together from that point on, and two years later, in 1926, we were married.

The navigator in charge of the 'transportation', the future Frau Weill, had already adopted the stage name under which Weill's music was to make her famous, and nobody ever spoke of her, or addressed her, by any other. 'Lenya', Kaiser had said to her. . . .

And indeed, although she pretended she no longer remembered, Weill had not forgotten that she auditioned for a part in his *Zaubernacht* two years before but decided not to accept the offer. Since that time she had lived from hand to mouth in minor theatrical roles until meeting Georg Kaiser and his wife earlier that year. The Kaisers took a fancy to her and invited her to stay in their villa as a kind of *au pair* to their children and maid of all work – her duties apparently including the ferrying of visitors, of which there were more than a few, from the local railroad station.

'Lotte Lenya', or 'Lenja', as she wrote it, was born when its owner was seventeen. Her real name was Karoline Wilhelmine Charlotte Blamauer. She was born in Penzing, a working-class district of Vienna, in 1898, one of four children brought up in a small two-room apartment where her mother, Johanna Teuschl, took in laundry. Her father, Franz Blamauer, from a firmly proletarian background, was a coachman. At the time Linnerl – as the family called her – was born, Franz Blamauer was thirty-three, his wife thirty. In America many years later Lenya gave her own brief, bitter outline of her life down to the moment of her encounter with Weill:

> I had come from the slums of Vienna. My father drove a fiacre and beat us up regularly. I danced first in the streets, walked the tightrope with a little street circus. I had gotten to Switzerland, worked as a clerk in a tobacco store while I studied dancing. I started then as a dancer in provincial opera houses, became an actress. . . .

In a way this is all that needs to be said. A narrative constructed around it cannot but be steeped in unpleasantness, albeit tinged with sadness. Blamauer had become an alcoholic, and brutalised the children, especially Linnerl, when he came home drunk in the evenings. Whether he sexually abused her also may be open to question. Not open to question is that she had become a child of the streets before she was twelve, and that her volatile relationships with men throughout her life had their psychological origin in what she could only feel as her father's violent rejection of her as a child. He deserted his family shortly before the outbreak of the Great War, and died, a physical and mental wreck, in 1928, only two years after his daughter's marriage to a man he never met and whose world he could have never shared.

Not beautiful, barely even pretty but attractively roguish-looking, the vivacious Linnerl was too bright a pupil for her run-of-the-mill companions at the local *Volksschule*, and at ten she was transferred to an intellectually more demanding *Bürgerschule* in a neighbouring suburb. Whether school discipline was too irksome, whether the family needed the money, whether tempted by the bright lights and the *frisson* of immoral adventure – perhaps all these played their part – she left the

Bürgerschule at thirteen and took to the world's oldest profession more or less full-time.

But she saw the future differently. 'As far back as I can remember,' she said later, 'there was nothing in my head but theatre. But it was never an escape for me: it was, shall I say, my life.' So when, having collected enough money to visit an aunt in Zurich, she let her secret ambitions be known, she succeeded in finding a family willing to help her attend classes in drama and dance at the Stadttheater in return for her domestic services. While still a student during the 1914–18 war she took small parts in productions at the Schauspielhaus, and after completing her ballet course, joined the company of the Stadttheater as a ballerina. Since she could 'sing a bit', as she put it, she was also given occasional bit parts in operettas.

Elisabeth Bergner, also in Zurich at the time, on the threshold of her own fame on stage and screen, found herself 'immensely fascinated by the Blamauer woman', her precise contemporary, who, she recalled,

> was always to be seen in the company of officers, who picked her up at the end of the show – different officers each time. The gossip about her promiscuity was never-ending. The nicest thing about her was that she was always cheerful, always in good spirits. At the same time there was a flavour of forbidden fruit about her which gave her a special attraction.

When she met 'the Blamauer woman' again a few years later as the star of the *Dreigroschenoper* in Berlin, the now famous Bergner could hardly believe how far the little bit actress had come.

Short, dark, provocative, sharp and streetwise from her proletarian childhood and exploitation of her sexual attractions, Lenya seemed predestined to take, sooner or later, the next step in her life. Whether in the company of another girl dancer or with her drama teacher Richard Révy – the accounts do not tally and Lenya was not always the most reliable of witnesses – she went to Berlin. The raciness, the decadence, even the sordidness and squalor of the place quickly took hold of her. But for every one young hopeful who managed to find a foothold in the cut-throat world of show business there were a hundred who were trampled underfoot in the mêlée. Certainly Berlin had not been waiting for the Lotte Lenya of 1921, and it was over a year before she found anything approaching regular work. At the time she presented herself at the Kurfürstendamm Theatre for a part in Weill's *Zaubernacht* and met, or almost met, its composer, she was playing Maria, Olivia's lady-in-waiting, in *Twelfth Night*. It was after one of these performances that she had met Georg Kaiser.

At her audition for *Zaubernacht* Lenya had been required to dance and to sing a little song. She always stood for the actress who sings, not, like the opera star, the singer who acts. Nor did she make any bones about it. 'Reading music is a skill I never learned,' she cheerfully admitted only a few years before she died, 'and Weill consistently refused to initiate me into the mysteries of harmony and counterpoint. He was certain that it was better to trust my good ear than to try and cultivate any ability I might have had in the area of theory.'

But Kurt Weill, the quiet, intense intellectual, had not made the trip to Grünheide in search of a wife. He had come to work – more accurately, to be given work, namely to discover in discussion with Kaiser how the one-act tragedy *Der Protagonist* might be given operatic form. Written in 1920 and first played in 1922, Kaiser's short but masterly piece of dramatic writing reveals, in a language of uncanny coolness and logic, the violent consequences of a tragic confusion of reality and illusion in the mind of the artist. On bicycle rides together through the Mark Brandenburg, in one of Kaiser's boats on the tranquil waters of Lake Peetz, side by side on walks through the glorious woods, with Margarethe Kaiser and Lenya behind them, the two men pondered how spoken drama might be turned into music drama, Kaiser tossing up one idea after another. It was one of his disconcerting habits during conversation to suddenly look away, fumble in his pocket for a piece of paper, jot down a thought that had just struck him, then stuff the paper back into his pocket. His pockets and drawers were crammed full with such impulsively scribbled, and rarely used, scraps of paper.

From the beginning Weill and Kaiser had a relationship that was as personally warm-hearted as it was professionally harmonious. It clearly helped that the Kaisers liked Lenya and were prepared to go out of their way to help her. But it went deeper than this. In the summer of 1924, as Busoni lay dying in Berlin, it was to Georg and Margarethe Kaiser that Weill turned for solace. 'The Kaisers have become dear friends,' he wrote to his sister Ruth, 'and are probably the only people who will be able to replace to any extent what I shall lose with the death of Busoni.'

The action of *Der Protagonist* takes place in a shabby English country inn at the time of Shakespeare. A troupe of strolling players, led by the Protagonist, is rehearsing a comic dumb-show, to musical accompaniment, for performance that evening before the Duke and his friends. After the rehearsal the Protagonist's sister, who lives with the troupe, confesses to him that she has a lover – a confession that shatters his incestuous dependence on her. After she has left to fetch her lover, a messenger arrives from the Duke with instructions that, because a Bishop has unexpectedly arrived and will unfortunately be joining the company at the evening performance, the bawdy comedy originally planned will have to be replaced by something more serious. The Protagonist converts the scenario of the mime from comedy to tragedy, with himself in the part of a cuckolded husband, and a new rehearsal begins.

Just as the point is reached at which he is about to stab his rival, his sister, who knows nothing of the changed scenario, joyfully bursts into the room with her lover. The actors and the musicians break off in confusion. The sight of his sister brings back to the Protagonist's mind the thought of her confession. The real-life confession, a statement of betrayal, mingles with the scene he is playing, and instead of murdering his rival, he plunges his dagger into his sister's throat.

This piece of black nihilism, in which the artist, the Protagonist, is betrayed both by life, in the form of his sister, and by art, which is by its nature founded on illusion, offered an admirable scenario for the sort of work Kaiser and Weill had in mind. On the one hand the strong storyline provided a foundation on which real opera-as-drama could be built, using the music to express in intensified form the agony of the Protagonist's experience. On the other, the presence at the heart of the play of two mime scenes enabled them to exploit the insights they had gained from their work on the pantomime-cum-ballet which they had only recently abandoned as a medium inadequate for conveying their artistic intentions.

For Weill it was like arriving at opera through the back door. *Zaubernacht* had given him an understanding of the visual aspect, the demands of the stage, music as interpretative commentary on action. In the setting of words to music he had already ranged from Rilke to the medieval poems of *Frauentanz*. At the same time he had been sharpening the technical tools of his trade, particularly his powers of orchestration, in a series of 'abstract' instrumental compositions. It all pointed towards an expectation, close at hand, that these strands of experience would be drawn together in a single creative act, a definitive statement of a position reached and an artistic outlook declared. The hour or so's music of *Der Protagonist*, 'the natural, almost fortuitous blend of opera and mime-show', as Weill described it, defines the position and exemplifies the outlook.

The twin climaxes of the work are the two pantomimes, or mimed rehearsals. For the comic pantomime Weill sets an eight-piece band of wind players on the stage to accompany the action; the tragic pantomime, and the five main singing roles of the opera proper, are accompanied by the orchestra in the pit. The formidable technical difficulty of these roles is matched by the harsh non-tonality of the melodic and harmonic idiom and the objective inner logic of the polyphonic writing. Weill has reached the summit of assured expression in the language he has been developing and refining over the past three or four years. The unsentimentality and disciplined intellectuality of that language have their roots in Busoni but Weill achieves an unremitting intensity that is his own. The comparative brevity and the continuous action of the work force from him a concentration of attention which makes Kastner's remark that there was 'not a single superfluous note' in his Violin Concerto a statement of strength, not of limitation.

Writing in 1932, by which time Weill's music for Brecht had come to overshadow everything he had composed earlier, the critic Herbert Fleischer perceived that the strength of *Der Protagonist* and the works that surround it lay in the power of the music to be, not the accompaniment or illustration of a situational reality but its complete, immediate expression: 'Gestic quality, mime, the clear definition of an individual will, directness of expression and address – this constitutes the heart of Weill's music, and has done since his earliest works. Weill talks and gesticulates in music: his art turns into language, into representation.' And in *Frauentanz* and *Recordare*, Fleischer continues, one can recognise Weill's aim of 'elucidating the content of the text by means of the musical expression' and achieving a 'unity of musical and verbal rhythm, of melodic and verbal gestus'.

Poetic texts exist in their own right and do not need music to 'elucidate' them. We can, however, accept from Fleischer that, in his settings of words to music, and whether the context be lyrical or dramatic, Weill aims at a new heightened unity which, as he sees it, meets the objective needs of the moment and is far removed from the ideals of late Romantics like Richard Strauss. A few years later, under the influence of Brecht, he explained in an essay called 'On the Gestic Character of Music' how he envisioned this unity in the form of 'epic opera' with its 'gestic music'. But he had always posed himself the basic question, he insisted, when pondering an opera, a ballet, a pantomime or a related hybrid: 'What grounds are there for having music on the stage?' And this provoked a second question: 'What is the nature of music for the stage, and are there particular qualities that brand certain music as theatre music?' The intimacy of musical identification with the poets and dramatists to whom he felt particularly drawn at different times in his life – Georg Kaiser, Ivan Goll, Brecht, later Maxwell Anderson – shows how seriously he took these questions.

Weill finished the score of *Der Protagonist* in March 1925, and it was published later the same year with a dedication to Lotte Lenya. On December 14, in the Berlin Staatsoper, Erich Kleiber conducted another first performance, one which Weill described as 'the most powerful event in Berlin musical life for years'. The work was Alban Berg's *Wozzeck*.

Pace the objection that one term, in itself imprecise, is being made to serve different functions, the description 'non-tonal' may be used to characterise the general musical language of both works, the idiom in which their broad musical argument is cast, and however many differences of technique and procedure may be identified. By the same token, both Berg and Weill also return to tonal, even triadic idioms at various points in their operas, to particularly calculated effect when such idioms occur as the last word in an argument which has up to that point been conducted in largely non-tonal terms. Such a procedure expresses the simple psychological reality that the interpolation of moments of diatonic consonance relaxes the tension inherent in dissonant, chromatic styles and allows the listener a passing glimpse of the familiar musical world in which he has grown up and which he accepts as by nature his own. Both *Der Protagonist* and *Wozzeck*, with their climaxes of murder and their presentation of human minds which collapse under the weight of an unbearable reality, need these moments for their dramatic purpose.

But to Weill, *Wozzeck*, powerful work though it was, formed 'the magnificent conclusion of a direct line of development starting with Wagner's *Tristan* and proceeding through Debussy's *Pelléas and Mélisande* and Strauss' *Elektra*.' It did not 'carry the seeds of the future in itself' – as, by implication, his own works did, or were about to do. On the occasion of a new production of *Wozzeck* in 1932, Max Marschalk wrote in the *Vossische Zeitung*:

> Looking back from today, we can see that modern opera has taken two clearly different paths. One leads from Wagner through Strauss to Berg, where it seems for the moment to have come to an end. The other, from Mussorgsky and Debussy to Janáček and Stravinsky, then to Milhaud and Kurt Weill, is in reality the new and modern path.

Whatever Marschalk saw at the time, we may suspect that it reflects a then fashionable leaning towards an objectivity and detachment which distinguish the 'gestic' manner of *Der Protagonist* from the total emotional involvement so shattering in *Wozzeck*. But so much has happened in the operatic world since then that a judgement which sets Berg against Weill to the former's disadvantage, then takes Milhaud and Weill as pioneers of the true way forwards, can only be seen as the victim of history. Perhaps history has also expressed a view by establishing Berg's Violin Concerto as one of the greatest in the modern repertoire while leaving performances of Weill's as collectors' items.

But comparisons aside, *Der Protagonist* can stand as a gripping work of musical theatre in its own right, a piece of *Neue Sachlichkeit* drama yet also with its moments of expressionist intensity. Is it too much to hope that some enterprising company may one day realise what a splendid evening's entertainment it and its *buffa* companion, *Der Zar lässt sich photographieren*, could provide?

CHAPTER VI

Journalism and Jazz

The musical and critical maturity of the twenty-five-year-old Weill, his keen mind exploring new avenues of expression, his immense creative energy fully committed, and his most sensational success only three years away, is a matter of public record. In a letter written in July 1925 he tells Universal, in an almost throwaway tone, that he intends to write some piano pieces for Claudio Arrau and a new string quartet for the Roth Quartet; he is also, he says, discussing plans 'with a well-known poet' (he often dangled such provocative pieces of semi-information in front of their noses) for a new stage work – which turned out to be *Royal Palace*. Neither the piano pieces nor the quartet materialised. But this does not detract from the reality of his vigour or his tireless imagination.

The private Weill, the man behind the quiet, composed exterior, emerges as an equally intense person, blending a desire for self-fulfilment with a philosophical overview of human conduct in general. A letter to Ruth, part of an exchange of reflections and intimacies of the kind which often passed between them, brings us close to the heart of the man. 'There are two kinds of happiness,' he tells her:

> there is a rapture for two, where one is more in one's partner than in oneself; and there is the blissful loneliness of creation, as one gazes silently upon life and mankind. You consider that I turn my back on what is unpleasant. I don't – I drink my fill of it, because it is part and parcel of the age into which I have been born and because it points the way to beauty, which blossoms today as it has always done. . . . I savour every emotion to the full, without wondering what it might lead to.

It is a statement of an almost naive honesty. It is also a philosophy that carries with it the certainty of self-inflicted pain and worry. As Weill acknowledged both the unpleasant and the beautiful, so his life reveals the inseparability of the honesty and the pain.

Even more revealing of his innermost thoughts is a long letter he wrote to his mother on New Year's Eve 1924. He is alone, not unwillingly so, confined to the city for the daily rehearsals of his *Stundenbuch* songs for baritone and orchestra at the Philharmonie, where they were to have their first performance in a few weeks' time. Lenya is with the Kaisers in Grünheide. He writes:

> My beloved Mamushka,
> As you are on your own this evening, I want you to at least have the pleasure of receiving this letter tomorrow morning. Console yourself with the thought that I shall spend New Year's Eve at home as well. I have rehearsals every afternoon until January 22 and shan't be able to get to Grünheide. I don't want to go anywhere else. I detest the thought of stumbling into a new period of my life in a state of intoxication after a night of carousing, and prefer to sit at home and reflect on life.
> Your remarks on Hannukah, half-jesting, half-scornful, lead me to make a few fundamental observations. Religion is a matter of conviction. It can be reached by three paths. The first is that of upbringing and custom, and you have performed a dutiful service by showing us this path. We think too much, and our young, critical minds cannot understand how, acting on our pure childhood faith, we can do things that set us beyond the bounds of custom. Today, having left the second path behind me, I feel much closer to the first. That second path is that of society. The observance of religious practices is made easier by one's membership of a community. I tried to join such a community, and thought I had found friendship in these circles but it was that very community which destroyed that friendship, leaving me with a feeling of such profound contempt for these Jewish circles that it is impossible for me to have anything to do with them. The other Jews – the assimilators and the Zionists – are in any case totally impossible.
> So there remains only the third path, namely, to start from the point of one's own development as a human being and gradually find one's way back to the faith of one's childhood. It takes a long while and is beset with many distractions but it is the goal towards which all great developments move. The Great Truth must be something quite simple. . . .
> Goodbye for now. Be sensible and don't over-exert yourself. Things still get done with half the effort.
> A thousand kisses from
Your
Kurt

It is a touching personal confession, the testament of a man intensely conscious of his origins yet deeply critical, even resentful, of some of the ways in which the development of his people has manifested itself. On a philosophical plane it envisions a cyclical schema of the evolution of human understanding analogous to the story of the Garden of Eden. Man's loss of natural goodness and spontaneous emotion is laid at the door of intellectual restlessness and the pursuit of rational, 'scientific' experience, and can only be restored by abandoning the cold prerogative of reason and analysis and returning to the childlike state of God-given innocence in which we were born.

Weill was not a man given to extended philosophical speculation – not, at least, in written form, although there was a lot going on behind those thick spectacles which the outside world never learned about. When he did turn his mind to theoretical matters, then it was to the conceptual principles underlying his music of the moment, or to the relationship between art and society, or to the historical continuum within which he viewed his activity. All the more precious, at this moment, are these insights into the intensity of his concern with the meaning and the quality of his life.

'We were together from that point on,' said Lotte Lenya of their meeting in Grünheide in the summer of 1924. To an outsider they must have seemed an unlikely pair. Weill, reserved but intense, keenly intellectual, his imagination constantly at work, had a personality heavily indebted to his middle-class Jewish background. He had abandoned the public observance of his faith but he maintained a loyal relationship to his parents, writing to them about his struggles to realise his artistic ambitions and knowing that they would understand. His two brothers, Nathan and Hanns, had both married within the faith, so had his sister Ruth. Nathan and Ruth, like their parents, embraced their Zionist birthright and eventually emigrated to Israel. It was the expectation, not to say assumption, of ex-Cantor Albert Weill and his wife that when the chosen moment arrived, young Kurt too would bring a Jewish girl into the family circle.

But he did not. Lotte Lenya's was a Gentile, proletarian world on to which had been grafted the notoriously fickle, footloose milieu of show business. And whereas the Weill family held together in the comfort of their religion and their solid bourgeois morality, in the strains of war as in the horrors of the inflation that followed, the Blamauers could do little more than scratch a day-to-day existence in an environment designed rather to escape from than to seek refuge in. The extrovert Lenya had an experience of raw life that Weill did not, and her years in and around the theatre had instilled in her an immense resilience and an intuition for survival. To be sure, Weill had to prove himself like anyone else – had to convince the public that he had something to say which was worth listening to. But Lenya had to fight material and psychological circumstances as well, and fight them without the tender understanding of a secure and comforting family.

Maybe it was those very differences that attracted them to each other. *Les extrêmes se touchent.* Certainly neither of them changed – Weill did not become a Bohemian, Lenya did not become an intellectual. The wit of Berlin cabaret in the 1920s, politically and musically, perhaps provoked a meeting of minds and provided them with an area of shared response and, later, of shared activity. But throughout their twenty-five years together, they each 'did their own thing', while yet deeply anxious to know, at the same time, what the other's 'thing' was.

A few months after their meeting at the Kaisers, Lenya left Grünheide and joined Weill in Berlin. First they found rooms in Halensee, at the western end of the Kurfürstendamm. Then in the spring of 1925 they moved closer to the centre and occupied two rooms on the first floor of the Pension Hassforth, Luisenplatz 3, which belonged to Georg Kaiser but which he only used on the rare occasions when he stayed in the city. The house, which still stands, carries a plaque commemorating Kaiser in large letters, with a postscript in smaller type adding (far from accurately) that it was 'in his [i.e. Kaiser's] flat that Kurt Weill wrote the music for Brecht's *Dreigroschenoper* in 1928'. In one of his two rooms Weill continued to give the private lessons from which he drew a not inconsiderable part of his earnings. Visitors remembered with surprise that although he had shelves full of books, his library of scores was selective to the point of self-denial – Mozart, Verdi, Bellini's *Norma*, Bizet's *Carmen*. For her part, Lenya added a modest contribution to the family budget from periodical engagements in suburban Berlin theatres.

The dark and dreary rooms of the Pension Hassforth, which faced the Charlottenburg Palace, were also home to the Marxist poet and dramatist Rudolf Leonhard, who aroused Weill's interest in the 'Gruppe 1925', a loose association of radical writers – Brecht, the philosopher Ernst Bloch, Walter Mehring, Johannes R. Becher, the Czech novelist Ernst Weiss and others – formed in the spirit of the 'Novembergruppe' which had emerged at the end of the war. The writer Hermann Kasack stated the common view of those in the 'Gruppe 1925' that the writer 'can no longer live out his private poetic idyll of contemplation or resignation detached from his age but must feel himself to be the conscience and the expression of that age'. This was the sense of the social dimension of art which had drawn Weill to the Novembergruppe and which was now revived in the rooms of the Pension Hassforth. He retained it, in one form or another, until the end of his life.

Indeed, it was about to receive a new and ideal platform for expression. Public service radio broadcasting in Germany had begun with the establishment in Berlin of a company called Funk-Stunde Berlin AG in October 1923. Regional stations quickly followed, and a journal, *Der deutsche Rundfunk*, was founded – a combination of *Radio Times* and the original-style *Listener* – both to inform the growing number of listeners of the programmes for the forthcoming week and to review the highlights of the week that had passed. As the potential of the new medium began to be realised, a separate new division was created by the Funk-Stunde company to handle drama and opera, which supplemented the musical programmes that had formed part of the staple diet of the day's broadcasts from the beginning.

As a by-product of the exciting new invention and the experiences it offered, there arose a need for a new kind of journalist, an arts critic with the breadth of knowledge and power of judgement of the old-style reviewer of plays, operas and concerts but also with the capacity to cover ten times as much ground in a given week and write about it ten times as fast. This was the cultural slaughter to which Weill now offered himself as a lamb.

Principally, one imagines, his motive was financial. Nobody, says the cynic, does that sort of thing for love. But the kind of deadline discipline it imposes, while attracting a dubious image of hastiness and shallowness, greatly concentrates the mind. By writing week in week out in *Der deutsche Rundfunk* for over four years, Weill forced himself to discover where he stood vis-à-vis the 'classics' and the whole spectrum of contemporary music, light and serious, for which the new medium had created a mass public. It also set him pondering what new opportunities for music radio had opened up. And although he later became disillusioned with its one-time promise, his *Berliner Requiem* and the Brecht-Weill-Hindemith *Lindberghflug* both owe their existence directly to it. And he was to compose again for the medium in America.

The range of subjects on which Weill wrote – more specifically, had to write, since he did not choose what items were broadcast – was staggeringly wide, and could only have been mastered by someone who for years had spent most evenings in the theatre or the concert hall, as well as keeping abreast of general developments in the arts. Many of his articles have the character of general reviews, others devote space to individual topics on which he had particular points to make, not only in music but also in drama: Kleist, Ibsen, Gorky, Georg Kaiser, Wedekind and Bernard Shaw take their place alongside Weber, Bruckner, Verdi, Mahler, Max Reger and, above all contemporary composers whose 'difficult' works were now being relayed to an ever-widening audience – Busoni, Schoenberg, Stravinsky, Hindemith, Janáček, Bartók. At the lighter, 'easier' end of the scale came Millöcker's *Der Bettelstudent*, Gershwin's *Rhapsody in Blue* and jazz, including articles on Paul Whiteman and Josephine Baker.

He even reported on a boxing match – which is perhaps not as quirky as it sounds, for boxing commanded a wide following in the 1920s. Max Schmeling, later heavyweight champion of the world, became a national idol, a symbol of renascent German power, and at the ringside one would find leading actors like Fritz Kortner and Hans Albers and writers such as Brecht – who had an unbridled passion for the sport – Leonhard Frank and Weill's fellow-lodger Rudolf Leonhard, not to mention the former

German Crown Prince Wilhelm, son of the ex-Kaiser.

Weill's career was gathering pace. His steady stream of articles for *Der deutsche Rundfunk* from the beginning of 1925 onwards ensured that his name recurred with the regularity every journalist cherishes. People looked forward to his column from one Sunday's issue to the next, and would open a conversation by asking, 'Did you read Kurt Weill on *Pierrot Lunaire* last week?' Then there was his work on *Der Protagonist* with the famous Georg Kaiser, a collaboration in itself tantamount to a seal of approval set on his abilities by Germany's second most popular contemporary dramatist. By March he had finished the score, but there was no immediate prospect of a performance. Two months later he went to Dresden to see the first performance of Busoni's *Doktor Faust*, left unfinished at the composer's death the previous year and now completed by Jarnach. He took *Der Protagonist* with him and gave it to Fritz Busch, who had said he would like to see it.

Interest of this kind was gratifying but it did not pay the bills. If, as seems to have happened with depressing regularity, his monthly hundred marks from Universal in Vienna did not arrive punctually, he was forced to send urgent telegrams demanding it. Later in the year Dr Hertzka agreed to increase the payment to two hundred marks a month – and the currency had now been stable for over a twelvemonth – but the money did not reach Weill's pocket any more quickly for that.

Indeed, up to and even beyond the sensational success of *Die Dreigroschenoper* the dominant tone of his correspondence with his publishers is one of sour dissatisfaction. Time and again he asks irritably why they are so slow in issuing his works; men like Klemperer, Furtwängler and Scherchen are ready to consider performing *Quodlibet* and the Violin Concerto but how, he complains, can they make up their minds if he has no printed score to show them? Irritating too was their habit of casually sending the one holograph score of a work to one conductor or opera-house director after another, allowing it to become tattered and torn in the process: if they were too tight-fisted to have a copy made, then at least they could try 'to treat my manuscript a little more carefully.'

Nor, he grumbles, are Universal raising a finger to help promote *Der Protagonist*: why would they not arrange for an article on him in the *Musikblätter des Anbruch*, their house journal, to generate some publicity in advance of its performance? The example of *Wozzeck* had shown the wisdom of publishing the piano score some months before the first performance, so that the public could become acquainted with the work and early sales generated, which was in everybody's interest. So why, asked the disgruntled and impatient Weill he was, after all, a young man in a hurry – did Universal not plan to do the same with his

Protagonist? Throughout his life Weill invested enormous energy in the promotion of his own music. Assembling as many write-ups as he could lay his hands on, he went to the lengths of telling Universal which sources to quote from in their publicity campaign to build up his public image. No wonder Hans Heinsheimer once said to him: 'If only I were as good a composer as you are a manager.'

In June 1925 came the first performance of his Violin Concerto, in Paris, followed by performances in Germany later in the year, including one in his home town of Dessau. The name of Kurt Weill was becoming one to reckon with. And not only in the realm of composition. For as he worked on *Der Protagonist*, at a moment when the vein of nineteenth-century music drama seemed exhausted, with Schoenberg, Stravinsky, Hindemith, Milhaud and others searching for new, 'objective' forms of musico-dramatic expression, Weill produced his own philosophy of the exercise.

It all rested, he explained in his essay 'Commitment to Opera' (1925), on a dual commitment: on the one hand, to the form of opera *per se*, a vote of confidence in the power of the genre to make manifest the emotions and values which the composer seeks to convey; on the other hand, to the principle that the music, far from being a mere accompaniment or illustration of the dramatic substance, carries that dramatic substance within itself, so that the evolution of the dramatic meaning and the unfolding of the musical argument are indivisible. 'In opera,' as he put it, 'we must be able to give our musical imagination the same totally free rein as in chamber music.' Or, in an extended essay the following year called 'Busoni's *Faust* and the Renewal of Operatic Form': 'Only the perfect fusion of all the expressive resources of the stage with all the expressive resources of music will produce that supremely heightened form of theatre which we call opera.' Imperiously pointing out the direction that modern opera should follow stood Busoni's *Doktor Faust*, 'theatre in its finest and purest form', as Weill described it, 'presenting in vivid form a great idea which unites the whole of mankind'.

If one takes Wagner's theoretical pronouncements as one's point of departure, as Weill seems to do, then one will indeed recognise the apparently unbridgeable gulf which Weill's historical postulate identifies. The theory of the *Gesamtkunstwerk*, and the principle, itself a protest against the undramatic, prima donna-dominated opera of the early nineteenth century, that the music should be made to serve the superior interests of the drama, represents just that attenuation of the power of music which Weill resents. But in practice, what are Wagner's music dramas but huge achievements in sheer music, works in which the profoundest meanings and emotions reside not in the concepts of the texts or the symbolism of the action but in the notes of the score? Here, surely, the musical imagination truly does enjoy the 'totally free rein' which Weill demands for it but which he apparently does not recognise in practice. Writing a year before Weill's 'Commitment to Opera', the inimitable Cecil Gray observed of the second act of *Tristan and Isolde*: 'If Tristan and Isolde were to behave on stage as they do in the orchestra, the police would soon stop the performance.' Today we have grown used to such behaviour on stage and the police would do nothing, but the serious point remains: the intensity of the meaning and action of the opera at this point – and not only at this point – lies in the uninhibited, almost uncontrollable music.

As his experience in musical theatre grew, Weill continued to accompany his compositions with statements of his critical position. Sometimes the articles were designed as interpretative commentaries on aspects of individual works – his *Mahagonny* opera, for instance, and *Der Jasager*; other pieces, predominantly on the problems confronting contemporary opera, he published in *Melos*, *Die Musik*, *Der Anbruch* and similar journals, and on occasion in leading newspapers such as the *Berliner Tageblatt*. All this in addition to his galley-slave labour for *Der deutsche Rundfunk*.

It had been Kaiser who brought Weill and Lotte Lenya together. It was also Kaiser who in the summer of 1925 introduced Weill to a poet who now made his own contribution to Weill's advancement. This was Ivan Goll, pseudonym of Isaac Lang, a Jewish expressionist-surrealist writer born in Alsace who, with his wife Claire, also a poet, had settled in Paris but spent considerable periods in Berlin. Bilingual by upbringing, Goll published lyrics and dramas in both French and German, sometimes translating them from the one language to the other. At the time Weill first met him in the Romanisches Café, he was thirty-four. In 1939, just before the outbreak of the Second World War, he and his wife emigrated to New York, returning in 1947 to Paris, where he died of leukaemia three years later – two months before Weill.

The Romanisches Café, a legendary haunt of artists and writers behind the Kaiser-Wilhelm-Gedächtniskirche, was an ugly nineteenth-century building which had acquired its fame by a bizarre accident. For years its two large barn-like rooms had stood almost empty, while in the hospitable Café des Westens nearby, in the Kurfürstendamm, intellectuals and literati had made themselves a convivial home from home, arguing with each other in smoke-filled rooms until the early hours. Irreverent Berliners dubbed the Café des Westens the 'Megalomaniacs' Café', which eventually so irritated the proprietor that he told his intellectual patrons to take their *Stammtisch* elsewhere. So these 'megalomaniacs' – poets such as Erich Mühsam and Else Lasker-Schüler, the philosopher Ernst Bloch, the painter Max Slevogt, Piscator and his production team,

Friedrich Holländer, the most successful light music composer of the day, innumerable literary critics – crossed the street and set up shop in the hitherto deserted Romanisches Café. Their custom, and the owner's astute management, turned the 'Romanisches' into a centre of intellectual life which flourished, effectively and noisily, until the banning of free speech and discussion by the Nazis. The house went up in flames during an air raid in November 1943, and the area surrounding the Gedächtniskirche has since been completely rebuilt.

Goll, a regular at the 'Romanisches', was the born refugee, the man with many homes – or with none – the poet with whom the 'lost' post-war generation could identify unhesitatingly. 'Ivan Goll has no home,' he wrote: 'a Jew by fate, born a Frenchman by chance, made a German by a stamp on a piece of paper.' The roots that had been torn up in life were those he sought to re-establish in his poetry through the expressive personality of the artist set not on indulging himself in the literary fashions and experiments of the subjective expressionist-surrealist moment but on exploring the unchanging nature of man in his inalienable humanity. This humanity he portrays in terms of the polarities that determine the immutable parameters of life: time and eternity, joy and misery, hope and despair, appearance and reality.

A perfect symbol of these antitheses, carrying within itself both the tensions of common humanity and the creative sufferings of the artist, presented itself to Goll in the figure of Orpheus. Into this symbolic figure, focus of his poem 'Der neue Orpheus', Goll poured the confused yearnings and sufferings of modern man, of the modern artist, Orpheus reincarnate in the Berlin of 1920. The musician of Greek myth with his lyre has variously become, in his contemporary metamorphoses, a hurdy-gurdy man, a church organist, the leader of a palm court orchestra, the conductor of a choir of war veterans singing patriotic songs, and an internationally famous virtuoso. His Eurydice, meanwhile, equally responsive to the opportunities offered by post-war society, has become a prostitute, and stands outside a mainline railroad station as a spokesman for the unredeemed in Hades. But she does not heed him. For, like those who surround her, she wants only to be left in her underworld. So, alone in the waiting room at the station, he shoots himself.

Originally written in French, the poem called 'Le nouvel Orphée' appeared as 'Der neue Orpheus' in a little German volume of Goll's poetry in 1924. It is cast in short, free, unrhymed stanzas and in an uncanny language at one moment close to desperation, at the next chillingly detached and parodistic, revelling in an imagery of incongruities. Expressionism and surrealism lie side by side in a bitter-sweet relationship which caught the imagination of young intellectuals who had lived through, and now escaped from, an atmosphere of broken promises and were viewing the human condition through the untinted glasses of *Neue Sachlichkeit*.

Weill found in this strange poem of Goll's an appeal to his own ever-widening powers of dramatic expression, and under the attraction of its dissonant originality he set it as his Op.15 – *Der neue Orpheus*, a cantata for soprano, solo violin and orchestra. Claudio Arrau, who was still among Weill's private students, later recalled in conversation that a group of friends used to meet to discuss matters of art and music – he mentions Weill's fellow-Busonian Vladimir Vogel, the cellist Gregor Piatigorsky and Hans Mersmann, editor of the music journal *Melos*, as members of the circle – and that on one occasion a number of them 'went over a sort of cantata Weill was composing at the time'. The mythical subject of the cantata led them to review 'old' Orpheuses, and 'one night,' Arrau said, 'we went through Monteverdi's *Orfeo*, which at that time was a discovery, since it had not been performed for years.'

Central to the aesthetic of surrealism is the intention to shock the observer out of his complacency and conventionality by creating incongruity, parody, a world stood on its head. Its artistic means, whether in literature, art or music, are derived from realism – or, more accurately in the historical context, from the form of realism that goes under the name of *Neue Sachlichkeit*. The incongruous, the parodistic and other inversions of 'normal' experience can only be grasped by reference to the familiar and the compatible of everyday existence as we know and understand it. The negative takes its meaning from the positive, and the terms of the antithesis have to be clearly recognised in their own right, otherwise the meaning of their juxtaposition, or of their 'unnatural' substitution for each other, is lost. There is no room for explanation or interpretation. Montage and collage, the agglomeration of elements familiar in their individuality but disturbing, even destructive, in their new composite function, became characteristic techniques for creating a surreal world.

The technical constituents of surrealist music – features such as the montage-like use of the idioms of jazz and dance music, the mixing of media, the shock tactics of incongruity and irreverent parody – find their ideal home in the Brecht-Weill world of *Die Dreigroschenoper* and *Mahagonny*. Adorno called the latter 'the first surrealist opera'. But already in Weill's *Der neue Orpheus* one catches the scent of the cabaret and the dance hall, the mocking march and the ironical waltz rhythms.

Weill himself sensed that something was happening. In an excited letter to his parents early in the New Year, 1926, he wrote:

> As a composer I am going through the years of sitting on top of a powder-keg. Untapped sources of energy are going to have to explode,

and a state of heightened awareness is making me feel perpetually tense. Only if you look at it this way will you understand certain things about me which might otherwise remain incomprehensible. I am now in the grip of work again. I am immersed in this new opera [*Royal Palace*] and only leave the house to deal with the most urgent matters. I have got to master a form of expression that is still new to me. And I have discovered to my pleasure what I first found out in *Der neue Orpheus* – that I am gradually working my way towards my 'true self' and that my music is becoming much more assured, much freer, much lighter – and simpler.

It sounds like the sort of music Busoni, to his displeasure, suspected that Weill might be working towards when, in the course of one of the master classes in the Viktoria-Luise-Platz, he said scornfully to his pupil: 'What do you want to become, the poor man's Verdi?' To which, according to Lenya, the poor man's Verdi had retorted: 'Is that so bad?'

In his New Year letter to his parents there is no disguising the pulsating energy and sense of breathless expectation surging through Weill's creative mind. It is a key moment in his development, a moment when he realises he is about to leave something behind but without yet seeing clearly the goal towards which his 'still new form of expression' is taking him. This gives *Der neue Orpheus*, like *Royal Palace* that followed it, a particular significance in his *oeuvre*, a significance independent of any judgement one may pass on the paradoxes and heterogeneities of the work itself. For like any symbol of transition, *Der neue Orpheus* looks two ways, and one must observe both where it has come from and where it is going to. The expressionist recitative of the virtuoso soprano part, with its mordant, witty declamation of Goll's provocative verses, belongs to the world of *Der Protagonist*; the use of non-triadic harmony within a tonal framework is a common feature of Weill's earlier style, and the instrumentation recalls the idiom of the Violin Concerto.

Lying cheek by jowl with the features of the 'difficult' Weill the world had come to know were the elements of the new 'simpler' style towards which he was desperately working. These elements appear in the idioms of cabaret song and dance music through which are portrayed the splintered modern reincarnations of Orpheus – as music teacher, as silent-movie piano player, as operator of mechanical instruments and so on – who occupy the centre of Goll's poem. To the surrealism of the text he adds the musical surrealism of the incongruous association of these popular, accessible dance music clichés with the cerebral music of the young post-Schoenbergian and post-Busonian. To some critics the result was an unfortunate lapse into incompatibility. As the process of musical integration intensified in Weill's mind, so the discrepancies became absorbed and his homogeneous personal style took shape. But at the time of *Der neue Orpheus* the paradoxes and uncertainties could not be ignored, although the music has a brashness and drive which sees it through much disparaging critical attention.

So has that of *Royal Palace*, the one-act opera to which Weill turned, almost without pausing for breath, the moment *Der neue Orpheus* was finished. Fired by a sudden new enthusiasm aroused by joining the conversations in Grünheide between Weill and Georg Kaiser, Goll now set opera, in his lyrical, non-dramatic definition of the form, at the pinnacle of the arts. 'The spirit of drama is action,' he wrote in the programme book for the première of *Royal Palace*, 'that of opera is rhythm. Drama rests on thought, opera on emotion. The raw material of drama is logic, that of opera is dream. Drama is life, opera is fairy-tale.'

All this is very precious and self-indulgent, with a suspicious flavour of disingenuousness. But, perhaps surprisingly, Weill saw a way to handle the libretto that the poet constructed on these premises – a way to pick up what Goll described, in an unexpectedly sporty metaphor, as 'the ball of words that I was constantly at pains to land in the composer's court'.

These 'balls of words' tell a melodramatic story set on the terrace of the Grand Palace, a luxury hotel on the shores of an Italian lake. An elegant, spoilt young woman called Dejanira is wooed by three men: her husband, 'Yesterday's Lover' and 'Tomorrow's Lover'. Each of these three in turn has the opportunity to show, in a scene danced and acted out before her, what pleasures he would offer her. The Husband envisages an extravagant banquet at the hotel, with jazz for the whole staff to dance to, followed by an airline trip to the capital cities in Europe. Yesterday's Lover mounts a ballet danced by the sun and the moon, by the stars and the signs of the zodiac, to recall to her mind their erotic ecstasies in the past. Finally Tomorrow's Lover cries: 'I will give you everlasting Nature!' and conjures up a phantasmagoria, also danced, in which Orpheus appears, followed by all living creatures who worship God, as the stage rocks to and fro to the movement of the waves. But Dejanira spurns all three suitors as pretentious confidence tricksters who have no understanding of her true inner needs, and drowns herself in the waters of the lake below. The three men look on helplessly, and in a surrealistic final section built on a persistent tango rhythm they do nothing but call out the name Dejanira in endless repetitions of its syllabic elements in varying combinations – Janirade, Nirajade etc. As their chanting grows softer and softer and the curtain falls, the Husband stumbles back on to the stage, then throws himself from the parapet.

Goll was overwhelmed by what Weill had made out of this one name in the final part of the work. 'This word has the principal role in the opera,' he rapturously claimed. It was the perfect paradigm of his demand that the lyric poet should see himself as an assistant to the musician: 'The greatest happiness that a poet can wish for is to hear his poetry transformed into music.'

A lot of sweat and toil went into the score. 'I have laboured away these last few weeks to such an extent,' Weill wrote to Peter Bing, 'that I am now in a state of utter stupor. But except for the two dances the score is now finished.' The full orchestral score has not survived; the piano reduction, however, published the following year, shows that a full orchestra was called for, including, significantly and for the first time in Weill's works, an alto saxophone, together with an eclectic chamber ensemble set on the stage. The work is dedicated to Georg Kaiser.

Like its companion piece *Der neue Orpheus*, *Royal Palace* betrays the Janus-like quality of Weill's musical personality at this point. Much of the writing is still highly dissonant and full of that complex polyphony which looks back to Busoni and which has become deeply engrained in that side of his activity which is sustained by technical skill and facility. Much of the operatic vocal writing, too, belongs to the world of *Der Protagonist* – angular contours, awkward intervals, a no-holds-barred intensity of declamation. But the symbolic appearance of a saxophone in the score, accompanied by harsh syncopations, dance-music rhythms and jazz-band instrumentation, with a prominent xylophone part, points in a quite different direction.

Jazz was in the air. That is to say, the European perception of jazz was in the air, white man's jazz as popularised and commercialised by the big bands of Paul Whiteman, Ted Lewis and Guy Lombardo. With the spectre of war banished, society lightheartedly, lightheadedly danced its way through the 1920s to the rhythms of foxtrot, Charleston and tango. Syncopation found its way into the general musical consciousness, giving that spicy, tangy touch to the four-square melodies of familiar experience. And as the vehicle for conveying the new mood of excitement there arrived the brash new timbre dominated by reeds, brass and percussion, both in the small jazz group and in the ballroom dance band.

Under the social conditions in which it operated as a mass consumer product – in contrast to its origins as a largely extemporised art in the black communities of the American South – jazz rapidly became both highly sophisticated and highly stylised, settling into standard forms with virtually normative power. This assimilating, 'civilising' process reached its peak in the flamboyant 'symphonic jazz' of Paul Whiteman, which to some was a triumphant demonstration of the unbounded potentialities of the medium, to others a shameful commercial betrayal of what true jazz stood for. Whichever side one took, it was impossible to gainsay the influence of such events as the concerts given by the Paul Whiteman Band at the Grosses Schauspielhaus in Berlin in the summer of 1926, which no 'serious' musician could afford to miss. Here Whiteman introduced

German audiences to the *Rhapsody in Blue*, which Weill can hardly fail to have heard. At the same time the recently established German radio stations broadcast regular daily programmes of dance music played by their own newly-formed bands. Since the supply of current gramophone records could not meet the day-in, day-out demand alone, the creation of 'in-house' orchestras was the only way in which the available air-time could be filled.

What filtered through to 'serious' composers was a kind of distillation of jazz elements which they used to invigorate their music in moments of frivolity or ironic detachment. Direct in impact, derived from an alien and more primitive tradition, these elements could relax tension, introduce incongruity or in some other way break up the uniform surface of a work. It is rather like a craftsman using, not unskilfully yet somewhat incongruously, tools that belong to a different trade. It may also reflect an intention to shock, by deliberately juxtaposing elements from unrelated levels and traditions, to the point where burlesque and parody become elevated to an aesthetic principle – the point occupied by, for example, William Walton's *Façade*.

Weill saw the flood of jazz and dance music that was sweeping over Europe as having a three-fold significance for the society of the day. Firstly, there was its role as a purveyor of commercialised romantic distraction and pleasure, even comfort, to a toiling, alienated population that no longer knew the true dance music which naturally and spontaneously expressed the values and emotions of a society. Secondly, modern commercial dance music is a synthetic commodity which, like cinema, reflects the instincts and values of the masses and thus possesses a certain comprehensive objective validity.

The quest for objectivity, ironically, also underlay the highly intellectual movement of so-called neo-Classicism in the 1920s, in which Stravinsky and Hindemith led the younger generation to the cultivation of a cool, anti-Romantic impersonality which yet, by a second and totally foreseeable irony, bears the unmistakable fingerprints of its creator as clearly as any unashamedly 'subjective' piece of music from the Romantic tradition. It is not by chance that Stravinsky and Hindemith should have been both dabblers in the exotic pleasures of jazz and practitioners of the abstemious, impersonal techniques of a revived classicism. There is even a parallel between the contrapuntal style and the performance of the jazz group in which each solo player weaves his own thread of melody through the piece from beginning to end. At the same time, in harmonic terms jazz was reassuringly based on familiar, tonal formulae that raised no eyebrows and challenged no instincts, and thus acquired the role of a delectable oasis in the midst of an increasingly atonal desert. The jazz movement of the 1920s, as Ernst Křenek put it, represented the last great attempt of tonality 'to hide its disintegration'. Milhaud's *La création du monde*, one of the earliest pieces of 'symphonic jazz', shows what he meant.

Finally in his survey of the social influence of jazz and dance music, Weill sees in this cultural import the most remarkable manifestation of 'the process of Americanization, which is spreading slowly but surely across the face of our entire social life'.

Europe in the 1920s was wallowing in a love-hate relationship with America. In Germany, the traditionally-minded saw in the New World a brazen land of anti-culture dominated by materialism and the worship of technology; man was encouraged to see himself as a ruthless, acquisitive animal and to relegate his intellectual and spiritual urges to the status of inessential and peripheral pursuits. Those on the left of the political spectrum in the Weimar Republic equally rejected the unrestrained cult of materialistic values but saw it in terms of capitalist exploitation, accompanied by the evils of poverty, social degradation and human misery.

At the same time America held a peculiar fascination for the onlookers three thousand miles away. The immensity of the place defied the imagination, and the range of opportunities, as proven by tens of thousands of immigrants from all corners of the Old World, was infinite. Events in the country's history like the Civil War and the gold rush, the world of Red Indians, of skyscrapers, of jazz, of the movies, a twentieth-century Eldorado – a glamorous jumble of such associations invoked excitement, grudging admiration, also envy. And as the Great War had shown, America was a country able singlehandedly to change the course of world history. To become part of such a dynamic enterprise was to ensure the uninhibited development of all sides of the individual personality, the opportunity to become a fuller man than the conditions of a confined, tired, old civilisation in Europe would allow.

'All of us were fascinated by America,' said Lotte Lenya,

> as we knew it from books, movies, popular songs, headlines. Weill loved Sophie Tucker's records. This was the America of the garish twenties, with its Capones, Texan Guinans, Aimee Semple McPhersons, Ponzis, the Florida boom and the stock market crash. Also the disastrous Florida hurricane, which we used in *Mahagonny*, and a ghastly photograph reproduced in every German newspaper of the murderess Ruth Snyder in the electric chair, Hollywood films about the Wild West and the Yukon, Tin Pan Alley songs. We all dreamed of going there.

The perfect symbol of these paradoxes, in his own career as in his depiction of the land where the sky was the limit but where many did not raise themselves much above the gutter, was Charlie Chaplin, idol of the intellectuals and the masses alike. And in the Germany of this time there was no greater admirer of Chaplin than the American love-hater *par excellence* Bert Brecht, who never escaped from the fatal attraction of the culture he affected to despise, and for whose hospitality he ultimately had cause to be profoundly grateful – if gratitude had been a word in his vocabulary. As Chaplin cooks and eats his boots in *The Gold Rush*, so in Brecht's *Mahagonny* the anti-hero Jimmy Mahoney, bored by the ordered existence that has been introduced into the town, considers eating his hat. 'This Jimmy Mahoney,' wrote Adorno, in provocative, if wilfully obfuscatory vein, 'is a subject without subjectivity – a dialectical Chaplin.'

Weill finished *Royal Palace* early in 1926. In the course of his work on it he wrote to his parents,

> . . . . I have become considerably more independent, more confident, more cheerful and less inhibited. Naturally a great deal of this can be put down to my living with Lenya, which has helped me enormously. This is the only way I could bear to have someone around me – two people with different, unconnected artistic interests, each helping the other along his own path. How long will it last, someone might ask. A very long time, I hope.

The direction of Weill's path was clear; that Lenya 'helped him along it', both as his wife and as his interpreter on the stage, is equally clear. Maybe she also saw a path of her own, along which he did not help her – she still, after all, had a career as a 'straight' actress ahead of her, alongside the singing roles in the Brecht-Weill works that made her reputation. He alone could never have been enough for her. But then, no one man could, at least for long. And he never left her in any doubt that his music came first. His question 'How long will it last?' has a poignantly ironic ring in its context, while for us his answer is laden with sadness. He was barely fifty when he died.

Kurt Julian Weill and Karoline Wilhelmine Charlotte Blamauer were married at the Charlottenburg registry office on January 28, 1926. It was a quiet occasion, so quiet as to be almost inaudible. No relatives came to Berlin to celebrate, either from his family or from hers. The witnesses were two casual acquaintances of Lenya's. And if the form of words used at the ceremony contained a phrase exhorting her to 'keep thee only unto him, so long as ye both shall live', it passed unheard. In the stormy course of their years together they both kept themselves unto several.

There is a touching photograph of the little couple, taken on their wedding day in the park of Charlottenburg Palace. Lenya, despite the cold, is bare-headed, smiling quietly and happily as she clutches two bunches of flowers. Weill wears a light-coloured felt hat which looks to be several sizes too big, and peers out from beneath its broad brim through thick spectacles, serious, unsmiling, almost suspicious. And while Lenya has on a bright coat with a cheerful check pattern and a light fur collar, her stance relaxed and unembarrassed, her husband has chosen to wear his formal black coat and his black trousers, which are too short and reveal an extent of unmatching socks. His black bow-tie is crooked, and he stands inelegantly splayfooted, clinging to his wife's arm with one gloved hand and holding what looks like a paper parcel in the other. Where she looks so outgoing and approachable, he exudes a dutiful sternness coupled with an awkward bashfulness, as though dressed up for an occasion at which he is not quite at his ease. It is a photo that brings to life Hans Heinsheimer's description of him a few years earlier as looking more like a student of theology – Old Testament, presumably – than a composer.

They went back to their rooms in the Pension Hassforth, with its jet-black painted furniture and its horrible pictures of what Lenya called 'bloodthirsty stag-hunts in the mountains'. It was an ordered existence governed by the disciplines of Weill's musical commitments – lessons to a few remaining pupils, the time-consuming preparation that went into his articles for *Der deutsche Rundfunk*, and above all composition. 'Kurt sat down at his desk every morning at nine,' Lenya recalled many years later:

> He scarcely used the piano at all, except to give his pipe a short respite. Once he was totally absorbed in his work, he was as happy as a sandboy. Fixed working hours were sacred to him; he would only interrupt them for a theatre rehearsal, if it really could not be avoided.

She was not finding it easy to land theatrical roles, and a life spent sitting by herself and waiting for him to appear at meal times was not what she had envisaged:

> I sat at the table and Weill came down for breakfast, then went back to his music. He came down for lunch, then went back to his music. After a few days I said to him: 'This is a terrible life for me. I see you only at meals.' He looked at me through those thick glasses and said: 'But Lenya, you know you come right after my music.' That was my place. Weill was a man who knew only music. Other composers had hobbies – Schoenberg and Gershwin painted. Weill, I think, had music as his hobby.

The sense of dissatisfaction, fifty years on, is still unconcealed. But it is not, and was not, bitter or reproachful. Lenya went into the commitment with her eyes open. She knew that she was consigning herself to a permanent second place in his scale of values. When, shortly after, she became a direct part of his musical production by singing roles that he had created for her, her feeling of discontent had a chance to recede, but even then she made no attempt to conceal that there were substantial parts of her life in which she still felt unfulfilled – beginning with sex. When Weill's life-long friend Maurice Abravanel challenged her over her waywardness, she protested: 'But I don't cheat on Kurt. He knows exactly what's going on!'

For his part, Weill probably did not understand how his attractive show-business wife could not be satisfied with her lot. Perhaps, subconsciously, he still maintained the Jewish assumption that the needs of the head of the household were paramount, and could not see what grounds she had for complaint. One little affection they had in common was for domestic pets. Lenya acquired a pet monkey to share the apartment with them, and in Kleinmachnow, as later in America, they shared a fancy for large, shaggy dogs.

In 1929, looking back on three years of married life with Lenya, Weill gave a Munich paper his description of what he saw:

> She is a lamentable housewife but a very good actress. She cannot read music, but when she sings, people listen to her as they do to Caruso (incidentally any composer whose wife can read music has my sympathy). She pays no heed to my work – which is one of her greatest assets – but she would be very offended if I took no interest in *her* work. She always has a number of men friends, which she explains by saying that she gets on so badly with women – though maybe she gets on so badly with women precisely because she always has a number of men friends. She married me because she wanted to know what it was like to get the creeps, and she maintains that this desire has been more than adequately fulfilled. My wife's name is Lotte Lenya.

Gently mocking, yes, but with too many barbed hints, innuendoes, and black-comic turns of phrase to be quite so harmless. There seems to be more between the lines than on them. But as many have said who knew them, both during these years in Germany and in their American second home, in some strange, perverse way they needed each other, and realised it. Hence their tolerance in each other of what would otherwise have been intolerable – and often was.

In March 1926, two months after their wedding, Weill and Lenya travelled to Dresden for the first performance of *Der Protagonist*, which Fritz Busch had promised to conduct there. From Berlin to Dresden is a mere two-hour train journey but even such expenses as these weighed heavily on the family budget. 'We were so poor,' Lenya remembered, 'that he had to hire a dinner-jacket to appear at the opening of his first big success.'

A great success in Dresden *Der Protagonist* surely was, and as such, a landmark in his career. Sustained applause greeted the grisly climax of the piece, and composer and soloists took one curtain call after another from an audience experienced in handling the premières of none-too-easy operas by contemporary composers. They had only just recovered from Busoni's *Doktor Faust* the previous year.

The critics too found much to praise. One after the other, having noted the stylistic influence of Stravinsky and Busoni as well as the effectiveness of the twin-orchestra instrumentation, they emphasised the quality of the work as musical drama – indeed, as drama *tout court*. For so completely has the music first absorbed, then re-expressed in its own terms, the essence and tragic meaning of Kaiser's play that the separation and comparison of text and music has become impossible. The *Dresdner Neueste Nachrichten* reported: 'This one-acter restores our faith in the future of opera . . . with its grand dramatic sweep it is pure theatre, theatre at its most vivid,' while the correspondent of the *Deutsche Tageszeitung* in Berlin described it as 'swaying to and fro between a rising and falling tension, its dramatic power never once faltering, leaving the audience almost breathless as they lived out the tragedy of the mime-hero. The applause was tremendous'. So often in the course of his life did Weill work himself to a point of near exhaustion that the word relaxation seemed almost to have forfeited all meaning – a condition not lost on Lenya. But after the success of *Der Protagonist* he did allow himself to unbend to the extent of taking her on a vacation to Italy and the French Riviera, where he always felt especially at his ease.

The impact made by *Der Protagonist* in Dresden quickly led other opera houses to take it up in the following years – Frankfurt, Hanover, Leipzig, the Städtische Oper in Berlin. The interest even extended to Russia, where, as Weill excitedly told Universal, Stanislavsky showed great enthusiasm for the work after having been shown it in a translation 'which contained slight modifications in order to draw attention to the revolutionary nature of the piece'.

Occasionally it fell on stony ground. A performance in Erfurt which Weill attended in December 1926 met with a wall of silence: at the end the audience just got up and left, without applause, even without the boos and whistles which had become a regular feature of musical life in the 1920s. But the critics' conviction that here was something excitingly new and progressive did not flag – a music, said Wilhelm Matthes of a performance in Nuremberg, 'totally without inhibitions, written with all the destructive rage of a young generation that has set out to overturn all the old concepts of style'.

Flattering testimony to his rising stature came from Willy Haas' influential journal *Die literarische Welt*, which posed the question 'What does Beethoven mean to young musicians today?' and invited him to join a select group of composers – Ravel, Ernst Křenek, Janáček, Milhaud, Georges Auric – in giving their replies. Milhaud answered the question in five words: 'I love Beethoven. Vive Beethoven!' Weill, who regarded

Fidelio as the world's greatest opera, responded by saying that since his generation was in the process of descaling the encrustation of 'ethico-humanistic concepts' that had settled on Beethoven in the course of the nineteenth century, they had 'for the time being to renounce a great deal of what they loved and revered in Beethoven'. Writing in the *Sozialistische Monatshefte* shortly afterwards, however, he reasserted his confident idealism, describing Beethoven *sub specie aeternitatis* as the triumphant exemplification of the principle that 'it is the artist's task to create works of art not from the events of the moment but from the immutable ideals of humanity as presented by his age'.

Weill was now type-cast by the musical world, and corresponding expectations were laid upon him. But two months before the première of *Der Protagonist*, itself completed a whole year earlier, he had moved on, stylistically, into the transitional 'freer, broader and simpler' mode of which he had written to his parents, the mode of *Der neue Orpheus* and *Royal Palace*. There was a time-lag between the state reached by the development of his creative personality and the public's perception of his position in the musical world. And as he was to experience with the highly critical treatment meted out to his two Goll works the following year, respect and goodwill earned by one piece is not automatically transferable to another.

The success of *Der Protagonist*, coupled with the reputation that his articles for *Der deutsche Rundfunk* were bringing him, led to a commission to write incidental music for a radio production of the tragedy *Herzog Theodor von Gothland* by the nineteenth-century dramatist Christian Dietrich Grabbe. This portrait of a man 'driven to his destruction by the demonic forces within him', as Weill described the work, was broadcast in September 1926, with Werner Krauss and Theodor Loos in the cast. Of the music a fellow-journalist on *Der deutsche Rundfunk* wrote: 'Kurt Weill has struck out in a completely new direction. . . . In this drama of great expressive power the music does not seek to accompany the action; rather, the drama and the music coincide in a unique way, producing a synthesis of lasting significance for both music and text'. But the music has not survived.

All but a fragmentary piano draft has also been lost of a full-length opera, or perhaps operetta, which occupied Weill's mind for the rest of the year. This was *Na und?* – roughly 'Well?' or 'What about it?' – the frivolous title of which matches his description of the work as 'a piece in a light vein'. The libretto was the work of his friend and one-time pupil Felix Joachimson.

Writing to his publishers in April 1927, Weill described the idea underlying the opera as 'the way in which people today are at cross-purposes with each other', and characterised it as a 'lighthearted work of a kind not seen since *Der Rosenkavalier*', consisting of seventeen independent numbers, interspersed with recitative or spoken dialogue. Maybe there is still room for hope that Weill's manuscript will one day turn up. No unambiguous information on its whereabouts has emerged since the day in the summer of 1927 when, having failed to persuade Otto Klemperer, then at the Kroll Opera in Berlin, or Hans Curjel, Klemperer's dramaturge, to put the work on, he picked up his manuscript and left. A few musical ideas in the surviving fragments of the draft recur in the *Mahagonny Songspiel* of the following year, and the fact that it is flanked, in chronological terms, by the *Songspiel* on one side and *Royal Palace* on the other, gives a context of expectation – jazz rhythms, dance-band instrumentation, the atmosphere of the cabaret – for imagining what its musical character might have been. But further than this one cannot go.

Weill's appeal to the Kroll was the last of his ill-starred attempts to arouse interest in his 'quite unproblematical comic opera in a totally new style', as he described it. With his piano draft ready early in 1927, he travelled down to Vienna in April, certain of receiving a vote of confidence from Universal Edition and its director Emil Hertzka.

Things worked out rather differently. 'Weill played the entire opera,' recalled Heinsheimer, who, with Hertzka, constituted the audience,

> singing softly with a veiled, pleasant expressive voice, playing the piano in a dry, matter-of-fact, unflourished manner. Hertzka and I followed with the libretto . . . We did not like the libretto, which was by a little-known playwright and musician who had never written a libretto before, and as we read on, we ardently wished he had let it go at that. We loathed the title of the opera, which seemed to reflect the worst asphalt cynicism of Berlin. The music seemed handicapped and weighed down by the story and the lyrics. As the composer played on, one could sense an aura of despair creep into the room.

The mischievous Heinsheimer was delightedly embroidering the situation. 'After Kurt had finished,' he gleefully went on elsewhere,

> we felt there was only one thing to do: to make this first performance of *Na und?* under all circumstances the last. . . . 'Kurt,' I said, and looked him straight in the eye, 'tonight you are going back to Berlin. Shortly after the train leaves Vienna, it crosses the Danube. When you are in the middle of the bridge, open the window, take your score and just drop it into the river.'
> Kurt looked back. He did not say a thing. He just took his music, put it in his briefcase and walked out of the room.

Weill did not take Heinsheimer's ungentle advice – yet. Instead, with Universal's consent, he offered it to Schotts, in Mainz, Universal's rival in the promotion of contemporary music. They too turned it down. So when Curjel, at the Kroll Opera, said no for the third time of asking,

Weill realised that he had come to the end of the road. 'A few days later,' said Curjel, 'he telephoned to say that he now shared my opinion and had resolved never to have the opera performed.' Later in the year, to forestall any unwelcome act of piracy, Universal considered it politic to accept *Na und?* into the fold and to raise Weill's retainer from two hundred to four hundred marks a month. So although it was never published, Weill's labour had not been entirely in vain.

The inhospitable treatment meted out to *Na und?* was no doubt provoked by the perceived shortcomings of the work itself, particularly, it seems, its libretto. But in the background lurked two contrasting pieces of circumstantial evidence which could not be overlooked, both conspiring to work in Weill's disfavour. One was the knock-out success of Ernst Křenek's revue-opera *Jonny spielt auf* at its launch in Leipzig in February 1927; the other was the frosty reception given to Weill's own *Royal Palace* three weeks later.

Jonny spielt auf ('Johnny Strikes Up') is a witty montage of jazz elements – syncopated melodies and rhythms, blues, shimmy, foxtrot – strung over a Dadaist libretto written by the composer himself, with stage props that include a train and an automobile. The story, such as it is, follows the frolics of an Italian violinist, a German composer and a Negro jazz musician (Johnny), who steals the Italian's Amati and ends up fiddling triumphantly as the rest of the cast dance to celebrate their departure for America, 'the unknown land of liberty'. A classic *Zeitoper* – 'topical opera', the term widely, sometimes indiscriminately used at the time to pigeonhole works with 'contemporary relevance', like Weill's *Dreigroschenoper* and Hindemith's *Neues vom Tage* – *Jonny spielt auf* was a one-off *succès de scandale* which made Křenek the talk of the town.

Born in Vienna in the same year as Weill, with a comparable technical facility and even greater productivity, Křenek was for a while to be found in the Busoni circle. Leaving behind the atonality of his early operas, which in style and 'feel' breathe a similar air to Weill's *Der Protagonist*, he called his *Jonny* 'a return to the tonal idiom, to the cantilena of Puccini, seasoning the whole with the condiments of jazz'. Jazz itself he described in defensive, almost prophylactic terms as 'a protection against atonality'.

But it was a short-lived return, a moment of romantic dalliance which he soon rejected – though not regretted, given the financial rewards it brought him. Back in Vienna in the early 1930s he became a close friend of Alban Berg and Anton Webern, and from then on he committed himself to the twelve-tone world. But in 1927 he represented the *Zeitoper* at its most triumphantly modern.

Jonny spielt auf was a difficult act to follow. And when *Royal Palace* was given its première three weeks later, comparison – unfavourable comparison – with *Jonny* was inevitable. The performance itself, at the Berlin Staatsoper under Erich Kleiber, formed part of a triple bill with Weill's *Der neue Orpheus* opening the programme and Manuel de Falla's puppet-opera *Master Peter's Puppet Show* concluding it. Franz Ludwig Hörth, who had handled the stage direction of Weill's *Zaubernacht* in 1922, had in the meantime become director of the Staatsoper, and used the occasion to introduce film sequences into an operatic production for the first time, taking his lead from Piscator's famous pioneering use of film material in his Volksbühne productions the previous year. For the scene in *Royal Palace* where the Husband offers Dejanira an airline ticket to the capital cities of Europe, Hörth filmed his actors and actresses leaving a luxury hotel, being driven to the airport and climbing up the steps into the waiting aeroplane. 'I then superimposed a number of suitable views of international cities,' Hörth explained, 'and inserted the complete scene into the action of the opera as a kind of cinematic interlude.'

Such imaginative gimmickry did not rescue the work. And although it says much for Weill's status that the Staatsoper should have accepted it, and that Kleiber, who had given *Wozzeck* there two years earlier, should have conducted, the venue offered no protection against hostile opinion. Adolf Weissman, who had reviewed most of Weill's works from the String Quartet of 1922 onwards, spoke for many:

> The impression made by this libretto is of a comic melancholy which borders on the ludicrous. Nothing especially interesting has been contributed by the composer. His use of jazz is competent but he also attempts to be lyrical in the spirit of today and it is these lyrical moments that are the dullest. . . . He is not to be classed with Křenek in any respect.

'A failed attempt at a revue-opera in the manner of *Jonny spielt auf* ', Herbert Fleischer called it. 'A defeat. Křenek was superior.' Paul Stefan probed a little deeper, sensing that the true Weill was somehow being cramped, held back by the inferior quality of the literary material within which he had to work and lacking a full commitment to what he was doing: 'Weill is so genuine a composer that he can only convince when there is a convincer who can set him free, when he speaks, not just because he *can* but because he *must* – for surely nobody can seriously question his ability any longer.'

Indeed they could not – now or at any other time. For if there is a constant in Weill's world of fluctuating styles, fortunes, pressures, it is his technical facility, the ability to respond to changing circumstances and challenges with an adaptability that some, not always benevolently, have called chameleonic. The issue that Stefan addresses when he calls Weill a 'genuine' composer is one that regularly presents itself when one faces a piece of 'light' music – whatever that means – written by a 'serious' composer. To what extent, runs the thought, has he 'written down' to a public with which he does not normally deal, introducing a calculated element of condescension into his activity which will ultimately take its revenge. Or – shifting the focus from the art to the artist – has he betrayed his highest calling to the pursuit of easier rewards?

The Berlin musical world of the 1920s offered many temptations of this kind, not least for the financial pickings to be had. Artur Schnabel, pianist and composer, remembered pointing out to a group of progressive young musicians, including Eduard Erdmann, Alois Hába and Ernst Křenek, how fatal it would be if they compromised their true natures:

> Křenek and Erdmann told me one day that they were going to write light opera, to make quicker money than with the heavier type of music they composed. I advised them against it, feeling certain that it would be a failure, for I am convinced that in order to produce a successful light opera, it has to be the best work of the composer. If he does it only as an act of condescension, he will not succeed. But they insisted, telling me that they had studied all the most popular and effective work in the field and would simply imitate it, and probably do it better. So they went ahead with their attempts . . . Erdmann had great fun with it but gave it up very soon, while Křenek was tougher and completed his light opera. His publisher wanted to provide for performance, so he asked Křenek to come and play his work for some people competent to judge its value. As Křenek told me afterwards, after he had played the first page of his score, the expert got up and said, 'Mr Křenek, much too good!'

'This is a very instructive story, as you see,' Schnabel went on. 'If the light opera composer, born and gifted to write that sort of music, were to compose an oratorio and play it for an expert, he would say, "Much too bad!" '

The intellectuals' flirtation with light opera and jazz laid itself open to this danger. Křenek's *Jonny spielt auf*, in the verdict of critics and audiences alike, showed how delightful the flirtation could be. Weill's *Royal Palace* did not. He had not swept his victim off her feet, was uncertain how far to go, how many past memories to carry with him, how confidently to embrace the new attractions. Hence the in-between character of his two Goll pieces. It was a moment of hesitation, even of suspense, but it was not to last for long, and by the time of their première Weill was set on a very different course.

CHAPTER VII

Weill and Brecht:
The Music of Epic Theatre

The performances of *Royal Palace* and *Der neue Orpheus* at the Berlin Staatsoper in March 1927 had left a sense of general discontent. *Der neue Orpheus*, a relatively small-scale work in which Weill himself seemed to take scant interest, mattered less. Even before the première he remarked to Max Butting that he attached little importance to it. But when the critics based their disapproval of *Royal Palace* on the impossible libretto, they were striking, by implication, as much at Weill's inability to create a convincing work of music out of Goll's text as at that text itself. Goll's conception of theatre was not dramatic but lyrical and symbolical, like Maeterlinck's. But Weill needed a strong, direct dramatic text to which to respond with a powerful, objective, original music – a 'gestic' music, as he was shortly to term it.

Such had been the nature of Georg Kaiser's *Der Protagonist*. And the success of their collaboration the previous year had given rise in theatrical circles to the proposition that the two men might produce a companion piece to round out a Kaiser-Weill double bill. The disappointment over *Royal Palace* fresh in his mind, Weill made his way to the lakeside villa in Grünheide one day and proposed that Kaiser, whose days of sensational success now lay behind him but whose name still carried great kudos, should write him an original libretto for an *opera buffa* to set alongside the tragic *Der Protagonist*. The result was *Der Zar lässt sich photographieren* ('The Tsar Has His Photograph Taken'), Op. 21.

Weill composed the music for his comic one-acter between March and August 1927, music which explores for the last time the through-composed, free-tonal world of expressionist derivation in which he had laid the foundations of his current reputation as an operatic composer.

Kaiser's text is witty in plot, with political overtones which audiences of the day would not have missed, and equally witty in repartee. The action takes place in the studio of a fashionable Paris photographer called Madame Angèle. A telephone call announces that a figure calling himself the Tsar – he is not named and there is no case for identifying him with any historical figure, Russian or otherwise – will shortly come to have his picture taken. Before he arrives, a gang of revolutionaries force their way into the studio, capture Angèle and her two assistants, and replace them with three imposters. Their intention is to conceal a revolver under the black cloth draped over the camera, then for their female imposter, pretending to be Angèle, to shoot the Tsar as he poses for his photograph. The Tsar, a modest young man in an inconspicuous lounge suit, arrives and is clearly more interested in the attractive False Angèle than in photography. She repeatedly tries to get him in front of the camera and the revolver, while he equally persistently tries to make love to her. She is on the point of giving in to him when the news arrives that the police have traced the revolutionaries to the studio. The False Angèle and her fellow-villains escape in the nick of time, the real Angèle returns, discharges the revolver harmlessly and sets up her camera again, and the mystified, though somewhat disappointed Tsar finally does have his photograph taken.

Describing at the time his own view of the genesis of the work, which he saw as the last of his series of one-act operas, Weill wrote in the *Leipziger Bühnenblätter*:

> The need arose to complement *Der Protagonist* with another work, this time *buffa* in nature, in order to provide a full evening's theatre. While visiting Georg Kaiser one summer, I reminded him of a jocular notion he once had of a camera containing a built-in machine-gun. We then invented the character of a typical post-war nobleman – the sort of figure portrayed on the screen by Adolphe Menjou. In a couple of days the two of us had put together a scenario, and Kaiser gave me the finished libretto soon afterwards.

At times this lighthearted concoction becomes almost knockabout farce, an aspect which Weill was far from loth to enhance with acidic musical comments in the spiky harmonic and instrumental tone of voice that is his trademark. But behind this there lie a dialogue and a characterisation of considerable subtlety which drew from the highly intellectual Weill a musical response that the flaccid prose of Ivan Goll could not. As Kaiser's Protagonist came to grief on his inability to distinguish between reality and illusion, so in the *Zar* things are not what they appear to be. The revolutionaries' preconceived notion of the Tsar is of a tyrant worthy only to be overthrown; in reality he turns out to hold democratic views and to bitterly resent that the representative role forced upon him prevents him from living the ordinary, natural life he craves, a life which includes the right to try and seduce an attractive woman when the opportunity arises. The gang's blustering demand for his assassination becomes a mindless shibboleth behind which they hide their own tyranny. And as for the False Angèle, their ringleader, the mindless hatred which sends her out on her murderous errand melts under the warmth of the flesh-and-blood character to whom in the end she is prepared to give herself – though not at the cost of being caught by the police.

The sustained, agitated action of Kaiser's libretto drew from Weill a seamless web of music, sung throughout, one episode in the adventure merging into the next in a highly effective piece of integrated operatic writing. More homophonic than its tragic counterpart, and tonal in harmonic idiom, though freely so, it was the last work he wrote in a 'through-composed' style, before turning to the number-opera form, with songs and interspersed dialogue. Kaiser provided for nine singing roles on stage; to these he later added, at Weill's suggestion, a male chorus set in the orchestra pit. This chorus, detached, as in Greek drama, from the adversarial action of the characters on the stage, interposes sardonic comments on this action and is used, musically speaking, almost as an instrument of the orchestra, drawing attention to this or that utterance by its interjections.

There is an interesting parallel to Weill's use of a detached chorus of Classical precedent in Stravinsky's scenic oratorio *Oedipus Rex*, a work described by Weill as 'a milestone in the development of modern opera'. The première of *Oedipus Rex* in May 1927 fell at the very time Weill was at work on his *Zar*, and his claim that he himself had added the chorus to Kaiser's *dramatis personae* raises the possibility that he did so after being impressed by the musical opportunities that this extraneous agent of objectivity offered. In particular, as he wrote of the performance of *Oedipus Rex* at the Kroll Opera under Klemperer the following year, it served, like the Latin text, to concentrate the essential meaning of the work on the music, with 'action, dramatic quality and visual effect being completely subordinated to the dictates of musical form and design'.

But where Stravinsky's chorus serves the sombre needs of his tragic neo-Classical masterpiece, Weill, whose traces of neo-Classicism had been growing fainter year by year, puts it to ironic, sometimes parodistic use. 'The Tsar is having his picture taken!' the men bark time and again, butting into the frolics on the stage. And at the end, when he really has had it taken, they triumphantly bellow the news *fortissimo* for the benefit of the world at large. The formal kinship between *Oedipus Rex* and the *Zar* was remarked upon at the time, and although the *Zar* did, as Weill intended, take its comic place on many occasions alongside *Der Protagonist*, it also frequently came to share a double bill with *Oedipus Rex* – an arrangement which he could hardly fail to welcome.

In the context of Weill's development the invention of the chorus is a step along the short road that led to epic opera, the musical equivalent of Brecht's epic theatre. Another sign of what was to come is the melodically and harmonically distorted tango that accompanies the love-making preparations of the Tsar and the False Angèle. And a typical stroke of Weillian effectiveness is to have the music of this 'Tango Angèle' pre-recorded and played on the stage gramophone, which the False Angèle only has to switch on to induce the atmosphere of seduction. As an intrusion by one medium into another it is a moment that matches Piscator's use of film projection in drama production, a technique later taken over by Brecht and Weill – and by Brecht alone – to promote 'epic' detachment. A gramophone was a familiar enough object, but not as a source of music on the operatic stage. It was as out of place as the automobile horns in *Royal Palace*. Weill was a master of the calculated incongruity, the confusing, shocking surrealist moment, in broad design as in inner musical detail.

In musical retrospect the year 1927, and more particularly the spring of that year, appears as a watershed both in Weill's inner development and in the public's perception of him. *Na und?*, which never reached the stage but which meant a great deal to him and for which he had made great claims, was finished in March. *Royal Palace* and *Der neue Orpheus* had their joint first performance in the Berlin Staatsoper the same month. Work with Kaiser – the composition of the *Zar* was well under way – had sharpened his sense of musical theatre and simplified his complex, intellectualised manner of the first half of the decade. The unlikely conjugation of Busonian clarity and discipline with the exciting idioms of jazz, above all in rhythm and instrumentation, had reached the point at which the inimitable Weillian ductus was about to crystallise, the sound which brings a knowing smile to the listener's face as he says, 'Ah, I can tell you who that's by.'

At this very moment, as though providence recognized its cue to intervene, two events occurred, the one linked to the other, which opened up to Weill the worlds that his maturity had prepared him to conquer. One was an invitation to contribute a work to the Baden-Baden Music Festival that July. The other was his meeting with Bertolt Brecht.

The Baden-Baden Chamber Music Festival was the successor of the annual Donaueschingen Festival founded by Prince Max Egon zu Donaueschingen on his Black Forest estate in 1921. The Prince, a patron of the old school, had taken upon himself the task of promoting modern music and of providing an occasion, away from the pressures of the commercial concert world, for young composers to have their works performed. There was to be no cult of personality, no pursuit of exclusivity, no championing of causes – just a relaxed and cheerful environment for musical performances and discussions of current issues – a Tanglewood of the 1920s. Each composer and performer even received from Prince Max a Black Forest cuckoo clock as a souvenir of his participation.

Unfortunately this initial liberality and informality did not survive for more than a few years. Perhaps inevitably, and not for the worst reasons, individual names tended to occur and recur, the owners of those names seeing the Festivals as a platform for the promotion of their own music. Hindemith was regularly represented, and from 1925 onwards no Festival was complete without the presence of Stravinsky. By 1927, when the scope of the event had outstripped the facilities available at Donaueschingen and the venue had been moved to Baden-Baden, it had become a market place at which all prominent composers of the day, especially Germans, were pleased to see their wares displayed.

The musical policy of the Baden-Baden Festivals lay in the hands of a triumvirate – Hindemith, Heinrich Burkard, music director to Prince Max zu Donaueschingen, and the composer Josef Haas. For the opening season they proposed Alban Berg's Lyric Suite of 1925–6; Hanns Eisler's *Tagebuch* (1926), vocal settings of his own texts; Bartók's Piano Sonata of 1926, played by Bartók himself; a programme of music for mechanical instruments by Hindemith, George Antheil and others; an evening of film and music written thereto; and a final evening devoted to four short chamber operas commissioned for the occasion – Milhaud's *L'enlèvement d'Europe*, Ernst Toch's *Die Prinzessin auf der Erbse* (from the fairy-tale 'The Princess on the Pea' by Hans Andersen), Hindemith's *Hin und zurück* (libretto by the cabaret and revue writer Marcellus Schiffer) and a piece by Weill.

At the time the invitation reached him, he was coming to the end of the unfortunate *Na und?* He first thought of fulfilling the welcome commission by doing a short scenic cantata based on a tragedy such as *Antigone* or *King Lear*. When Festival time arrived, however, he offered something very different, a *succès de scandale* that marked the turning-point in his public career – *Mahagonny. Ein Songspiel nach Texten von Bert Brecht.*

Bertolt Brecht was – is – one of the most contentious figures in twentieth-century European literature. Born into a well-to-do family of paper manufacturers in the Bavarian town of Augsburg, he was two years older than Weill. Two years may seem of scant significance, but they distinguish those who, like Brecht, served in the war from those, like Weill, who did not. In the two years that Brecht spent as a medical orderly in a military hospital lie the roots of the savage pacifism, sometimes almost cynical in its savagery, that he retained throughout his life, cheek by jowl with the Communist's characteristic justification of the use of violence in what he sees as a politically righteous cause. To the political aspect of this pacifism he linked an inflexible moral conviction, spurning the decadent culture of post-war Germany and affecting, in a language as strident as that of the expressionists he despised, a deliberately offensive predilection for what are usually regarded as the baser aspects of human nature.

To complement the *épater les bourgeois* roughness of his plays and to make apparent his denial of his bourgeois origins, Brecht cultivated in his appearance and deportment a proletarian image through which to project his native wit and cunning, not to say his inspired deviousness in the pursuit of his own interests. It made for a strange medley of qualities in a man who in 1928, at the age of thirty, 'looked not as though he had aged prematurely but as though he had always been old', wrote Elias Canetti in his memoirs. 'He had the profile of a Jesuit,' said Willy Haas, founder and editor of the journal *Die literarische Welt*:

> the steel-rimmed glasses of a schoolmaster, the close-cropped hair of a convict and the tattered leather jacket of an old member of the Bolshevik party. It was a combination that I did not like at all, whatever my views might have been about the constituent elements individually. He spoke in a very supercilious tone, harshly and in abstract terms. What I liked least was his evident desire to make a favourable impression on me, obviously regarding me as bourgeois through and through.

Ernst Josef Aufricht, the impresario who was to put on *Die Dreigroschenoper* the following year, perceived a similar bundle of paradoxes:

> His long face often bore the ascetic expression of a monk, at other times the craftiness of a gallows-bird. He had dark, piercing eyes which hungrily and greedily soaked up everything that they encountered. He was skinny, with sloping shoulders. The unkempt proletarian garb that he adopted, with cap and jerkin open at the neck, always seemed to me to be a typically Brechtian 'alienation' effect. Although his appearance tended to put one off, he nevertheless attracted people.

In particular he attracted women, for whom he had an insatiable appetite, exercising his *droit de seigneur* over the young actresses in his plays and over the wives of his friends and colleagues. By his first and perhaps only great love Paula Banholzer ('Bi') he had a son, Frank, who was killed in the Second World War; his daughter Hanne, who took the stage name Hanne Hiob, was born to his first wife, the actress Marianne Zoff, and Stefan and Barbara (wife of the actor Eckehard Schall) are the children of his second wife, Helene Weigel, one of the classic interpreters of his female roles, who died in 1971. Then there are the many collaborators and 'personal assistants' who placed themselves at his utter disposal – Elisabeth Hauptmann, Ruth Berlau, Margarete Steffin, Marieluise Fleisser and a host of others. Two years before his death he indicated to the dissident East German philosopher Wolfgang Harich that he would like his wife Isot Kilian, for a while: 'Divorce her now,' he said, 'and have her back again in a couple of years' time.' And for those last two years Frau Harich belonged to Brecht – exclusively.

'All Men are Thieves in Love,' declares Mrs Peachum in Gay's *Beggar's Opera*, 'and like a Woman better for being another's Property.' Quite so, said Brecht.

The hedonistic self-centredness of his private life had its counterpart in the way he viewed his professional interests. Contracts would be heavily weighted in his favour at the expense of his partners, witness the famous, or infamous, division of the royalties from the *Dreigroschenoper* into $62\frac{1}{2}\%$ for himself, 25% for Weill and $12\frac{1}{2}\%$ for Elisabeth Hauptmann. In matters of stage production people either did things his way or, as far as he was concerned, did not do them at all. When his friend the dramatist Carl Zuckmayer said to him, 'Your idea of a collective enterprise is one in which a group of intelligent people work together to do what one person wants, that person being you,' he beamed approvingly.

At such moments he was being himself. But often he seemed to be acting a role, with the unshaven stubble and the working-class garb promoting an image of deliberate alienation. Weill once noticed a book lying on the bedside table in his flat and picked it up. The dust jacket said 'Karl Marx: *Das Kapital*'. Inside was an Edgar Wallace thriller.

But when these and other quirks of a complex, commanding, less than lovable personality have been paraded and relished, there remains the controversial phenomenon of the uncomfortable poetic talent who remains the greatest German dramatist of the twentieth century and whom many see as the greatest European dramatist since Ibsen. In the 1920s Brecht had acquired the status of an *enfant terrible* in the society that was slowly but surely consolidating itself within the framework of the Weimar Republic. When he left Germany in 1933, it was as the author of the sensationally popular *Dreigroschenoper*, satire on the mores of bourgeois society which the delighted denizens of that society flocked to see. He had established squatter's rights on a plot of literary land called epic drama, and in the course of the 1930s he liberally fertilized this soil with a patented product designated *Verfremdung*, 'alienation', 'detachment', a rationalistic means of breaking down the empathetic process by which the actor identifies with his role and the audience identifies with the actor.

From a succession of places of refuge – Switzerland, Denmark, Sweden, Finland and finally the United States, 'changing my countries more often than my shoes', as he put it – came *The Life of Galileo, Mother Courage and her Children, The Good Person of Sezuan, The Caucasian Chalk Circle* and most of the other plays on which his fame rests. He left America in 1947 for Switzerland and two years later made his home in East Berlin, where the Berliner Ensemble was put at his disposal. When he died in 1956, he had an East German theatre, an Austrian passport, a West German publisher and a Swiss bank account. The archetypal survivor.

At the time he and Weill first met, Brecht had just begun a systematic study of the work of Karl Marx, and was gripped by a conviction that what was needed was a politicised literature, in particular a political drama which should demonstrate how the world could, and must, be changed. Since, as Marx presented it, this dynamic of historical evolution was inevitable, man's obligation lay in understanding what he was witnessing, and of what he was a part, rather than in becoming emotionally involved in it. This political analysis reinforced the opinion which Brecht had already formed, that the objective processes of social reality could not be accommodated within the forms of drama hitherto developed in the Western world. Hence the concept of epic drama, a concept inseparable from the name of Brecht, although in this political sense the term had already been coined by the great protagonist of proletarian theatre, Erwin Piscator. The principle of objective, 'observer's' theatre, moreover, is already present in the ritualised Japanese No-plays – which Brecht had recently discovered and admired – as well as in the dramatic tradition of other cultures.

Art as communication, and as such embedded in, not preciously preserved away from, the rest of life, remained an unshakeable principle for Brecht. Artist and public face each other on the same plane, and the work of art must be seen by the 'consumer' as an object worthy of earnest scrutiny, not as an ideal creation to be worshipped. It is not the notional beauties of a serene, ideal Nature that are the proper subjects of literature but the brutal realities of the rat race in the grimy, impersonal city to which the majority of men and women in industrial society are condemned. Nor need one fear that by subjecting a true work of art to examination, one will destroy it. 'Pluck a rose,' said Brecht, 'and each petal is beautiful.'

It sounds plausible enough. But even Brecht could not balance the terms of his equation. The sociologist Fritz Sternberg, who had a considerable influence on Brecht's thinking in the later 1920s, pointed out to him that whereas in Shakespeare's time, for example, people knew their place and a person could be seen by all to be the King, the prince or the slave that he was, in the twentieth century the individual's social function was no longer publicly perceptible, and contemporary society could only be understood by rational analysis. But, Sternberg continued, if Brecht viewed society, i.e. human beings, solely through the approved exercise of *ratio*, the poet in him would be struck dumb – the natural integration of rational knowledge into his consciousness would stifle his intuitive poetic gifts. Fortunately for posterity, *pace* his inveterate theorising and his political posturing, Brecht's *ratio* was subdued and the *poète malgré lui* usually emerged victorious.

To accompany the image of the angry young man projected by his early dramas, Brecht published in 1927 a volume of poems with the ironic title *Bert Brechts Hauspostille*, a 'domestic breviary', arranged as a mock-liturgical anthology of prayers, rogations and other spiritual exercises, largely in the form of ballads on men and women in peace and war, on love, hate, friendship and the other emotions that bind us. 'This collection of homilies is intended for the reader to use,' his prefatory injunction prescribes. 'It is not meant to be mindlessly sopped up.' In other words this is *Gebrauchslyrik*, 'utility poetry', a kind of lyrical anti-lyricism, companion to Hindemith's *Gebrauchsmusik*, a sub-genre to which Weill, Hanns Eisler and others were also attracted on occasion.

The abrasive ballads of the *Hauspostille*, like all ballads, were meant to be sung, and many remembered how, surrounded by his friends, Brecht would perform them to his own accompaniment on the guitar, for all the world as though he were performing in a political cabaret. 'He had complete mastery of the instrument,' wrote Carl Zuckmayer, who first met Brecht in Munich in 1923,

> and liked complicated chords difficult to finger, like C sharp minor and E flat major. He sang in a hoarse, piercing voice, sometimes with the roughness of a street-singer and the unmistakable intonation of his native Augsburg, at other times in a manner one could call almost beautiful, lilting without emotional vibrato, every syllable, every semitone precise and accurate. One could say of his voice what Herbert Ihering said of the language of his early dramas: 'It has a brutally sensuous quality on the one hand and a tender melancholy on the other, something vulgar, nasty, but with a sense of doom-laden grief – savage wit alongside plaintive lyricism.'

In an appendix to the *Hauspostille* Brecht printed his own melodies to fourteen of his poems, some of which had figured in his performing repertory for a number of years. They are not what would be called fully-fledged 'settings' of the texts but have a provisional, open-ended character reflective of the improvisatory social context in which they were born. And although Brecht was not a 'trained' musician, he had an innate musicality which gave him very clear conceptions of the kind of music his poetry required. He could not have composed the music that Weill, Eisler, Dessau and others wrote to his poems. But nor could they have done so if, to their often less than wholehearted joy, he had not constantly looked over their shoulder or jogged – more likely twisted – their arm.

Early in 1927 Weill stood poised to enter the den of the young lion Brecht. The Baden-Baden invitation had just arrived. Brecht's *Hauspostille* had been published at the beginning of the year, and Weill was only one of many to be gripped by the sound of this powerful new voice in the poetry of the day. Then, in March, Berlin radio announced a performance of Brecht's play *Mann ist Mann*, a cynical presentation of the individual as a helpless, dispensable, replaceable object in society. Brecht himself composed and sang the 'Mann ist Mann' theme-song, and incidental music was written by Edmund Meisel, Piscator's music director. Weill, in his regular column for *Der deutsche Rundfunk*, described it as 'perhaps the most original and most powerful drama of modern times'. The time was ripe for a meeting of minds.

It may have been Georg Kaiser who added the personal touch that finally brought Weill and Brecht together. The two men met one evening in Max Schlichter's recently-opened restaurant in the Lutherstrasse, down the road from the Romanisches Café. Max Schlichter's younger brother Rudolf was a gifted artist of Communist conviction who attracted to his brother's establishment George Grosz, Otto Dix, John Heartfield and others of the 'Rote Gruppe' devoted to the cause of revolution through art. Schlichter's sketches and portraits turned the walls of the restaurant into a permanent art exhibition, in the middle of which sat Piscator, Tucholsky, Döblin, Brecht, Helene Weigel and their radical friends.

For Weill Brecht was the great poetic and dramatic force of the future, a man to open the door to new worlds. For Brecht Weill was merely an ex-pupil of Busoni's who composed 'rather complex, psychologising music', 'atonal, psychological operas', as he put it – hardly a promising candidate for a joint enterprise of Brechtian character. Financially too their ratings were very different. Brecht had recently made a deal with the Ullstein Verlag, guaranteeing him 30,000 marks over five years in return for exclusive publication and performing rights; Weill, one of Universal Edition's captive young hopefuls, had

had to badger them for the mere two hundred marks a month he was now getting.

That the days of Weill the composer of 'atonal, psychological operas' had passed, was something Brecht could hardly have known. In any case opera, as generally understood, did not come high on his list of preferred artistic genres. But the two men soon discovered common ground. 'At my first meeting with Brecht in the spring of 1927,' said Weill

> we were discussing the potentialities of opera, when the name Mahagonny cropped up, together with the notion of a 'Paradise City'. The idea immediately seized my imagination, and in order to pursue it further and to try out the musical style that I envisaged for it, I set the five 'Mahagonny Songs' from Brecht's *Hauspostille*, linking them together to form a small-scale dramatic work, a '*Songspiel*', which was performed that summer at Baden-Baden.

Brecht's five 'Mahagonny' poems, two of them in a characteristic Brechtian pidgin English (though they may actually have been written by Elisabeth Hauptmann, Brecht's 'assistant'), make up the Fourth Lesson of the breviary. Behind them lies a satirical love-hate vision of an immoral capitalist America that both attracted and repelled him. At the same time the 'Paradise City', with its hedonistic adventures, its alcoholics, its prostitutes, but also with its *Angst* and its boredom, embodies the evil reality of bourgeois society in the world at large. So to make explicit the situation of which his poems were like individual snapshots, and to meet Weill's conception of the dramatic form of the piece, Brecht rounded off his 'libretto' with a final admonition: 'This whole Mahagonny exists only because everything is so bad, because there is no serenity, no harmony, and nothing to hold on to.'

According to the expressionist writer Arnolt Bronnen, who belonged to Brecht's circle of friends in Munich in the early 1920s, the name Mahagonny – which is in fact only an idiosyncratic spelling of the German *Mahagoni*, i.e. 'mahogany' – came to Brecht's mind at the sight of the posses of brown-shirted SA-thugs marching through the streets at the time of Hitler's attempted *Putsch* in 1923. It was also the sort of word that appealed to him for euphonic reasons, like Alabama, Benares, Pensacola and other 'exotic' names which he throws indiscriminately into the argument. The final words of the text give the game away:

> For it does not exist, Mahagonny;
> For there is no such place as Mahagonny;
> For it is only an imaginary word, Mahagonny.

Imaginary it may have been – as a word. But what it stood for, as the Weimar Republic stumbled towards its doom and German society prepared to throw itself into the arms of the Nazis, was tragically real. 'If Mahagonny ever comes,' Brecht once said to Bronnen, 'I go.' It did. So did he. So did Weill.

As a narrative context into which to set the *Mahagonny* songs and the social satire, Brecht and Weill, in company with the stage designer Caspar Neher, a schoolmate of Brecht's whose name became inseparable from Brecht-Weill productions over the years, devised a scenario requiring six characters. Four hard-drinking, whoring, poker-playing gold-diggers called Charlie, Billy, Johnny and Bobby set out for Mahagonny, a city that sounds to them like paradise; on the way they are joined by Bessie and Jessie, two prostitutes. Once there, they discover that the only law of the land is that of money. Disillusioned, they decide to leave for Benares, 'where the sun is shining', but news comes that Benares has been destroyed in an earthquake, and they are forced to stay in Mahagonny. When God descends and sees what a den of iniquity the place is, he condemns the inhabitants to hell; but they rebel, protesting that they had been in hell all along. What they had dreamt of as a Utopia had turned out to be a capitalist Gehenna, where there is 'no serenity, no harmony and nothing to hold on to', as the gold-diggers and their women sing in the final sextet.

The novel genre of 'Songspiel' – the name very deliberately coined for its associations with the *Singspiel* of operatic history – was born in this piece for the Baden-Baden Festival and continued its triumphant existence in the *Dreigroschenoper* and *Happy End*. To produce a seamless musical work – a complete performance takes some thirty minutes – Weill composed an instrumental introduction and conclusion, together with interludes linking the vocal items, so that there is music from start to finish. But the essence of the work, both musically and conceptually, lies in the emotional world of the songs.

In the Brecht-Weill world the word 'Song' is virtually a technical term. These are no Lieder. New products require new names, and the inventors patented for the German market the neologism 'Song', leaving English to make the best of the situation. Brecht's friend and translator Eric Bentley facetiously proposed that English speakers adopt the Central European pronunciation of the word and call them 'zonks'.

But the Brecht-Weill 'zonk' *is* something special, a force born of a unique collaboration in unique circumstances, a medium in which, through their release on to Brecht's poems, Weill's creative powers grew and discovered themselves. And because those poems had their roots in a committed social consciousness, the final work of art that emerged spoke to, and for, the whole of the society to which it belonged, to this extent acquiring an objective, 'epic' validity, in Brecht's sense. The critic Herbert Fleischer, looking back in 1932 at a 'Weill-style' as unmistakable as a 'Stravinsky-style' or a 'Debussy-style', saw the 'Songs' in those terms:

> A Weill song is not a common-or-garden hit tune but a ballad. Someone from the lower classes, someone of the streets, sings his or her little bit of life, or little bit of romance, of love, of longing for adventure. The songs are in essence one continuous lamentation, one continuous attack... they are language, philosophy, life in musical sound. Weill found his real self in this song style, the power to let music become language. And his sense of social reality provided the ethos of his work, opened up everything to him – which is precisely what most present-day artists lack.

The *Mahagonny Songspiel* is the first work in which what the world has come to recognise as the inimitable voice of Kurt Weill is heard from beginning to end. It is a voice which, having been trained to say complex things, has reverted to the familiar tonal language of common experience in which listeners recognise that they are being directly addressed. It is an unique voice, one which makes people sit up and take notice. But it had learned, in the course of its development, to say things in remote tongues before settling for the poetry and the prosody of the medium in which it could most effectively communicate. As Schoenberg once observed, there is still a great deal to be said in the key of C major.

In an obvious sense the *Mahagonny Songspiel* represents a kind of trial run for the full-scale *Mahagonny* opera completed two years later – Weill himself called it a 'stylistic study' for the opera. It is also a work of astonishing effectiveness in its own right, with the mocking satire directly translated into 'gestic' musical terms. This gestic music does not reflect, or somehow correspond to, the perceived meaning and intention of the enacted events – it *is* that meaning and that intention. 'The music itself became, so to speak, the agent of the muck-raking, the provocation and the denunciation,' as Brecht put it in his notes 'On the Use of Music for Epic Theatre'. On their own level, a level not too far away from Weill's, cabaret and operetta, says Brecht, have for some time also cultivated gestic music in this sense.

To take one familiar example out of many. When Bessie and Jessie sing their pathological craving for the nearest whisky bar, their craving, and the mocking presentation of it – for in a decent society such a craving would not be known – live in the music and in the scornful discrepancy between a trivial little three-note jingle and the accompaniment that pulses insistently beneath it. Not only that. The accompaniment is ironically rich in the fourths and the 'semitonal slip' which are as basic to the 'difficult', Busonian Weill as to the Weill of this moment:

And all their maudlin, whisky-sodden sentimentality is then poured into the burlesque dance-music lamentation of the 'Alabama Song', this time with a slimy semitonal movement quietly burrowing away in an inner part:

The score of the *Mahagonny Songspiel* calls for a ten-man, jazz-type ensemble dominated by woodwind, brass and percussion, with just two violins as the 'outsiders'. Like the slightly smaller instrumental groups for the *Dreigroschenoper* and *Happy End*, it is a body of forces that descends, technically, from Stravinsky's *L'histoire du soldat*, with the same precision of utterance, the same power of pointed comment, that comes naturally to non-legato instruments. The very opening of the work, *fortissimo*, utters a suitably brash warning of what is to come, its vigorous dotted march-rhythm driven home by an acerbic chromatic harmony expressive of the ambiguous pleasures, the betrayed expectations and inner contradictions of life in the seductive 'Paradise City'.

This musical world is Weill's creation. Yet Brecht cannot be quite kept out of it. Technically his musical knowledge stretched to little more than the occasional notation of his own melodies in an odd personal form. But many recognised, as Zuckmayer had done, that much of his poetry concealed a musicality of its own, which gave him clear conceptions of the sort of music his poetry would, and would not, welcome.

The Finnish conductor Simon Parmet saw this at close quarters. 'He was not musical in the deepest sense of the word,' wrote Parmet, 'but he had an infallible instinct when it came to imagining what sort of music would best match his kind of drama. . . . Sooner or later I would find myself captivated by the tune he proposed and would realise that that, and only that, was the melody appropriate for the scene under discussion.' Brecht took his tunes wherever he found them, and encouraged his composers to do the same (sometimes he also took his texts wherever he found them, witness his plagiarism in the *Dreigroschenoper* of K. L. Ammer's translation of Villon).

From Parmet comes the story that Weill's most famous melody, the 'Mackie Messer Song' in the *Dreigroschenoper*, is 'in fact a Russian folk-tune which Brecht appropriated and handed over to his composer'. Maybe so, maybe not. 'To be sure,' said Zuckmayer, 'the music of the *Dreigroschenoper* is by Kurt Weill but anyone who knew Brecht's tone of voice and individual melodic diction also knows that it was his idea and his prompting that gave birth to the famous hurdy-gurdy song about Mackie Messer.'

Indeed the *Dreigroschenoper* music *is* by Kurt Weill, and by no one else. Yet when a collaboration is as close and as spectacularly productive as that between Weill and Brecht, the notion of a clean and absolute division of responsibility between the two parties cannot reflect the true nature of the relationship. The give-and-take axiomatic to any collaboration – even one involving the dictatorial Brecht – will mean that, as the music moulds itself to the text it is given, so it may demand, in its own interest, that changes be made in that text – passages shortened or extended, perhaps whole scenes added or excised. The claims of musical form will be weighed against those of conceptual and dramatic form: the poet becomes part-musician, the composer, part-poet. It is like watching a mysterious process of symbiosis or osmosis.

Brecht's own tunes to the Mahagonny poems in his *Hauspostille* have scant melodic charm, though sometimes a quirky interest. The 'Benares Song' is an outrageous concoction of 'There is a Tavern in the Town' for the verse and 'One Fine Day' from Puccini's *Madame Butterfly* for the refrain. Brecht's tongue must have been firmly wedged in his cheek. But, probing a little deeper, we find that the rhythmic pattern of his 'Alabama Song', in both verse and refrain, is identical to that of Weill's setting of a few years later. Weill himself pointed out this natural identity of the two basic 'gestic' formulae in his essay 'On the Gestic Character of Music', written in 1929.

Then we make an even more interesting discovery. Some time before he and Weill first met in spring 1927, Brecht wrote the words and melody of a song called 'Seeräuberjenny', of which an arrangement had recently been made by a young Berlin cabaret musician called Franz Servatius Bruinier. This is the refrain of Brecht's song as it appears in Bruinier's manuscript:

And this is what Polly sings in the *Dreigroschenoper*:

It can hardly be doubted that the formal conception of the 'Pirate Jenny Song' as a whole, and of its refrain in particular, down almost to the last melodic and rhythmic detail, is Brecht's. But nor can it be doubted that the finished product, vocal line and accompaniment, that we know from the *Dreigroschenoper*, is Weill's. It does not detract from the quality or the originality of his finished product to know that vital parts of the raw material come from elsewhere. Any composition that rests on folk music, for instance, is in this situation, so is a set of variations on somebody else's melody. There is no concealment of priority, no squabbling over plagiarism. Weill himself habitually re-used material from his earlier works, presenting it in a quite different guise in a quite different context – self-pillage, some might wish to call it. The only point at issue is that the circumstances be recognised for what they are. It means, on the one hand, acknowledging the musician in Brecht without exaggerating what this musicianship implies, and on the other, not trying to pretend that the music of *Mahagonny*, *Dreigroschenoper* and the rest is by anyone else but Weill. Running battles across this territory between Brechtians and Weillians in recent years have thrown up so much smoke that sight has been lost of a simple, albeit sensitive central truth.

*

On the evening of July 17, 1927 Weill and Brecht found themselves at the final events of the Baden-Baden Chamber Music Festival. The short chamber operas by Milhaud, Toch and Hindemith had come and gone, and the audience was using the intermission before the final item to take a stroll in the grounds of the Kurhaus.

When they returned to the auditorium, they were bewildered to find stage-hands erecting a boxing-ring – a platform with wooden posts at the corners, joined by ropes, with a bucket of water in one corner. Inside the ring stood an American bar. Behind the ring was a large screen on to which were projected illustrations, texts and slogans designed by Caspar Neher, to make visually explicit the events and sentiments that bound the songs together and conveyed the 'message' of the piece. As in Piscator's 'epic theatre' productions at the Berlin Volksbühne, the line that divided audience from actors has been erased. The concertgoer who has come to hear a chamber opera, or at least a staged cantata, finds himself at a boxing-match, his sense of surrealist alienation further intensified by the intrusive projections and slogans to which he is subjected.

There was no 'acting' in the conventional sense, no emotional interplay between characters. It was all very cool, very rational, very 'epic'. The six singers – two sopranos, two tenors, two basses – all came from a background of opera except for Lotte Lenya, here performing Weill for the first time. They all wore identical evening dress – black dinner jacket, white shirt, black tie, the men with hard black hats like bowlers, the women with white boaters – and stood in a row, side by side, in the middle of the boxing-ring as though giving a concert performance of an opera. Brecht, who directed the proceedings, shuffled in and out of the ring during the music, puffing on his cigar. More than once Brecht put forward the proposal to institute an 'Epic Smoking Theatre' in which the audience would be allowed to drink and smoke, as they do in cabarets and boxing matches, in order to promote the attitude of detachment integral to his 'epic' theatre. Such a theatre, needless to say, would have been devoted solely to performing Brecht's own works.

The *Mahagonny Songspiel* opened with the crack of a pistol shot (planned) and ended in a riot (unplanned but not unpredictable). The gold-diggers and the prostitutes told their tale, and Lenya rounded off the proceedings with the mocking revelation 'For it does not exist, Mahagonny. . .' Then, picking up placards bearing slogans such as 'Up with the Mortality of the Soul!', 'Down with Syphilis!' and 'Up with Weill!' (Lenya's contribution), they marched to and fro in the boxing ring, provoking the outraged response they knew would follow.

Most of the *cognoscenti* of the atonal avant-garde, the pillars of the Donaueschingen and Baden-Baden Festivals, felt offended and insulted.

Hoots and whistles broke out, rotten apples were thrown – the spontaneous protests had evidently been well planned – while others clapped and cheered. Brecht, cunning old fox that he was, had foreseen trouble. 'The entire audience stood to cheer and boo and whistle all at the same time,' recalled Lenya. 'Brecht had provided all of us with little whistles of our own, and we just whistled right back.'

Those who had taken the trouble to read the programme would have realised that they were in for something of a revolutionary experience. At the bottom of the page, following a few brief facts on his career, Weill had added a little paragraph about his intentions:

> In his latest works Weill has been moving in the direction of those who, in all spheres of artistic activity, foresee the liquidation of the arts as social graces. The little epic piece *Mahagonny* simply draws the conclusion that emerges from the irresistible collapse of the existing social classes. It addresses itself to an audience that unsophisticatedly demands to be entertained in the theatre.

Anyone acquainted with Weill's social attitudes knew his insistence on art as communication, on the immediacy of the relationship between artist and public. But prescriptive terminology like 'liquidation of the arts as social graces' and 'irresistible collapse of the existing social classes' has its own obvious doctrinaire origin, and it is hard not to suspect that we are also hearing the voice of Brecht, who was in the full flush of his discovery of the Marxist interpretation of history.

As the audience greeted the *Mahagonny* 'happening' with a mingled chime of cheers and boos, so the critics, in no less of a state of shock, went their separate ways. Those who chose to be outraged concentrated on the unacceptable politicisation of the work of art and protested that the serious aims of the Festival had been mocked, especially in the gratuitously offensive and totally dispensable placard-waving at the end. Aaron Copland found Weill to be in the painful posture of 'trying too hard to be revolutionary', sacrificing his gifts at the altar of 'a questionable dramatic effectiveness'.

But others saw it as a very serious work indeed, above all in musical terms. 'It is impossible to escape its magnetic attraction,' wrote Max Marschalk in the prestigious *Vossische Zeitung*: 'one is kept in a state of tension but without knowing why, expecting something to happen but not knowing what.' More spontaneous in his enthusiasm, Adolf Weissmann, of the *BZ Am Mittag*, called it 'infernally clever' and declared: 'This man Kurt Weill does things that others can't.'

At the reception after the performance the mood matched the violently divided response in the auditorium. Would the supporters or the opponents win the day? 'Suddenly,' said Lenya, looking back on the occasion,

I felt a slap on the back, accompanied by a booming laugh: 'Is there no telephone?' It was Otto Klemperer.

With that the whole room was singing the 'Benares Song', and I knew the battle was won.

Klemperer's relationship to Weill's music is the story of an unhappy ambivalence and of missed opportunities. In the early 1920s Klemperer, a manic depressive of emotional extremes, built up a reputation as a passionate champion of contemporary music. When he was appointed to the Kroll Opera in 1926, he let it be known that he was looking for new works, but when Universal Edition offered him the première of Weill's *Der Zar lässt sich photographieren* the following year, he turned it down. After first raising hopes, then dashing them, he said no to *Der Protagonist* as well.

After the *Mahagonny Songspiel* at Baden-Baden, however, his interest returned and he asked Weill whether he had a new work on the stocks. When Weill offered him the recently finished *Na und?*, Curjel, Klemperer's dramaturge, was as curtly dismissive as Heinsheimer had been in Vienna. But the saddest episode occurred over the première of the full-length *Mahagonny* opera in the 1929–30 season. Curjel and the production team at the Kroll were firmly convinced it was just the work they needed. Klemperer could not make up his mind. After Weill had played through the third act of the opera to him, he declared himself willing to take it on. Two hours later, as Weill described the events to Hertzka, Klemperer telephoned in a state of great agitation and wanted to come round immediately. 'He arrived,' said Weill, 'looking utterly distraught, and explained to me with tears in his eyes that he had been struggling with himself for the past two hours but it was no good. He said that he realised the importance of the work and could recognise the beauties in the music but that he found it alien and incomprehensible as a whole.'

Weill, who would have been given a great boost by a Klemperer première at the Kroll, had some nasty things to say about the temperamental maestro at the time. Fences were eventually mended. But Klemperer never changed his mind over the *Mahagonny* opera, still calling it almost fifty years later 'awful', 'obscene' and a '*Schweinerei*'. Great conductor that he was, he had his blind spots.

CHAPTER VIII

Art and Politics

When Weill went to Schlichter's wine restaurant in the spring of 1927 to meet Bertolt Brecht, he had little idea what, if anything, would come of it. As the recent song-settings by Franz Servatius Bruinier had shown, Brecht was keen to see his ballads set to music by 'proper' composers, so giving Weill his 'Mahagonny' poems could, if he were lucky, serve as welcome publicity for his own cause. If he were unlucky and the settings made no impression, he would not have lost anything.

But the two men's conversation went a good deal further than this. Weill later recalled that they had discussed the question of opera, and that in this connection the name 'Mahagonny' had been mentioned, the 'Paradise City'. The idea of an opera on the subject had already crossed Brecht's mind some years earlier, and among a list of names and subjects for possible dramatic treatment jotted down in his diary for July 1924 is 'Mahagonny-Oper'. In his notes to the completed *Mahagonny* opera Weill calls the Baden-Baden *Songspiel* a test run for the opera on which they had already started work; the test run having proven successful, they turned their attention back to the opera, taking almost a year of on-and-off discussion to put together a libretto. Yet as early as April 1927, three months before Baden-Baden, Weill had told Hertzka that the subject for a 'large-scale tragic opera' was already prepared. In short, there is a kind of Mahagonny complex which stretches from Weill's first meeting with Brecht in early 1927 to the première of *Aufstieg und Fall der Stadt Mahagonny* in March 1930 – even beyond, since changes to the opera were still occupying their minds in 1931.

Both men were out to break the comfortable middle-class, art-as-consumer-goods domination of the cultural market, with its pretentious elitism and its philistine values; both assumed that it was the responsibility of art to speak to the heart of man, both as a private creature and as a social being, not just to provide a superficial gratification or to minister to a fleeting fashion. Each in his own way, therefore, they found themselves drawn to such politicised enterprises as the proletarian 'agitprop' theatre movement associated with Erwin Piscator and Karlheinz Martin, which laid its emphasis not on the fate of the individual but on the objective problems of the age and the drama of the masses. Subjective emotionalism was spurned, a theory of 'objective acting' was evolved to complement the theory of 'epic drama', and an appeal to rational understanding took the place of the cult of inspiration and the expression of passion. Brecht's contribution to this movement was the theory of 'alienation' and the practice of 'epic theatre'. Weill's was the concept of 'gestic' music.

But whereas by 1927 Brecht was firmly marching down the road marked 'Art as an Agent of Social Change', Weill – like Hindemith, to this extent – had his mind rather on attracting a wider public to the experience of art, and thus on creating the kind of art that would promote this accessibility. This is one route of entry into the related phenomena of *Gebrauchsmusik* and *Gemeinschaftsmusik* ('Music for the Community'), concepts that could also effortlessly embrace jazz, an art-form expressive of the instincts and responses of the untutored masses – contemporary folk-music, in other words. 'A glance at the dance halls of every continent will go to show that jazz is as much an external expression of our own age as was the waltz at the end of the nineteenth century,' observed Weill.

The first question that Brecht asked about a work of art was 'How can we best use it?' Weill's sights, however, were set on the work of art *per se*, on how its range and appeal could be extended in their own terms. Brecht had a theory that subjected art to ideology; Weill was in search of an aesthetic. And this, without reference to whatever intentions Brecht might have had in his devious mind, was how Weill viewed the remarkable prospects that their collaboration opened up. What he already knew, and what he expected from the future, he made clear to Hans Heinsheimer in a letter which reads like a chapter of intellectual autobiography. 'What attracts me to Brecht,' he wrote a few weeks after the Baden-Baden *Mahagonny*,

> is above all the way in which my music becomes so powerfully interlocked with his poetry – something which took all the leading critics at Baden-Baden by surprise. I am convinced that collaboration between two equally productive minds can lead to something fundamentally new. There can be no doubt that a completely new kind of work for the stage is emerging at the present time, addressed to a far larger audience and with an impact over an extraordinarily wide area. . .
>
> Long discussions with Brecht have led me to the conclusion that his views on an operatic libretto largely correspond to my own. The work we intend to produce is not going to make use of contemporary material that will be out of date in a year's time but sets out to present our

1. Cantor Albert Weill and his wife Emma, Kurt Weill's parents, in 1897, the year of their marriage.

2. The Weill children: Ruth, Hanns, Kurt and Nathan.

3. Kurt Weill at the piano in the family apartment adjoining the Dessau synagogue, 1915.

4. Programme of a recital given by Weill and the soprano Elisabeth Feuge in Halberstadt in 1920. The recital opened with 'Introductory Comments' from Weill and included two of his own songs.

5. The Court Theatre in Dessau in Weill's day.

6. Georg Kaiser, 1925.

7. Busoni and his master class, 1922. From left to right: Kurt Weill, Walther Geiser, Luc Balmer and Vladimir Vogel.

8. Weill and Lenya on their wedding day, January 26, 1926.

9.   A rehearsal of the *Mahagonny Songspiel*, Baden-Baden 1927. Lotte
Lenya as Jessie (left) and Irene Eden as Bessie (right) in the boxing-ring;
behind them, outside the ring, the golddiggers, wearing black hats. Weill is
on the extreme left of the ring; the second figure to the right of him, facing
front, is Hindemith. Brecht stands alone to the right of the ring. The
screen in the background shows one of Neher's projections.

10.   At the Baden-Baden Music Festival, 1927. Front row: Lenya on the
left, Walther Brügmann, the conductor, in the middle. Centre: Brecht and
Heinrich Burkhard, co-director of the Festival. At the back, on the left,
talking to Burkhard and quite uninterested in the group photo being
taken, sits Weill.

11.   Caspar Neher, 1931.

12.   The Neues Theatre am Schiffbauerdamm, Berlin, scene of the sensational success of the *Dreigroschenoper* in 1928.

13.   Playbill for the première of the *Dreigroschenoper*, August 31, 1928. Lenya, in the role of Jenny, was overlooked, to Weill's considerable indignation (see p.144).

(see p.144)

Theater am Schiffbauerdamm

Direktion: Ernst Josef Aufricht

Die Dreigroschenoper

(The Beggars Opera)

Ein Stück mit Musik in einem Vorspiel und 8 Bildern nach dem
Englischen des John Gay.
(Eingelegte Balladen von François Villon und Rudyard Kipling)

Personen:

Jonathan Peachum, Chef einer Bettlerplatte	Erich Ponto
Frau Peachum	Rosa Valetti
Polly, ihre Tochter	Roma Bahn
Macheath, Chef einer Platte von Straßen-banditen	Harald Paulsen
Brown, Polizeichef von London	Kurt Gerron
Lucy, seine Tochter	Kate Kühl
Trauerweidenwalter	Ernst Rotmund
Münzmatthias	Karl Hannemann
Hakenfingerjakob	Manfred Fürst
Sägerobert	Josef Bunzel
Jimmie	Werner Maschmeyer
Ede	Albert Venohr

Filch, einer von Peachums Bettlern	Naphtali Lehrmann
Smith, Konstabler	Ernst Busch
Huren	Kuffner / Jeckels / Helmke / Kliesch u. a.
Bettler	Schiskaja / Ritter / Heimsoth u. a.

Banditen, Huren, Bettler, Konstabler, Volk.
(Ort der Handlung: London)
Eine kleine Pause nach dem 3. Bild.
Große Pause nach dem 6. Bild.
Die Walzen des Leierkastens wurden hergestellt
in der Fabrik Bacigalupo.

Übersetzung: Elisabeth Hauptmann
Bearbeitung: Brecht
Musik: Kurt Weill
Regie: Erich Engel
Bühnenbild: Caspar Neher
Musikalische Leitung: Theo Mackeben
Kapelle: Lewis Ruth Band.

age in a definitive form. Its influence will thus extend far beyond the moment in which it is written, and it is our task to create a new genre appropriate for the expression of the totally new concerns and values of our age.

The hammering-out of a libretto with Brecht for the full-scale *Mahagonny* opera took the best part of a year. The publicity gained by the *Songspiel* at Baden-Baden was welcome and had helped to offset the generally unfavourable reception of *Royal Palace* in Berlin earlier in the year, but it had not translated itself into the hoped-for succession of royalty-bearing performances elsewhere. *Na und?* was consigned to a drawer, and remained there, while *Der Zar lässt sich photographieren*, newly completed, had not yet found a firm venue for its première. And for months he had been losing, one by one, his private pupils.

So to support his wife and himself, Weill was left only the monthly two hundred marks from Universal Edition and, as his main source of income, his weekly articles for *Der deutsche Rundfunk*. This did not even stretch to a summer holiday, it seems. For the weeks that he and Lenya spent in August and September in Prerow, a quiet little resort on the sandy Baltic coast, were subsidised by Dr Hertzka, who had been captivated by Lenya's performance at Baden-Baden and sent her a cheque to enable her to take a holiday.

Weill's quandary was that his principal source of income was precisely what he most wanted to get rid of. 'These articles rob me of my best working hours,' he complained to Hertzka, 'and in view of the speed with which I am working at present, this naturally puts me under considerable stress.' The situation could be remedied immediately, he adds, if his retainer were raised to six hundred marks a month, a sum he describes as 'absolutely essential'. In the event Universal agreed to four hundred marks, but only for the coming six months.

After the flurry of excitement at Baden-Baden and the relaxation of their seaside holiday, Weill and Lenya returned to their ordered life in the Pension Hassforth. For Lenya, gregarious and extrovert, it was too ordered. She needed the stimulus of company, preferably male, and since her husband had no time to attend to her needs, she looked for men who did. She struck up a relationship with Rudolf Leonhard, the Marxist poet who lived in the same house, then with the dramatist Leo Lania, one of Piscator's collaborators in the cause of political theatre, for whose play *Konjunktur*, ironically, Weill later composed incidental music and songs. How much Weill knew of her affairs we cannot tell – probably almost everything. Lenya always ingenuously claimed that he knew perfectly well and that she made no attempt to deceive him – though whether it left him as emotionally unscarred as his external demeanour implied is another matter. In any case, the discipline he imposed on himself left little time for speculation on what else he might do with his life. Once ensconced within his own four walls and immersed in composition, he needed nothing, and nobody, else.

Discussions on the form of the *Mahagonny* opera generally took place in Brecht's studio flat in the Spichernstrasse, a fifteen-minute walk from the Luisenplatz. The flat was a spartan affair, without carpets or curtains, and dominated by a huge cast-iron stove; there was a heavy table with a typewriter on it, an easel on which stood some sketches for stage sets and costumes, and a large, long-suffering couch pushed against the wall.

As an archetypal rebel and iconoclast, Brecht had around him a coterie of admiring young men and women whom he harangued and questioned as he walked to and fro, enveloped in a cloud of tobacco smoke that hovered above him like a halo. The cult of meanness and scruffiness belonged to his act – an ostentatious demonstration of solidarity with the working classes of whose real nature he had little idea.

When he and Weill made it clear that they wanted to get down to work, the acolytes would disperse and leave the two men alone in the shabby studio; sometimes Lenya too would stay, together with Elisabeth Hauptmann, the most loyal and most creative of Brecht's female companions. At their working sessions Brecht, naturally, took the lead. He knew what he wanted of his collaborators, and was sufficient of a musician to be able to convey his intentions to Weill. Sometimes he would make his point by picking up his guitar and singing or strumming a few bars; Weill would listen, note down Brecht's ideas and consider how, or whether, to incorporate them when he got back to the privacy of his own surroundings.

In his own right, discussing a particular work in *Der deutsche Rundfunk* or making a declaration of critical principle about the direction in which he intended that his own music should go, Weill struck a tone of assurance and conviction. Yet when working with others, he was always open to suggestions, always willing to consider doing things differently. When Universal proposed changes in the accompaniment of the 'Alabama Song' to make the harmony milder and less acerbic – in other words, blander and easier for the masses – he accepted without demur. Transposition of a song to accommodate the tessitura of a particular singer, re-orchestration imposed by the exigencies of the moment – such things were close to the spirit of the *Gebrauchsmusik* of the age, and the technical skills needed to make these on-the-spot modifications had been in his possession since his days as Kapellmeister in Lüdenscheid and Dessau. He was not the man to protest that variations offended the sanctity of his score.

Once asked whether a particular number should be taken slower or faster, he replied: 'I don't care. If you want to do it faster, do it faster.'

Although he felt himself to be, and in practice was, the senior partner in the enterprise, Brecht became increasingly aware how intelligent and inventive a musician he had as a colleague. Whatever service he had had from men like Bruinier and Edmund Meisel, here, in Weill, was an artist in a totally different class, both intellectually and technically, and the basis of their relationship was mutual respect. Yet in personal terms it never went much further than this. They had very different ideas on how to conduct their private lives, and Weill found the growing authoritarianism in Brecht's Communist stance far from appealing. Neither now nor at any later time in their lives did they use the intimate 'du' in addressing each other.

The popularity of the Brecht-Weill works, offset by a widespread unawareness of what Weill had written before and what he was to write afterwards, has created the impression that their collaboration flourished over many years – an association comparable, say, to that between Richard Strauss and Hugo von Hofmannsthal. In fact it lasted only from 1927 to 1930, with a somewhat ambivalent postscript (*The Seven Deadly Sins*) in 1933. Furthermore, the poems of the *Mahagonny Songspiel* and the *Berliner Requiem* of the following year were not written either for or with Weill, and some of them go back many years, which further reduces the scope of their directly collaborative activity.

But it is not in its brief, if brilliant history that the central interest of this socio-aesthetic partnership lies. Rather, its fascination emerges from the observation of how the two men, each proceeding in the context of his own *métier* but with liberal glances at the way his actions impinged on the other's domain, found common aims and made common cause to achieve them.

In the course of the 1920s, under the particular stimulus of the political theatre of Erwin Piscator, where the phrase was born, Brecht pursued the implications of 'epic theatre', a concept set up in deliberate opposition to Aristotelian 'dramatic theatre'. Where, in the Aristotelian tradition that we have inherited, the spectator is drawn to identify with the emotions being portrayed on the stage, Brecht appeals for critical observation. Reason should prevail over feeling – not replace it, for there is no such thing as a situation without feelings, but learn to dominate it. What we need is not a closed 'dramatic' plot woven from a selection of blended strands and reminiscent of the old Aristotelian unities, but an open, episodic, 'epic' narrative in which each moment stands for itself. The thrust is directed towards jolting the audience out of its complacent cult of entertainment – what Brecht called the 'culinary' approach – and breaking the spell of the conventional theatrical experience by the disruptive use of film and projected images, the posting of scene titles and slogans, the introduction of music, the use of half-curtains, and above all the adoption of a detached, critical style of 'epic' acting.

Finally, moralising as openly and unashamedly as Schiller or George Bernard Shaw, Brecht announces a policy of 'emphasising more and more the didactic at the expense of the culinary, thus converting luxury goods into vehicles of education and places of entertainment into media of communication.' Opera as a form, despite the admiration he maintained for Mozart, did not much interest him: the central task of the stage was to convey a message through the medium designed for the conveyance of messages, namely language. If such ambient elements as music can intensify the message or speed its conveyance – and Brecht took very seriously the question of what music should be allowed into his dramas – then by all means encourage them. But only as servants of the ideologico-dramatic aim.

Such were the ideas, theoretical and practical, that Brecht, dramatist with a sense of music, brought to the conference table, so to speak, in his working sessions with Weill in the Spichernstrasse. Weill, musician with a sense of theatre, had been preparing for this moment in his own way. In the years immediately following his tutelage under Busoni his concern had lain principally with the formal aesthetic issues involved in an attempt to rejuvenate opera in a post-Romantic world. The music, he argued, with the recent example of Busoni's *Doktor Faust* vividly in his mind, cannot be just an illustration of events carried by a dramatic text, or a mere commentary on the spectacle being enacted before the audience's gaze. 'Only the complete and utter fusion of all the means of dramatic expression with all the means of musical expression will produce that supreme genre of theatrical art that we call opera,' he wrote in 1926 in his essay 'Busoni's *Faust* and the Renewal of Operatic Form'. His search for clarity and precision of expression in his own musical language, both theatrical and instrumental, runs parallel to this.

At the time of his first encounter with Brecht, and even more so immediately after it, Weill shifted the balance of his arguments from the inner-musical, the aesthetic, to the circumstantial, the sociological. Narrative fiction and lyric poetry speak directly and privately to the individual, without the mediation of an external force or the interpretation of a third party. Drama, by contrast, is an open spectacle and cannot but have a communal and social dimension; moreover it can only communicate, like music, through agents, through public exhibition. Although every age has its artists who shrink from the material realities around them and withdraw into their private world, the *Zeitgeist* of the 1920s in Germany lay heavily on the values of social 'relevance', on subject matter drawn from the tangible facts of everyday experience, on the presentation of crises clamouring for contemporary solutions.

Among progressively-minded writers, artists and musicians issues such as these involved considering the constitution of the public for whom their works were intended, and thus the nature of the relationship between the work of art and its consumers. At the same time any art worthy of the name must retain a validity that is not exhausted by and in the age to which it owes its existence. But society was changing and, as these intellectuals saw it, the pace of change could only quicken. So while themselves also working to hasten this change, they were at the same time preparing to address the society of the future.

Weill recognised this twin-pronged challenge. Writing in 1927 on the prospects for opera, he regarded as ineluctable the 'coming liquidation of the arts as social graces'. But he also saw the consequential need for opera 'to take account of the fields of interest of that wider public at whom opera will in the immediate future have to be directed, if it is to have any justification for its existence'. This is not a commitment to the Brecht-Piscator view of art, specifically drama, as an instrument of social change, but it does make clear a conviction that there are such things as artistic needs in a society, and that an art which does not minister to these needs in one way or another will not survive. Equally, new artistic forms can only come into existence as a response to a new view of the world and of man's relationship to it.

Yet within this sociological reality Weill consistently seeks to retain a sense of permanent values as well as the principle of timeless validity in a context of heterogeneous timebound characters and phenomena. 'Stravinsky's *Oedipus Rex* is no less a mirror of our age than, say, Chaplin's *Gold Rush*,' he observed.

Aware that music is a more general medium of communication than literature and cannot, except in its external trappings, respond to each successive shift of interest in the fashionable *Zeitgeist*, Weill held to the central immutability of the experiences that music transmits:

> The complexes of emotions and thoughts that music can represent are fairly circumscribed and have remained basically unchanged for centuries. What has changed has been the objects of attention and the forms employed. The human quality that music is able to express has

remained the same. But man has changed – he now reacts differently to external influences, events and emotions.

Posing the twin questions 'What reasons are there for having music in the theatre?' and 'What is the nature of music written for the stage?' Weill reaches the heart of his philosophy of musical theatre, and at the same time the synthesis of his activity with Brecht's, in the concept of what he called 'gestic' music. *Gestus*, a term also used by Brecht in this new, quasi-technical sense, denotes the objective demonstration in speech and action of the essential relationship of one human being to another, stripped of all psychological and subconscious elements that cannot be absorbed into the new convention of externalised, concrete expression. Gestic language and gestic acting are integral parts of Brecht's epic theatre. Gestic music is the equivalent expression, in its own terms, of the same objective reality, the correlative of determinedly non-Romantic, epic theatre, the music of the Brechtian principle of alienation.

'We find gestic music wherever there is a musical representation, in direct, naive form, of a situation in which one person is involved with another,' Weill puts it. 'It is at its most striking in the recitatives in Bach's Passions, in Mozart's operas, in *Fidelio* ('*Nur hurtig fort und frisch gegraben*' [the duet between Leonore and Rocco in Act Two]), and in Offenbach and Bizet.'

Because it is easier to illustrate the phenomenon of gestic music than to define it, Weill quotes in his essay the case of the 'Alabama Song' from the *Mahagonny Songspiel*. The basis of the *Gestus*, he argues, lies in 'fixing the rhythm of the text', i.e. converting the verbal material and the cadences of the language into musical terms. This much Brecht had already done in the skeleton melody he printed in the appendix to his *Hauspostille*. When he came to turn the text into a 'proper' song, Weill retained the same gestic rhythm, because what Brecht had instinctively lighted upon already expressed the basic *Gestus* and was only waiting to be 'properly composed', as Weill put it.

So closely intertwined were Weill's and Brecht's thoughts during their work on the *Mahagonny* opera that the precedence of particular formulations – even the word 'gestic' itself – cannot always be known beyond doubt. There is some Weill in what passes for Brecht, who was in any case a notorious poacher of other people's thoughts, a propensity he airily dismissed as 'a basic laxity over matters of intellectual property'. Equally, above all in matters of sociological tendency, the phraseology of some of Weill's essays suggests that Brecht was looking over his shoulder. And there is a third contributor to the common enterprise, a man to be found at Brecht's pad in the Spichernstrasse as often as Weill, and an artist without whose insights and skills the impact of 'Brecht-Weill' would not have been what it was. This was the stage designer Caspar Neher.

Like Brecht and Weill, Neher stood on the threshold of a career that was to capture international acclaim. Senior to Brecht by one year and to Weill by three, the tall, craggy 'Cas', as he was known, had attended the same school in Augsburg as Brecht. He designed the sets and costumes for almost all the Brecht premières of the 1920s, as well as for all the Brecht-Weill stage works performed in Germany from the first – the *Mahagonny Songspiel* – onwards. 'Neher's projections are as integral to the *Mahagonny* opera as Weill's music and the libretto,' said Brecht. Since his arrival in Berlin in 1924 Neher had had commissions for Max Reinhardt's Deutsches Theater and Piscator's Volksbühne, and he was soon in great demand throughout Germany, both for dramatic and operatic productions.

To many people's surprise he did not leave the country when Hitler came to power. His political sympathies could be readily implied from the company he kept, but he spent the war years unharmed in Germany and afterwards quickly picked up the threads of the international career he had established before 1939. One of Brecht's first acts on his return to Europe from the United States in 1947 was to seek 'Cas' out and persuade him to spend part of each year with the Berliner Ensemble. But, unlike Brecht, he would never have committed himself to live in that part of the world. Neher's sets and costumes were everywhere in demand – Glyndebourne, the Salzburg Festival, La Scala, the Metropolitan Opera, Covent Garden, Zurich, not to mention all the major opera houses of Germany. Like Brecht he took Austrian citizenship after the Second World War for tactical reasons, and went to live in Vienna in 1959, where he died in 1962, the longest survivor of the *Mahagonny* and *Dreigroschenoper* trio. 'Cas is a truly fine man,' Weill once said to Lenya, 'and I find his way of looking at things very much to my liking.' It is not the sort of remark he would have made about Brecht.

To the outside world in Berlin in 1927 and 1928 Brecht, Weill and Neher appeared as a trio of radical innovators, working almost like a group of conspirators with their own sets of values and their own terms of reference. Hans Curjel tells how the three would drop in to his office at the Kroll Opera and lay out before him the principles of the 'music theatre of the future', exemplified at that moment by the *Mahagonny* opera. Curjel's office was at the time something of a meeting-place for left-wing intellectuals and artists – Klemperer, Brecht, the philosophers Ernst Bloch and Adorno, the critic Walter Benjamin, and the constructivist painter and designer László Móholy-Nágy, whom Weill knew from the Romanisches Café in the years immediately after the First World War. Móholy-Nágy had just returned to Berlin from teaching at the Bauhaus in Dessau, and now found a congenial ambience for his work with Piscator and the Volksbühne.

It may not be true, as Curjel later claimed, that it was he who, bowled over by the *Mahagonny Songspiel* at Baden-Baden, first proposed to Weill that he turn the story into a full-length opera. But he certainly moved heaven and earth to try to persuade Klemperer to change his mind over his refusal to accept it for the Kroll – a refusal which still provokes a wagging of heads in disbelief.

Curjel had a clear memory of Weill at this time:

> He was very forthright in his opinions, seeing the evolution of music in terms of the evolution of a society that was undergoing great change. He was small of build but he gave the impression of being of average height. He wore heavy glasses with very large frames, behind which glistened observant and thoughtful eyes. His movements were relaxed and friendly – indeed, there was a general air of friendliness about him. He often used to sing and play me excerpts from pieces on which he was engaged. He played the piano like a proficient but by no means consummate repetiteur; his voice, on the other hand, was unforgettable – soft, gentle, utterly unsentimental but full of feeling, the accents firm, yet never harsh or violent. . . .
>
> Politically, to the best of my knowledge, he was left-wing, like all of us, without belonging to any particular party. And although he did not scorn material considerations, he was anything but a moneygrabber.

From autumn 1927 to spring 1928 the *Mahagonny* opera, specifically its libretto, continued to dominate Weill's thoughts, as he gradually manoeuvred his partner into providing the precise form of text he required. 'I am working with Brecht on the libretto every day,' he wrote to Universal, 'and it is being moulded entirely according to my instructions. This kind of collaboration, where the shape of the libretto is determined by purely musical considerations, opens up totally new possibilities.' These possibilities extended to plans for an 'epic opera' based on the industrial society of the Ruhr. Where *Mahagonny* focused on consumption and the pursuit of leisure in capitalist society, this 'Ruhr Epic' would have centred on work and on the inhuman conditions in the coal mines. But the plans did not leave the paper.

Weill's free play with words like 'entirely' (*vollständig*), 'purely' (*rein*), and 'totally' (*ganz*) may overstate the case. Nor is a libretto 'determined by purely musical considerations' anything new. Wagner's texts, a kind of memorandum from Wagner the dramatist to Wagner the composer, a form of words that has fulfilled its purpose the moment it gives rise to music, would meet Weill's demands without further ado. The deepest meaning of Wagner's art lies in the music, and nowhere else, and this music is as 'gestic', in its own terms, as that defined by Weill and Brecht.

Ironically, it was just this Wagnerian world that Weill and his generation pledged themselves to supersede.

In the 1920s, moreover, as at many other times before and since, suspicions were abroad about the credentials of the 'exotic and irrational entertainment' that is opera. To Brecht the supervention of music meant an intensification of the epic experience. Piscator, however, who employed music in his productions as a matter of course – *Gebrauchsmusik* in the strictest sense – saw a potential conflict of interests, a threat to the precise word-borne political message from the irrational and ultimately more powerful, because more immediate, impact of music. 'Throughout my life', said Piscator,

> I have always fought for the primacy of the word – its significance, its precision, its power of expression. Music, of course, has the power to intensify the word, but at the same time it introduces an atmospheric quality that blurs the clarity of the verbal utterance. There is even a danger that the whole meaning of the text will be swamped by the music.

It is more than a danger – it is a virtual certainty. What Piscator feared as a threat to the text, to precision of language as the evidence of clarity of thought, was what Nietzsche infallibly sensed in Richard Wagner – a music that undermines the critical faculty and invites a self-abandonment to the delights assembled under the banner inscribed 'Romanticism'. Music will always tend to dominate a joint artistic enterprise of which it is part, and the greater the music – which is to say, the closer to the core of its inner spirituality – the more complete the dominance. Piscator was better off with a subservient musician like Edmund Meisel than he would have been with a Kurt Weill.

However confident Weill sounded that Brecht's emerging libretto of the *Mahagonny* opera would fully meet his musical demands, Hertzka at Universal Edition had considerable reservations about the material Weill sent him. It seemed too undramatic, he objected, too non-operatic, and he compared it to Delius' *A Village Romeo and Juliet*, which he had just seen – idyllic, full of beautiful music, but totally undramatic. Weill was not amused. 'The great disadvantage of Delius' opera,' he replied tartly, 'is – forgive my bluntness – that it is boring. I can assure you here and now that *Mahagonny* will not contain a single boring moment.' Hertzka accepted the assurance, and had no cause to regret it.

Although *Mahagonny* claimed the lion's share of his creative energies, Weill still had time for other things, both of his own choice and by way of commission. In the Third Lesson of Brecht's *Hauspostille* he found 'Vom Tod im Wald' ('Death in the Forest'), a sombre ballad of eight stanzas, in the rough, cruel, ice-cold language in which Brecht could be so gripping. Weill sets the poem as a recitative-like dirge for bass solo and ten wind instruments. It is a brooding, starkly atmospheric piece in a sinister, non-tonal idiom which it seemed he had left behind and to which he never again returned.

According to Count Harry Kessler, German diplomat and cultural man-about-town, plans were afoot for a Diaghilev ballet for which he would write the scenario and Weill the music. Weill apparently envisaged his music as mainly vocal – to this extent an anticipation of *The Seven Deadly Sins* – but we know nothing about the subject matter or whether Weill ever composed a note. In any case Diaghilev had no time for Weill's music and told Kessler that what he needed was a 'proper composer'.

Weill's ability to make a musical point in the space of a few bars, coupled with his skill in scoring for small and often unusual combinations of instruments, brought him a number of invitations in the 1927–28 season to write incidental music for prominent stage productions in Berlin and elsewhere. Among these were the Brecht-Feuchtwanger version of Marlowe's *Edward the Second*, Arnolt Bronnen's frenzied drama *Katalaunische Schlacht* ('Battle of the Catalaunian Plains'), produced in the Berlin Schauspielhaus in April 1928, and Leo Lania's anti-capitalist *Konjunktur* ('Oil Boom'). Later in the year he again became involved with the oil industry, convenient whipping-boy for the evils of multinational capitalism since Upton Sinclair's novel *Oil*, when he wrote three songs for Feuchtwanger's play *Petroleuminseln* ('Petroleum Islands'). Some of these musical items have survived, others have been lost.

Breaking into the new plans and challenges crowding in on Weill's mind at this moment came the première in February 1928 of *Der Zar lässt sich photographieren* in Leipzig. So much had happened in his life in the six months since he completed the work that its public launch had something of a retrospective quality about it. Not that it looked that way to Weill, who had travelled down to Leipzig several times in recent months, visiting his parents *en passant* but mainly in order to attend the vital early rehearsals. He had been trying to secure acceptances of the work from as many other opera houses as possible, and urging Universal to do the same. Plans for a performance in Russia met with doctrinal problems, an adviser at the Moscow State Opera replying gravely that 'the ideology of the work makes it impossible to perform it in the Soviet Union', above all because the hero 'adopts no firm political stance'.

Ideally, Weill wanted the *Zar* to be paired with its tragic predecessor *Der Protagonist*. Its companion piece at the first performance, however, was Nicola Spinelli's *A basso porto*, a one-acter from the *verismo* world of Mascagni's *Cavalleria rusticana*. Conducted by Gustav Brecher, the *Zar* was enthusiastically applauded. The swiftness of the comic action, the raciness of Georg Kaiser's libretto and the wit of Weill's music combined to sweep the audience off its feet. The 'Tango Angèle', played through a gramophone on the stage as a theatrical gesture of incongruous, montage-like alienation, caught the imagination immediately. Universal rushed out a piano version, showing that they could act quickly enough when the sweet scent of financial profit was in the air, and the Parlophon-Beka company, which had made the record used in the performance, issued it commercially within a few weeks – Weill's first popular hit.

Not that some of the smaller theatres, or even Weill himself, took success for granted. For a combined performance of *Der Protagonist* and *Zar* in March at Altenburg, where Maurice Abravanel conducted, the management took the precaution of driving him to the theatre by car because they were afraid – perhaps remembering what had happened at the end of the *Mahagonny Songspiel* – that there might be a riot. 'All the more surprising,' Weill wrote afterwards to Universal, 'was the applause that came from the entire house for both works – thirteen curtains for *Protagonist* and fifteen for *Zar*.'

There were also disappointments. Hans Curjel, at the Kroll Opera, had assured him that Klemperer would 'almost certainly' take on the *Zar* later in the year, while Weill himself had heard that Bruno Walter had started rehearsing it. Such names would have done much for his cause. In the end neither of them tackled the work. But by the following year it had been given in over twenty German opera houses, and it retained its popularity – second only to that of the *Dreigroschenoper* – down to the time when the Nazis banned all performances of Weill's 'decadent' music.

In March 1928 Heinsheimer had cause to write to Weill about the gratifying reception of the *Zar* and about some of the many other matters which sustained the voluble correspondence between the composer in Berlin and his publishers in Vienna. In a postscript, his tone suspicious, almost threatening, lest something be going on behind Universal's back, Heinsheimer added:

> We gather from an item in the newspaper that you are engaged with Bert Brecht on an adaptation of *The Beggar's Opera*. We should be very interested to learn more about this.

Very interested indeed, we may assume, not least for financial reasons. It was not long before the whole world learned more about this 'adaptation', destined to become one of the greatest successes in the history of musical theatre.

CHAPTER IX

The *Dreigroschenoper*

Far from being the end-product of a singleminded strategy rigorously planned and unwaveringly executed, the *Dreigroschenoper*, most famous of all Brecht-Weill collaborations, had its origins in chance, evolved at bewildering speed under unpredictable external pressures, and received its triumphant première in conditions of near chaos.

The story starts, as so many of Brecht's undertakings, with Elisabeth Hauptmann. Since coming to know Brecht in 1924, this intelligent, devoted woman had taken it upon herself to collect quietly material which he might one day put to use, particularly material from English literature. One work of which she had recently become aware was John Gay's *The Beggar's Opera* of 1728, which she now set out to translate, slipping it scene by scene into the plans and sketches with which Brecht's table was littered – 'so that he would do something with it', she said.

The Beggar's Opera had been something of a talking-point in European cultural circles since Nigel Playfair's revival at the Lyric Theatre, Hammersmith in 1920. Originally seen as a mere stop-gap in the theatre's programme, it ended up running for years, and Frederic Austin's new arrangements of the old airs and ballads had their place alongside the foxtrots and tangos of the modern dance-band world. 'The beggars have come back to town,' said *The Times*, 'and taken up their abode at the Lyric Theatre, Hammersmith, where, to judge from the enthusiasm of their welcome on Saturday night, they should be able to disport themselves for as long as they will.'

Brecht, always a connoisseur of life among thieves, pimps and prostitutes, found Elisabeth Hauptmann's succession of racy scenes highly entertaining. The conversion of the *Mahagonny* material into opera had left the 'Songspiel' standing isolated in its environment, whereas the success of the 'Songspiel' form, and the possibilities it opened up, encouraged both Brecht and Weill to exploit it further. Here, in this most famous of English ballad-operas, they found both their formal historical antecedent and a stimulus to the extension of their artistic frontiers.

The potentialities of *The Beggar's Opera* for the German market had already been seen by the publishers Schott, who had proposed to Hindemith in 1925 that he do a modern version of the music, leaving Gay's text and characters in their eighteenth-century home. But Hindemith found no attraction in the idea.

For Brecht and Weill too the musical point of departure had initially been the airs which John Christopher Pepusch arranged for *The Beggar's Opera* according to Gay's instructions. But there was no question of a straightforward translation of the text from English into German, and the song-texts that Brecht envisioned had a character quite at odds with the idiom of the eighteenth-century tunes. These tunes had something pleasantly nostalgic about them, something cosy and reassuring. For Brecht's alienated, 'epic' world these were the last qualities to be cultivated. What was needed was 'gestic' music, a music designed for the exigencies of the contemporary age, using a language proper to that age. There would have to be new verses set to new music.

With this much evident, there now appeared on the scene a man who was to catalyse the whole undertaking. His name was Ernst Josef Aufricht.

Of the same generation as Brecht, Weill and Neher, Aufricht was the son of a well-to-do Jewish wood merchant from Silesia. After the First World War he embarked on a not overly successful career as an actor in Berlin with the left-wing group 'Die Truppe' under the avant-garde director Berthold Viertel. At the beginning of 1928 Aufricht inherited a large sum of money from his father with which he was determined to make his mark on Berlin theatrical life. His first move was to lease the Theater am Schiffbauerdamm, an ornate little nineteenth-century establishment tucked away on the banks of the Spree behind Max Reinhardt's voluminous Grosses Schauspielhaus. Aufricht had engaged Erich Engel, a young director who already had a handful of Brecht premières to his name, to handle the first production. The problem now was to find a suitable play – not some established classic or a novelty which would enjoy a *succès d'estime* but a blockbuster that would cover Aufricht with the theatrical glory denied him as an actor.

Approaches to radical dramatists like Ernst Toller and Lion Feucht-wanger led nowhere, partly because they had nothing sufficiently advanced on the stocks, but partly also because of a suspicion of this young *parvenu*'s ability to actually get a show off the ground. Engel then suggested that Brecht, whose mind was overflowing with plans for this work and that, might be their man. So one day they went to Schlichter's and found Brecht there. Engel introduced Aufricht, and Brecht revealed that he was doing a version of *The Beggar's Opera* to be called *Gesindel* ('Rabble'), and that the first six scenes were already written. Aufricht suddenly sat up, and the following day he sent his assistant Heinrich Fischer round to the Spichernstrasse to collect what Brecht had written.

Immediately he had finished reading it, he decided that here was something with a future. However, when told by Brecht that the music was to be written by Weill, he hesitated, fearing that Weill, on the evidence of *Der Protagonist* and *Zar*, was too heavy and highbrow a composer for what he saw as 'a lighthearted literary operetta shot through with occasional flashes of social criticism'. So to be on the safe side, he asked his friend Theo Mackeben, a dance-band leader and arranger, to look at the old Pepusch tunes with a view to jazzing them up for the new occasion. If Weill's music turned out to be unacceptable, Mackeben, with the jazz musician's skill in improvisation, would be able to cobble something together out of the old songs at short notice. None of this, of course, could be allowed to reach the ears of Brecht or Weill.

Aufricht had set his opening night for August 31, some four months away. Brecht, who hated deadlines, saw no chance of having the work ready in time as long as he remained exposed to the constant distractions of life in Berlin, so he proposed to Weill that they take refuge on the French Riviera for a few weeks and work together there undisturbed. He rented a house on the esplanade at Le Lavandou, between Toulon and St Tropez, and drove down there – he was addicted to fast sports cars – with Helene Weigel and their four-year-old son Stefan.

Weill had already planned a vacation on the Riviera, and asked Universal for an advance on his allowance to pay for the trip. With the help of this he and Lenya took the train via Paris to Marseilles in June and joined the Brechts on the coast. The Weills took a room in a hotel-pension in St. Cyr-sur-Mer, and gradually the two men moulded their *Beggar's Opera* into shape, breaking off from time to time for a dip in the sea. That is, Weill did: he enjoyed swimming and was never happier than when at the seaside.

As with the *Mahagonny* opera, Weill was not just the musical agent in a production line, receiving literary material from one side, setting it to music, then passing it on to the next stage in the manufacturing process. From the beginning, he was a co-creator. Weeks of work with Brecht on text and dramatic form were needed before the foundation was firm enough to receive the music – thereafter the speed and variety of Weill's inventiveness could be relied upon to take over on its own. Not for nothing does the published text of the work in Brecht's *Versuche* acknowledge its tripartite authorship at the end of the final scene: 'Brecht. Hauptmann. Weill.'

By early July they had broken the back of the work. Brecht finished off the final scenes in the tranquillity of his cottage by the Ammersee, leaving Weill to return to Berlin to sort out the purely musical problems. Absence from the metropolis may be relaxing and welcome for a while, but life there does not stop because one looks the other way, and a regular columnist cannot afford to get out of touch. For four weeks Weill had written nothing for *Der deutsche Rundfunk*, and the massive shadow of the *Mahagonny* opera hung over him. Back in March he had confidently told his publishers that he would have the composition sketch of *Mahagonny* ready by May and the full score by the end of the summer – but maybe this was only the kind of unrealistic assurance with which many an author has sought to retain his publisher's goodwill. Even his offer to play them some of the hit-tunes from the work next time he came to Vienna was something of a smoke screen, for the 'Alabama Song', the 'Benares Song' and the other numbers needed only to be taken over, more or less ready-made, from the *Songspiel*. In the event it took him another year to finish the *Mahagonny* opera. At least Universal's confidence in him stretched to a rise in his monthly retainer from four hundred to six hundred marks a month from the end of June, though not before he had firmly pointed out that the recent success of his *Zar* and the expectations for *Mahagonny* and the *Dreigroschenoper* more than covered such an increase.

The new work was something of a diversion from the demands of *Mahagonny*, and whether because of this or in spite of it, Weill plunged wholeheartedly into the composition. 'I am greatly enjoying it,' he told Universal. 'It will be written in an easily singable style, since it will be actors who perform it.' Just what 'it' was, he did not say. Altogether he held his cards close to his chest. 'When I visited Weill in his apartment close to the Charlottenburg Palace in 1927,' wrote his friend, the critic Hans Heinz Stuckenschmidt, 'I noticed lying on the grand piano some pages of manuscript paper, freshly written. "I'm doing something that might well be a success," he said, with a smile, his doleful eyes twinkling behind his thick glasses. A year later all of us, the entire intelligentsia of Berlin, were sitting in the Theater am Schiffbauerdamm, listening to the *Dreigroschenoper*.'

With the final scenes and songs more or less complete, he went along to the theatre with Lenya to introduce his music to the apprehensive Aufricht. He was only a moderate pianist. When he played some of the songs from *Happy End* to Theo Mackeben and Aufricht the following year, Mackeben jumped up, snatched Weill's manuscript from the piano and exclaimed: 'Give it to me! This music is far too good for you to play!'

But on this occasion Mackeben, Heinrich Fischer and another young production assistant called Robert Vambery – a man of the theatre whose path crossed Weill's on a number of future occasions – took their places with Aufricht in the auditorium. A piano was wheeled out of the storeroom and Weill sat down in front of it. 'The gentle little man with the glasses,' recalled Aufricht,

> began to play and sing in a soft, metallic voice which expressed just what he wanted. At first, I think, we were all taken aback. Then Vambery crept over to me and whispered in my ear: 'The music could be as big a success as the play!' The longer Weill played, the quicker my prejudices melted away. For all its strangeness, this music had a naive quality that moved me, while being at the same time sophisticated and exciting.

The battle was won – if there ever was a battle. Mackeben realised that his services as a composer were not going to be required. Instead, catching the scent of something special, he eagerly set about investigating Weill's plans for the instrumentation of what he had played. Aufricht and Engel had already put together a provisional cast, and Caspar Neher, who in his own field was as quick as Weill to see what a theatrical situation required, had sketched the sets and costumes. A month later, after an unbelievable sequence of mishaps and miscalculations, the product of these labours finally hit the Berlin theatrical scene as *Die Dreigroschenoper*.

As a satire derived from another satire, the work laboured from the outset under the threat of ambiguity and uncertain reference as far as subject matter was concerned. John Gay's *Beggar's Opera* was an exercise in mockery and satire on two counts. Formally it burlesqued the Italian opera of the day, stimulated in particular by Handel – an imported aristocratic entertainment with affected plots, flowery libretti, heroic male roles sung by castrati and a host of other unnatural devices. In its place, representing a total inversion of the outlandish scheme of things that was the object of its derision, came the democratic home-grown product of the ballad-play. Here men acted as men, women as women, popular airs and ballads in the vernacular, familiar for all to whistle and sing, supplanted florid arias in a foreign tongue, restoring nature and healthy normality.

But beyond the aesthetic dimension lies the social and political satire of *The Beggar's Opera*, a satire that arose from, and can only be understood in the context of, conditions in early eighteenth-century England. The audience knew exactly what it was watching in the scenes from London's underworld – the poverty, the abuses of power, the network of crime, and above all the omnipotence of money, which divides society into the haves and the have-nots. But although the highwaymen exchange Robin-Hood-like sentiments about the corruption that issues from an unfair distribution of the world's riches, Gay launches no head-on attack against society and urges no programme of reform. There is satire and ridicule but no indignation, righteous or other.

Brecht's *Dreigroschenoper* is anything but a translation of Gay's text. Brecht does, however, retain the basic story as he found it, bringing it forward in time to the age of late Victorian capitalism and locating it in Soho, headquarters of the London underworld. The gangster boss 'Captain' Macheath, here Mackie Messer – 'Mack the Knife' – secretly marries Polly, daughter of Jonathan Jeremiah Peachum, in Gay a fence of stolen property, in Brecht the organising genius behind the Mafia of professional beggars who ply the London streets. Peachum, feeling betrayed by his daughter, vows to deliver Macheath into the hands of Scotland Yard; warned by Polly, Mackie flees but is caught in a brothel by the police chief Tiger Brown after a tip-off by Jenny and her fellow-prostitutes. Tiger Brown's daughter Lucy, an old flame of Mackie's, helps him to escape but he is again betrayed by the whores and condemned to be hanged. Before being taken to the gallows, in a masterly moment of dramatic irony, he meets for the first time the Beggar King Peachum, the man who is both his persecutor and father-in-law.

Then, as the noose closes round Mackie's neck, Peachum turns to the audience and announces that, since this is opera, where mercy must prevail over justice, there will be an obligatory happy ending: to mark her coronation the Queen has decided to pardon Mackie, elevate him to the peerage and settle on him an annual allowance of ten thousand pounds.

Yet the last word does not rest with this piece of parody nor with the mood of general jubilation into which it dissolves. It rests with Peachum, who reminds the company that such happy endings cannot be relied upon, that the poor in capitalist society do indeed have an unhappy lot, and that men like Mackie Messer will not escape justice so easily when the proletariat casts off its chains and the new Communist social order comes, as come it will. First reform the physical environment of society, and the moral reformation of man will follow: '*Erst kommt das Fressen, dann kommt die Moral*,' as Mackie had elegantly put it – 'Grub first, morals later.'

Brecht instructed that the part of Mackie Messer be played in such a way as to make clear that he is the representative of the declining bourgeoisie. But audiences did not readily perceive this – indeed, saw no need to, especially as the swashbuckling, charismatic Mackie made such a splendidly libidinous hero. Whatever the political meaning Brecht wanted to convey, *Dreigroschenoper* remains a play by a bourgeois dramatist for a bourgeois public.

History has an ironical postscript to add to the story. In the wake of the lampoons in plays like *The Beggar's Opera*, its equally popular sequel *Polly*, and other works that fell victim to the Licensing Act of 1737, the corruptions of government were exposed and Sir Robert Walpole, the prime minister, was forced from office. Two hundred years later the *Dreigroschenoper* changed nothing – political, social, literary, operatic. The bourgeoisie said to be on its way out still provides the theatre with its public, while the theatre of the proletariat, by the proletariat, for the proletariat remains a fringe pastime. Maybe Gay had been more successful in 'changing the system' than Brecht.

And 'changing the system' was what fired Weill also – not the political or social system but the consumer music industry, in particular the consumption of opera. As in any market situation, the equation embraces two factors – the consumer, i.e. the public, and the product, i.e. the work of art. Weill was acutely sensitive to the relationship between the two. As, when writing in *Der deutsche Rundfunk* and elsewhere about the artistic needs of the contemporary public, he had firm proposals to make about how those needs can be met, so, as an artist, he composes not for art's sake, or even *ad maiorem Dei gloriam*, but for a modern, identifiable audience which he has decided to address directly and uncompromisingly. It was because this equation of demands, the receptorial and the artistic, came so close at this moment to the interests of Brecht that such a unique creation as the *Dreigroschenoper* came into existence.

On the role of his music Weill offered the following explanation in 'On Composing the *Dreigroschenoper*':

> It became possible, with *Dreigroschenoper*, to embark on the work of reconstruction [of the opera] because here we had an opportunity to start from scratch. What we set out to do was to create the basic form [*Urform*] of opera. With each new work written for the musical theatre the question arises, how is music possible in the theatre – above all, how is singing possible? In the *Dreigroschenoper* this problem has been solved in the most primitive manner. I had a realistic plot, and had to set my music alongside it, since I do not believe that music can ever have a realistic effect. Thus either the action was interrupted to make room for the music, or it was deliberately directed towards a point at which singing had to take over. . . .
> This return to a primitive form of opera was accompanied by radical simplification of the musical language. I needed to write music that could be sung by actors, that is, by musical amateurs. But what at first seemed a limitation turned out in the course of my work to be a source of immense enrichment. Only the creation of an accessible and readily intelligible musical idiom made possible what has been accomplished in the *Dreigroschenoper*, namely, a new type of musical theatre.

Taken together, the use of singing actors rather than acting singers and the achievement of 'an accessible and readily intelligible musical idiom' show the working of his 'gestic' music in practice. His music is direct, objective, detached – detached both from the situations it presents and from the text that carries the dramatic action. Separate autonomies are at work: when dialogue holds the stage, the music is silent; when the dialogue has run its course, a song takes over. The song – to this extent a relation of the aria in classical opera – is not a vehicle of the action: on the contrary, the action stops so that the song can make its own psychological or symbolical point.

At the time, the *Dreigroschenoper* stood for the deliberate antithesis, not only of the musical idiom of late Romanticism in general but also, pointedly, of the sentimental world of contemporary operetta. A month after it opened came the Berlin première of Lehár's *Friederike*, starring Käthe Dorsch and Richard Tauber. These were the names that filled theatres, and this was where the competition came from. Weill even allowed himself to wonder whether his new form might take the place of the operetta. But this is local history – the constellation of specific circumstances, in time and place, to which *Dreigroschenoper* belongs. On the broader generic view it belongs in the tradition of musical theatre with vernacular spoken dialogue, a tradition traceable back to the eighteenth-century ballad opera, thence forward to the German *Singspiel*, to operetta in Paris (Offenbach) and Vienna (Johann Strauss, Lehár), to Gilbert and Sullivan and to the twentieth-century musical.

Nor does Brecht's text, *qua* drama, break new formal ground. It has wit, its dialogue effervesces, and there are moments of real poetry in the songs, though the poetry may sometimes be Villon's or Kipling's rather than Brecht's. But while it is not a libretto, neither is it a play to be performed without its songs (*vice versa* the music, deplorably, is often performed and recorded in sequence without the spoken dialogue). Formally, much depends on the way the dialogue is driven to a point of pause, a moment of reflection, at which the meaning of the work passes to song. Brecht even prescribes a specific shade of lighting – a golden 'Songbeleuchtung' – in which the songs are to be sung.

Which leaves us contemplating the realm in which the true originality of the *Dreigroschenoper* resides – the realm of its music. And as the first mock-pompous bars of the anti-Handelian overture, punched out by the incongruous forces of an eight-man dance band, are drilled into our ears, we are jerked into a startled suspicion that here is a music which will speak with a forked tongue, and that before us lies an evening's entertainment rich in irony and ambiguity – also no less rich in unfeigned joy and musical high jinks.

No sooner has the overture bumped to an ungainly halt than a ballad-singer appears on the stage. Draping himself over his hurdy-gurdy, he grinds out, verse for unrelenting verse, his *Moritat* of Mackie Messer, Brecht's Macheath, with its sinister, uncanny little tune which can hardly get started, which, once started, could go on till Doomsday, and which has become the most famous of Weill's melodies:

And all this before the action has even started.

It is an extraordinary pastiche that Weill has produced in his twenty-one numbers, songs, duets, choruses. On the one hand there are the jazz tempi of blues, tango and foxtrot, on the other the mock gravity of the Protestant chorales at the beginning and end of the stage action – the former, 'Peachum's Morning Chorale', being the one token tune retained from Pepusch and the old *Beggar's Opera*. In between comes the waltz, symbol of grace and an ordered society, to accompany Mackie's and Polly's fatalistic, almost cynical love-song as they prepare to share their marriage bed in the stable. Incongruity and satire lie here in the music itself, a music sometimes pretending to convey a genuine joy and an honest lyricism but in reality concealing a sense of emptiness and arid cynicism. It is not a question of illustration of a dramatic sequence on the stage but of the objective embodiment of that sequence in musical terms. This is the Weill-Brecht 'gestic' music, expressed initially, as Weill defined it, in 'the rhythmic disposition of the text', then driven home by the insistent rhythms and spiky harmonies of the accompaniment and given its final penetrative edge in the brash, intrusive jazz-band instrumentation, the sharpest weapon in Weill's satirical armoury.

And maybe it is in terms of satire that Weill's musical style and manner are most appropriately perceived. It is not merely that this music satirises *something* – something by definition outside itself – which it often does: it is that the satire is an integral element of the musical language itself, inseparable from the musical utterance as a whole, as vital to its meaning and existence as, say, the expressions on the faces of George Grosz's caricatures of the contemporary bourgeoisie or the sometimes brutal tone of Brecht's poetry.

The poetry and the music, harmoniously blended in the conventional song, may also be played off against each other to satirical effect, setting up an incongruity or a contradiction. How often Weill writes a sentimental tune to bitter words, or casts doubt on the emotional genuineness of an utterance through a harsh, impersonal music! At the opening of *Dreigroschenoper* the ballad-singer shuffles on to the stage to warn the audience what sort of gangster-hero they are about to meet. Strophe by strophe his criminal career is laid out before us. And Weill's response? A trite little barrel-organ ditty which wanders listlessly round the notes of the sugary added-sixth chord and could meander harmlessly, droningly on for as long as there were crimes to report.

Satire demands the retention in the mind, on equal terms, of a positive and a negative, thesis and antithesis. The positive is the tonal, triadic musical language at the root of the *Dreigroschenoper*, the familiar terrain to which, via *Royal Palace* and the *Mahagonny Songspiel*, Weill has returned from the severities of dissonance and free tonality. The negative is the sudden, unprepared injection into this familiar idiom of contradictions and discrepancies which unsettle our sense of equilibrium and induce a feeling of malaise, or at least of irritation. Then, through the acceptance of these carriers of incongruity into the creative process, a resolution, a synthesis emerges with its own meaning and its own logic, claiming our attention in its own new right.

The main active ingredient in this synthesis is chromaticism, now selectively applied but only a few years earlier the dominant melodic and harmonic feature of Weill's works. The familiar 'semitonal slip' is still there, so is the old contrapuntal Weill, who reappears in the fugato section of the Overture. Equally effective for his purposes is the strategically-placed 'wrong' note in chords or harmonic progressions, calculated to unsettle and ultimately alienate the innocent ear. Similarly ambiguous are added-note chords, in which the discrepantly added note sets up fresh tensions within the chord to which it belongs – or more properly, does not belong. The added-sixth chord on the major triad – c-e-g-a in C major – is a treacly commonplace in the world of jazz and dance-band music, and in the music of 'serious' composers, including Weill, who raided that world. The minor added-sixth chord, on the other hand (c-e^b-g-a), sets up a tension between the minor third and the major sixth, a tension which creates an insecurity and uncertainty that look for resolution. The obvious resolution is to slide from the minor third to the major third, that is, to the 'jazzy' added-sixth chord. This slide, the alternation between minor and major, between tension and release, is a basic term in Weill's harmonic vocabulary – a musical visiting card which serves as proof of identity.

The tension and ambiguity communicated by this harmonic complex become all the greater if, in a technique developed by Weill to a calculated perfection, the melody that such chords accompany is an artless little diatonic tune from a seemingly alien world. So destabilising can added-note chords be that they can make a melody of simplicity and innocence seem unnatural and out of place.

'Wrong' in a different sense, and no less productive of a mingled surprise and pleasure, are the unexpected lurches of the bass to a point of harmonic implication which is at odds with the harmony implied by the melody and could not possibly be deduced from it. Take the refrain of the 'Barbara Song'. It opens with what is to all intents and purposes the gypsy folk tune 'Dark Eyes':

Hand this to a music student to harmonise, and one would hardly expect what Weill gives us:

The deliberate distortions in Weill's music, his calculated abuse of stylistic purity and unity, his yoking together of realms and elements that do not want to be yoked together – this provokes the intellectual *frisson* which so delights his audience, seducing them with a delicious sense of impropriety and relativising their conventional values. It is the counterpart of the Brecht syndrome: audiences relishing the spectacle of their own impotence and historical irrelevance, instead of taking steps to change things, as the author intended.

*

While Brecht and Weill, first in the south of France, then back in Berlin, were putting their piece together, Aufricht and his director Erich Engel had been assembling a cast, and rehearsals started in early August. The enterprise seemed to be jinxed from the start. For the two principal characters, Mackie Messer and Polly, Aufricht had engaged the musical comedy star Harald Paulsen and Carola Neher (no relation of Caspar), an attractive, emancipated young actress known to Brecht from his director's couch in Munich. Aufricht was not competing with the state theatres, either in originality or in quality: he was looking for a hit, and a hit needed stars – from theatre, from musical comedy, from cabaret. But stars, in their turn, looked for material that would illuminate their stardom, and from what Aufricht could tell them of this rather frightening avant-garde combination of Bert Brecht and Kurt Weill, some doubted whether the *Dreigroschenoper* would do their reputation any good.

Hardly had rehearsals begun than the first blow fell. Carola Neher had married, only three years earlier, the dramatist and cabaret performer Alfred Henschke, who went under the pseudonym of Klabund. Terminally ill with tuberculosis, Klabund was lying in a Swiss sanatorium with only a few days to live, and his wife decided she had to be at his side. Klabund died soon after but when she returned to Berlin, Carola found that the script had been so mutilated during her absence that she was no longer prepared to have anything to do with the play. Barely a week before the first performance, Aufricht found the music-hall artiste Roma Bahn, wife of Karlheinz Martin, to take over the role.

There were other troubles. The original Mr Peachum – Lenya thought it was to have been Peter Lorre, one of Brecht's regular actors – fell ill and had to be replaced. Helene Weigel was due to play Mrs Coaxer, the brothelkeeper, and proposed to do so as a legless figure à la Lon Chaney, confined to a wheel chair, but mercifully she succumbed to an attack of appendicitis and the role was cut. The brassy cabaret singer Rosa Valetti, well cast as the coarse Mrs Peachum, suddenly refused to sing the 'obscenities', as she called them, in the 'Ballad of Sexual Slavery' and refused to have anything more to do with 'this filthy play'.

Then it was the turn of the hero. Harald Paulsen, 'extraordinarily conceited, even for an actor', as Lenya described him, decided that he needed a bigger build-up for his entry, and demanded that Brecht write an extra song for the purpose. So Brecht strung together the strophes of his *Moritat* and gave his poem to Weill, who turned up at the theatre next morning with the little hurdy-gurdy tune that has since travelled the world.

Not that Brecht was concerned just to do Paulsen a favour. Having virtually created a new character and written a new one-man scene, he cast the ballad-singer in the role of Chorus and had him perform the

Moritat from the front of the stage at the very beginning of the play. Not only that. The song was given to Kurt Gerron to sing – the burly baritone who already had the part of the crooked police chief Tiger Brown. So the corrupt spokesman for law and order in the community turns out to be the one who had built up the hero's reputation by reciting his criminal achievements.

As item after item of disastrous news filtered out of the Schiff-bauerdamm Theatre, with few people aware – even in the production itself, one suspects – just how their strange new hybrid creature was going to turn out, the prophets of doom in the Berlin theatrical world were already writing it off. Sometimes it looked unlikely to open at all. Brecht and Erich Engel argued over points of staging, Aufricht tried to pacify recalcitrant performers and the text had to be amended time and again to satisfy their whims. Even the equable Caspar Neher threatened to walk out if Aufricht and Engel persisted in scrapping the final chorale because, they complained, Weill's setting made it sound like Bach, and what had Bach to do with the *Dreigroschenoper*? The only oasis of relative calm was the musicians' corner, where Weill discussed practical matters with the conductor Theo Mackeben. This enviable ability to shut out the surrounding sights and sounds reflected a power of concentration which never deserted him. Still in his American years he could be found sitting in a corner of the theatre during rehearsals, scoring part of this or that scene, undisturbed by the action taking place on the stage.

Friends, supporters, men and women of the theatre, interested out-siders – a constant succession of visitors dropped in on the proceedings. Fritz Kortner, one of the leading actors of the day, came to satisfy his curiosity, so did the great Viennese satirist Karl Kraus, who happened to be in Berlin at this time. Kraus was much taken by Brecht and his play, and according to Aufricht, provided the second strophe of the 'Jealousy Duet' sung by Polly and Jenny in Act Two, 'because the audience, in his opinion, would not be satisfied with only one'. The novelist and dramatist Lion Feuchtwanger, a close friend and ideological colleague of Brecht's, paid close attention to the rehearsals and was responsible for proposing, at the eleventh hour, the title of *Dreigroschenoper* for what up to then had only had a series of working names.

August 30: dress rehearsal in the evening – a farce that lasted until five o'clock the next morning. Hans Heinsheimer had travelled up from Vienna during the day to represent Universal Edition at the première and went straight from the railway station to the theatre:

> I found the stage filled with shouting people wildly gesticulating, yelling at each other, and only making common cause in bodily threatening the director, who outshouted everybody else. A huge piece of scenery

suddenly descended, almost crushing half-a-dozen people to death, and put a sudden end to that outburst of violence and obviously saved the director's life . . . Pandemonium was not limited to the stage. I saw excited groups debating in the orchestra and in the boxes. Smoke filled the air; crumpled papers, empty bottles and broken coffee cups littered the floor. . .

I went to look for Kurt Weill and found him quietly sitting in the orchestra, his mocking smile on his lips, as unconcerned as if he were just a disinterested outsider calmly enjoying the débâcle of a crowd of complete strangers.

By five o'clock in the morning a collective stalemate of mingled rage, despair and exhaustion had settled over the proceedings. A strong body of opinion pressed Brecht, Weill and Aufricht to call the whole thing off before they made themselves the laughing-stock of Berlin. The rest did not care one way or the other, convinced that the first night, if there were one, would also be the last.

But there was now too much at stake, and the punch-drunk cast were told to report for a further dress rehearsal at noon. This was somewhat less chaotic, but by six o'clock, when it was forced to break up, with playwright and composer still thoroughly dissatisfied, the cleaners were already at work sweeping the auditorium for the performance at eight. Then suddenly Weill discovered that Lenya's name was missing from the playbill. 'It's a bloody shambles!' he shouted furiously and was on the point of forbidding her to appear. 'It was the first and last time in his entire career in the theatre,' Lenya said, 'that Kurt completely lost his self-control.'

As Brecht stormed out after the final rehearsal, he raved: 'This is the last time you'll see me in this theatre!' 'The same goes for us!' Weill and Neher chimed in. To which Heinrich Fischer, Aufricht's assistant, sardonically retorted: 'Would you gentlemen be kind enough to put that in writing?' In the end, wrote Aufricht, 'since they were real men of the theatre, they all turned up for the opening night punctually at half-past seven.'

That night, August 31, 1928, has its place in theatrical history. No one knew what to expect. Much was still in a state of flux, even as to who should sing what, and when. Everything was done from manuscript, the words as well as the music. Neither Brecht nor Weill regarded the verbal or musical text of the première as a fixed and final statement. A month elapsed before Weill sent Universal Edition the score for publication, and it was not until October that Brecht's 'official' text was available and that Universal were in a position to publish a piano score that put most of the uncertainties to rest – though by no means all. Even over the 'Barbara Song', a number that has since become so famous, eye-witnesses disagree over whether it was sung by Polly (Roma Bahn) in Act One, or by Lucy (Kate Kühl) in the prison scene of Act Two.

The overture, played by the Lewis Ruth Band grouped around a large fair-ground organ at the back of the stage, had the audience bewildered. So did the following *Moritat*, especially as the hurdy-gurdy failed to work for the first two strophes. The whole of the first scene fell flat; the obscenities of the wedding scene may have helped to raise the temperature a little but the reception given to Polly's 'Seeräuber Jenny' remained cool.

The lighting changed to announce another song, and a Neher projection announcing the 'Cannon Song' was flashed on to one of the screens at the side of the band. Everything exploded. As Macheath and Tiger Brown thundered out the march rhythm of their anti-imperialist, anti-army tirade, the audience began to clap their hands and stamp their feet. When the song finished, they jumped to their feet and shouted for an encore. 'From that moment on,' wrote the relieved Aufricht later, 'every line and every note was a success.'

Not merely *a* success but the most spectacular in the history of the German theatre in the 1920s, and one that neither Brecht nor Weill, as a team or individually, ever equalled. In Berlin it ran for a year, and within a week of its opening had been booked for more than fifty theatres all over Germany; by the end of the following year it had also been played in Italy, Switzerland, Hungary, Poland and Russia, and the Théatre Montparnasse in Paris had performed an *Opéra de quat' sous*. Universal Edition rushed out separate voice-and-piano versions of the most popular songs at 1 mark, 50 pfennigs a time, together with arrangements for salon orchestra and jazz band. At the end of the year Weill himself put together, at the suggestion of Otto Klemperer, a potpourri of eight numbers arranged for full-size wind band which he called the *Kleine Dreigroschenmusik*, and which Klemperer conducted to great applause in Germany and abroad.

Gramophone companies – HMV, Telefunken, Columbia and others – fell over each other in their eagerness to sign up the stars of the show for recordings of the songs and the ensembles. In these the singers were by no means confined to the numbers they had performed on the opening night but laid claim to whatever items took their fancy. Brecht himself made a recording, in his inimitable Augsburg dialect, of the 'Mackie Messer Song', and Lenya founded her own legend on recordings of the 'Barbara Song' and 'Pirate Jenny'. Sections of a live performance in the Schiffbauer-damm Theatre were filmed by Karl Koch a few weeks after the première, and in 1930 an original film version of the whole work was made, with Rudolf Forster, Carola Neher, Lotte Lenya and Ernst Busch in the cast. People hummed and whistled the tunes as they walked down the street, and a '3-Groschen-Bar' opened in Berlin, playing only '3-Groschen' music. One could even buy rolls of '3-Groschen' wallpaper, depicting characters and scenes from the work in pale shades of pink, yellow and green.

As a composer writing not for a sophisticated coterie but for as broad an audience as he could reach, Weill saw in all the popularisations and imitations of his song-style a measure of the quality of his achievement no less than of its momentum. 'The fact that my *Dreigroschenoper* music has been industrialised,' he observed, 'speaks for it rather than against it, and we should be lapsing into the errors of our old ways if we were to deny the importance and quality of a piece of music simply because it had become popular among the masses.' True, the *Dreigroschenoper* could not be copied, even by Weill himself, and the *Mahagonny* opera shows how quickly he moved on; indeed, his whole career has the character of a constant succession of 'movings-on'. But this does not detract from the impact of the *Dreigroschenoper* phenomenon in its own right.

The '3-Groschen' mania tells a story in itself. It becomes the more remarkable when seen against the background of the contemporary theatrical scene. For 1928, far from being a lack-lustre year in which anything a little bit special was bound to shine, showed the Berlin theatre at its height. Max Reinhardt, Leopold Jessner, Piscator were in full flow, while in Fritz Kortner, Alexander Moissi, Gustav Gründgens, Hans Albers, Tilla Durieux, Lucie Höflich, Elisabeth Bergner and a host of others the capital had a treasury of priceless acting talent unequalled in any period before or since.

And if one chose to object that the *Dreigroschenoper* was not in direct competition with the works of 'legitimate' theatre, there were operettas, musical comedies, the immensely popular satirical revue *Es liegt in der Luft* ('It's in the Air') by Marcellus Schiffer, with music by Mischa Spolianski and starring Marlene Dietrich and Margo Lion, Heinrich Mann's comedy *Bibi*, with its inlaid dances and songs, and plenty of other pieces of musical theatre to set up as rivals. Further down the cultural line, popular taste was being catered for by the new medium of sound film, with its lavish displays of *Kitsch* imported from America. 1928 marked the clamorous arrival in town of Al Jolson and *Sonny Boy*; the previous year it had been Gershwin's *Strike up the Band* and *Funny Face*. A mere year later Wall Street collapsed, the Great Depression set in, the bubble of prosperity and cultural confidence burst, and the Weimar Republic began to slither into the open arms of the Nazis.

But in 1928 the *Dreigroschenoper* caught the raw nerve of Berlin as nothing else. The young Elias Canetti, novelist and later Nobel Prize winner, was at the première and felt how Berlin-ish the whole thing was. 'A cunningly effective performance, coolly and deliberately calculated,' he described it in his memoirs:

> It reflected that Berlin in every detail. It was themselves that the audience clapped and cheered – it was them on the stage, and they liked what they saw. 'Grub first, morals later' – *their* grub, then their morals.

None of them could have put it better, and they took it literally. And now it had been said openly, everyone felt as happy as a pig rolling in the mud. Steps had been taken to abolish punishment – hence the royal messenger mounted on a real horse. The sense of strident and unashamed self-satisfaction engendered by this show could only be credited by someone who had experienced it for himself.

Unlike the unanimous enthusiasm shown by the public, the work's reception by professional reviewers reflected either delight at the discovery of something totally new or disgust at something so crude and offensive. Herbert Ihering, very much a Brecht man, wrote the next day in the *Berliner Börsen-Courier* of a 'triumph of open form. What Brecht and Weill have succeeded in doing is to go beyond the revue and invent a new genre, fusing the ingredients of vaudeville into an expression of living theatre'. After a performance in Frankfurt a few weeks later Adorno went so far as to call the *Dreigroschenoper*, on the basis of a single hearing, 'the most important event in musical theatre since *Wozzeck*'.

But there was no shortage of offended dissent. 'The only sort of people who could work up an enthusiasm for this flashy, loud-mouthed "hero" Macheath,' said Franz Servaes in the *Berliner Lokal-Anzeiger* the day after the première, 'would be the perverse residents of Berlin's elegant West End who, having caught the Paris bug at one time and the Moscow bug at another, go mad over international criminals and gallows-birds but would be the first to tremble at the knees if they received a professional visit from one of these gentlemen during the night.'

Diaghilev, who never had any time for Weill's music, dubbed *Dreigroschenoper* the work of a latter-day Donizetti, 'though camouflaged by the requisite number of "wrong" notes, which always put in their appearance at the appropriate moment'. The English camp, too, when the work crossed the Channel in the early 1930s, had their difficulties in coming to terms with it, not least because of their lingering affection for the Playfair *Beggar's Opera* of glowing recent memory. 'Bert Brecht the librettist and Kurt Weill the composer,' wrote William McNaught in *The Musical Times*, 'have done a queer thing. The one has lifted and altered Gay's plot, the other has thrown away the well-loved tunes and substituted his own post-war jazzy inanities. It is all very crude and painful.'

Maybe one should not be too surprised at such a reaction from an establishment figure like McNaught, who takes pity on the poor Germans for not having had a proper Gay and Pepusch of their own. But the decidedly non-establishment Constant Lambert, too, identified a 'crudeness' in the work, while conceding 'a certain Hogarthian quality, a poetic sordidness, which gives a strength to what otherwise might have been a completely worthless work.' And before the attitude of McNaught and Lambert is put down to British po-faced insularity, we may care to recall that Aufricht's production of the *Opéra de quat' sous* in 1937 in Paris, a city with its own experience of revue and highbrow flirtation with jazz, had no lasting success, and that there it was the public that showed no interest. 'We played the work fifty times,' Aufricht said: 'the intellectuals praised it but the general public stayed away.'

Initially the *Dreigroschenoper* had been for Weill a kind of intercalation – interruption, even – in his sustained work on the *Mahagonny* opera. 'An entertaining project', he called it when he happened to meet Max Butting, his old friend of Novembergruppe days, 'but not terribly important.' When Rudolf Wagner-Régeny said he would like to attend one of the rehearsals, Weill replied: 'Don't go. There's nothing to it.' But when Wagner-Régeny telephoned him after the opening night, he had changed his mind. 'They'll still be doing it in a hundred years' time,' he said.

A week or two later Weill met Butting again. Greeting him cheerfully, he said: 'Well, is *Dreigroschenoper* my new path, or isn't it?' This was the earnest young disciple of Busoni who five years earlier had seen his career in terms of the intellectual severity of his String Quartet and reproached Hindemith for having 'danced rather too far into the land of the foxtrot'. The astonishing transformation was not lost on Butting. 'The interesting thing about our conversation from my point of view,' he recalled,

> was to observe that public success in no way caused this highly talented man to repudiate the excessive complexity of his earlier works. I am sure that formerly he would never have asked himself whom he was actually writing for. . . . Now the question of how he should write had very quickly received its answer, as far as he was concerned, for he believed that he had found his public.

It is a public that looks for the songs rather than for the dialogue, for Weill rather than for Brecht. Perhaps inevitably, the *Dreigroschenoper* has become a work of individual moments, the experience described by the Hungarian dramatist Julius Hay, who knew the *Dreigroschenoper* from an early production in Budapest but was disappointed with what he later saw in Berlin:

> I found every detail as delightful as ever but the work as a whole left me with a dissatisfied 'Is that all?' sort of feeling. I loved the music and I particularly liked the words of the songs. But the rest of the libretto left me cold.

In other words, to reverse a familiar dictum: the whole is less than the sum of its parts. But what parts!

CHAPTER X

'Off to Mahagonny!'

The proceeds from the *Dreigroschenoper* – royalties from performances, from sales of the piano-vocal score, of instrumental arrangements and individual numbers, from the sale of the film rights – laid to rest once and for all Weill's fears for his financial future. A few weeks after the spectacular première he and Lenya left their gloomy Pension Hassforth, after three years of challenge and achievement, and moved to spacious quarters at Bayernallee No. 14, a tree-lined street in Berlin's Neu-West-End district, a quieter and superior neighbourhood. The painter Emil Nolde lived in the next house but one. Weill's rising status in the musical world led a prominent dealer to place a grand piano at his disposal, and he also bought the obligatory status symbol, an American car – a Graham-Paige of appropriate show-biz flamboyance which he used not only for local excursions but also for visiting his publishers in Vienna. Gone were the days when he had to ask them to send him the money for his rail ticket in advance.

In December Franz Blamauer, Lenya's father, died. He had deserted the family when she was little more than a child, and she had not seen him since she left Vienna for Zurich. Weill had never met him, and Blamauer would have had no inkling of the rising fame of his son-in-law. Lenya herself, little known during her early years in Berlin, her career frustratingly stagnant since her marriage, was on the way up. She had attracted attention to herself as Jenny in the *Dreigroschenoper*, and in the month that followed, new offers came her way: in a new production of Feuchtwanger's *Petroleum Islands*, for which Weill composed three incidental songs and Neher did the decor; in *The Pioneers of Ingolstadt* by Brecht's young protégée Marieluise Fleisser, where in a particularly shocking scene, she has sex with a soldier while leaning against a headstone in a cemetery; and as Ismene in Jessner's production of *Oedipus Rex* and *Oedipus Coloneus* at the Schauspielhaus. Later, at the Volksbühne, she appeared with Peter Lorre in Wedekind's *Spring's Awakening*, and as Lucile in Büchner's *Death of Danton*.

Gratifying as she found these opportunities to emerge from the ever-growing shadow of her husband's fame, the road of independence took her away from the community of interests, personal and artistic, that she shared with him. She could never have remained the little woman in the background. *Dreigroschenoper* had put her on the map, yet it was to be four years before, in *The Seven Deadly Sins*, she again created a role that he had written with her in mind. The big vocal works of these four years – *Mahagonny, Die Bürgschaft, Der Silbersee* – were written with concert or operatic singers in mind, and Lenya was neither. The school opera *Der Jasager*, the cantatas *Das Berliner Requiem* and *Der Lindberghflug* – there is nothing here for her. Even the première of *Happy End*, with the famous songs she later made her own, took place without her.

Weill, the composer of the moment, was in growing demand. Invited to contribute to the spectacular festival 'Berlin im Licht', held that October, when the whole of the centre of the city, from Kurfürstendamm to Alexanderplatz, was bathed in light, he wrote a song in slow tempo which also doubled as a march for military band (the opening phrases recur note for note in 'Hosanna Rockefeller' from *Happy End* a few months later; and the first four-note phrase is not Weill's at all but that of Brecht's 'Mann-ist-Mann' song. Weill always looked to get maximum mileage out of good material). Also in October his two one-act operas *Der Protagonist* and *Der Zar lässt sich photographieren* came to the Städtische Oper in Berlin. 'Great success. Brilliant reviews. *Heil*!', he wired to Universal the next day, with characteristic sunny confidence.

Another commission, more substantial than that for the 'Berlin im Licht' occasion, came from the national broadcasting corporation for a radio cantata. November, the month in which he started work on this, marked a ten-year anniversary of dual significance – the end of the Great War of 1914–18, and the abortive November Revolution. Weill had been through the war as a schoolboy, suffering the privations of its last two years with his parents in Dessau and fearing lest he be conscripted into the army at the last moment. After the war, like so many of his generation, he had found in a radical socialist idealism an antidote to the conservatism and imperialism that had poisoned the German body politic under the Kaiser, and had joined the ranks of the Novembergruppe. Bonding these memories under the powerful personal influence of Brecht, he put together a sequence of Brecht poems and set them to music as *Das Berliner Requiem* – 'one of my best and most original pieces', he adjudged it at the time.

The *Berliner Requiem*, scored for three male soloists and an ensemble of wind instruments and harmonium, underwent changes in its constituent numbers at various times, but the two focal points of interest in the Brecht poems on which Weill drew remain firm: a sometimes brutal, sometimes ironic, powerful anti-war sentiment, and the figure of the Spartacist leader Rosa Luxemburg, murdered in 1919, with whose fate two of the poems are directly concerned. In these two dirges, with the two magnificent 'Reports on the Unknown Warrior' that follow them – Brecht at his savage best – lies the emotional and musical heart of the work.

Ever resentful of the domination of concertgoing by what he called the 'educated and moneyed classes', Weill saw in radio a medium for reaching all levels of society. Introducing his *Berliner Requiem* in the pages of *Der deutsche Rundfunk* a few days before its broadcast in May 1929, he wrote:

> For the first time the serious contemporary composer is being challenged to write works that can be appreciated by a large number of listeners. The content and form of these compositions must therefore be such as to interest a mass of people from all groups, and the means of expression must not pose difficulties for the untutored listener.

This was the spirit in which Weill wrote his cantata, and this the universal public he wished to address:

> There is no doubt but that the substance of the *Berliner Requiem* accords with the emotions and attitudes of the broadest possible cross-section of the population. In it an attempt has been made to express the attitudes of the city-dweller of today towards the phenomenon of death.

The result is a microcosm of Weill's art at its most original, at its most deadly ironical, at its most intense and most subtle. From the strident brassiness of the blood-chilling 'Grosser Dankchoral' (thanksgiving for what?) to the gripping neo-Classical recitative of the 'Second Report on the Unknown Warrior' – a refugee from a contemporary Bach Passion – at the end; from the incongruous whining waltz which haunts the 'Epitaph' for the murdered Rosa Luxemburg to the mocking fugal march of the 'First Report on the Unknown Warrior'; aggressive marching rhythms and ambiguous harmonic progressions – the whole Kurt Weill is here:

Das Berliner Requiem
'First Report on the Unknown Soldier'

It is the music of its time, a time of brash self-confidence and unrepentant sensuousness but also of studied irony and ambiguity. The self-confidence, in a time of rising material prosperity and of man's growing control over his physical environment, rests on a basis of technical expertise and exploitation of skills; the irony is born of the knowledge that man does not live by technical expertise alone yet has no body of confident moral and spiritual values to set above it, or even alongside it. So one shuttles, non-committed, to and fro between the two worlds, or sometimes straddles the no-man's-land between them, enjoying the view in both directions. Weill has all the self-assurance that issues from the combination of a fertile imagination with a brilliant and formidably adaptable technique. But as an heir to the moral and social uncertainties of the Weimar Republic, and as a composer who chose to set texts which met these uncertainties head-on, he encountered the reality of transience and human fallibility at every step. And as the paradox remained unresolved in life, so he converted it into the substance of his music, with unresolved dissonances, mordant wit, the detached, ironical tone of the objective *Gebrauchsmusiker*, and above all the cult of ambiguity, the tension between what is desperately important and how society has trivialised it. The music of the *Berliner Requiem* is held in the grip of this ambiguity and this tension.

Behind the scenes at the Reichsrundfunkgesellschaft there had been an argument over Weill's piece. One faction hailed it as an exciting novelty. Others resented Brecht's anti-war sentiments and regarded the resurrection of the memory of the Communist Rosa Luxemburg as highly offensive in a work called a requiem. These reactionary censors succeeded in delaying the broadcast for three months. Weill was greatly annoyed, so much so that he made this the immediate reason for ending his association with *Der deutsche Rundfunk*. For four years, missing only the occasional issue, he had contributed his column on Berlin's musical and cultural life. It had helped to keep him solvent over years of uncertainty; it had widened his cultural experience and sharpened his critical judgement; it had kept his name in the public eye. But now he no longer needed it, on any of these counts, and it deprived him of time that could be better spent. His last articles, among them an account of his *Berliner Requiem*, appeared in May 1929.

For the *Berliner Requiem* Weill had made a free choice of texts from among Brecht's existing poems. For a second radio cantata, *Der Lindberghflug* ('Lindbergh's Flight'), composed for the July 1929 Chamber Music Festival in Baden-Baden, Brecht wrote an original script inspired by Charles Lindbergh's historic solo flight across the Atlantic in the 'Spirit of St Louis' in May 1927. In ideological conception, the work belongs to the group of experiments in didactic drama that Brecht perpetrated between 1928 and 1930 and called *Lehrstücke* – pieces designed, not to convey an emotional experience but to exemplify certain social and moral precepts, Communist in derivation, firstly to those acting in the play, then to the audience.

The centre of Brecht's attention is not the figure of Lindbergh himself – whose Nazi associations later led him to delete all mention of Lindbergh's name from the text and rename the work *The Ocean Flight* – but his achievement in partnership with the successes of modern science. The form is confrontational: on the one side stands the Radio, the new medium, reporting the airman's progress and representing the physical circumstances of his adventure, including the natural forces against which he had to fight; on the other side stands the Listener, who represents Lindbergh and thus personally experiences, as an instructional exercise, what the hero undergoes. As first published, Brecht's text bore the title *Lindbergh, A Radio Play for the Baden-Baden Festival. With music by Kurt Weill.*

The text is divided into sixteen numbers, three of them to be recited, the remainder to be sung, and as the title states, the music was to be Weill's. In what was performed at Baden-Baden, however, only seven numbers, plus one of the halves of a bifurcated section, were written by Weill, while the remaining five-and-a-half numbers were supplied by Hindemith. A second *Lehrstück* by Brecht, *The Baden Lehrstück of Acquiescence*, was also scheduled for the Festival, and for this Hindemith had already been commissioned to write the music. In fact the entire Festival took place under the twin signs of the didactic cantata and music for radio, the two being brought together under the aegis of *Gebrauchsmusik* and *Gemeinschaftsmusik*, 'communal music', of which Hindemith was the leading protagonist.

In the Kurhaus at Baden-Baden, scene of the *Mahagonny Songspiel* riot two years earlier, *Lindberghflug* was performed twice in succession. The first time was through loudspeakers as a radio cantata, produced by Ernst Hardt (author of the play *Ninon de Lenclos*, from which Weill had planned to make an opera during his time in Lüdenscheid). The second was a concert performance, produced by Brecht. On one side of the platform, identified by a large board inscribed 'The Radio', were singers and orchestra, together with the gramophone through which the sound effects were transmitted – the roar of the aircraft's engine, the breaking of the waves, the cheers of the crowd. On the other side, beneath a board marked 'The Listener', stood the antiphonal figure of Lindbergh, who recited and sang his didactic role from beneath a familiar Brechtian backdrop bearing slogans such as 'Doing is better than Feeling'. The work is scored for tenor (Lindbergh), baritone and bass soloists, chorus and orchestra. Both performances were conducted by Hermann Scherchen.

At the time he agreed to do Brecht's *Lindberghflug*, Weill was working under greater pressure than even he could cope with. He was finally coming to the end of the frequently interrupted *Mahagonny* opera but revisions needed to be made and the première was still a year away. Aufricht had already approached him and Brecht for another play-with-songs with which to celebrate the anniversary of his occupancy of the Schiffbauerdamm Theatre in August. Having got so far with the *Lindberghflug*, Weill appears to have broken off and devoted himself to tasks that could not be delegated; Hindemith then provided the items that were still missing. Weill, who had no close personal relationship to the man with whom he found himself sharing the musical billing, thought little of Hindemith's contributions and later in the year returned to set for himself those numbers originally contributed by Hindemith. 'Given our different natures,' he said, 'we were fully aware that there could be no question of artistic unity.'

The first performance of the all-Weill *Lindberghflug* was conducted by Klemperer at a concert in the Kroll Opera in December. When he came across Weill some time later, Felix Joachimson greeted him jovially:

> I saw you take a bow with Otto Klemperer. Six foot seven next to five foot one. You two looked like a circus act. I wouldn't have missed it for the world.
>
> Kurt Weill laughed. 'When we went backstage after the fourth curtain call, I said to Klemperer, "You know why they're applauding, don't you? Not because they liked the piece. They just want to look at us." '

Differing musical natures as Hindemith and Weill may have had, they shared at this moment a community of interest and outlook:

> A composer should write today only if he knows what purpose he is writing for. The days of composing for the sake of composing may well have gone for good. At the same time the demand for music is so great that composer and consumer ought definitely to come to some form of understanding. . .

This is Hindemith speaking, but it could as well be Weill.

> The urge to write simple, popular music is something I share with many of today's composers. We do not want music to be a private affair that we confine to the drawing-room – on the contrary, we are searching for ways and means to make a broader impact. . . .

The words are Weill's, but Hindemith would not have disowned them. As a lifelong teacher, Hindemith had a stronger didactic streak than Weill. But Weill, in his own way, was no less committed to the social function of music, and although he was not much concerned, any more than Hindemith, about the narrowly political purposes that Brecht pursued in his *Lehrstücke*, the usefulness of the general format remained, and he yoked the *Lindberghflug* and the *Jasager*, written the following year under the specific instructional rubric of *Schuloper*, 'school opera'. Participation was all-important. 'It is better to make music than to listen to it'.

Amateur music-making, moreover, demands flexibility – of standards, of practical procedures like the constitution of the vocal and instrumental forces, and in the simplification, transposition, even omission of this or that section of a work. In his preface to the *Badener Lehrstück* Hindemith wrote: 'Whole musical numbers can be left out, the dance can be omitted, the scene for the clowns can be shortened or left out altogether, other musical items, dances and readings can be interpolated as necessary.' This absence of an authority issuing from the composer's definitive statement of his intentions led Schoenberg, for one, to repudiate the whole collectivist, 'democratic' trend of the *Zeitgeist*. 'Such music,' he wrote, 'could be taken to pieces and put together in a different way, and the result would be the same nothingness expressed by another mannerism.' Like Brecht's *Mann ist Mann*, in fact. As Marc Blitzstein, one-time pupil of Schoenberg's and author of the famous English version of the *Threepenny Opera* produced in New York in 1954, confirmed: 'To the twelve-tone-row boys the whole of Kurt Weill was treated as so much craftsmanlike trash.' It was the view of the Twelve-Tone Master himself: 'Franz Lehár, yes; Weill, no. His is the only music in the world in which I find no quality at all.' One feels sorrier for Schoenberg and the twelve-tone-row boys than for Weill.

In the spring of 1929, as Weill had almost reached the end of the composition of the *Mahagonny* opera and was also giving thought to the *Lindberghflug*, Aufricht raised as a matter of urgency the question of another popular piece to replenish his coffers. A tendentious *Lehrstück* of the kind that currently dominated Brecht's thinking was the last thing he wanted – rather, not to mince matters, an entertainment guaranteed to match the success of the *Dreigroschenoper*. While Brecht had no financial objection to a repetition of that success, he was averse to lowering his ideological sights in order to achieve it. So, as so often, the problem was laid at the door of Elisabeth Hauptmann. She turned out a story about Chicago gangsters and the Salvation Army which, in a haste bordering on panic, she and Brecht then proceeded to put into dramatic form, she with her customary diligence, he with little interest or effort. It was to be called *Happy End*.

In May, with two acts having been somehow put together, Brecht and Weill decided to repair to the French Riviera in order to work on the songs, as they had done before *Dreigroschenoper* a year earlier. Weill also had modifications to *Mahagonny* which he wanted to discuss. They left Berlin together in their cars, Weill with Lenya, Brecht with Helene Weigel.

But Brecht, for whom an automobile symbolised power and aggression and who drove accordingly, crashed his Steyr north of Frankfurt, broke a knee-cap and had to be transported back to Berlin. Weill and Lenya continued southwards more circumspectly in their Graham-Paige, and after what he described as 'a wonderful journey lasting six days', they reached the Mediterranean and returned to their little hotel in St. Cyr-sur-mer. Since April Universal had raised his monthly stipend to 1,000 marks in return for a commitment to offer them two more full-length stage works after *Mahagonny*.

When, on his way back to Berlin in July, he called on Brecht at the Ammersee, the third act of *Happy End* was still not written, and Brecht was talking of withdrawing his name from the production. Meanwhile, in Berlin, Aufricht had assembled a strong cast, including Carola Neher, Heinrich George and Peter Lorre, together with the entire production team from the *Dreigroschenoper* – Vambery and Heinrich Fischer, Caspar Neher as designer, Erich Engel as director and Theo Mackeben to conduct the Lewis Ruth Band. Rehearsals started in August on the basis of such material as was available, while Brecht, to general indignation, announced that he would come to the theatre and write the third act while rehearsals were in progress. George left the cast in disgust; Engel resigned, then relented; tempers ran high and abuse proliferated. By the opening night a proper script of the third act was still not in sight, and much of the other two had been chopped and changed.

The banal tale that Elisabeth Hauptmann thought up – George Bernard Shaw's *Major Barbara* is not far away – takes place in an improbable milieu inhabited by Chicago gangsters and the Salvation Army. Lilian Holiday, a lieutenant in the Salvation Army, falls in love with Bill Cracker, a gangster boss (in Brecht-Weill he is a shady bar-owner), and is dismissed from the Army for her indiscretion. She converts him to a Christian morality, and the gangster and the Salvationists make common cause, the latter being presented as a 'front' organisation serving to deflect attention from the crimes of the former, who are the natural spokesmen for a capitalist society.

Brecht altered this storyline here and there and subsequently reworked some of the Salvation Army material for his play *St Joan of the Stockyards*. But in the end the text of *Happy End*, coyly attributed in the programme to one Dorothy Lane – the baffled search for whose identity was to claim hours of fruitless scholarly investigation – has little interest and even less poetic or dramatic quality. The only justification for its survival lies in the songs. Superb songs. Four in each of the three acts, among them the unforgettable 'Surabaya-Johnny' and the 'Matrosen-Tango' with its languid refrain '*Ja, das Meer ist blau, so blau*', plus the rip-roaring finale 'Hosannah Rockefeller!' – all cast in the same mould as those of *Dreigroschenoper*, with the same jazz instrumentation, spiky rhythms, acid harmonies, drooling sentimentalities and other ingredients of Weill's sardonic Berlin accent.

Maybe it was indeed the prospect of such songs from the Brecht-Weill studio that drew most of the sophisticated audience to the Schiffbauerdamm Theatre that night at the beginning of September 1929. But, like patriotism, the songs alone were not enough. People had also come to enjoy a properly-scripted play, and they knew when they were not getting it. Aufricht, who was in a state of fear and trembling the whole evening, later wrote up his own colourful account of the proceedings:

> Up to the interval after the second act it was as big a success with the audience as *Dreigroschenoper* had been. Then came the third act. Palpably disappointed, they started coughing and fidgeting. I was standing behind the stage, counting the minutes. The act came to an end, and the only thing left was a Finale to be sung on the stage by the assembled cast.
>
> Then to my amazement, hardly able to believe my eyes, I saw Helene Weigel [who had played the role of the gangster boss, called 'The Fly'] advancing to the front of the stage. Reading from a scrap of paper, she shrieked out into the auditorium in a piercing voice, 'What's a picklock compared to a share certificate? What's robbing a bank compared with founding a bank?' and similar bits of crude Marxist propaganda. The bored audience, violently shaken out of their listlessness, clamoured for the curtain to come down. Two stained-glass windows depicting Henry Ford and John D. Rockefeller dropped from the flies, and sitting at the piano, Theo Mackeben sang and played the Finale of the piece, 'Hosannah Rockefeller, Hosannah Henry Ford', at the top of his voice, the tears running down his cheeks. He was the only one left singing and playing – the voices of the others were drowned in the tumult. Weigel's outburst was her response to suggestions from curious characters who considered that *Happy End* did not have a satisfactory ideological infrastructure.

The critics panned the work. Apart from the feeble and half-baked text, they scorned the blatant intention, miserably executed, to capitalise with a minimum of effort on the profitable formula of the *Dreigroschenoper*. Even the skill and musical subtlety of the best numbers could not disguise a sense of *déjà vu* or save the work from disaster. After two more performances the show closed. The day after, Georg Kaiser's *Two Neckties*, with music by Mischa Spolianski and a cast headed by Hans Albers and Marlene Dietrich, opened at the Berliner Theater to an enthusiastic reception and quickly wiped the non-event of *Happy End* from the public memory.

'I bore Brecht no grudge,' Aufricht concluded. 'Both of us had gambled and lost, each in his own way. In my case the losses amounted to 130,000 marks.' And ruefully contemplating his burnt fingers, he added: 'My theatre now took a rest from Brecht.' Not long afterwards Weill did the same. But not before they had brought to fruition their largest joint venture.

The intention to make out of Brecht's *Mahagonny* idea a full-length musico-dramatic work had been in both men's minds from the beginning. For Weill this primacy was linked with the evolution of a new style totally divorced from the 'song-style' of *Happy End* and *Dreigroschenoper*, a style which he was convinced, as he wrote to Hans Heinsheimer, 'had a seriousness, a "grandeur" and an expressive power that exceeds everything I have written up to now'.

Like the one-acters *Der Protagonist* and *Der Zar lässt sich photographieren*, and the later *Die Bürgschaft*, but unlike *Dreigroschenoper*, *Happy End* and the operettas-cum-musicals of his American years, Weill's *Rise and Fall of the City of Mahagonny* is true opera, with recitative, arias (including the songs), duets, trios, quartets, ensembles and orchestral interludes. The singing roles, moreover, unlike those in *Dreigroschenoper*, *Happy End* and in the *Mahagonny Songspiel*, were written for opera singers, not cabaret performers or actors-who-could-sing-a-bit.

But it was opera of a new kind, as different in conception from 'conventional' opera as Brecht's 'epic' theatre is from 'dramatic' theatre. Not by accident did Brecht make his 'Notes on the Opera *Rise and Fall of the City of Mahagonny*' the occasion for first laying out in tabular form his celebrated distinctions between the Aristotelian theatre of familiar experience and his new epic theatre, with its demand for narrative objectivity and rational detachment. In his 'Notes on my Opera *Mahagonny*', published in the periodical *Die Musik*, Weill described the conception of the work in terms common to them both:

> The subject of this opera is the story of a city – its foundation, its early crises, its moment of glory and its collapse. It consists of scenes depicting the mores of our time, projected on to a larger screen, and in keeping with this subject matter we were able to adopt the purest form of epic theatre, which is at the same time the purest form of musical theatre.

In his 'Preface to the Stage Instructions for the Opera *Mahagonny*' he spelt out the implications of this for the musical composition:

> Epic theatre, as a form, is the juxtaposition of a sequence of situations. As such it is the ideal form for musical theatre, since it is only such situations that can be turned into music in closed forms. A juxtaposition of situations in musical terms produces the heightened form of musical theatre that we call opera ... The subject matter of the opera *Rise and Fall of the City of Mahagonny* made it possible to create a work according to purely musical laws, for the chronicle form adopted is nothing other than just such a 'juxtaposition of situations'.

As in earlier collaborations with Brecht, to the latter's suspicious disapproval, Weill is clearly concerned that, whatever the fascination of the plot, the attractions of the text and the importance of the socio-political message, it shall in the final analysis be the interests of the music that assert themselves in the common enterprise. Brecht had a different scale of values, and any suggestion that he had just provided a libretto put him in a bad mood. Their differences were more than mere variations of emphasis: they went to the heart of the question of what the nature of opera should be, and they show how inevitable it was, after successes which to the outside world seemed to have sprung effortlessly from a perfect marriage of minds, like Gilbert and Sullivan or George and Ira Gershwin, that Weill should soon part company from his increasingly doctrinaire partner. Brecht, for his part, quickly found in Hanns Eisler a more consentient colleague, both musically and ideologically.

Of the characters in the *Mahagonny Songspiel*, the four gold-diggers and one of the two women, now renamed Jenny, are taken over into the opera (Brecht constantly juggled the names of his characters, and those in the text of his collected works are quite different from those in the score of the opera. 'Since the pleasure-seeking city of Mahagonny is international, in the broadest sense,' he explained, 'the names of the heroes can be changed to such as are familiar in the country where the work is being performed.'). The rest of the cast is made up of the unholy trio of the Widow Leokadja Begbick (also a character in Brecht's *Mann ist Mann*), Fatty the Procurist and Trinity Moses, with a group of six Mahagonny prostitutes on Jenny's side of the action and a male chorus as the men of the city.

As the agitated orchestral prelude begins, the news is flashed on to the curtain screen that Begbick, Fatty and Trinity Moses, convicted of procuring and embezzling, have escaped from jail and are being pursued by the police. Their car breaks down in the middle of nowhere, so they decide to stay where they are and establish a 'paradise city' called Mahagonny in which men can lead quiet, contented lives devoted to drinking, whoring and poker. But such an idyllic existence, based on rules of good behaviour laid down by Begbick and her companions, becomes boring, and the inhabitants prepare to revolt. News suddenly arrives that a hurricane is heading towards the city. In the terror of the moment Jim Mahoney, spokesman for the four gold-diggers at the centre of the action, discovers a new principle for the achievement of happiness: 'Do what you like. Everything is permitted.'

As if to give divine blessing to this new philosophy, the hurricane changes course at the last minute. Mahagonny is reprieved and left free to reconstitute itself as the pleasure capital of the world, devoted to eating, drinking, fornication and boxing.

Its fortunes rise again – so do its prices, and the motto becomes 'Do what you like, provided you can pay for it'. But Jim Mahoney has committed the cardinal capitalist sin of being unable to meet his debts; Jenny, the tart whom he loves, refuses to help him, and he is sentenced to die in the electric chair. His execution provokes a massive demonstration against inflation. A chaotic mob marches to and fro across the stage, carrying a bizarre medley of banners proclaiming 'For a Fair Distribution of Otherworldly Goods', 'For an Unfair Distribution of Earthly Goods', 'Up with Venal Love', 'Long Live the Golden Age', while in the background the city of Mahagonny goes up in flames. There is nothing anyone can do about it. '*Können uns und euch und niemand helfen,*' as the massed demonstrators chant at the end: 'Can't help ourselves or you or anybody.'

The story, said Weill, is 'a parable of modern life in which the principle character is the city itself'. Mahagonny, the capitalist world as Brecht saw it in the years that accompanied the rise of Nazism, arose to meet the needs and desires of the people, and it was these same needs and desires that brought about its destruction. Although Weill called the work a parable, Brecht viewed the happenings in his fictional city as thoroughly realistic. For money did indeed rule the world, dividing society into exploiters and exploited. At the same time, sharing the fascination of his age with the flamboyance, the glamour and the violence of contemporary America, Brecht decked out his reality in the fancy-dress of gold rush and Wild West – brutal realities for those swept along by the tide of material necessity but model romantic fictions for adventure-loving spectators in an unrelated time and place. In *Dreigroschenoper* those spectators, in a differently unrelated time and space, chuckled over the attacks made on the society they represented and blunted the barbs of satire by making them open sources of squealing delight. The *Mahagonny* opera permits no such inversion, or perversion, of intended meaning and effect. Its language is calculatedly crude, its explicitness often *outré* and offensive. But its thrust is inescapable – nor did the age escape it.

Mahagonny comprises twenty-one closed musical numbers asymmetrically divided into three acts, the musical statements being geared to the pace and content of the evolving action. 'Thus the music is not an agent propelling the action forwards,' wrote Weill: 'rather, it emerges at those moments when situations have been arrived at' – those situations being the objective elements out of which epic drama is made. So to express these situations in all their variety, Weill calls on the kaleidoscope of inventive skills which the world had come to expect of him, though now with the resources of an operatic cast, full-blown operatic production facilities and full opera-house orchestra.

Through the breadth of its conception and the multiplicity of its artistic means the *Mahagonny* opera has a sustained power and conviction which absorbs and concentrates, though not necessarily unifies, the earlier Weills – the Weill of the Violin Concerto, *Der Protagonist*, the *Mahagonny Songspiel*, then of the *Dreigroschenoper*, the *Berliner Requiem* and *Happy End*. And the music is indeed an extraordinary assimilation of disparate, profoundly incompatible elements – Baroque counterpoint, neo-Classical arioso, the open melodiousness of operetta, melodrama, *a cappella* outbursts, accompanied recitative, foxtrots, blues – and, of course, the famous 'Songs'.

For all its calculated incongruities, and the reappearance of the sleazy night club music of the 'Alabama Song' and 'Benares Song' from the *Songspiel*, the mood of the opera is serious, even sombre, proper to a *Götterdämmerung*. There is a powerful dynamism behind the advance of the operatic action, sustained by Weill's mastery of the tension engendered by the interaction of soloists and ensembles, and by the effectiveness of his orchestration. The result was what Hans Heinsheimer, to Weill's considerable satisfaction, perceived to be a 'synthesis of the rhythmic and melodic substance of your "song" style, accessible to the public at large, with a creativity that bears the hallmark of the highest artistic standards'.

For months after the score was virtually complete – and even before – Weill had in his usual industrious way been corresponding with opera houses throughout Germany to try and 'sell' them the work. The venue of the première itself was of prime importance but so too was the assurance of back-up performances in other strategically chosen centres. Berlin, specifically the Kroll Opera, seemed ideal, though as Heinsheimer warned him, the cultural pre-eminence that the aggressive, self-confident German capital had built up since the end of the Great War had generated resentment elsewhere in the country, and the provinces, far from taking their lead from Berlin, were now developing their own artistic policies.

There were also more sinister forces rumbling in the background. Ever since the humiliating Treaty of Versailles Germany had smarted under the imposition of what she regarded as unfair and unreasonable reparations. In theory the astronomical inflation of 1923 had wiped out the debt but as the Republic stabilised and began to prosper, the question of realistic repayments again became the subject of international negotiations. In 1928 the Young Plan settled new levels of payment, to the predictable accompaniment of storms of protest from Left and Right alike, and a severe economic retrenchment set in. The situation became worse with the Wall Street crash of October 1929: the German state faced bankruptcy, unemployment soared, anti-Semitism flourished, and the soil was ready ploughed for Hitler to sow the seeds of Nazism.

The cutbacks in public expenditure struck particularly hard in the cultural sector. Subsidies to state theatres and orchestras were cut, profitability and cost-effectiveness became the order of the day. This meant a policy of 'safe', uncontroversial productions and the discourage-ment of experiment and innovation, anything blatantly 'modern' being left to the private speculator willing, like Aufricht, to gamble on its success. The occasional operatic novelty did find its way through the net, like the Staatsoper's production of Milhaud's *Christophe Colomb* in May 1930, but the Kroll Opera, scene of many avant-garde events and aesthetic home of the intellectual left-wing, was a sitting target for the conservative and increasingly reactionary authorities, and the government closed it down at the end of the 1930–31 season.

At the end of 1929, however, when the decision over *Mahagonny* had to be taken, the prospect of a première at the Kroll under Klemperer had its attractions. And if Klemperer, to Weill's and the Kroll management's considerable annoyance, had not shilly-shallied for so long, then finally said no, it could have come to pass. But it did not. In the end – after Brecht had been persuaded to tone down some of the more unsavoury passages, in particular the dialogue accompanying the prurient scene of the men excitedly waiting their turn in the Mandelay brothel ('Patience, gentlemen, patience. You will appreciate that each client has to be allowed a little time to enjoy his sex.') – it had its opening at the Neues Theater in Leipzig in March 1930. The conductor was the local music director Gustav Brecher, who had conducted the first performance of Weill's *Zar* in the same theatre two years before. Caspar Neher was responsible for the sets and for the projections which were a central feature of Brecht's methodology, with Walter Brügmann, a veteran of the *Mahagonny Songspiel* and the *Zar*, in charge of the stage direction. Thus the fortunes of the evening, artistically, at least, lay in the hands of a seasoned team.

What lay beyond their power to control, however, were the elements of the occasion that had nothing to do with music and drama. Any opening night of a work by Brecht and Weill could be counted upon to provoke some kind of disturbance, and the battle lines were drawn up well in advance. This was now 1930. Thousands were joining the dole queue from one day to the next. Gangs of brown-shirted Nazis were tramping through the streets, shouting abuse at the Jews, at 'cultural Bolsheviks', at the liberal-republican politicians who had 'destroyed the pride of the German nation'. Rival mobs of Communists, chanting anti-Fascist slogans, marched against the storm-troopers. At the general election in September the National Socialists suddenly became the second largest party in the Reichstag.

Weill was both a Jew and a left-wing sympathiser, a composer of both decadent 'expressionist' operas and 'degenerate' music derived from jazz, despicable product of the subhuman culture of the negroes. Brecht, foul-mouthed *enfant terrible* of the German theatre, spurned the true national German tradition and preached the repellent doctrine of the international class struggle and Marxist revolution. What better occasion for a sortie against the anti-art of the Judaeo-Communists than a Brecht-Weill first night?

Nazi agitators had already demonstrated in the afternoon outside the theatre. 'They carried banners and placards,' recalled Heinsheimer, 'signs protesting against the new opera by Weill and Brecht. Men who looked as if they had never seen the inside of an opera house and did not know what they were demonstrating against screamed their indignation from the street corners.'

At the performance itself groups of SA men in uniform took their seats in various parts of the house. The first act passed off without incident. Then after the interval shouts of protest began to be hurled at the stage; counter-shouts of support came from other quarters, followed by boos and whistles, counter-boos and counter-whistles. Brecher struggled to keep the performance going, while some of the more frightened members of the audience left in panic when scuffles broke out. At the end the protesters rose to their feet *en masse*, only to be drowned by the applause from the rest. Klemperer, who had travelled to Leipzig from Berlin in search of self-justification, hurried out of the theatre without a word. Hostilities were not brought to an end until the police arrived and finally cleared the theatre.

For Weill and Lenya it was a shattering experience. For Weill's father and mother, who had been living in Leipzig for some years and who sat through the performance at the side of their son and daughter-in-law, it must have seemed like a nightmare. The uproar and the threat of physical violence were bad enough – but what could they have made of the extraordinary work, deeply distasteful and alien to them in story, in language and as music, that was at the centre of it all?

Albert Weill had long made his peace with his son's defection from the Jewish faith. He and his wife had also welcomed their Gentile daughter-in-law into the family without demur. 'They look on her as an honorary Jewess,' said Kurt gratefully. But his father had always disapproved of his association with Brecht. 'Religion and Marxism don't mix,' he said. And although he shared, as a father, in the joy of his son's successes, it rankled with him that they should be based on collaboration with an unrepentant atheist.

Next day the *Leipziger Abendpost* carried a report of the occasion under the headline 'Strong Public Protest. Brecher Promotes Communist Propaganda in the Neues Theater.' The report begins:

> On Sunday evening Leipzig experienced a theatrical scandal the like of which the city has not seen for a long time. Brecher, our director of music, undertook to perform a work which is the vilest and most blatant Communist propaganda. With great patience and tolerance Leipzig audiences have in the past put up with a number of dubious experiments on Brecher's part but this time he has gone too far, and the sound instincts of the public rebelled against the spirit of degeneracy which is threatening to destroy the Leipzig opera as a cultural institution.

One of the performances in Frankfurt later in the year was actually brought to a halt when a detachment of SA-men forced their way into the theatre and threw stink-bombs at the performers and the orchestra. In other centres which had agreed to put it on, however, planned series of performances passed off without disturbance, and often, in fact, to great enthusiasm. The production in Kassel, three days after the 'Battle of Leipzig', earned over twenty curtain calls. A local review recorded that 'the applause mounted from one act to the next, finally turning into a sustained and virtually unanimous demonstration of enthusiasm for Weill, for Abravanel, the conductor, for the producer and for the entire cast'. In Brunswick the same evening the delight of those inside the theatre had to reckon with the threatening behaviour of the rent-a-crowd outside: 'The tumultuous applause from the majority of the audience became even louder in the face of the antagonism of certain elements who, incited by the outrageous events in Leipzig, were seeking to cause a scandal . . . In the street outside people who had not even seen anything of the performance were trying to break it up and had to be dispersed by the police.'

Critical opinion, as expected, was divided. To be sure, Weill never stood still for long: the inimitable novelty of his most successful works was by nature 'non-copiable', to use Heinsheimer's description, and Weill himself was always at pains to emphasise how far his style had developed from one work to the next. *Mahagonny*, moreover, a full-length opera demanding all the modern resources of its genre, was very different from anything he had produced before, and was entitled to be judged in the context of Alban Berg's *Wozzeck*, Hindemith's *Cardillac*, Schoenberg's *Von heute auf morgen* and other major operatic works of the 1920s and 1930s.

But there was also an immediately recognisable Weillian language, a musical trade mark, proof of the ownership of certain intellectual patents on the exploitation of idioms derived from contemporary jazz and dance music, and critical attitudes to this language, once struck, tended to remain fixed. As the turbulent Marc Blitzstein put it: 'Jazz as an aesthetic resembles very much the Machine: a single work or two of real but isolated value, and the thing has been said completely.'

So as Brecht's anti-capitalist message has become boring and irrelevant – to portray man in his contemporary brutishness and immorality, wrote Hugo Leichtentritt, calls for a Dante, not a Brecht – Weill's once modish jazz has become hackneyed and mannered. 'A self-styled reformer of opera has greater obligations than this,' complained one critic, while Stravinsky, who had enjoyed the *Mahagonny Songspiel*, later said of the opera: 'There are good things everywhere in the score, only it is not good everywhere.' 'Yet despite many reservations,' wrote one of the anonymous writers quoted by Paul Stefan in his collection of reviews for the *Musikblätter des Anbruch* in 1930, 'it must be emphasised that the sets and the music are bursting with theatrical effectiveness and reveal immense ability, particularly in a dramatic respect.'

With his gift for looking on the bright side and his conviction of the importance of what he was doing, Weill spoke of the première of his opera in almost apocalyptic terms as marking 'a parting of the ways which will determine the course of musical life over the coming years', and as comparable with the famous riot at Wagner's *Tannhäuser* in Paris in 1861. Urging his publisher to immediately issue publicity material to promote the work, he suggests with almost embarrassing immodesty that the keynote be struck by his friend Hans Heinz Stuckenschmidt, who had written in his review: 'From a historical point of view *Mahagonny* stands at the very summit of contemporary musical works for the theatre.'

Who would not bask in such praise from a respected critic of the day? Yet the tone of his letters to Universal Edition on his own behalf has a raw edge of self-importance, almost of incredulity that anyone of discernment could fail to share his conviction that he had given the world a work of epoch-shattering importance, rather than just the brilliant music to a piece of entertaining theatre. What mattered was recognition, both by those charged with the responsibility of knowing quality when they saw it – the critics, that is – and by the public. Quiet and unassuming of manner he may have been. But he never underestimated himself.

CHAPTER XI

Farewell to All That

Aufstieg und Fall der Stadt Mahagonny was a work which, for a number of in-dwelling reasons and despite a series of sometimes profitable interruptions and agreeable distractions, insisted on being written. For one thing it had been the first joint enterprise Weill and Brecht discussed. For another, as by far the largest such enterprise, it held out the prospect of the most substantial success. Above all, it represented the practical demonstration of ideas which playwright and composer, each in his own way, were anxious to exhibit, ideas designed to set the composite genre of theatre-plus-music moving in a new direction.

Der Jasager ('The Boy Who Said Yes'), to which Weill turned his mind immediately after the première of the *Mahagonny* opera, has no such history or aesthetic compulsion behind it. It is a quick response to a precise challenge, a custom-made piece which first created a need for itself, then satisfied that need. But playwright and composer did not see eye-to-eye over the nature of the need, or, consequently, over the purpose of the piece constructed to fulfil it. That the *Jasager* was to be the last of this group of collaborations between Weill and Brecht – although thoughts for joint projects were still to pass between them over the years – is to observe a foregone conclusion.

In 1929 Elisabeth Hauptmann discovered Arthur Waley's English translations of Japanese No-plays from the fifteenth century and put four of them into German. One, called *Taniko* (literally 'The Casting into the Valley'), took Brecht's fancy. It tells of a boy who asks to be allowed to join a pilgrimage into the mountains in order to pray for his sick mother. His teacher, who is leading the pilgrims, fears that the strain will be too great but the boy implores him to be allowed to go, and the teacher finally consents. As the going becomes more difficult, the boy begins to feel unwell. The pilgrims then draw attention to the 'Great Custom' of their religion whereby anyone who falls ill on such a journey has to be cast into the valley below. The boy says that he knew, when he embarked on the pilgrimage, that this was the sacrifice the rite demanded, and he consents to his own sacrifice, though not without a sad thought for his sick mother. The pilgrims throw him into the depths but also pray that he may be restored to life. Their prayers are answered when a Spirit appears carrying the boy in her arms.

Ignoring the motif of redemption, Brecht chose to see in this religious parable a paradigm of subservience to a higher law which could be reproduced in modern secular terms. His Communism was becoming increasingly Stalinist, governed by the principle of 'my Party, right or wrong', except that the Party was never wrong, and Brecht, on his own later declaration, never joined it. The individual must acquiesce in his fate, an acquiescence founded on his rational acceptance of the underlying forces of collective necessity. Society is all; the individual is nothing.

Weill was not slow to see the musico-dramatic potentialities of Brecht's terse, pithy text, which, with a few changes in motivation to accommodate the modern ambience, stays close to Elisabeth Hauptmann's translation of Waley. And since the hero was a boy, they conceived the piece, dramatically and didactically, as addressing itself to schoolchildren and called it a 'school opera'. Ideologically Weill saw it in the same terms as his partner:

> We wanted pupils to learn that a community of which one is a member demands that one accepts the consequences of membership. By saying Yes to being thrown into the abyss, the boy lives out his life in the community to the full.

Not only was *Jasager* written for schoolchildren, it was intended to be performed by schoolchildren, who would learn the message from the inside, so to speak. There are three solo parts; the choir functions as a classical Chorus, underscoring the significance of the action and drawing the requisite morals from it, with the school orchestra binding the ensemble together. Aware that the resources of one school would differ from those of another, Weill posited a basic accompaniment of strings (excluding violas) and two pianos: if flute, clarinet and alto saxophone were available, so much the better, otherwise a harmonium could take over their parts; similarly, plucked instruments (guitar, mandoline) and percussion would be desirable but not indispensable. There are eleven separate musical numbers, arranged in two short acts, and the whole piece takes thirty-five minutes to perform. 'As you see,' said Weill, 'the basic principle of this school opera is simplicity.'

In the Weill-Brecht context *Jasager* stands in line of succession from the *Lindberghflug* of the previous year – conceptually as a didactic piece addressed to children, formally as a succession of self-contained musical scenes in which the action is step by step revealed like a series of film projections. Common to both works is also a strong reliance on the expressive power of the rhythm, especially of ostinato figures in the accompaniment, which underline key statements in the text and lodge themselves firmly in the memory of the children who watch and listen. Directness and lucidity are of the essence, in the means as in the end.

So *Jasager* returns us to Weill's 'gestic' music, a music which does not accompany or illustrate but which 'is', an objective artistic statement that needs no reference point outside itself. Weill himself attached particular importance to it at the time as proof that he had changed course since the days of his 'song style', and as a riposte to those 'who are always trying to type-cast me in terms of *Dreigroschenoper*'.

Enthusiastically taken up by the schools and youth groups for whom it was intended, *Jasager* became second in popularity, measured by number of performances, only to the *Dreigroschenoper*. Stokowski, whom Weill met in Berlin just after he had completed the score, agreed to perform it in the United States and over the coming years it found its way to places as far apart as Amsterdam, Paris and Tokyo. But although they did eventually sanction professional concert-hall performances, both Weill and Brecht wanted it basically confined to the educational milieu. When Klemperer intimated that he would like it for the Kroll Opera, Weill kept him at arm's length.

Musically it is a slight work: slick and effective, yes, but restricted in emotional range and power by the limitations of its purpose and scope. Music pedagogics, however, was big business at the time. The 'sociology of music' and 'social reception of art', areas of attention turned into fashionable intellectual playgrounds by Adorno, Ernst Bloch and other left-wing thinkers, became 'in' slogans. The production of works of art runs parallel to the manufacture of industrial goods, with the wants of the consumer governing the activity of the producer. There is a programmatic spirit in the air, a strong whiff of *dirigiste* centralism.

When he arrived in America a few years later, Weill again learned how market forces compelled the artist to adapt his product to what the public was prepared to buy. In America it became a matter of survival. At the time of *Jasager*, his financial and artistic position assured, it was a matter of choice.

Equally a matter of choice, though not to the liking of his publisher, was his reluctance to move away from his exclusive devotion to music for the theatre. Heinsheimer had urged Weill to write a new orchestral piece, both to prevent him from becoming type-cast in the public mind and also – Heinsheimer was too much of a businessman to offer merely disinterested advice – because conductors were on the look-out for attractive modern works. Erwin Stein, then head of the orchestral division at Universal Edition, expressed himself bluntly:

> I can understand very well why a man like you, who feels the need, as an artist, to exert a direct influence on the social and intellectual life of our age, does not find it easy to write 'absolute' music. But in order to widen your sphere of influence and make your work felt in circles which, because of your subject matter, have hitherto been up in arms against you, I consider it necessary for you to make a reappearance as an absolute composer. And don't tell me that you don't give a fig for such people – make an effort to win them over as musicians in the first instance.

In other words, the name Weill could bring audiences in, whereas the name Brecht tended to drive them away. In fact any link with words was suspect. When, after finishing the *Mahagonny* opera but before starting on *Jasager*, Weill considered an offer to write a handful of songs for a Berlin folk comedy, Heinsheimer was curtly dismissive: it was not at all the kind of activity, he said, that he wanted to see.

Then thoughts of a musical dramatisation of Hašek's *Good Soldier Schweyk*, or of a story by Kafka, or of one or other of Jack London's novels, crossed his mind. And two months later he started work with Caspar Neher on a new opera. Stein and Heinsheimer might as well have saved their breath. It was to be another three years before Weill wrote that piece of 'absolute' music they were looking for – and by then he was no longer in Germany.

The successful launch of *Jasager* by the Prussian Academy of Church and School Music in June 1930, coming hard on the heels of the *Mahagonny* opera in Leipzig, Kassel, Frankfurt and elsewhere, ensured that the name of Kurt Weill did not stay out of the musical headlines for long. One work sells another, and a number of theatres, particularly those under provincial or municipal control which faced considerable financial cut-backs, were looking for works with smaller casts and lower production expenses. This combination of pressures led to a flurry of interest in the *Mahagonny Songspiel*, for instance. But gratifying as this attention was in itself, hard commercial considerations led Universal Edition to prescribe, lest the cheaper *Songspiel* should queer the opera's pitch, that only theatres which had performed or accepted the full-length opera would be allowed to do the *Songspiel*. Weill, as concerned as ever to scrutinise the ways in which his works were marketed, found the tactic well grounded.

With *Jasager* in circulation, Weill and Lenya drove down to the French Riviera together for a summer vacation at Le Lavandou, where he and Brecht had written most of the *Dreigroschenoper*. Brecht also arrived there a few weeks later in the company of Elisabeth Hauptmann, with whom he was working to salvage from the wreckage of *Happy End* the material he eventually turned into *St. Joan of the Stockyards*. Here, under the warm Mediterranean sun, Weill relaxed with an intensity almost equal to that with which he worked.

Lenya, for her part, was still picking up regular theatre engagements. Since Marieluise Fleisser's *Pioneers of Ingolstadt* and Büchner's *Death of Danton* the previous year, she had appeared in Valentin Katayev's satirical comedy *Squaring the Circle* with Peter Lorre and Heinz Rühmann, and in Paul Kornfeld's dramatisation of Feuchtwanger's great novel *Jud Süss*, which opened in Berlin later in the year. Gramophone companies also invited her to make recordings of numbers from the *Dreigroschenoper* and elsewhere.

In July, shortly after their return from the French Riviera, Lenya went to London for negotiations over a film role (nothing appears to have materialised), and Weill travelled over to visit her – his first trip to England. Later in the month he drove down to Bavaria to discuss a project with Brecht that was to have far-reaching consequences for them both – the proposed film version of *Dreigroschenoper*.

With the arrival of the 'talkies' in 1929 German film makers found themselves confronting a bewildering mass of new, as yet imperfectly understood opportunities. One of these was the involvement of music, not merely to illustrate and heighten the movements of the visual action but as an integral feature of the action itself. *The Blue Angel*, with Marlene Dietrich 'falling in love again', showed what the illustrative approach had to offer. The *Dreigroschenoper*, filmed in the same year, was ready-made material for the integral approach.

Weill had a keen awareness of the musical opportunities that the new medium opened up. There was the obvious potential for spectacular 'shows', vehicles for glamorous stars and lavish displays of song and dance. There was also the cartoon world of Mickey Mouse, a world 'governed by purely musical laws', as he put it – 'films defined in terms of rhythm, which establish an entirely new and original form we might call "film ballet"'. With a shrewdness striking in its historical context barely a year after the arrival of talking pictures in Germany, he concludes that the overriding need is for film to recognise its independent being and discover its own personality as a creative force, not content itself with a set of values derived from drama, opera, stage musical or any other medium.

In May 1930 the Nero Film Company, with financial backing from Warner Brothers to the tune of 800,000 marks, made a contract with Brecht and Weill for the film rights of the *Dreigroschenoper*. It provided for a payment of 40,000 marks, plus additional fees for whatever work was involved in adapting the work to the new medium, such as the provision of additional words and music. Caspar Neher was engaged to help Brecht with the script, and Leo Lania undertook to produce the screenplay. As in the theatre, Theo Mackeben conducted, and the film was to be directed by G.W. Pabst, creator of some of the most strikingly realistic German films of the silent age, most memorably those starring Louise Brooks. Such was the producers' confidence in the work's commercial success that they planned both a German and a French version, using the same set: immediately after a scene of the *Dreigroschenoper* with its German cast they would shoot the same scene of *L'opéra de quat' sous* with the French cast. In the original version Macheath was sung by the handsome Rudolph Förster, Jenny by Lenya and Polly by Carola Neher; doubling for Lenya in the French version was the cabaret star Margo Lion, friend and rival of Marlene Dietrich, with Albert Préjean as Macheath.

As good luck would have it, the ground for the film of *L'opéra de quat' sous* was to be prepared by a run of performances of the play at the Théâtre Montparnasse in October 1930 which had the Parisians whistling the tunes in the streets like the Berliners two years earlier. 'We knew nothing about Brecht,' recollected Simone de Beauvoir in her autobiography, 'but we were enchanted by the way he depicted the adventures of Mack the Knife. The work seemed to us to reflect a totally anarchic attitude ... Sartre knew all Kurt Weill's songs by heart and we often used to quote the catch phrase about grub first and morality afterwards.'

Though Pabst and Nero Films could hardly have been ignorant of the troublesome Brecht's reputation, the events of the ensuing months caught them totally unawares. Nero and their backers had not unnaturally expected a script that kept reasonably close to that of the Schiffbauerdamm success; the whole point of the cinematic exercise, after all, was to repeat this success.

But they had fatally underestimated their man. The Brecht of 1928 had been content to toss off a bit of witty, lightweight social persiflage derived from an eighteenth-century English satire. The Brecht of 1930, an intransigent, stern-faced Communist who saw the world in terms of capitalist black and Marxist white, was not. Changing the title to *Die Beule* ('The Bump on the Head'), he now came up with a story in which Peachum has become head of a Beggars' Trust and Mackie Messer the boss of a 120-strong gang of criminals. War between the rival factions ravages the streets of London. Mackie has married Peachum's daughter Polly, as in the original play, and is betrayed to the police by the prostitute Jenny but in the meantime Polly and her husband's gang have 'acquired' the National Deposit Bank and use its funds to get him released on bail. When one of the beggars, a man called Sam, is beaten up by Macheath's men for tipping off the police about a burglary they were planning, the beggars threaten to revolt. Tiger Brown, the corrupt chief of police, appeases the mob who are looking for the execution of Macheath by putting the beggar Sam in the death cell instead, with Peachum's treacherous approval. At the end all three – Macheath the banker, Peachum and Tiger Brown – are seen walking arm in arm, pillars of a bourgeois society that welcomes them as its rightful spokesmen.

Nobody had bargained for a situation like this. With a quite unacceptable scenario on their hands, the producers offered to pay Brecht his money on condition that he withdrew from the project and leave them to find their own solution. But again they had mistaken their adversary. The contract contained a clause that embodied a principle vital to both Brecht and Weill: 'The producers guarantee the authors the right to participate in all decisions concerning the final editing of the material [i.e. the final cut].' This clause was followed by an undertaking that no additional textual material would be used in the film unless it had been written by Brecht, and no music used unless it had been composed by Weill. Armed with these rights, Brecht and Weill jointly applied to the courts for an injunction to prevent Nero Films from doing any more work on the film. It had in any case already become clear that Pabst intended to treat Weill's music very freely, not to say roughly, leaving out material here, reallocating and redistributing songs there, even having extra bars composed which Weill knew nothing about – all to conform to his concept of the film's overall dramatic effectiveness. Pabst sympathised with the play's social thesis but his main interest lay in the emotional relationship between the characters, especially Macheath and Polly, which for Brecht had mere incidental interest.

When he saw the outrageous things that were happening on the film set, Weill was aghast. Furious at the 'Kitsch being manufactured there', he wrote to his publishers:

> When I sought to avail myself of the right to make my voice heard, and protested against what seemed to me a particularly objectionable scene, they simply fired me, without the slightest cause. So my lawyer, Otto Joseph, immediately sued them. The hearing has been put down, together with Brecht's, for October 17.

For both men the principle at stake was that of the integrity of the work of art and the artist's control over the use of his own material. But in the unhappy muddle that now bogged the whole enterprise down Weill had in effect suffered a double betrayal. Brecht knew full well that the scenario he had supplied was to all intents and purposes a new work, and that, whatever the contract said, his moral position was far from being as convincing as he made out. Weill, on the other hand, assuming that, with reasonable concessions to the new medium, his original music would remain as it was, found not only that the producers were riding rough-shod over his score but that his partner had been doing the same, pursuing his new, politicised storyline with little or no regard for where the 'Barbara Song', the 'Cannon Song' and the other highlights of the original production were going to fit in – if at all. Pabst and his production team must have shaken their heads in disbelief.

Judgement was delivered in November 1930. Brecht, held to have withdrawn his cooperation on the script, and thus to have broken his contract at a certain point, lost his case and was ordered to pay costs but received an out-of-court payment of 16,000 marks from the film company in return for a promise to keep his distance. Since filming had gone on uninterrupted during the legal hostilities, and Brecht had already made his influence felt on the script, there was no way in which his voice could be completely stifled. But his distance from the centre of the action could not be disguised when the film was finally released in February 1931 with the story described on the placards as 'freely adapted from Brecht'.

Weill, on the other hand, won his action. It was a proud and important victory, establishing the artist's rights over his property and guaranteeing that not a single note of music in the score should be written by anyone else. In return for accepting the reordering and deletion of some of his original numbers, he too agreed a settlement with the production company, which included a commitment to allow him a key role in three future film projects, and withdrew his objection to the film.

One change was to have a dramatic effect on the career of Lotte Lenya. As in the stage production, she took the part of Jenny but now, as a result of the new text, was also given the 'Pirate Jenny' song to sing, which originally belonged to Polly (sung in the film by Carola Neher). From that moment on 'Pirate Jenny' was Lenya's, and Lenya, slinky, provocative, with more of Jenny's blood in her veins than many knew, stole the film. For a pot-pourri of numbers recorded in December 1930, immediately after the shooting of the film, she also sang Polly's equally famous 'Barbara Song', together with Lucy's part in the 'Jealousy Duet', thereby identifying herself in the eyes – or ears – of the world with the music of virtually all the female roles in the *Dreigroschenoper*.

Having launched their suit on the high moral ground of artistic integrity and the sanctity of the work of art, Weill and Brecht now found themselves accused of betraying their principles for material reward. With Brecht one could never be quite sure. But Weill, who all along had shown more tolerance and readiness to compromise, played a more honest and open game and had nothing to be ashamed of. Nevertheless he owed it to himself, he considered, to set the record straight. 'I did not settle with the company in order to receive a sum of money in compensation,' he stated crisply in the journal *Licht-Bild-Bühne*:

I took legal action in order to ensure that certain practices damaging to art or harmful to individuals be prohibited in the field of film production, and I was prepared to settle because the company guaranteed that these practices would be banned in any future films. I brought the action in order to ensure that the author is granted the right to share in the decision-making process where questions of production are concerned, and I was prepared to settle because the company undertook to consult me in future over such questions.

The months of wrangling and uncertainty about the fate of the *Dreigroschenoper* film left Weill drained of energy, and immediately after judgement was given, he took himself away from the bustle of Berlin for a vacation in the mountains of the Riesengebirge, in a remote south-east corner of Germany near the border with Bohemia. His doctrinal differences with Brecht, especially since *Jasager*, had opened up a chasm which, as all could see, was rapidly becoming unbridgeable. But their minds had interlocked too closely, as each worked his way towards successive positions of principle, for them to part company with a clean break. As their artistic and political convictions were drawing them apart, the law suit brusquely brought them together again in defence of a common interest. Even while the world was waiting for the court's decision, final rehearsals were being held of a production of Brecht's *Mann ist Mann* for which Weill had written new incidental music. And at the end of 1931 the Berlin première of the *Mahagonny* opera thrust them once more into each other's by now unwilling arms, an occasion that provoked behaviour from Brecht which no relationship, personal or professional, would be likely to survive.

But for a collaboration that would leave behind the constant tensions and uncertainties which the unpredictable Brecht inflicted on his environment, Weill had already begun to look elsewhere after finishing *Jasager*, some months before the *Dreigroschenoper* film dispute exploded. In the course of a letter to Universal back in August he vouchsafed the news: 'I have been working for the past two weeks with Caspar Neher on the libretto for an opera.' He added that they had already sketched a plot, and that the title would probably be *Die Bürgschaft* ('The Guarantee').

Neher had always been a congenial and level-headed colleague. His association with Weill went back to the boxing-ring set, film projections and costumes of the *Mahagonny Songspiel* at Baden-Baden in 1927, and had continued through *Dreigroschenoper*, *Happy End* and the *Mahagonny* opera, but there had been no sign that he cherished a desire to see himself as a librettist. Little of the sharp Brechtian diction has rubbed off on the rather characterless libretto, part prose, part verse, of *Bürgschaft*, and the dictum 'Man does not change; it is circumstances that change man's attitudes', which runs through the work like a socio-psychological Leitmotiv, belongs to the commonplaces of Marxist theory.

At the heart of *Bürgschaft* lies a parable by Herder called *The African Judgement*, which Weill printed at the beginning of his score. Alexander the Great visits a rich province in Africa in order to learn its customs. He is taken to the market place, where the King is sitting in judgement over the disputes between his citizens. A man appears before him and tells how he found a bag of gold in a sack of grain that he has just bought from a dealer: when he tries to return the gold, the dealer refuses to accept it, saying that what he sold was the sack and everything in it. The King's judgement is that the one man's son shall marry the other man's daughter, and that the gold be given to them as a wedding present. Alexander cannot hide his amazement at this verdict: in his country, he tells the King, the two disputants would be put to the sword and the gold confiscated. Horrified by such inhumanity, the King responds: 'If your country, like mine, receives the blessings of the sun and the rain, it can only be for the benefit of the innocent animals, for human beings who behave like that do not deserve such blessings.'

This little anecdote could be made to bear a variety of applications, from the realm of basic common morality to which the great humanist philosopher Herder assigned its primary relevance, to local historico-political situations in which the conflicting forces could be clearly identified. Weill and Neher used it on the one hand to illustrate the dogma that man is the product of his environment, on the other, to allude to the threatening invasion of a civilised community by a barbarous tyrant. Nobody in 1932, when *Bürgschaft* was first performed, could fail to recognise who the tyrant and his barbarians were – not even the barbarians themselves.

The Prologue to the three-act opera, set in a fictitious country called Urb, defines the nature of the honest relationship between Mattes, a cattle farmer, and Orth, a grain dealer who pledges (the 'Bürgschaft' of the title) to redeem Mattes' debts. Act One, set six years later, embarks on the narrative of Herder's fable: Mattes discovers money in one of the sacks of grain he has bought from Orth, decides first to keep it to pay his debts, then to return it, only for Orth to refuse to take it back; the two men resolve to put the matter before a judge, claiming to be the same upright citizens they have always been, while the Chorus, standing apart from the action, reiterates the precept that circumstances cause men to change.

At the beginning of Act Two the judge delivers the same verdict as the King in Herder's fable. But when Urb is invaded by a neighbouring 'Great Power', the Commissar of that power overturns the verdict: Mattes and Orth are arrested and the money appropriated. Act Three, set a further six years on, reveals Mattes and Orth as re-established, well-to-do citizens. During this time, however, Urb has suffered the ravages of war: the people are poor and starving, while Mattes has prospered at their expense. They set out to take revenge on him; he flees to Orth and begs for help. But the world has changed, and after a fight Orth, in self-protection, turns his one-time friend over to the mob, who batter him to death. And why has this tragedy happened? Because, whispers Orth at the end of the work, everything is ultimately governed by the law of money and the law of power – which is to say, as contemporary audiences needed little prodding to realise, by monopoly capitalism in the affectionate embrace of the Nazis. Seasoned operagoers will also have had thoughts of the accursed gold in *Der Ring des Nibelungen*.

Bürgschaft occupied Weill from August 1930 to October 1931. Its first performance took place on March 10, 1932, three days before the presidential election confirmed the frightening rise in popular support for Hitler at a time when unemployment stood at six million. The political situation, indeed, threatened Weill's concentration and peace of mind throughout the time he was at work on the opera. First there was the shudder of apprehension that ran through the ranks of the politically conscious when, in October 1930, 107 duly elected brown-shirted Nazi deputies marched into the Reichstag instead of the mere twelve in the previous parliament. Then, as if to show how tragically justified that apprehension had been, no fewer than forty-five people were killed in political street fighting in Prussia alone during the first nine months of 1931, chiefly between Nazis and Communists.

As the South of France had always proven conducive to both recreation and creative work for him in recent years, Weill travelled down to Le Lavandou in April with Neher, leaving Lenya in rehearsal for Katayev's *Squaring the Circle* in Berlin. From the Riviera they drove westwards to San Sebastian, returning home via Biarritz and Paris to a Berlin of menacing unpleasantness. 'Conditions here are terrible,' he wrote to Heinsheimer in July. 'At the moment nobody has the slightest idea what is going to happen, though the general feeling is that there is virtually no hope of averting a total collapse.' He also took the precaution of asking Universal to send his monthly retainer of 1,000 marks to a bank account in Switzerland in future – 'given present-day circumstances, I want to protect myself against all eventualities and ensure complete peace and quiet to work on my opera.'

Emotionally the 'peace and quiet' of his apartment in the relaxed, tree-lined Bayernallee, a part of the city spared the rowdiness of political demonstrations and battles in the streets, was far from unruffled. Lenya was in Russia. Piscator, struck by her performance as Jenny in the *Dreigroschenoper* film, had engaged her to play the part of a sailors' whore in a joint German-Russian film version of Anna Seghers' novel *The Revolt of the Fishermen of Santa Barbara*. Cast and film-crew left for Odessa in July; after three months dominated by bureaucratic bungling and by arguments between Piscator and the Russians, not a single scene had been shot. Weill missed his wife and had even considered visiting her in Odessa, but when the film money finally ran out in October, the German contingent returned home.

For Lenya the premature homecoming brought not only a professional disappointment but also a personal shock. Herself no plaintiff for the cause of one-woman-one-man, she came back to find her husband having an affair with Erika Neher, Caspar's wife, which had developed during the months of close family contact over *Bürgschaft*. However the affair started, and whether it was directly or indirectly related to the homosexual predilections which Neher had allegedly shown since the birth of his son Georg in 1924, the urge for its continuance and its intensification lay primarily with Erika. In letter after importunate letter, sometimes more than one in a day, often discussing casual trivialities with an intensity which showed how desperately she needed him, she poured out her heart to Weill in search of his companionship. Gently he sought to deflect her passion but many months went by before some semblance of emotional equilibrium – externally, at least – was restored. Lenya, for her part, watched and waited, keeping her feelings to herself.

The permissive openness characteristic of Weill's relationship to Lenya survived to the end of his life – as, indeed, did the relationship itself, despite its centrifugal tendencies and its manifest strains. His almost paternal concern for her and her problems led him at this moment to get Universal to deduct one hundred schillings from his monthly royalty and pay it regularly to her mother, who was eking out a miserable existence in Vienna under the drunken domination of her second husband. And as for his involvement with Erika Neher, its motive force was more likely to have been pity than passion.

Bürgschaft is Weill's largest work, a full-scale opera in aim and manner. The libretto may not have the savage penetration of a Brecht or the psychological subtlety of a Kaiser but it is no weaker than many that have spawned great musical works and has a directness to which Weill unhesitatingly responded. Compared with Brecht, Neher had both a better understanding, in principle, of what the operatic composer required of his librettist and a more generous willingness to adapt his text to what Weill convinced him would be musically more effective. Brecht, for his part, resented the ease with which his two friends slipped into productive collaboration; he poured scorn on the moral concerns of *Bürgschaft* and tried hard, in his jealous way, to prize them apart. Alongside the relaxed pleasure of working with Neher, Weill found it a relief, as Lenya later recalled, to compose full, uninhibited opera again after the restraints of writing for small groups, untrained singers, children, and the special demands of Bertolt Brecht. 'Now I must let all that music out of myself again,' he told her.

As far as conceptual intention is concerned, Weill wanted *Bürgschaft* to be viewed both as a tragic opera and as a piece with a 'message'. 'The tragedy,' he explained, 'lies not so much in the death of Mattes as in the final words uttered by Orth, while the "message" for the audience to take away with them lies in the recognition of the hopelessness conveyed by these words.' Above all it is a work for and of its time: '*Bürgschaft* makes an attempt to deal with things that concern us all. Such an attempt must needs provoke controversy. That is part of its function.'

Musically – and not merely because of its breadth of conception – *Bürgschaft* marks a new phase in Weill's development. The intellect-ualised pseudo-jazz of *Mahagonny* and *Dreigroschenoper* has all but disappeared, the songs have become arias, recitative has developed into emotional monologue, and the ensembles, no longer basically homophonic, chorale-like utterances, revel in a new contrapuntal strength that had lain dormant since the days of the severely intellectual, 'difficult' Weill of the early 1920s. The vocal lines, often reminiscent of Busoni, are clean, direct and basically diatonic, though free in their tonality. Structurally the work, musically continuous, with only an occasional moment of spoken dialogue, is built as a series of more-or-less self-contained numbers, some of them long and complex, each with its own inner musical logic. In many respects, indeed, it has a lucidity and precision of line that recall the *Neue Sachlichkeit* and neo-Classicism of the 1920s.

There are seven main singing roles, and the score calls for a full orchestra, including two pianos but without the saxophones, harmonium and assorted exotic percussion to which he had become attached during the years of his 'song style'. The characteristic Weillian ostinato in the orchestral accompaniment, however, is still much in evidence, while the use of a chorus to link stage-action and audience, and to point the didactic message of the piece – as at the beginning and the end of *Jasager* – led critics to draw parallels with Stravinsky's *Oedipus Rex* and Milhaud's *Christophe Colomb*. The choral parts of the work, in fact, carry much of the musical as well as the philosophical argument.

Why *Bürgschaft* is rarely talked about, has not been commercially recorded and is hardly ever performed, are questions best addressed to the captains of the music industry. Maybe it flags here and there; maybe the episodic form of its 'epic' scenes encourages the feeling that Weill's ideal format is smaller than that of full-dress opera. But it has moments of great dramatic power, such as the 'Four Gates' sequence in Act Three, in which the people are made to pass through the ordeals of War, Inflation, Starvation and Disease. It also has scenes of poignant lyrical beauty, like Anna Mattes' lament for her lost daughter, compared by Ernst Bloch to 'Marterl' in the *Berliner Requiem* and characterised as having 'an element of Jewish Verdi about it'.

Two years later Count Harry Kessler, then in Paris, wrote in his diary:

> One evening at Madame Homberg's Kurt Weill played us large parts of his *Bürgschaft* . . . The effect left by the work is like that of a book by an Old Testament prophet – Isaiah, Jeremiah, 'messianic', a people in the depths of misery awaiting their Redeemer, and in this respect also a great historical document testifying to the condition of the German people in 1930 as they waited for Hitler. A work of immense power and stature.

To this aesthetic judgement – cast in terms that make *Bürgschaft* an ironic sequel to Johannes R. Becher's play *A People Sally Forth to God*, on which Weill had based his First Symphony – Kessler added a chilling postscript:

> Madame Homberg nevertheless considered it would be dangerous to perform the work in Paris at that moment because it would frighten the public with its revolutionary ardour and harm the cause of the refugees.

Such was the social reality that overrode artistic quality and exposed the isolation of the emigré.

As usual, even before the score was finished Weill invested much time and energy in seeking declarations of interest from as many opera houses as possible, then in planning the strategy of the première and subsequent early performances. After the experience of the *Mahagonny* opera he had to tread warily. Leipzig was out of the question, and other centres had either no funds for adventurous new productions or a fear of the repercussions of putting on a transparent anti-totalitarian allegory by a Jewish composer, or both. Maybe, he began to think, he should pay greater attention to securing performances abroad, especially in America.

However before *Bürgschaft* could reach the stage, there was another important matter that had to be attended to. This was the long-awaited, long-frustrated introduction of the *Mahagonny* opera to the Berlin stage in December 1931.

The state opera houses, including the Kroll, had refused to tackle the work, and it fell to the ubiquitous Ernst Josef Aufricht to save the situation. Aufricht had had his eye on *Mahagonny* for some time. He knew it was a very different proposition from the other two Brecht-Weill works he had put on. But by mounting it in a theatre rather than an opera house, and by engaging for the leading roles singers whose allegiance was not to opera but to lighter forms of musical theatre, he thought to promote it for a somewhat different public, without sacrificing the dramatic or musical substance.

Brecht and Weill agreed to make certain further revisions to the work. In particular, gladly meeting Aufricht's wish to have Lotte Lenya in the cast as Jenny, Weill transposed certain material and wrote a new setting of the 'Havanna-Lied' for his wife. Lenya could not have sung the original version but she now made this new song ('*Ach bedenken Sie, Herr Jakob Schmidt*') inseparable from her interpretation of it. The company also included Harald Paulsen, the original Mackie Messer, as Jimmy Mahoney, the popular cabaret singer Trude Hesterberg as Widow Begbick, and the as yet unknown Lale Andersen as one of the Mahagonny girls.

At the same time other familiar landmarks, like the '*Lasst euch nicht verführen*' chorale and the 'God in Mahagonny' number, were dropped and the whole work compressed, both in time and in space, largely in deference to the conditions of the venue. Neher was recruited as stage designer, and, again thinking of old times and old friends, Aufricht wanted Theo Mackeben to conduct. But Mackeben would have been out of his depth in opera, and with Weill's approval the baton was handed to Alexander von Zemlinsky, brother-in-law of Schoenberg and Klemperer's assistant at the Kroll Opera.

Weill had lost none of his old skill in adaptation and arrangement. At one point in rehearsals, the composer Wagner-Régeny remembered, the proceedings stuttered to a halt when the singers found themselves at odds with the orchestra. Director, composer and conductor held an urgent conference in the middle of the stage. Then Weill came down into the auditorium with a sheaf of orchestral parts under his arm. 'Spreading the parts out on a table,' said Wagner-Régeny,

> carefully and with great concentration, a smile sometimes flitting across his face, counting the bars and calculating the rests, he began to write music on loose sheets of manuscript and insert them in the parts. In less than an hour, without having recourse to the score, he had entered a section of the music, albeit a short one, directly into the orchestral parts, and the rehearsal was able to resume.

Aufricht had taken a lease on the Theater am Kurfürstendamm, where Weill's first stage work, *Zaubernacht*, had been put on nine years ago, and here the *Mahagonny* opera had its greatest success, with a run of over fifty performances. But not before playwright and composer had almost come to blows.

It was the old problem of all opera: Which comes first, the words or the music? Brecht's answer was simple. The function of words is to convey ideas; stage drama presents stylised situations which similarly embody ideas; music may heighten the effectiveness of that presentation but it can never have more than a secondary role, and that it might arrogate to itself the position of dominant partner was unthinkable. In other words Brecht had little idea of what opera was all about and had no wish to revise his priorities.

Weill, on the other hand, clung to the legitimate claims of music in its own right, a music true to itself – and, by extension, to the society it serves – only when allowed to follow its own course. The furore that had greeted *Mahagonny* in Leipzig and elsewhere had shown Brecht that he was making his political point, but Aufricht's plan for this Berlin production seemed to him to be aimed at turning the work, with Weill's connivance, into a piece of 'culinary' entertainment to rival *Dreigroschenoper*, the social criticism in which had been swamped by the jazzy delights of the tunes. Box-office appeal was paramount in these tight-fisted days of three million unemployed, when only the likes of a Richard Tauber, a Hans Albers or an Elisabeth Bergner could be depended upon to fill the house.

Brecht's simmering resentment finally boiled over during rehearsals. Muttering about a dastardly plot to trivialise his sacrosanct text, he brought a lawyer to the theatre and threatened to put a stop to the proceedings. Weill issued a counter-warning against interfering with his music. 'Brecht knocked the camera out of a press photographer's hand for taking a picture of him and Weill together,' wrote Aufricht, waspishly enjoying the spectacle. 'Then, as Weill made to leave, Brecht shouted after him: "I'll put on my war-paint and throw that phony Richard Strauss down the stairs!"'

Neher, well-disposed towards both parties, tried in vain to mediate. In the end Aufricht managed to buy off the irate Brecht by offering to put on his newly-written play *The Mother* in the familiar home of the Schiffbauerdamm Theatre. Pacified by this offer, Brecht withdrew his troops and left the *Mahagonny* camp in peace.

The public that went to the Kurfürstendamm Theatre enjoyed what they saw and heard, and the astute Aufricht distributed copies of the hit tunes to the city's hotels and bars for the resident bands to play. Most of the critics, on the other hand, gave it the thumbs-down – and not only those from organs with an impeccable record of blinkered opposition to almost everything that Weill did.

He collaborated with Brecht only once more – on *The Seven Deadly Sins* in 1933. In 1944, in American exile, they considered doing a version of Brecht's *Good Person of Sezuan* together, and there was a good deal of talk about a musical dramatisation of Hašek's novel *The Good Soldier Schweyk* (the idea of a musical *Schweyk* had first occurred to Weill back in 1929). But nothing came of either project, nor of the idea of an all-black *Dreigroschenoper* for the American market.

The relationship had concealed the seeds of its disintegration from the beginning. The confident, established Weill of the *Mahagonny* opera and *Die Bürgschaft* was a very different proposition from the diffident petitioner who had made his modest way to Schlichter's restaurant five years earlier. For Brecht music was one of the means to an end. Weill perceived it was its own end. The final break was inevitable. But can we be other than grateful that it was deferred for so long?

Clearly as he recognised the importance of the Berlin *Mahagonny*, Weill yet had an uneasy feeling that it might get in the way of what was to him a far more urgent concern – the launch of *Bürgschaft*. The world of *Mahagonny* now lay behind him and he wanted to be seen for what he was now, and not for what he had been. 'We must make it abundantly clear', he wrote to Universal, 'that the *Mahagonny* opera brings to an end a period in my creative life which started with the Baden-Baden *Songspiel* but now has been superseded, and that *Bürgschaft* is the first large-scale product of a new line of development which began with *Lindberghflug* and, more particularly, with *Jasager*.' He knew that his work would always be attacked from certain predictable quarters: at least he could do his best to ensure that the attacks were properly aimed.

Bürgschaft, directed by Carl Ebert – son of the former President of the Weimar Republic and the first director of the Glyndebourne Festival – conducted by Fritz Stiedry and with designs by Caspar Neher, opened in the Städtische Oper Berlin in March 1932 to a barrage of paranoid hate from circles proud to identify themselves with the Nazi clarion, the *Völkischer Beobachter*. Calling the Städtische Oper's action 'a slap in the face for German values', the paper pontificated:

> At a crucial moment like this a decision has been made to hand over the theatre to a composer who had the impudence to put before the German people works like the *Dreigroschenoper* and *The Rise and Fall of the City of Mahagonny*, quite apart from his other third-rate pieces. This

Jew was made to experience the uproar that the latter work caused in Leipzig, and that disgraceful piece of trash, the *Dreigroschenoper*, has been snubbed by everybody. It is incomprehensible how a composer who supplies such thoroughly un-German works can again have an opera performed in a theatre subsidised by German taxpayers' money.

But the public was not going to be bludgeoned. 'The immediate impression it made was so powerful,' wrote the critic Oskar Bie after the first performance, 'that the audience began to applaud even while the action was still continuing. And after Act Three the applause went on and on, bringing the whole cast back time and again to take their curtain calls.' *Die neue Zeit* in Berlin called it 'an unforgettable day in the history of music, when modern opera scored a victory which, after the many conspicuous failures of recent times, was like an act of deliverance.' Weill was struck by the ironical fact that the right-wing press, whose antagonism might have been taken for granted, actually found much to praise. 'I never did believe,' he told Universal, 'that it was only nationalist and anti-Semitic circles that stood in the way of the progress of the modern theatre, and now I believe it even less. The blame lies at least as much with the wishy-washy, spineless attitude of the liberals.'

Nevertheless political pressure succeeded in removing *Bürgschaft* from the stage of the Städtische Oper after only three performances. It also intimidated all but two – Wiesbaden and Düsseldorf – of the eight or so houses that had originally expressed interest in the work into beating an abject retreat. 'The coming months will decide,' Weill wrote to the Düsseldorf director Walter Iltz, 'whether Germany will continue to have anything resembling civilised theatre or not.' The answer quickly became clear.

For a time after *Die Bürgschaft* Weill considered a number of other projects to undertake with Neher, from pieces for choirs of the Workers' Musical Association (a genre which Hanns Eisler had made very much his own) to a chamber opera that could be performed in a small private hall and thus escape the spiteful eye of censorship. But nothing came of them, or of other plans – a folk opera based on *Romeo and Juliet*, another on *Uncle Tom's Cabin*, a musical treatment of Georg Kaiser's play *The Jewish Widow*, and a new type of piece on the Old Testament story of Naboth's Vineyard that he called a *Laienoper*, 'opera for amateurs', an adults' successor to *Jasager*.

A proposal arrived from an unexpected quarter when the impresario Erik Charell – remembered particularly as co-author of the hugely popular musical *White Horse Inn* – invited him to collaborate in a musical stage version of the famous silent film *The Cabinet of Dr Caligari*; but Charell's aims smacked too much of the ephemeral values of show business for the socially and politically conscious Weill of 1932.

More congenial was the thought of a work based on George Bernard Shaw's *Caesar and Cleopatra*, an idea mooted in correspondence later in the year.

Characteristically, Weill made no proprietary claims on Neher and was happy to see him engaged in fruitful collaboration with others. Rudolf Wagner-Régeny, who described Weill as 'a thoroughly kind and generous man, one of the simple and uncomplicated kind,' paid grateful tribute to his magnanimity: 'The finest proof of his unselfishness came when, after the first performance of *Bürgschaft*, he introduced me to Caspar Neher and gave me the encouragement that led Neher and myself to write four full-length works together.' Whether Weill was as 'simple and uncomplicated' as all that may be open to doubt, but Wagner-Régeny's sense of gratitude is not.

A few days before the Berlin opening of *Bürgschaft* Weill and Lenya moved into a modest two-storey house that he had bought, Wissmannstrasse (now Käthe-Kollwitz-Strasse) No. 7, in the prosperous wooded suburb of Kleinmachnow on the southwest edge of the city. 'The arrangements for moving kept us very busy,' Lenya wrote in an excited little note to her mother: 'we are moving in at the middle of March.' 'We' involved a third resident in the form of a large sheepdog called Harras, to whom they were both greatly attached. When Weill left Germany for France the following year and Lenya was no longer in the house, their maid took him to Paris where Weill looked after him for the rest of his time in Europe.

The relaxed, almost rural ambience of Kleinmachnow attracted the well-to-do middle class who, especially in these days of retrenchment, wanted to be free from the constant spectacle of the unemployed, the beggars, the prostitutes and the other embarrassing victims of economic recession who spilled over on to the streets of the city. It also became a popular area for the actors, writers and producers who worked at the UFA film studios in nearby Babelsberg. Marlene Dietrich and Curd Jürgens lived here, so did Arnold Schoenberg during his years at the Akademie der Künste.

In April Weill and Lenya travelled together to Vienna, where Lenya was to sing her inimitable Jenny in a truncated version of the *Mahagonny* opera, directed by Hans Heinsheimer, at the Raimund Theatre – so truncated, indeed, that it is remarkable that Weill permitted it. Critics and audiences received it enthusiastically, and for most of them the star of the show was Lotte Lenya, with her shameless eroticism and captivating vulgarity. 'She was working-class through and through,' said Heinsheimer, 'and never pretended to be anything else.'

For Lenya, however, the star of the show – and not only the show – was the handsome, fair-haired young man who sang opposite her as Jimmy Mahoney. 'I knew, when I saw the gleam in her eye,' said Heinsheimer, who did not miss much, to Lenya's biographer Donald Spoto, 'that there was trouble.' The 'trouble' was called Otto von Pasetti. He was the son of a colonel in the Austrian army, and for the next three years he was to be the man in Lenya's life. It was a relationship built on sex and gambling, and the couple quickly built up considerable debts in Monte Carlo, of which Lenya's share Weill, when asked by his wife, had the indulgence to meet. But there was to be more to the relationship than froth, for it was to be Pasetti who burst Lenya's emotional frustration and led her to take the impulsive step, two years later, of asking her husband for a divorce.

However, for the moment such unpleasant formalities did not cloud her bliss. After sparing a moment to visit her mother she left joyfully with her lover for the French Riviera as soon as the last of the *Mahagonny* performances was over. In the words she had just been singing to her Jimmy Mahoney on the stage, 'I know that there will never be a time like this again.'

Weill made his lonely way back to Kleinmachnow and to the search for new projects. 'I'm looking forward to the time when Lenya is old,' he said wistfully to a friend. 'Then she won't leave me any more.'

Well aware of the deteriorating political situation and the effects it was having on his career, Weill had shown something approaching contempt for managements which, after first appearing eager to put on his works, meekly caved in to threats of what would happen if they did so.

But the threats were real. Courage to resist, whether politically or culturally, was in short supply, not least because it endangered individuals' careers and livelihood. The director of the Brunswick theatre was dismissed by the Nazi Minister of Culture for not pursuing rigorously enough the interests of the 'German national spirit'. So was the director of the famous Nationaltheater in Weimar, in the province of Thuringia – which, in a cruel irony of history, elected the first Nazi provincial government in 1933 and celebrated the event by establishing the concentration camp of Buchenwald on a hill overlooking the town.

Weill too knew that the situation was closing in. In an unusually irritable tone he wrote to Heinsheimer telling him 'to seek out new contacts and new opportunities for performance, and create new markets abroad', instead of 'sitting around in Vienna, hanging your head in despair'. He urged him in particular to launch a publicity drive in America and declared his willingness to travel across the Atlantic immediately if prospects looked encouraging. And although, naturally, his eye was focused in the first place on his own interests, Universal, with its impressive list of contemporary composers – Delius, Mahler, Schoenberg, Bartók, Alban Berg, Janáček and many others – would itself stand to profit from such an exercise, as he was not slow to point out. Sadly, nothing came of the initiative. Had Emil Hertzka, managing director of Universal throughout the 1920s, not suddenly died, the firm's policy might have been different.

In the summer Weill took a vacation with the Nehers and their young son at a resort on the Baltic Sea, testing out with Caspar whether a libretto would emerge from any of the subjects in his mind. It did not. Neher put his literary services at the disposal of Wagner-Régeny, and Weill turned back, not for the last time, to his first love – Georg Kaiser.

Since providing Weill with the text of *The Tsar Has His Photograph Taken*, Kaiser had gained a new lease of literary life as a purveyor of comedy revue texts, signally in 1929 with *Two Neckties*. In a way, a work like this was an insult to Kaiser's talent but it helped pay the bills, which had shown little sign of becoming more modest over the years. If Kaiser were willing to collaborate, Weill told Universal, they would have to find some money for him 'up front'.

In 1932, however, Kaiser suddenly turned his back on these lightweight diversions and returned to 'serious' drama with an allegorical work in three acts called *Der Silbersee* ('The Silver Lake'). The allegory lies in its subtitle, 'A Winter's Tale', a title to evoke for a German readership associations less of Shakespeare than of Heine's *Germany: A Winter's Tale*, a mordant satire on conditions in a mid-nineteenth-century Germany held in the clutches of political reaction and tyranny. Subliminally preconditioned by this literary parallel, and living in a Germany itself slipping into an age of winter cold and darkness, Kaiser's public found themselves watching events in an ostensible fairy-tale world, unlocated in time or place, but in reality their own unmistakable place and own unmistakable time. *Der Silbersee* is an example of the kind of work which, by shrouding itself in a veil of literary fantasy, could escape the suspicious eye of the totalitarian censor not subtle or intelligent enough to convert allegorical motivation into realistic meaning.

Not that he survived much longer. After the Reichstag elections of March 1933 had left the National Socialist Party firmly in control of the nation's destiny, Kaiser, along with Franz Werfel, Jakob Wassermann and other Jews, was expelled from the Writers Congress and a ban was placed on performance and publication of his works. He worked with various proletarian underground organisations for a few years but in 1938, after having his house ransacked by the Gestapo, he took refuge in Switzerland, where he died, impoverished and a broken man, two months after the end of the Second World War.

The story that Kaiser tells in *Silbersee* takes place in the woods surrounding a lake, where a group of unemployed youths from the nearby city have set up camp. Starving and desperate, they rob a grocery store in the city but are intercepted by the police; Severin, their leader, is shot and wounded by Olim, one of the policemen, and taken to the prison hospital. Olim is filled with remorse and changes his report on the incident so as to imply Severin's innocence and ensure his release from jail. Then, having won a large sum of money in a lottery, Olim resigns from the police, buys a castle and devotes himself to looking after Severin there; at this stage Severin, who vows vengeance against the man who shot him, does not yet know that it was his protector.

As well as the two men there live in the castle two servants, Baron Laur and Frau von Luber, former members of the gentry, and Frau von Luber's niece Fennimore, who is used by her aunt to discover the relationship between Severin and Olim. Fennimore innocently reveals Olim's identity to Severin, who threatens to kill his benefactor. Frau von Luber, under the guise of helping Olim, gets him to sign over the castle to her and Laur, reckoning that Severin will carry out his threat. Fennimore brings about a reconciliation between the two men but as they can no longer stay in the castle, they are forced out into the forest and make to drown themselves in despair in the Silver Lake, which, though winter has now passed, is miraculously still frozen over. Fennimore, the voice of purity and idealism, tells them that the lake will sustain anyone who has the will and the strength to cross it. 'The hours of darkness will be swallowed up in the brightness of a new dawn,' proclaims the chorus, and the two men, joined in friendship, set out across the lake towards their new future of serenity and trust.

Much can be, and has been, read into the details of this odd, none-too-happy mélange of satirical realism and sentimental idealism. The strange, homosexual relationship between the victim of capitalist callousness and his new-reformed tormentor, like the disembodied, flesh-and-bloodless figure of Fennimore, leaves a curiously uneasy feeling. And to what are Fennimore's siren tones beckoning the two men on the other side of the lake? For Kaiser, looking out from his villa on the shore of Lake Peetz across the glistening expanse of ice before him towards the dark woods on the horizon, the symbolism of the scene was plain. But what kind of future awaits the two men?

Kaiser's text is not a libretto, and Weill's music is not an opera. *Silbersee* is a play with music – three hours of the former and a little over one hour of the latter. It consists of sixteen musical numbers, encompassing so many different styles and techniques that the score almost becomes a compendium of the stages through which Weill's musical development has passed in the ten years since his time with Busoni. At one end of the spectrum are recitatives and contrapuntal choruses in the 'serious' operatic idiom of *Bürgschaft*; at the other are flashes of the bitter-sweet sentimentality, the satirical tango-sexiness and the 'Cannon Song' roughness of *Dreigroschenoper*, while hardly a page of the score goes by without an appearance by two or three of the patented harmonic and rhythmic hallmarks of Weill's craft. We even meet again the joyful, crashing dissonances of the First Symphony.

To this extent, the episodic music, incidental and illustrative in character rather than the vehicle for a self-generated argument, *Silbersee* assigns its own limitations to its status. *Dreigroschenoper* shocked, overwhelmed, captivated by its brashness and impulsiveness; *Silbersee*, partly, to be sure, because of its more diffuse, more opaque text but also in purely musical terms, is a less compellingly cohesive experience and tells us little new about its composer.

Much of the shiny Berlin revue style has gone, and with it the brittle dance-band orchestration built into that style. There are no wailing saxophones, no plangent banjos, no whining harmoniums; only the ubiquitous piano is left to supplement a conventional orchestra of woodwind, horns, strings and percussion, with five principal singing parts, a handful of smaller vocal and speaking roles, and a mixed chorus. There is a greater mellowness, one might dare to say sincerity, in the songs that leaves those of *Dreigroschenoper* in a world of the past. This does not make them any better than their predecessors – some of the extended sections in triple measure, like that with Fennimore and the chorus which ends the work, become clogged in an embarrassing sentimental monotony before they finally drag themselves to a close. But it does establish a changed context, one that shows Weill on the move from the Berlin which had taught him his politics and nurtured the musical language in which he addressed the society in which he had been brought up, to the Broadway into which he was soon to find himself pitched and whose quite different expectations he adapted himself to meet.

The music for *Silbersee* occupied Weill from August to November 1932, and as befitted a work by a dramatist with the standing of Kaiser, the première had been set for Max Reinhardt's Deutsches Theater in Berlin the coming January. As the time approached, however, the management, all too aware of what Kaiser's text meant, got cold feet and reversed their decision. So, for the same reasons, did the Dresden opera. However, not all theatres were so servile, and in the end it proved possible to arrange simultaneous opening nights in Magdeburg, Erfurt and, of all places, the Altes Theater in Leipzig, scene of the *Mahagonny* scandal in 1930, where the loyal Gustav Brecher now again declared his willingness to put his reputation on the line.

At the end of the year, however, before these performances of *Silbersee* could be synchronised, Weill experienced a moment of triumph which the insidious pressure of politics had no power to dim. Active in Paris at this time was a chamber music society which called itself 'La Sérénade', a rather precious but strongly motivated group pledged to the promotion of new music. Among its members it counted musicians like Darius Milhaud, Francis Poulenc and Igor Markevitch, together with well-to-do patrons with both the will and the resources to provide a public forum where modern works could be heard. The two most prominent such benefactresses were the Vicomtesse Marie-Laure de Noailles née Bischoffsheim, and the American-born Princesse Edmond de Polignac.

At Milhaud's suggestion the committee of 'La Sérénade' decided to mount two concerts of music by Weill in December – first a private audition in the Vicomtesse de Noailles' salon, then a public performance in the Salle Gaveau the following evening. Two works were envisaged: the *Jasager*, for which a group of twenty-five schoolchildren would be brought especially from Berlin; and a version, prepared particularly for the occasion, of *Mahagonny*, consisting of the numbers of the original *Songspiel* with the addition of a few items from the full opera but without dialogue. This Paris *Mahagonny* was also given the following year in Rome and London.

Although the stage production of *L'opéra de quat' sous* in Paris in October 1930 had had a poor reception, the film was a great success and kept Weill's name in the public eye for months after its release the following year. 'Friends of mine who have just come back from Paris,' he wrote cheerfully to Universal at the end of 1931, 'have confirmed once more how popular my music is there. There is great demand for records and copies of my works and people are singing the "Mackie Messer Song" as they walk down the street.'

The Vicomtesse spared no expense. Weill was invited to Paris to oversee the occasion, Hans Curjel to supervise the production, Caspar Neher to do his boxing-ring set and the costumes, and Maurice Abravanel to conduct. Most important of all, perhaps, the singers of the composer's choice were imported as part of the occasion, led by Lenya, for whose primary benefit the numbers from the opera had been added. Also in the cast was her paramour of the moment, Otto von Pasetti. To coach one's wife as she sings to her lover in a brothel, with men queuing in the background for the girls' services, is a scene as ruefully ironical to us as it was perversely cruel to him. But the show had to go on.

And from all accounts it was a brilliant show, one that dazzled its new audience. Among the Vicomtesse de Noailles' invited guests at the private performance were figures not only from the world of music – Honegger, Auric, Stravinsky – but from the Parisian cultural scene as a whole. André Gide and Jean Cocteau were there, so were Picasso and Fernand Léger, while in the audience at the Salle Gaveau the following day was Le Corbusier, who sent a note to Weill the next morning to say how much he had enjoyed the music. Milhaud was lecturing in Holland at the time but predicted that Weill would take Paris by storm. 'Little did I realise how right I had been,' he wrote when he got back:

> The delirious enthusiasm that had greeted the works lasted for days. The Montparnasse clique put the concert to political use, interpreting it as an expression of the lethargy and pessimism of the age. Smart society, on the other hand, as I was told by one of the ladies present, was swept off its feet, as though hearing the first performance of a Bach Passion.

Nor was it only the music that swept Paris off its feet. The star of the occasion was Lotte Lenya, and the critics fell in love with her. 'As well as sureness of taste,' said Marcel Moré,

> she has supreme experience and that sincerity of feeling shared by all great German singers, together with a certain acidic quality. This makes her the irresistible interpreter of that music which belongs to the borderland between romanticism and music-hall. We have no-one like her in France.

A husband-and-wife success for a couple who were not to be husband and wife much longer. Lenya, indeed, seems to have first raised the question of divorce at this time, buoyed up by the emotional delights of her life with Pasetti and by this sudden new success in her professional career. And although full-bloodedly heterosexual, she now also rediscovered the lesbian attractions she had occasionally felt and explored in Berlin, attractions which Cocteau and his homosexual circle willingly helped her to gratify.

January 1933, a sinister month in German history, found Weill back in Kleinmachnow, following the preparations for the opening of *Silbersee* and discussing here and there the possibility of new ventures. The row over the Berlin *Mahagonny* did not prevent him from wondering whether Brecht might have a fruitful idea or two – few people succeeded in keeping themselves clear of Brecht for good, whether personally or professionally – but although Brecht put up a few semi-ideas, nothing coherent emerged. A letter to Universal – with the news, in passing, that he has crashed his car, though without personal injury – also mentions doing something with one or other of the immensely popular naturalistic stories by the mysterious writer who called himself B. Traven.

More to his liking was the prospect of a film on Hans Fallada's *Kleiner Mann – was nun?*, an enormously successful novel about life in post-war Berlin which had been published the previous year. Part of his settlement with Tobis-Warner after his court action over the *Dreigroschenoper* film consisted of the right to be involved in three future productions, and *Kleiner Mann – was nun?*, with its seedy, if sometimes sentimental realism but uncannily gripping depiction of lower-middle-class life in the age of mass unemployment, captured his imagination. With Berthold Viertel as director and Caspar Neher also on hand, he worked intensively on a script for a number of weeks but abandoned the idea soon afterwards, less for reasons arising from the subject matter and its adaption than for the uncertainties of a threatening political situation. Wendhausen's film of the novel made in Germany in 1933, with Viktor de Kowa and Hertha Thiele, shows the success that might have come Weill's way. But as Mr Peachum said, 'the conditions were not right'.

On January 30, 1933 Hitler was appointed Chancellor of Germany by President Hindenburg, old and senile, but only taking what his advisers told him was the one reasonable course. Torchlight processions wove their way through the streets of Berlin, cheering the advent of totalitarianism, the end of personal liberty, the destruction of the instruments of justice and the final collapse of the Weimar Republic. Government was no longer to be by the constitution and the rule of law but by Emergency Decree, which is to say, by the uncontrolled and uncontrollable will of the Führer. Anyone who had taken the trouble to look at *Mein Kampf* knew what to expect. But not enough had.

In the dark shadow of these events, two weeks after Hitler's enthronement, the three simultaneous premières of *Silbersee* were given in Leipzig, Magdeburg and Erfurt, the Leipzig performance being regarded as *primus inter pares* and the one which Weill attended in the company of Lenya and his parents. The Nazis had already threatened disruption, and on the very morning of the première Carl Goerdeler, mayor of the city, advised the director, Detlef Sierck (later, as Douglas Sirk, director of *Magnificent Obsession, Written on the Wind* and other Hollywood movies), to 'go sick' for a few weeks so that it could be postponed and the work allowed to slip out of the public's consciousness. Otherwise, Sierck wrote, 'if the situation became critical, Goerdeler said he would not be in a position to protect me'. Backed up by Kaiser, Weill and Neher, Sierck had no intention of grovelling in the face of this blackmail, and the première went ahead on the appointed evening. When Goerdeler was sentenced to death in 1944 for his part in the July plot to assassinate Hitler, there was no one in a position to protect him either.

But although Nazi rowdies booed and cat-called at the end of the Leipzig performance, they were drowned by the applause which called author, composer, director and conductor back on the stage time after time. At Magdeburg, however, where the production, rather than either Kaiser's text or Weill's music, carried the day, the evening was frequently disrupted, and the following night, in what the Nazis hailed as a triumphant victory for the 'Aryan' cause over the destructive forces of 'cultural Bolshevism', the performance had to be abandoned altogether. 'Herr Weill,' wrote the *Deutsche Bühnen-korrespondenz*, 'this will assuredly be the final chapter in your career of destruction and put an end to your activities once and for all.'

It did. *Silbersee* was the last work Weill composed in Germany and his last piece to be performed there until the National Socialist tyranny had been ground to dust.

Except for one ironical moment. In 1938, as part of what they called a 'National Festival', the Nazis mounted an exhibition of so-called 'Degenerate Music' – the music of Mendelssohn, Meyerbeer, Schoenberg, Mahler and other Jews, jazz, as the music of the 'subhuman' negro race, together with jazz-inspired works by modern composers, like Křenek's *Jonny spielt auf*, and anything else that could be perverted into an 'un-German' product. Weill, naturally, had his own privileged corner.

But the event backfired. By playing items from *Dreigroschenoper* to illustrate the 'decadence' of the jazz idiom, the organisers of the 'Festival' attracted crowds of admiring listeners. The prevailing reaction was not contempt but barely-concealed delight, coupled with resentment at having been deprived of this entertainment for the last five years.

On February 27, 1933 the Reichstag building went up in flames, set ablaze by a band of SA men at the instigation of Goebbels. Hitler accused the Communists, who, he claimed, were about to launch an uprising against the organised state. And who, at the time, could have said that it was not so? A better pretext for the suspension of personal and civil liberties and for the concentration of policy and power in one pair of hands, could not be imagined. The elections in March a few weeks later, when the National Socialists reduced the other parties to near-invisibility, proved what trust the people had in that pair of hands.

In the beginning it was above all the political opponents of Hitler who realised what this meant and packed their bags. Brecht left with his family for Czechoslovakia the day after the Reichstag fire. Klaus Mann went to France, Alfred Döblin to Switzerland, two of the substantial, tragically mistaken group of intellectuals who had convinced themselves that the Nazi nightmare would soon pass, and that it was therefore not worth while going too far from home. 'We'll just wait till the storm blows over,' said Döblin to his friends, as he set out for the border.

Back in 1929 Weill too had seen little reason to take the Nazis seriously. 'Neither Kurt nor I was worried about Hitler,' wrote his friend Felix Joachimson, recalling that year. A far greater source of danger, in their eyes, was Alfred Hugenberg, press baron, embodiment of monopoly capitalism and leader of the German Nationalist Party. But that was four years ago. They could not know that Hitler would ride to power on the back of people like Hugenberg.

The purging of Jews from the musical life of the nation was also well under way. In May Schoenberg was expelled from the Akademie der Künste and relieved of his master class, while Artur Schnabel and Carl Flesch were dismissed from the curatorium of the Mendelssohn-Bartholdy Foundation – Jews no longer welcome in a body that would not have existed but for Jews. Jewish members of state orchestras lost their jobs; the once influential Leo Kestenberg was dubbed the 'Jewish musical dictator' and fled first to Prague, later to Israel.

Those who stayed knew what to expect. Carl von Ossietsky, editor of the liberal weekly *Die Weltbühne* and winner of the Nobel Peace Prize in 1936, was arrested on the very night of the Reichstag fire; so too were the novelist Ludwig Renn and the poet Erich Mühsam, and in the coming weeks the same fate befell writers like Anna Seghers and Willy Bredel. The expressionist dramatist Ernst Toller and Erich Maria Remarque, world-famous author of the anti-war novel *All Quiet on the Western Front*, had seen what was coming and had already fled. Thomas Mann, who was abroad at the time of the Reichstag fire, was warned by friends of the consequences of going back, and to the end of his life trod the soil of Germany only as a visitor. The critic Hans Heinz Stuckenschmidt wrote in the journal *Modern Music* at the time:

> Cultural affairs in Germany are being forced daily into an ever more dangerous dependence on social and political forces. As is now well known, German cultural policy since the summer of 1932 has been to wage war on all vanguard tendencies, particularly on 'cultural bolshevism', today the favourite slogan to denote all progressive tendencies in modern art and science. Modern painting, whether by Van Gogh, Picasso or George Grosz; architecture with flat roofs; the literature of large cities; pacifist poetry; atonal music; jazz – all of these and more are 'culturally bolshevistic'. Whoever espouses them is the enemy of a divinely-ordered world.

Surrounded by this stark, inescapable reality, the object of increasingly virulent attacks by the Nazi propaganda machine, his livelihood, perhaps even his freedom, under threat from hysterical paranoids liable at any moment to career out of control, Weill took the only possible decision. He confided it to no one except his wife and the Nehers. Lenya's position was less clear-cut. Anti-Semitism, as embodied in the Nuremberg Laws, had not yet reached its full, institutionalised horror, and having a Jewish husband would not at this moment have automatically made her *persona non grata*. Unlike Brecht, Weill and Neher, she was not a direct creator of 'decadent art' but merely its interpreter, and to this extent no different from Trude Hesterberg, Rosa Valetti or any other cabaret performer or actress.

But for Weill himself there was no room for manoeuvre. Drawing the same conclusions from the Reichstag fire as Brecht, he made a few quick preparations which would not arouse the suspicion that something unusual was afoot. The villas in the leafy quietness of Kleinmachnow were a far cry from the anonymous bustle of city apartment blocks. People noticed when cars came and went, and the last thing he could afford was a conspicuous coming and going on the cobbled streets outside. Hans Curjel recalled that one night in March Weill and Lenya turned up at his Berlin flat with a large box of books, copies of revolutionary works that he had acquired from the days of the Novembergruppe onwards, some of them with personal dedications. He asked Curjel to store them for him until happier times returned. But 'generically' Curjel was also a 'Jewish left-wing intellectual' and no less at the mercy of the Nazis than Weill (later that year he escaped to Zurich). So having torn out the pages with the dedications, Curjel and Lenya put the books in the car, drove out through the Grunewald woods along the famous dead-straight carriageway called the Avus, and tossed the books out one by one into the bushes.

On March 21, the pompous so-called 'Day of Potsdam', when Hitler and Hindenburg publicly sealed the union of the old Prussian Reich of Bismarck with the new Third Reich of the National Socialists, Weill quietly packed a few personal belongings, including his musical 'work in progress'. From the suburb of Zehlendorf, a few minutes away, Caspar Neher and his wife Erika, as deeply in love with Weill as ever, drove up in their car, put his bags in the boot and set off for Paris. Lenya waved them goodbye and headed off for Otto von Pasetti.

It was not a moment too soon. Barely ten days afterwards, on April 1, a general boycott of Jewish shops was proclaimed, and six days later the removal of Jews from public office began. In May came the public burnings of Jewish literary and scientific books; and so on and so on, down to Belsen and Auschwitz.

Weill's letters from 1930 onwards had struck a tone of mingled anger and resignation whenever the subject turned to the political situation. He had been a sensitive observer of the political scene since his last years at school, when the senseless waste of human life in the Great War had helped to turn him and many of his generation towards the politics of the Left. One would expect this experience to have told him that revolutions which become tyrannies – as most do – are not given to vanishing overnight. Or did he believe, like Döblin, that the storm would soon pass and that before long he would be back in the 'little house', symbol of his success, where he had lived for barely a year?

History decided otherwise. He never saw the house, or his native Germany, again.

CHAPTER XII

'J'attends un navire':
Intermission in France

Weill and the Nehers crossed the border into France on March 22, 1933. He had hoped that they might emigrate with him, as much for personal reasons as for the artistic stimulus and encouragement which Neher unfailingly offered. But after a week or two with him in Paris they returned to Berlin. Whatever official disapproval attached to Neher for his left-wing associations, he was in no personal danger and over the coming years he navigated his way through the shoals of the Third Reich without coming to grief. He and Erika went back to visit Weill in Paris a number of times and were able to act as messengers and mediators in dealings with Lenya – personal dealings over the divorce on which she had now set her mind, and practical arrangements over the possessions that he had left in Kleinmachnow. Lenya was not petty-minded. Conscious of his tragic predicament, she was willing to help where she could, and the letters that passed between them bore no animosity. She even engaged the services of her lover's father, Colonel Florian von Pasetti, to get some of Weill's property sent to Paris.

The choice of Paris as a safe haven may well have been guided by his recent success there and by the hope that his friend Darius Milhaud would open more doors for him to the musical life of the French capital. He had become a typical Berlin intellectual, thoroughly German in formative background and in his chosen field of operation. Vienna or Prague would have felt culturally nearer, and both knew his work. Maybe he sensed, as many others did not, that politically speaking they were too near.

Paris was playing host to many German refugees, most of them intellectuals and artists whose presence their native country would not have tolerated much longer. Painters, sculptors and musicians may have reckoned on a degree of access to an audience in their new environment; but for poets, dramatists, journalists, all whose livelihood depended on the written word, the lines of communication had suddenly been snapped, their natural public – natural both linguistically and culturally – blocked off. Dependent on the good will of friends and colleagues, they sat around in groups in cafés on the Champs Elysées and in Montmartre, drinking endless cups of coffee and driving away the proprietors' regular clientèle. What had risen on a wave of altruistic sympathy foundered soon after on the rocks of economic reality and personal inconvenience.

Memories of the Great War, moreover, were not much more than a dozen years old. Elderly Frenchmen could remember the war of 1870 as well as that of 1914, and what increasingly seemed to many countries, including Britain, as the excessive harshness of the Treaty of Versailles represented for the French a bastion of protection against the thrustful tendencies of their dangerous neighbour across the Rhine. Even a strain of *Schadenfreude* crept into the situation, as they watched the Germans masochistically inflict on their own people the suffering formerly reserved for others.

After a few weeks in the Hôtel Splendide, near the Étoile, Weill was offered a suite in the town house of the Vicomte and Vicomtesse de Noailles on the Place des États-Unis, where he stayed throughout the summer. As sponsor of the performances of *Mahagonny* and *Jasager* the previous December, the Vicomtesse was his natural first hope for establishing himself in his new surroundings. Count Harry Kessler mentions in his diary a plan to put on Alban Berg's *Wozzeck* and the Kaiser-Weill *Silbersee* at the Théâtre des Champs-Elysées, with Klemperer conducting. And Weill had not come empty-handed for in the luggage that he had brought with him from Berlin was the draft of the first movement of a symphony commissioned by the Princesse de Polignac in the wake of the enthusiasm that had greeted his December concert.

But the generosity of his hosts could not disguise the fact that he was a refugee, with the uncertain economic and social status of the refugee. With his works virtually banned, Universal Edition in Vienna had lost performance royalties and were receiving next to nothing from the sale of sheet music. As at the beginning of his career, when he had signed his first contract, he had become once more a financial liability. So to lamentations over the economic situation and assurances of deep regret, they first proposed to pay him nothing at all for the next few months, then, when he threatened to sue them for breach of agreement, reluctantly agreed only to halve his monthly stipend from 1,000 to 500 marks from April onwards. Since he was resident abroad, his bank accounts in Berlin were frozen, and a plan to sell his investments to Universal and transfer the proceeds to Paris was frustrated when permission to export the money was refused. A final blow came when a production of the *Dreigroschenoper* at the Empire Theatre in New York, by which he had set great store, was taken off after a miserable twelve performances.

Then, out of the blue, came an exciting invitation which changed the depressing outlook overnight. A ballet company calling itself 'Les Ballets

1933' had recently been formed 'in an atmosphere of dedicated poverty', as they put it, by two young Russians, George Balanchine, one-time chief choreographer of Diaghilev's Ballets Russes, and Boris Kochno, formerly Diaghilev's personal assistant. As musical director they had engaged Maurice Abravanel, who had stayed in Paris after the Weill concert the previous December and was completely at his ease in a French-speaking environment. Like all fledgling enterprises, however, Les Ballets 1933 needed sponsorship to get itself off the ground.

Enter the extraordinary Edward James, extraordinary by virtue both of his immense wealth and of the causes to which he devoted it. Twenty-six years of age, at one time rumoured to be an illegitimate son of King Edward VII, James had inherited a huge fortune, part of which found its way over the years into the pockets of a variety of artists, writers and musicians he deemed worthy of support – Poulenc, Magritte, Salvador Dali, John Betjeman among others. In 1928 he saw the dancer Tilly Losch in the Noël Coward revue *This Year of Grace* at the London Pavilion and fell in love with her. The following year he pursued her to America and they were married in New York in 1931. That same year she appeared on Broadway with Fred and Adèle Astaire in *The Band Waggon*.

Back in England, Tilly ached for an artistic triumph in the theatre, and the only hope James had of keeping her affections was to buy it for her. He did so by acquiring Les Ballets 1933 and getting Balanchine to design a work in which she could star – 'one of the most grandiose bids a rich man ever made to recapture the wife he loved', observed a contemporary wag.

James had been in the audience at the Salle Gaveau for *Mahagonny* and *Jasager* and found the Brecht-Weill manner highly attractive. Equally attractive was the figure of Lotte Lenya. Musing on how the Brecht-Weill-Lenya constellation could be made to serve Tilly's ambitions, James conceived the idea of a stage work that would represent the divided nature of woman through two contrasted dancers, the one embodying the passionate side of her being, the other the practical. Abravanel introduced James to Weill and the two began to draft a scenario. Weill proposed that the split personality be conveyed, not by two dancers, but by a dancer and a singer; he suggested inviting Brecht, who was in Switzerland, to write a text and Neher to come from Berlin to do the sets. The old triumvirate would be in business again.

So emerged the 'spectacle in nine scenes', as Weill described it, part ballet, part *Songspiel* of *Mahagonny* provenance, called *Die sieben Todsünden* ('The Seven Deadly Sins'). It was put together over a few weeks in April and May and first performed as one of a group of six short ballets at the Théâtre des Champs-Elysées in June 1933. Unhappily for Edward James himself the event did not suffice to guarantee Tilly's fidelity, and later in the year, after a lip-smacking law suit on which the tabloid press feasted for weeks, they were divorced.

Taking his lead from the concept of a divided female personality and from the formal requirement that the action of the fable should be played out by two figures, a dancer and a singer, Brecht created the characters of two sisters, both named Anna, and sent them out on a series of adventures through America. Anna I, the storyteller and singer, speaks for the bourgeoisie, commenting on the actions and problems of her sister, Anna II, the dancer, who sets out to earn enough money to build a little house for the family back home in Louisiana. 'My sister is beautiful, I am practical,' sings Anna I. 'She is a little crazy but I have my head screwed on properly. We are not really two persons but one.'

The odyssey of the two Annas takes the ironic form of a sequence of seven 'stations', like the Stations of the Cross, stopovers in Memphis, Los Angeles, Philadelphia and so on where the sisters experience the seven mortal sins of the scholastic Christian tradition – Sloth, Pride, Anger, Gluttony, Lust, Covetousness and Envy. To each of these in turn Brecht devotes a partly narrative, partly reflective poetic text sung by Anna I and the four members of the family they have left behind.

But Brecht being Brecht, and the Marxist view of society being what it is, the apparent meaning of the parable is stood on its alienated head: the allegory is presented not as thesis but as dialectical antithesis, and to make his message clear, Brecht extended the title of the work to *Die Sieben Todsünden der Kleinbürger* ('. . . of the Petit-Bourgeoisie'). For Sloth, Pride and the rest are, in themselves, not vices but virtues – they are vices only to the petit-bourgeois mentality which has subjected itself to a pattern of values which rests solely on venality. Everything, and everybody, has its price, and it is wrong to refuse to do something for which payment has been offered. Refusal amounts to an offence against the established order; in fact, by being natural, 'being oneself', one constitutes a threat to this order. 'Think what would happen,' says Anna I to her sister at the end, 'if you did what you felt like doing.' In a society founded on capitalist exploitation one cannot survive and be good at the same time.

Anna II, the warm-hearted sister who works her way through the system in a number of seedy occupations, shows traces of 'normality' – 'real' Anger, 'real' Lust and so on – from time to time, but her *alter ego*'s watchful eye prevents the situation from getting out of hand, and after their seven-year pilgrimage through seven sins in seven cities, they have achieved what their anxious family and the system expected of them. They return to the little house by the Mississippi and the circle is complete.

To the nine sections of the dramatic text Weill wrote a line-by-line music, now sentimental, now sardonic, in the alienated manner the world has come to recognise as Brecht-Weill. The two men's rancorous separation at the time of the Berlin *Mahagonny* never quite had the grand gesture of finality that Brecht tried to give it. The context of that quarrel, moreover, was full-blown opera and their disagreements over the relative importance of text and music in that irritatingly hermaphroditic genre. In works of *Songspiel* derivation, thankfully, such troublesome issues of principle did not arise, and Weill could propose, and Brecht accept, a collaboration that fell within the terms of their tried and tested formula. But it was for the last time.

As well as the ballet roles – Anna II and a group of dancers – and the soprano role of Anna I, Weill, in a stroke of brilliance, created a quartet of male voices to represent the family back home as they greedily follow the news of the girls' sluttish progress from one city to another.

Unmistakably from the same workshop as the *Mahagonny Songspiel*, *Dreigroschenoper* and *Happy End*, the music of the *Seven Deadly Sins* is, despite its mocking, parodistic elements, less abrasive, less redolent of the atmosphere of the revue and cabaret world of Berlin. To a large extent the change derives from the instrumentation. Where the 'classic' Brecht-Weill product owed its musical atmosphere to a handful of dance-band individuals, the *Seven Deadly Sins*, like *Silbersee*, calls for full orchestra. There is a greater mellowness, fewer jagged outlines and staccato outbursts. Much of the harmonic subtlety is given to the orchestra to reveal, both in the choreographic sequences and in the accompaniments to the sung texts. The familiar march rhythms are there, the familiar tango, the familiar ostinatos and other details of his musical language. But beyond this there is a sustained sense of musical conviction not always present in his work, a richness of timbre that was to persist through the symphonic work that was also in his mind at the time. The Epilogue, sung and danced by the two Annas, with its hauntingly beautiful final cadence, must be among the most touching pages that he ever wrote.

This is perhaps the music in which the Weillian sentimentality, offset in *Dreigroschenoper* and *Mahagonny* by mockery and parody, edges forward to shift the centre of musical gravity, however subtly, from Berlin to Broadway. 'Weill has a warm heart and a first-class prosodic gift,' wrote Virgil Thomson from Paris at the time. 'The rest is moving enough, perhaps too moving. It smells of Hollywood.' Thomson had a prophetic sense of smell – though what he called the Hollywood aroma in Weill's music would be wafted on the Parisian air as early as the following year. Not that this justified affecting an air of snooty superiority: 'Let him who has never wept at the movies throw the first stone at Weill's tearful but elegant ditties,' challenged Thomson. In sum, and more seriously:

> Kurt Weill has done for Berlin what Charpentier did for Paris. He has
> dramatized its midinettes and their family life. He has touched hearts.
> He has almost created style. . . Its authenticity, plus the fact that it is
> all very easy to understand, is why it is so eagerly received by the Paris
> fashionables ever alert for a new kind of gutter.

But in general the 'Paris fashionables' who saw the Ballets 1933's mixed
bag of offerings could not do much with *The Seven Deadly Sins*. 'In spite
of Weill's popularity here,' wrote Count Harry Kessler in his diary, 'it had
a bad reception from both press and public.' '*C'est de la pourriture du
ballet*,' fumed Serge Lifar. An English version, with the same cast and the
same conductor, was put on at the Savoy Theatre in London a few weeks
later, under the title *Anna-Anna*, when the complete Paris programme
was repeated. Constant Lambert called it 'the most important work in
ballet form since *Les Noces* and *Parade*'. But the British public did not
see it that way, and the venture left Edward James almost £100,000 out
of pocket.

Beset by an irritating inability to get under the skin of Weill's ironical
yet very German music – irritating as much to themselves as to anyone
else – the London critics and their public were equally sceptical of the
Mahagonny (the Paris version of the previous year) which rounded off
Edward James' summer season at the Savoy Theatre. The sight of Lenya
and her seedy associates singing their unedifying ditties from inside a
boxing-ring gave them little pleasure. 'A note in the programme,' wrote
The Times icily, 'compared the music with that of Mozart and "Cole
Porter in his best moments". Owing to the lateness of the hour, we were
unable to wait for the Mozartian passages, after having heard, but not
understood, a great deal of very dreary stuff sung partly in German and
partly in English.'

Lenya had arrived in Paris for *The Seven Deadly Sins* in the predictable
company of Otto von Pasetti, who took one of the two tenor parts in the
male-voice Family quartet. On their way they had stopped in Berlin, where
Lenya attended to some of the practical matters left by Weill's sudden
departure, in particular to the sale of the empty house in Kleinmachnow
and some of its contents. As to what happened to the personal possessions
he had left there, in particular what must have been a considerable library
of books and scores, we can only speculate. No one of the family seems
to have intervened; Lenya, though willing to do what she could, had
other thoughts on her mind and would hardly have embarked on the
complicated business of shipping crates to France. Maybe the Nehers took
some things into their custody. We do not know. But with biographical
material still coming to light in unexpected circumstances, we yet may.

After the performances of *The Seven Deadly Sins* Weill spent a four-
week vacation with the Nehers on the Adriatic, in the course of which, in

Positano, he met his sister Ruth and her husband, who were waiting for a boat to take them from Naples to Palestine. The strain of recent weeks had brought on an attack of the psoriasis that plagued him throughout his life, his ideal remedy being to seek the healing power of relaxation by the sea.

On his return to Paris he met Marlene Dietrich, a fan of *Dreigroschenoper* from its earliest days, who invited him to write a song or two for her. One of these was to a text by the popular lyricist and novelist Erich Kästner, and another, it seems, to a poem by Jean Cocteau, but neither corresponded to what Dietrich had in mind and she did not accept them. Cocteau, who had had his interest in Weill's music whetted by *Mahagonny*, raised the possibility of a collaboration on the subject of Faust, but this idea too was stillborn. Nor did anything come of plans, conveyed the following year in a flurry of telegrams, that Josef von Sternberg should direct a film for Paramount starring Dietrich and with music by Weill. (Weill's financial demands, incidentally, were for a fee of 6,000 dollars plus 250 dollars per week expenses and his travel costs. What a contrast between this, the cost of a beginner's labour, and the 55,000 dollars paid to George Gershwin for the Fred Astaire–Ginger Rogers *Shall We Dance?* four years later!)

Weill's most substantial musical commitment during the latter half of 1933 was a very different proposition, one which, by his standards, it took him an unusually long time to finish. This was a new symphony, the finished first movement of which had been in his baggage when he fled from Germany.

As the performance of *Jasager* and *Mahagonny* in Paris had come about through the sponsorship of the Vicomtesse de Noailles, so this symphony – now known as No. 2 but called by Weill at the time No. 1, since his symphony of 1921 had been neither performed nor published – arose in response to a commission offered him by Winaretta Princesse de Polignac, eldest daughter of the sewing-machine millionaire Isaac Singer and widow of Prince Edmond de Polignac. The symphony that Weill gave her, the first purely instrumental work he had written for years, is an attractive, tuneful piece in three movements, with a slow introduction, scored for a conventional orchestra almost identical to that of his First Symphony. Its musical idiom is that of the works that led up to it, that is to say, it has the lyrical qualities (one critic compared his song-like themes to those of Mahler) and the direct harmonic appeal of *Silbersee* and *The Seven Deadly Sins*. The lucidity of the orchestral writing recalls the neo-Classicism of the 1920s, and the whole work has a frank entertainment value which gives it the character of a sinfonietta rather than a symphony. Less solemn and insistent than the Symphony No. 1, it sometimes seems to defer, voluntarily and naturally, to the Parisian world in and for which it was written.

It was in some ways an ironical moment. Here was Kurt Weill, once of the radical Novembergruppe, protagonist of the social responsibility of the artist, unshakeably associated in the public mind with Brecht and the cause of proletarian anti-capitalism, now becoming, like Heine a century earlier, the darling of a Paris salon and the purveyor of artistic goods bespoken by the privileged rich. Or, seen from the other side of the equation, here were the Princesse de Polignac and her 'fashionables' relishing their support of anti-aristocratic causes and artists. 'His aristocratic patrons were readier to hear his music than were the proletariat with whom he identified,' wrote a critic about Erik Satie, one such cherished *enfant terrible*. The audiences who had revelled in *Dreigroschenoper* had acted the same charade.

But perhaps the Princess got what she expected – symphonic echoes of the theatre music that so fascinated her. By the same token, critics looking in a work calling itself a symphony for a measure of 'symphonic thought' – maybe an arbitrary concept but a quality clearly to be 'felt' in contemporary works by Prokofiev, William Walton, Roy Harris, Shostakovich and others – considered that it did not deliver what one was entitled to expect. Reporting on the first performance for the *Musical Times*, Herbert Antcliffe expressed his disappointment: 'What promised to be an event of unusual interest petered out as the production of a work that, while pleasant and well-written as far as the orchestration is concerned, proved to be of no great consequence.'

That first performance was given in October 1934 by the Concert-gebouw Orchestra of Amsterdam, conducted by Bruno Walter, now also a refugee from Nazi Germany, whom Abravanel had interested in the work. The audience enjoyed it, and Weill was called on to the platform several times to acknowledge the applause. Walter too thought highly of the work and performed it again shortly afterwards in other Dutch cities and at Carnegie Hall, but without persuading orchestras to make it part of their repertoire. Like Antcliffe and other critics, Bruno Walter regretted that the 'remarkable popular tone, half ironic, half tragic, which constitutes the charm of the work' should ever, as he wrote to Weill, have led to the description of the piece as a symphony. For the New York performance he even temporarily changed the title, apparently with the composer's consent, to *Three Night Scenes*, after having tried in vain to get Weill to give it a fancy impressionistic name of his own. But the work is not programmatic. In the event the change of title did nothing to get it past the critics' opposition, and it remains the Symphony No. 2. It also remains a very attractive work, and it is not difficult to share the uncomplicated delight with which Weill wrote to Lenya after a rehearsal in Amsterdam: 'It is a good piece and sounds splendid.'

While still at work on the symphony, Weill left the town house of the Noailles and moved into the second floor of what had once been a servants' cottage, Place Ernest Dreux No. 9, in the grounds of Madame du Barry's chateau in Louveciennes on the western outskirts of Paris. This remained his home for the rest of his time in France. A new publishing agreement with Heugel in Paris led to commissions for chansons for the popular cabaret singer Lys Gauty; there was the support of the Princesse de Polignac; and he also made efforts to get some of his foreign royalties sent to France from Italy by, in effect, transferring his membership of the German performing rights society GEMA to its Italian counterpart. 'I am feeling very well,' he wrote to Universal, whom he continued to keep informed of his activities,

> and working very hard. I am doing the music for a dramatisation of *Marie Galante*, the well-known novel by Jacques Deval. I have also started work on an 'operetta', for which I am being provided with an excellent libretto [*Der Kuhhandel*, or *A Kingdom for a Cow*], and Reinhardt's American plans also seem to be coming to fruition [a reference to the Jewish epic pageant *Der Weg der Verheissung* (*The Eternal Road*)].

He had a number of works under way – he was never a man for one project at a time – with a place of his own in which to sit and work, and the quiet conviction that, his art would gain the critical and popular approval of his new public as it had back home. It was a situation with a quality of reassurance that could be counted providential for a man who less than a year ago had arrived in the French capital with a suitcase and less than half a reputation.

And with less than half a marriage: Lenya had already talked about divorce at the time of the Paris *Mahagonny*. Application to dissolve the marriage was made in June 1933, and the final decree was issued in September from Potsdam, the administrative centre to which Kleinmachnow belonged. Since the divorce was by mutual consent, the court costs, a mere 150 marks, were to be divided equally between the two parties, and a statement of these costs was sent to each of them at the Wissmannstrasse address. On one of her occasional visits to the house Lenya forwarded Weill's copy to Louveciennes but not before scribbling at the bottom of the page, 'I have the same and am not going to pay anything'.

A trivial detail, but it betrays the tone of frustration and bitterness, that had crept into Lenya's perception of their relationship. It was she, after all, who had forced the break, and she, in conventional parlance, who was the 'guilty party', so why should he bear the whole expense? And since she had no thought of marrying Pasetti or anyone else, and was happy to live under Weill's roof in Louveciennes, London and elsewhere before leaving Europe with him two years later, why did she seek a divorce at all? In any case they made no great public announcement of the step they had taken, and as with their marriage, the only ones they told were those in their inner circle. When Aufricht met them in Paris in 1935, he had no idea they were no longer married and simply wrote in his memoirs of his joy at seeing 'Kurt Weill and his wife Lotte Lenya' again.

It had been a complex, discrepant relationship from the beginning. Lenya went her way, Weill went his. Yet in a paradoxical, infuriating way they needed each other, and any attempt to deny or destroy this need brought dissatisfaction and unhappiness in its train – a kind of disturbance of the natural order of things. The note of petulance in the remark Lenya wrote on the divorce costs document soon passed. She sent him amicable postcards from Germany, Italy and wherever else her travels with Pasetti took her, and he listened patiently to her tales of woe over her sundry ailments and gambling debts. There was hardly any time, it seems, when he would not have welcomed her back with open arms. For her it was a wilful act for which, later, she never ceased to reproach herself. He offered her a stable, in part almost paternal relationship which with one subconscious part of her being she desperately needed but was reluctant to admit, while believing with another and highly conscious part of her being, that what she also needed was the exciting and passionate partner which he was not.

Professionally too it was a partnership that would never be dissolved. At the end of 1933 Lenya, Pasetti and Weill were all in Rome at the invitation of the Accademia di S. Cecilia for performances of the Paris *Mahagonny* and *Jasager*, in which the familiar partnership of Curjel, Neher and Maurice Abravanel was also involved.

Settled in his little stone house on the outskirts of Paris, Weill looked out on the spring of 1934 with a measure of confidence. A concert in the Salle Pleyel the previous autumn, at which Madeleine Grey sang three numbers from *Silbersee*, had been accompanied by pro-Fascist and anti-Semitic jeering instigated by the composer Florent Schmitt, which had shocked him at the time. But the cheers that greeted the songs drowned the sound of such passing unpleasantness. 'I am living a peaceful, tranquil life out here in this little house of mine,' he wrote to Universal, 'working continuously and with a feeling of ease and relaxation such as I have not known for a long time.'

Nor did he lose that tolerant willingness to help others for which Lenya, in particular, had cause to be grateful. In the course of one of their letters to him Universal mentioned the plight of Georg Schoenberg, the composer's son, who was ekeing out a pitiful existence in Paris: could Weill, they wondered, find him some copying work with a music publisher there? It would not be easy, he replied, but he would do what he could, which turned out to be enough to help young Georg Schoenberg survive.

He could do nothing, however, in response to a sad cry, almost a whimper, from a past that was slipping faster and faster away. The voice was that of Georg Kaiser in Grünheide, pleading for Weill to get him an invitation to America. 'Kurt Weill is a subject we never cease to talk about,' he writes. Depressed, unbalanced, he would dearly love to come to Louveciennes, he says, but he is afraid of dogs, and Weill has the shaggy Harras in his apartment. Even after Weill had left for America, Kaiser continued to cherish a hopeless vision of achieving fame and wealth in the New World through Weill's mediation.

Weill's time in Louveciennes following the completion of the Second Symphony was dominated by work on two projects – the operetta *Der Kuhhandel* (known in its English version as *A Kingdom for a Cow*) and the Old Testament drama *Der Weg der Verheissung* (*The Eternal Road*). The former, to a libretto given to him by Robert Vambery, Aufricht's dramaturge at the time of *Dreigroschenoper* in the Schiffbauerdamm Theatre, occupied him over two spells in 1934 and was completed at the end of the year.

The composition of *Der Weg der Verheissung*, an immense undertaking, requiring 'as much music as an opera', he said, was started in Louveciennes, continued in London and Salzburg, and finished at the end of 1935 in New York. The idea had originated with the American impresario Meyer Weisgal, who put it to Max Reinhardt with the proposal that the text be written by Franz Werfel; Reinhardt then suggested Weill for the music, and at a meeting in Venice in the summer of 1934 the three men discussed their strategy. Weill now determined to give this work precedence over all other. 'I have been working literally day and night on our project,' he wrote to Reinhardt at the beginning of October, 'with an enthusiasm such as I have not felt for a long while.'

But then, unexpectedly, this enthusiasm was forced to give way to claims from a different quarter. In February, under no particular pressure, as he thought, he had agreed to do the music for Jacques Deval's dramatisation of his recent novel *Marie Galante*, a melodramatic tale set in the murky world of violence, crime and sex in which Weill, thanks to Brecht, had spent much of his creative musical life. Now, just back from the excitement of his visit to Reinhardt, he received Deval's final book and lyrics accompanied by the information that the piece was scheduled for the Théâtre de Paris before the end of the year, to follow the run of Deval's popular romantic comedy *Tovarich*.

Artistically it had been an eminently resistible offer – commercially it was not. So, in the interests of solvency, he laid his other work aside and cobbled together the incidental music and the seven songs that the text called for, lightening the task by recycling some of the melodies he had used in the ill-fated *Happy End* five years earlier.

Not that they brought a commercial success much nearer in their new environment. Opening just before Christmas 1934, with a cast led by Florelle, the musical comedy star who had sung Polly in the French film version of *Dreigroschenoper*, *Marie Galante* lasted less than a week. Marc Blitzstein considered that a couple of the songs might 'pick up and have a career of their own in the music-halls', where a singer like Margo Lion, then appearing at 'Les Noctambules', could have helped them on their way. Heugel, Weill's new French publisher, issued the seven songs as a vocal album in the hope of arousing interest, but the response was lukewarm. The sentimentality of the melodies, free of the ironic overtones characteristic of his Berlin manner, has been seen as skilful adaptation to the spirit of the French popular music market. If it really does represent such an adaptation, it was not skilful enough to rescue the show. Nor could such a circumstance make any difference to the quality of the music as it is, any more than can the association of the maudlin theme-song 'J'attends un navire' with the French Resistance during the Second World War. 'About rock-bottom in melodic cheapness', reckoned Blitzstein, when he heard the song again the following year at a concert of Weill's music in New York. Fortunately, having invested only a modest amount of time and creative 'soul' in *Marie Galante*, Weill was able to ride its failure with relative composure.

Not that of *A Kingdom for a Cow* however. This operetta, as he styled it, started life as a satirical play by Robert Vambery called *Der Kuhhandel* ('Horse Trading'), in which a love-story of simple village folk on an imaginary Caribbean island is acted out against a cardboard political background. Vambery, now also a refugee, brought his play to Weill early in the year, and by May two-thirds of the music had been written.

Arranging a performance in a German-language milieu outside Germany, however, proved not so easy. Weill had hoped that his friend from Kroll Opera days, Hans Curjel, now director of the Corso Theatre in Zurich, might take it up. Curjel had engaged Lenya for a role in a popular operetta at the Corso later in the year, and also had the idea that Weill might get together with the surrealist painter Max Ernst, then living in Paris, to devise some kind of stage work. Instead, Ernst got together, in a different sense, with Lenya. It was a brief but intense affair, passionately chronicled in his letters to her, and no secret to Weill, who responded with his quiet, frequently required shrug of the shoulders. A Weill-Ernst collaboration never came about. And since Curjel considered that Weill was wasting his time on Vambery's operetta, nor did a performance of *Kuhhandel*.

Weill had become too engrossed in the work, however, to give up willingly. An introduction to the producer C. B. Cochran led to the suggestion that, in English translation, it might find a home in London, and from then onwards, under the title *A Kingdom for a Cow*, the talk was only of this English version, for which Weill had high hopes. 'Maybe I can be a new Offenbach,' he mused to Abravanel. It was not a casual comparison. Offenbach had always ranked high in Weill's esteem. At the time of his great successes in Berlin he had set him in the company of Bach, Mozart and Beethoven as an exponent of 'gestic' music, the highest and purest form of dramatic expression. Later he considered him, with Johann Strauss and Gilbert and Sullivan, to be triumphant proof that the best light music, often set to texts with a sharp socio-satirical edge, like *La vie parisienne* and *The Grand Duchess of Gérolstein*, could express artistic values second to none.

London theatregoers of 1934, who had just fallen for Noël Coward's *Bitter Sweet* and Jerome Kern's *Music in the Air*, not to mention revivals of dear old *Merrie England*, were hardly looking for a latter-day Offenbach. Nor was Vambery's heavily politicised story likely to cut much ice. So when Weill went to London in January 1935, he found himself under pressure to bring it closer to the form and spirit of musical comedy as the English understood it: otherwise, he was told, the work would stand no chance. An agreement was signed to produce the work in the summer at the Savoy Theatre, scene of the generally ill-received *Seven Deadly Sins* and *Mahagonny* two years earlier, and the home ground of the much loved D'Oyly Carte productions of Gilbert and Sullivan.

Over the following six months he made a number of trips from Paris to London, staying first in a West End hotel, then in Chelsea, and finally renting a flat in Earl's Court. Lenya later joined him here, although there was no part in the work for her. The Pasetti episode was now over, and the theme of her rondo-like life, her Kurt, was about to return. She could never live alone, so where else should she turn?

Weill set about making the concessions to English musical taste, or what he had gathered was English musical taste, which his backers urged. New English lyrics were supplied by Desmond Carter, who had contributed to some of Gershwin's shows of the 1920s, and as well as rewriting many of his original numbers in simpler and lighter vein, he re-used material from his recent *Marie Galante*. Of the two numbers that became known outside the show – 'As long as I love' and 'Two Hearts' (a waltz lifted note for note from *Marie Galante*) – one could say that they are no better and no worse than hundreds of others of their kind.

His efforts were of no avail. Popular singers like Jacqueline Francell and Webster Booth could not endear the hybrid work to the London public. Equally disappointed, for different reasons, were friends and admirers of his works from Berlin days, like the famous art-dealer Alfred Flechtheim, now living in exile in London, who could not fathom what had happened to the sparkling iconoclast of the *Dreigroschenoper*. The critics liked it no more, either its subject-matter or its musical content. 'It sank,' wrote one, 'under the weight of its own pretensions after a fortnight, taking Webster Booth, Jacqueline Francell, Vivienne Chatterton, some silly dogma and sub-standard music with it,' *The Times* saw it as

> hovering uneasily between comic opera, musical comedy with the inevitable shuffling of the whole company in ungainly mass movements, and extravaganza . . . The duet 'Goodbye, my love' of Juanita and Juan was slush – though it is certainly a matter of some difficulty to tell when sentimental music is satirizing itself and when it is being itself. Weill writes a particularly nauseous kind of jazz with every beat of a bar of common time made into a strong beat, and his waltzes are more sympy(!) than the old-fashioned kind.

Quite why Weill took this failure so much more to heart than that of *Marie Galante*, apart from the cumulative despondency of a second failure following hard on the heels of a first, can only be surmised. To be sure, in terms of intellectual substance there was more to engage his attention in Vambery's socio-political drama than in Deval's romantic adventure story, which he frankly saw from the beginning as a pot-boiler. It must also have been galling to be told that a decade earlier George Gershwin had swept the land of Gilbert and Sullivan off its feet in two successive years, first with *Primrose*, then with *Tell Me More*, for both of which – a further twist of the knife – Desmond Carter had written lyrics.

The modifications that he had made to his original conception of *Kuhhandel* for his English sponsors had changed the nature of the work in midstream. It had become half one thing and half another, the musical numbers assembled piecemeal and inserted in appropriate slots, an unhappy attempt to meet the expectations of a public he did not know. He must have felt that it was not 'of a piece' and could not stand comparison with works that sprang from a single-minded vision of an artistic goal. We can only hope that Curjel did not say: 'I told you so.'

Between 1935 and 1940 London had a film industry which ran Hollywood a good second, and Weill used his stay in the capital to visit Alexander Korda's studios at Denham in the hope of picking up a commission to do a score. Korda had attracted a sizeable foreign community of actors to Denham, many of them refugees, like Elisabeth Bergner, Conrad Veidt and Edward G. Robinson, who subsequently moved to Hollywood. Weill too had to wait until he got to Hollywood before the opportunity to write film music came his way.

Back in Louveciennes after his mauling at the hands of the English, Weill found still lying on his desk large sections of the Reinhardt-Werfel Jewish project which had now been on the stocks for over a year. The originator of this extravagant project was a larger-than-life character living on the other side of the Atlantic called Meyer W. Weisgal. Son of a chazan, Weisgal had emigrated to the United States from Poland as a boy at the turn of the century and devoted his entire life to the cause of Zionism, distinguishing himself by an extraordinary ability to raise money for the Zionist cause. He was obsessed with the history of the Jewish people, and at the Chicago World's Fair in 1933, as Hitler consolidated his anti-Semitic power on the other side of the world, he produced a three-hour pageant called *The Romance of a People* in which, before an open-air audience of 130,000 in Soldier Field, a huge cast of dancers, singers, actors and narrators unfurled the drama of Jewish history from Abraham to the rebuilding of Zion. The climax was a message from Chaim Weizmann, President of the World Zionist Organisation and later first President of the state of Israel.

Reading in the newspaper that the great director Max Reinhardt was among the thousands of Jewish artists and intellectuals forced to flee from Nazi Germany, Weisgal, as he told in his autobiography, impulsively sent a cable: 'To Max Reinhardt, Europe. If Hitler doesn't want you, I'll take you.' 'The cable never arrived,' Weisgal added, 'but the idea stayed with me' – the idea, that is, that Reinhardt would undertake a sequel to *The Romance of a People*, an act of Jewish cultural self-assertion to set against the barbarism sweeping through Germany. At the end of 1933 Weisgal had travelled to Paris, where Reinhardt was working, and put his proposition.

Reinhardt's dynamic career stretched back to the great days before the War of 1914–18 when he bought the Deutsches Theater in Berlin. Never out of the limelight for long, a man who dominated every situation in which he appeared, he remained a potent influence on German theatre in the years of the Weimar Republic, and his country estate of Schloss Leopoldskron, outside Salzburg – whose Festival he co-founded in 1920 – became half discussion-centre, half place of pilgrimage for a stream of visitors. He had no 'method', in the technical sense, but his trademarks were grandeur of format and the exuberance of a brilliant, fast-moving style. An example of the kind of large-scale challenge to which he rose was Vollmöller's *The Miracle*, a huge spectacular for over two thousand actors, musicians, dancers and others, part drama, part Catholic ritual, which he had produced in London in 1911 and later in New York.

The Eternal Road sounded to Reinhardt like a Jewish *Miracle*, something very much to his liking, and he welcomed Weisgal's proposal. With Werfel commissioned to prepare the dramatic text, and Weill the music, Weisgal returned to America well satisfied and set about organising the financial backing.

In May the following year, 1934, in a political atmosphere which could be defined by reference to a single event – the murder by the

Nazis of the Austrian chancellor Dollfuss in July – the four men had met at Schloss Leopoldskron. Werfel read his first draft of the drama, to general admiration. Here, as Weisgal described it,

> three of the best-known un-Jewish Jewish artists, gathered in the former residence of the Archbishop of Salzburg, in view of Berchtesgaden, Hitler's mountain chalet across the border in Bavaria, pledged themselves to give dramatic expression to the significance of the people they had forgotten about till Hitler came to power.

Had Weill forgotten about his people – until Hitler reminded him? The intense Jewishness of his upbringing had slipped away from him under the liberal, cosmopolitan pressures, material and intellectual, of life in the metropolis, where in the affairs of the mind and spirit the question of who was Jewish and who was not did not arise. There is nothing in Weill's music, from the First Symphony of 1921 to *Marie Galante* and *A Kingdom for a Cow*, that makes it the music of a Jewish composer, any more than there is in that of Mendelssohn or, for that matter, George Gershwin and Jerome Kern. Aaron Copland's jazz is not racially distinguishable from Constant Lambert's, or Milhaud's from Hindemith's. But Weill was not the only one to feel what Weisgal made explicit, and to rekindle a flame of loyalty to the people who were once again being spurned as a tribe of wandering outsiders.

Werfel, ten years older than Weill, an immensely accomplished and popular writer whose expressionist poetry had already gripped Weill's attention back in his schooldays, had his own struggles with his un-Jewishness. At the core of his being lay an intense religiosity, idealistic and universal in character, bound to no one faith or creed, coupled with a vision of a humane society governed by brotherly love and a passionate conviction in the goodness of man. As time went on a strain of subjective mysticism became more prominent within him, a mysticism that he might have identified with Chassidism but which, in the event, led him to Roman Catholicism. It was the same road as that trodden by Gustav Mahler whose widow, the formidable Alma, Werfel had married in 1929.

At the time of his collaboration with Weill and Reinhardt, Werfel was living in Austria; in 1938, just before the Anschluss, he left for France, then in 1940, always one step ahead of his pursuers, made his way via Spain and Portugal to the United States. Like Thomas and Heinrich Mann, Theodor Adorno, Schoenberg and many other refugee intellectuals and artists, he settled in California, where, famed above all for his novel *The Song of Bernadette*, he died in 1945.

Calling for a complex stage divided into five different levels, Werfel's drama depicts a Jewish congregation on the point of being driven out of their homeland. As they wait in their synagogue, the rabbi reads from the Scriptures, each passage merging into its dramatic enactment. At the end the congregation take to the road, like Abraham and Moses before them, singing Psalm 126 as they go: 'When the Lord turned again the captivity of Zion, we were like them that dream.' The work was undertaken, said Werfel, 'in order to praise God through His own words and to display to the world the divine plan that has been enjoined upon the people of Israel'. Or more succinctly, as he wrote to Weill: 'Our task is and remains to bring the entire Bible to life.'

To Werfel's broad, highly effective text, part prose (the synagogue scenes), part verse (the Biblical scenes), Weill brought a corresponding breadth of historical approach, writing to his parents to ask them to send him original Jewish chants for incorporation into the synagogue scenes and consulting sources of Hebrew music in the Bibliothèque Nationale. He had sketched over half the work by the time he broke off for *Kuhhandel* in November 1934, and went back to it after his return to Louveciennes from London the following summer.

Early on, according to Weisgal, 'there was a dispute between Werfel and Weill as to whether it was going to be a musical drama or a drama with music'. What emerged was a kind of staged oratorio – a dramatic pageant painted in flowing strokes, addressed to a mass audience commensurate with the Gargantuan production, using recitative, aria, song, chorus, with interposed orchestral episodes and spoken passages. The musical idiom is solidly diatonic and direct, not to say simplistic, again consonant with the aims of a piece of passionate ethno-religious propaganda. At the same time it remained axiomatic for Weill that his music would not simply illustrate, or even intensify, the dramatic text: rather, as he had always maintained, it should be an autonomous music with parity of importance, a vehicle of communication in its own right.

The public were going to have to wait some time to hear this music. The American composer Marc Blitzstein, then living in Paris, had a pre-audition of it and passed a typically provocative and inconsistent verdict:

> A private piano-performance of this work [*The Eternal Road*] indicates to me that it is Weill's best score, and also his most uneven. Weill has one theatre-attack ... The ghetto-ballads, the more severely-paced choral numbers, the hurries and the sharp, easy-rhythmed orchestral interludes, comprise his equipment; and he uses it all, and in the same way, for almost every work ... The questionable intelligence involved in using the same general style for the Middle-Western *Mahagonny* and the Old Testament *Road to Promise* [i.e. the original German *Weg der Verheissung*] evidently does not bother him.

As a comment on *The Eternal Road* this does not take one far. It does, however, lead into the heart of the phenomenon of Weill's music *an sich*. There is an unmistakable Weill musical accent, a Weill 'sound', identified in most people's minds with the *Dreigroschenoper* and the works surrounding it, down to *The Seven Deadly Sins*. But there had been signs in the last two years that this characteristic sound was becoming less characteristic, blander, almost more commonplace. There had been a flattening-out, a dulling of the cutting edge. The tensions and conflicts of the old Berlin environment had been the goad that drove him forwards. Take away these conflicts, remove the forces of opposition, and the *raison d'être* of the work evaporates. Paris was not Berlin. For reasons as much of survival as anything else Weill turned from confrontation to accommodation, to serving a market for which in Germany he had spent much of his time showing scorn. The cabaret songs for Lys Gauty and Marlene Dietrich, the sentimentalities of *Marie Galante*, the 'popular' musical-comedy-type melodies of *A Kingdom for a Cow* had all contrived to induce a soft-bellied sameness in his music which could hardly be kept out of the otherwise so different world of *The Eternal Road*.

Indeed, there are numbers in the religious pageant where the most solemn religious utterance is accompanied by music that might have been written for a mass-production Hollywood musical, and where his once penetrating march rhythms have given way to the flat, ponderous conventionalities of Salvation Army music. To sing 'May God reward me happiness or sorrow', from 'The Song of Ruth' in *The Eternal Road*, to a commonplace tune that might have escaped from musical comedy is to expose the non-differentiation of idiomatic levels about which Blitzstein waxes so sarcastic.

Weill was far too intelligent a musician not to know what he was doing, and far too alert for it to be put down to insouciance or weariness. He claimed to have studied the local market for which *The Eternal Road* was being prepared, and its reception was to bear him out. A lapse of taste? A lowering of sights? Or beyond this perhaps an early expression of that urge to accommodation and adaptability which was to become so strong in America.

When, after a long series of mishaps and disputes, *The Eternal Road* finally reached the stage, the work made the overwhelming impact on its audiences that Reinhardt and his colleagues had promised. But this is more a statement about the psychology of a particular ethnic minority in a particular place – New York – at a particular moment of tragedy in their history than a judgement of artistic quality. The majesty of the Biblical theme has not spawned a majestic artistic achievement, nor should it be expected to. The greatness of *Messiah* is Handel's, as that of *Elijah* – perhaps in Weill's mind at times, especially in its choral grandeur – is Mendelssohn's. It is not the Bible's. God may help those who help themselves. In *The Eternal Road* Weill did not help himself sufficiently, alas, for the Almighty's intervention to become operative.

During the time Weill was preoccupied with getting a hearing for *A Kingdom for a Cow* in London, Max Reinhardt had been in the United States, principally for a production of *A Midsummer Night's Dream* in the Hollywood Bowl and the film version that followed, but also to further the cause of *The Eternal Road*. His engagement of the flamboyant Norman Bel Geddes as designer reinforced his own taste for spectacle, and after his vision of a production in a big top set up in Central Park had been reluctantly discarded, he took over the Manhattan Opera House, the interior of which Bel Geddes proceeded to strip and completely rebuild for the purpose. Potential backers needed strong nerves. A typical reaction, wrote Weisgal, was to say 'Okay – Reinhardt is all right, and Weisgal may be bearable, but who could stand a combination of the two – not to mention Bel Geddes. Who's going to control this million-dollar baby?' The opening was optimistically scheduled for December.

With Werfel in Austria, Weill in Paris and Reinhardt flitting to and fro as opportunities beckoned, any kind of sustained collaboration was impossible, so it was decided that they must all assemble in New York. Weill had been looking forward to such an opportunity for some time, not least because he had long believed that Universal had been dragging their feet over the promotion of his works in America. So after a holiday in Yugoslavia, by the Adriatic, and final discussions with Reinhardt, Werfel and Weisgal at Schloss Leopoldskron, he eagerly prepared for the voyage.

A year, or even half a year earlier he would probably have expected to be travelling alone – less from his choice than from Lenya's. But slowly, right from the day of the final divorce decree, she had been realising that their separation did not 'feel right', that she had from him a quality of understanding and reassurance which no other man could give her. A year ago, in a fit of depression after returning from a painful errand to Berlin to deal with the sale of the house in Kleinmachnow, she had tried to commit suicide. Maurice Abravanel tells how she telephoned him in panic from a pension in Paris. When he rushed round to her room, he found her with bloodstained bandages wrapped round her wrists. She begged Abravanel, the Milhauds – who were fond of him but disliked her – and other friends to persuade Weill to take her back. As if he would ever have refused. In her impulsive, untutored way (a graphologist would have a field day with her handwriting), endearingly calling him 'Weillchen', throwing herself at his feet, she wrote imploringly to him during his stay in London: 'I will do anything, even housework. You can be completely independent. I won't disturb you at all.' It was the concession of the priorities he had gently laid down at the beginning of their life together, when she had complained of feeling neglected: 'But Lenya,' he had protested, aggrieved, 'you know you come right after my music.'

And now she was back, willingly, gratefully, in her old position, right after his music. He too felt gratitude, a gratitude born partly of the conviction that, for all its paradoxes, it was the 'right' condition of life, for him as for her, but partly also of a relief that this conviction had survived the tensions it had been made to endure. 'After ten years,' he wrote to her, a few weeks before relinquishing his home in Louveciennes and assembling his few possessions, 'you still give me things, essential things, that no one else can give me.'

On September 4, 1935 Weill and Lenya joined Meyer Weisgal aboard the *S.S. Majestic* in Cherbourg and arrived in New York six days later. They came as visitors, not as immigrants – he, as a collaborator in the production of a great musico-dramatic spectacle, cuttingly called by Feuchtwanger 'that Jewish-American Oberammergau'; she, as – well, simply as Mrs Kurt Weill, whatever her papers may have said. He arrived in the New World with an open mind. The longer he stayed, the more he understood why he had come.

CHAPTER XIII

The New World

When he landed in New York on September 10, 1935, Kurt Weill knew more about America than America knew about him. What he 'knew' was a mixture of fact and fiction, the characteristic bundle of assorted admirations, envies and suspicions carried in their minds by Europeans who had never been there. The unimaginable size of the place, with its limitless possibilities for expansion and self-advancement, and thus for the acquisition and exercise of power, held the European mind in thrall. Here was the world's richest country, where the streets were paved with gold and dollar bills grew on trees.

At the same time there was an intellectual resistance, almost opposition, to this cult of economic salvation, above all to the exportation of its values to Europe. 'Americanisation' became a fashionable term of abuse to Left and Right alike. Even Brecht could not escape the fascination of the place, with its skyscrapers, its king-size automobiles and technological wonders, its dazzling movies and its vibrant jazz. The Fords, the Rockefellers and the Vanderbilts may stand for America but so also do Charlie Chaplin and Louis Armstrong.

The stock market crash of 1929 dented the chromium-plated confidence in what had been held to 'make America great', and recovery from the depression was slow. At the beginning of 1932 there were 13 million unemployed, and no social security. Yet traditional trust in rugged individualism and self-help survived almost unscathed. Even Roosevelt's New Deal, seen by some at the time as a kind of creeping socialism, aimed in reality at the restoration of the free enterprise system by creating jobs for the unemployed and putting purchasing power back into the economy. Under such circumstances businessmen were looking longer and harder at whether it made sense to invest in theatre and the arts, especially if there were a dubious scent of something high-brow, or even middle-brow.

Against this background, as a measure within the framework of the New Deal, the Works Progress Administration had under its wing the Federal Theatre Project, a nationwide programme to create work for professional actors through the provision of what Harry Hopkins, President Roosevelt's assistant, called 'free, adult, uncensored theatre' for the public. In New York alone, where the dramatist Elmer Rice headed the board of administrators, Federal Theatre gave employment to over 5,000 actors in a repertoire of classics and modern plays, until the increasing politicisation of its policies attracted more and more resentment and led Congress to abolish the Project in 1939.

Weill knew that in America dog ate dog. The social world, no less than the natural world, was subject to the laws of Darwinism. But at this moment, having just walked down the gangway of the *Majestic*, he did not need to deal with this particular circumstance. He was not entering the country as an immigrant, like thousands of his fellow-countrymen, but had been invited to do a particular job of work, and no more: having done it, he would leave. The house at Louveciennes was still available to him. The confident expectation was that *The Eternal Road* would open around the end of the year.

Weill and Lenya found themselves royally accommodated at the Hotel St. Moritz, overlooking Central Park, surrounded by the dazzling lights, the frantic haste, all the sights and sounds they knew from the movies. Like Ravel, when he visited the city in 1928, they eagerly sought out the jazz clubs to hear in the flesh the instrumentalists and singers – Weill had a particular love of Sophie Tucker and Louis Armstrong – whose records they had collected in Europe. Language proved little of a problem. Weill had a foundation of school English from his *Realgymnasium* in Dessau and had survived for six months in London while getting the production of *A Kingdom for a Cow* off the ground, so he felt few inhibitions in an ethnic crucible like New York, where German English, or Polish English, or Russian English was sometimes more readily understood than English English. His natural adaptability stood him in good stead, and within a short time he was writing letters in English with a remarkable assurance.

Lenya had more difficulties. There was one particular experience she used to dine out on. 'I went to Saks Fifth Avenue and bought a sweater,' she related, 'and in my horrible English I asked the clerk: "Would you rape it for me?" "Sorry, miss," he answered, "but it isn't my type." '

New York had hardly been waiting anxiously for Weill's arrival – or Lenya's, for that matter. A production of *The Threepenny Opera* in English translation two years earlier had collapsed after twelve performances, and the film, like the gramophone recordings, was a minority interest. Avant-garde circles that did know his music, however, and had followed reports of his career in Europe greeted him warmly and had him invited to social gatherings to make contact with people from the world of music and theatre.

One such invitation took him to a party at the luxurious apartment of George Gershwin on 72nd Street, the sight of which must have taken the Weills' breath away and perhaps even nudged him to wonder whether he too might one day hold his own parties in such a place. Gershwin was a self-centred extrovert who held court in this huge, fourteen-room duplex with its art gallery, its gymnasium, its music studio and its host of living and dining rooms. The two men had met briefly in Berlin during the Gershwins' whistle-stop tour of Europe in 1928. Now Gershwin was able to tell Weill that he greatly enjoyed the recording of the *Threepenny Opera* – except, he added, not knowing the identity of the woman at Weill's side, for the 'squitchadicka' voice of the leading lady. Gershwin being Gershwin, Weill and Lenya could do little more than raise a wan smile.

Ira Gershwin, George's elder brother and writer of some of the most sparkling lyrics to come out of Broadway or Hollywood, was at the same party. With a degree of self-confidence remarkable in a man so new to the country and normally so reserved, Weill expressed to Ira the hope that they might work together some day. Ira was taken aback by this directness from a stranger, and in any case held the view that 'all collaborations are marriages of uncertain durability, stabilised even temporarily only with finesse'. How could he or anyone else know that his first major work after his brother's tragically early death, a mere eighteen months away, would be a Broadway musical with Kurt Weill? Weill's reward for his initiative was an invitation from Ira to join him at a rehearsal of *Porgy and Bess* which was due to open at the Alvin Theatre (now the John Simon Theatre) on October 10 – music which made a deep impression on him, the more intense for being experienced from within the culture in which it was born.

In the December after his arrival the American League of Composers arranged, as a corporate gesture of welcome, an 'Evening in Honor of Kurt Weill', to which they invited an audience of composers, critics and music publishers. The intention was twofold: on the one hand to present a selection of Weill's music for the theatre, an eight-year European retrospective to acquaint the New York cognoscenti with the range of his achievement down to the previous year's *Marie Galante* in Paris, and on the other, to provide an occasion for him to meet influential people in the musical establishment. Lenya sang numbers from *Mahagonny* and *Dreigroschenoper*, and a group of singers performed excerpts from these and later works, with a two-piano accompaniment. But even the hand-picked invités found that they could not stomach so much Weill at one sitting. Half of them made their apologies and left after the interval, and no one offered him anything more tangible than a smile and a valedictory 'Good Luck'.

This was soon to change. The change came in the person of Harold Clurman, a young theatrical director and one of the driving forces behind the organisation that called itself the Group Theatre.

Clurman had been an actor with the Theatre Guild, the prestigious body that did so much for serious drama in America after the end of the Great War with its productions of Shaw and Eugene O'Neill in particular. No American theatre organisation put on so many excellent plays. But by the end of the first post-war decade some of its younger members felt that it had lost much of its sense of missionary purpose. Clurman described it as 'symbolic of a Greenwich Village grown prosperous. They were destined to become an institution.'

The Depression shattered the nation's assumption that it was destined to march triumphantly and irresistibly towards a future that became rosier by the minute. Physical hardship and a crippling sense of anxiety penetrated the world of the stage like any other walk of life. In the 1929–30 season there had been 239 productions in New York; in 1930–31 there were 187. And such were the commercial uncertainties that by 1938–39, the physical effects of the Depression long shrugged off, the number dropped to 100. In 1931, in the immediate shadow of the Depression, Clurman and two fellow-actors from the Theatre Guild, Lee Strasberg and Cheryl Crawford, founded the Group Theatre in order to promote values of spiritual and moral renewal through a theatre committed to face the great humanitarian issues of the day and to help bring mankind closer together. They inevitably struck a left-wing political stance, which equally inevitably made them many enemies, but their enthusiasm for the cause sustained their optimism. 'Our heat would melt the city's ice', was Clurman's conviction. It was theatre in the service of life. 'The Group,' said a friend of Clurman's, 'is really a training-ground for citizenship.'

This sense of mission kept their spirits alive through the leanest of years. 'During the period of the Group Theatre's personal depression,' said Brooks Atkinson, doyen of New York theatre critics, 'most of the actors lived in a ten-room tenement on West 57th Street, for which they paid fifty dollars a month. Meals came out of a common fund; two of the actresses did the marketing, and a few of the men did the cooking. It was like a metropolitan kibbutz.' Among the penurious actors and actresses in this 57th Street tenement at one time or another who later achieved fame were Lee J. Cobb, Sylvia Sidney, John Garfield, Franchot Tone, Stella Adler (Harold Clurman's wife) and her brother Luther.

The Group Theatre's opening production in 1931 was Paul Green's study of Southern poverty and racial prejudice *The House of Connelly*, which met with the kind of success that proved triumphantly that there was a market for the serious play of ideas. At the beginning of 1935 the revolutionary *Waiting for Lefty*, by the leading contemporary dramatist of social protest, Clifford Odets, cut even more deeply into the American consciousness, and its six months on Broadway, together with *Awake and Sing!*, *Till the Day I Die* and his other plays, made Odets the darling of the American Left, as well as the financial salvation of the Group Theatre.

Waiting for Lefty had come off only a few weeks before Weill arrived in New York, and its ripples were still being felt. The direction of Weill's social and political sympathies was apparent enough to Clurman from *Dreigroschenoper* – a 'Group pastime', he called it – and whatever else he might have known of Weill's work. So when it was suggested that the Group might widen its activities by going into musical theatre, Clurman's path led immediately to Weill. One-hundred-per-cent American though he was, Clurman, a friend and fellow-student of Aaron Copland's, had studied in Paris during the same post-war years as Weill had spent with Busoni in Berlin, and brought a European dimension to his intellectual policies and judgements. Lee Strasberg and Cheryl Crawford agreed that Weill's involvement might add considerably to the Group's fortunes, although a musical would take them into unexplored territory.

'Short, thin, almost mousy,' Clurman found their new recruit, 'with a mouth pursed as though he were withholding some special secret. He might easily have passed unnoticed at a large gathering. He never wanted attention.' 'Copland remarked,' Clurman went on, 'that the enormously gifted Weill always reminded him of "the smartest boy in the class, the inconspicuous runt who receives the highest grades".'

'The smartest boy in the class' was smart enough to feel both flattered and challenged. A mere three or four months in his new country, known to the few, unknown to the many, he found himself being courted by a progressive and highly respected stage company. *The Eternal Road* had suffered another of its countless postponements, and he needed work. Early in 1936 Clurman was visiting with Paul Green in his home in Chapel Hill, North Carolina to talk about another play for the Group, and mentioned that Kurt Weill had appeared on the scene. Green showed interest in the idea of a piece of musical theatre, and a few weeks later Weill and Cheryl Crawford made their way to Chapel Hill to see what might emerge from a few days' discussions in the Carolina countryside.

Paul Green, six years Weill's senior, belonged to the drama faculty of the University of North Carolina but invested much of his emotional and spiritual energy in the writing of plays on the downtrodden Southern blacks. In 1927 he won the Pulitzer Prize for his play *In Abraham's Bosom*. An ardent patriot, in the deepest sense of the word, he found his values in his native soil and in all that constituted the spirituality of the people who lived on it – their legends, their ideals, their folklore, their history. For the presentation of these values he envisaged great open-air pageants which, in hill-side amphitheatres built especially for the purpose, should re-enact noble moments from the American past.

Cheryl Crawford travelled to North Carolina by car, Weill by train. 'Paul Green was always to remember this event vividly,' noted the writer Ronald Sanders, drawing on Green's own memories:

> He waited at the station for the appointed train, but Weill did not get off it when it arrived, and Green finally returned home in bewilderment. At last the telephone rang. It was Weill, calling from a remote farmhouse, to which he had wandered after getting off mistakenly at a siding that had not been used as a passenger stop for years. Green ascertained the spot, got into his car, and drove to it. The early North Carolina summer had already struck, and he found his prospective collaborator waiting outside in the hot sun, forlorn, bareheaded, and wearing a baggy suit that, as it turned out, was to be his sole attire for the rest of the summer. Green sensed that this was a man in some financial need but also admired his courage as he got into the car quietly and without complaint.

In the forefront of Green's mind was the idea of a play on the degradation and futility of war. A kind of American Wilfred Owen, Green had served with the American army in Europe during the Great War and not only brought home with him a personal experience of the brutality and dehumanisation of warfare but also knew the hollowness of the claim that it had been a war to make the world safe for democracy, a world 'fit for heroes to live in'. Thoughts of the victimisation of the common man and the inhumanity of war reminded Weill of earlier thoughts he had had of a musical dramatisation of *The Good Soldier Schweyk*. Carl Zuckmayer's *Der Hauptmann von Köpenick*, an immensely successful comic satire on authority and the cult of military trappings, also came into the conversation, together with Büchner's *Woyzeck*, harrowing drama of the sadism of army life and the abuse of the simple soldier. By the time Cheryl Crawford and Weill returned to New York, it had been agreed that Green would set to work on a play conveying their shared anti-war attitudes through the experiences of a semi-autobiographical American hero – anti-hero – in World War I.

That summer the Group Theatre took up residence, as was their custom, in an out-of-town resort where they could escape from the New York heat. This year they went to a summer camp at Nichols, Connecticut, trying out plays for new productions and meeting the cost of the rent by giving public performances. Weill and Lenya went with them, and Paul Green travelled up from Chapel Hill. Green supplied Weill with scenes and sections of his script as he completed them; Weill would study how music could be incorporated into them, make suggestions for changes on musical grounds, try out his first thoughts on the actors – who, like those in *Dreigroschenoper*, were not meant to be trained singers –

and slowly work his way towards a comprehensive image of the finished product. 'Kurt worked at his piano below my bedroom, so the songs were drilled into my head day and night,' wrote Cheryl Crawford. 'I also taught him to like applejack,' she added, 'the cheapest drink we could buy during Prohibition.'

He had found a task, and that was what mattered. He could not stand inactivity for long, and he was eager for success. He got hold of what background material he could in order to empathise with the common American view of the Great War – a very different view from those which he had experienced in his native Germany in the 1920s – then pooled with Green his own scepticism of military solutions and dislike of violence. 'We called the script *Johnny Johnson* after our hero,' wrote Cheryl Crawford, 'an ordinary, simple soldier who hated war and tried to stop it. The story was told in terms of vaudeville, fantasy and poetry.'

There is no mistaking the glow of well-being that was spreading over Weill's view of his situation, a well-being that he could not imagine enjoying anywhere else at that moment. 'As you see,' he wrote to Franz Werfel from the Group Theatre Summer Camp,

> I am still in America. I have been living in the countryside for some months, in a lovely area, and am working with Paul Green, one of America's best young dramatists, on a musical play which is to be performed in October by the Group Theatre. It is work that gives me a great deal of pleasure, as I am cooperating with enthusiastic young people and feel, for the first time in years, the ability to really create something.

Not only a tone of rising confidence but no longer any doubt as to where his future lay:

> The longer I am here, and the better I get to know the country, the more I like it. And at the moment there is certainly not much to attract anyone back to Europe.

The eponymous hero of *Johnny Johnson* is a young monumental mason living in a small town in the American south in April 1917, the month that the United States enters the war. He is for peace, while Minny Belle, the girl he loves, is for war, as is his rival for Minny's love, Anguish Howington. Hearing President Wilson declare that this will be 'a war to end war', Johnny changes his mind and enlists, hoping thereby to win Minny's love.

Act Two takes place in France, where Johnny is fighting in the trenches. He makes friends with a German soldier he has captured and releases him to spread the message of peace among the German troops but is hit by a bullet in the buttocks – hardly a mark of courage – and taken to hospital. Here he steals a cylinder of laughing gas from the medical stores, sneaks out of the hospital and makes his way to military headquarters, where he discharges the gas at a meeting of the Allied High Command. Laughing and happy, the Generals declare a cease-fire, which Johnny rushes off to declare to the jubilant front-line soldiers. But when the Generals recover, they order the fighting to go on; Johnny is arrested, shipped back to America and put into a mental hospital.

In the final act, set ten years later, Johnny is in a lunatic asylum called 'The House of Balm', where the inmates assume the roles of distinguished men of the past and discuss, with more humanity than politicians of the present, the issues confronting mankind. He is finally discharged from the asylum and becomes a hawker, selling toys from a tray. Minny Belle, who has since married Anguish, passes by with her son without a hint of recognition; peering at what Johnny has to sell, the boy loses interest when Johnny tells him that he does not, and will not, sell toy soldiers. Mother and son move away, leaving Johnny sad but not without hope for the future of the world – so long as men like him and the 'madmen' of the asylum still survive.

With the naive, almost childlike directness of its anti-war propaganda and the tear-jerking sentimentality of the love sub-plot of Johnny, Minny Belle and Anguish, Green's sprawling play is very much a child of its time. Its honesty reflects the moral concerns of liberal America against a glowering European background dominated by the Spanish Civil War and the seemingly inexorable onward march of Fascism. The very presence in their midst of men like Weill made it impossible to turn a blind eye to what was happening on the other side of the Atlantic – why, after all, were such men here at all?

Formally the play has a tendency to disintegrate into a series of episodes. Partly this is due to the huge size of the cast. But it also proceeds from an uncertainty in Green's mind – and, indeed, in Weill's and in that of Lee Strasberg, who directed the production – about what kind of 'mix' of drama and music their end-product should contain. At times *Johnny Johnson* is a musical: the talking stops, leaving a character to reflect on the situation, to lay bare his heart in a song, the functional equivalent of the operatic aria. At other times it is a play with incidental music, as for a film, superimposed on the action in order to raise the dramatic temperature and intensify the emotional reflexes of the audience. An unevenness hangs over the work, paralleled by the patchwork of open influences lying on the surface – Büchner's *Woyzeck* in Johnny's enlistment scene, Zuckmayer's *Hauptmann von Köpenick* in his brief assumption of power with his cylinder of laughing gas, Johnny as an American 'good soldier' Schweyk.

Musically too *Johnny Johnson* has something of the collage about it – bits of the old and bits of the new lying side by side, an in-between work. The 'Song of the Liquor Merchant' from *Happy End* is pressed into service as the opening theme of the instrumental Introduction; the old 'Bilbao Song' from *Happy End* provides the opening of 'Mon ami, my friend', and the predictable Weillian tango of European days is also here. Above all the orchestral 'sound', to the extent that it derives from woodwind and brass, still has the hard, gritty feel of that created in the Schiffbauerdamm Theatre. To the here-and-now of America in 1936, on the other hand, belongs a pop-song sentimentality far from the ironic, tongue-in-cheek sentimentality of *Dreigroschenoper*, heightened by the use of a handful of strings and the synthetic lamentations of the recently invented Hammond organ.

This bilingualism, so to speak, makes *Johnny Johnson* a revealing piece. For the known, instantly recognisable European Weill and the new, emerging American Weill do not share a free, random side-by-side existence but occupy their own individual areas of expression. In the numbers concerned with the events of war and the historical background, whether sombre in treatment or satirical, the Weill of old is at his striking and powerful best – though he does not stay as long as we might wish. The lyrical numbers that carry the personal relationships, on the other hand, show how far the fuzzy hit-parade flaccidity of his new environment has encroached on the scene. As the motto of the *Bürgschaft* has it: 'Man does not change: it is circumstances that change man's attitudes.'

As Weill told Werfel in connection with *The Eternal Road*, from the moment of his arrival in the United States he had investigated what the American public needed and would accept – a kind of musical market research. He was not always right. But successes like *Knickerbocker Holiday*, *Lady in the Dark* and *One Touch of Venus* were to show with what uncanny skill he could pitch the appeal of his works and, as a total outsider, take his place alongside the Gershwins, the Kerns, the Rodgers and the others for whom Broadway was their birthright.

Johnny Johnson suffered a few depressing previews – depressing because the 44th Street Theatre was too big for the production, because the cast, which included Morris Carnovsky, John Garfield and Lee J. Cobb, had difficulty making themselves heard, especially in the songs, and because the longer the performance went on, the more determined the exodus from the auditorium became. 'The panic that ensues on an occasion like this has nothing to do with art,' Harold Clurman wrote. 'It is hysteria that combines the fear and shame of economic ruin with the humiliation attendant on a blow to one's pride. We had had such a hard time getting this play on the boards; and now – this!' In order to condense the production, many of the musical numbers were cut but still the Group's admirers begged them not to open.

When the first night came in November 1936, Messrs Clurman, Strasberg and Crawford were 'flabbergasted'. Wild applause greeted the piece. 'The first imaginative and exciting entry in a season of old, dead-tired waxworks,' cried Robert Benchley in the *New Yorker*. But most critics wrote the kind of polite, approving reviews that keep people away. Brooks Atkinson called it 'a sincere and generally exalting attempt to put on the stage an imaginative portrait of recent history' – fine words that butter no parsnips and sell no tickets. 'Admired but not liked', he concluded. It was an expensive production to run and it closed after nine weeks. But it brought Weill friends and contacts – and a modest financial reward. 'At all events,' he wrote to his brother Hanns, who was still in Germany, 'it is a wonderful thing for me to have such a fantastic reputation here and to be able at last to do something about my disastrous financial situation.' There could have been worse debuts for a stranger in an alien land.

After returning from the Group Theatre summer camp in September, Weill and Lenya had left their residential hotel on Riverside Drive and joined Cheryl Crawford and her friend, the actress Dorothy Patten, in a shared apartment on East 51st Street, which became their home for the next twelve months. Shortly after the opening of *Johnny Johnson* a further and – to general incredulity – genuinely final date was set for the première of *The Eternal Road* at the beginning of January 1937. Apart from extending the stage to the very roof and sides of the theatre, and ripping out row upon row of seats in the orchestra stalls to make room for his mammoth sets, Norman Bel Geddes had recently drilled down through the foundations of the building and perforated the water mains, flooding the theatre and putting rehearsals back still further. Moses may have smitten the rock at Meribah for the water to gush forth but, as one wit observed, Bel Geddes was no slouch either. The road to the opening of the show had indeed been eternal.

But the moment of arrival was overwhelming. 'Everything was on a colossal scale,' wrote Brooks Atkinson, with the faintest of indulgent smiles:

> The cast included forty-three principal actors and singers. The scenery represented not only the earth, where Moses morosely trudged across sand dunes, but also a modern synagogue on the lower level, with heaven above, where a choir of angels burst into song in the blue empyrean . . . Max Reinhardt and his many assistants have evoked a glorious pageant of great power and beauty.

As well as the forty-three principals that Atkinson counted – among them Lenya in the two not overly important roles of Moses' sister Miriam and the Witch of Endor – the cast included sixty dancers, a large chorus and over a hundred extras, all working to a remarkable English translation of Werfel's text by Ludwig Lewisohn.

In the event these 'heavenly lengths' proved incompatible with the demands of life in the everyday world. The opening performance did not finish until three in the morning. To meet their deadline for their reviews in the next day's papers, the critics had to leave at the end of the second act. Many of the general public too found that seven hours of epic pageant exceeded their powers of concentration – Wagner's demands seemed modest by comparison – and from the second performance onwards the last two acts were quietly discarded.

To Weill's considerable annoyance. All along he had had to struggle with Werfel, and to an equal extent with Reinhardt, to preserve the conceptual integrity of his music, a music deployed not as a series of illustrative episodes but as a symphonically planned structure with its own inner dialectic of stasis and kinesis, tranquillity and tension. His musical climaxes, as he put it in a letter to Reinhardt, stand as 'highly integrated musical structures which cannot be meddled with – unless one is going to utterly destroy them'. A third of his music, he protests, has already been cut, and he concludes: 'In the course of my own development I have observed that when I have let people destroy the form of my works, the result has invariably been failure.'

Werfel, as he never tired of pointing out, had made many cuts in his text to prevent the work from becoming unmanageably long, and he saw no reason why the music, by its nature an agent of deliberation and protraction, should not make its own sacrifices. 'Why all the scenery, why all the music?' he complained. Perhaps it is just as well that he did not wait long enough in New York to see what the producers had done to his original *Weg der Verheissung* by the time its English version reached the boards – though this did little to pacify the much-abused Weill.

In obedience to the demands of the labour unions a handful of musicians performed live from a perilous position high in the flies, but since Bel Geddes' Gargantuan set left no room for a full orchestra, the music was pre-recorded – at a cost of 100,000 dollars – and relayed through loudspeakers. Weill had used pre-recorded music in his *Zar* and *Bürgschaft*, and saw the technical advantages of a recording, definitive and unchanging in form, over the vicissitudes of successive live performances. At the same time he had misgivings about how the conductor – Isaac Van Grove, who had composed and conducted the music for *The Romance of a People* at the Chicago World's Fair in 1933 – could weld the live singing of soloists and chorus to the mechanically produced orchestral sound. Reassurances from Leopold Stokowski, a man of experience in these matters, set his mind at rest.

After a stuttering start *The Eternal Road* picked up and began to play to full houses. Yet even this could not recoup the initial outlay. A week's full houses brought in 24,000 dollars, the weekly operating costs amounted to

30,000 dollars, and Weisgal was still desperately searching for sponsors weeks after the show had opened. He laid the bulk of the responsibility at the door of the labour unions for their policies of consistent overmanning – a dozen stage hands would have been sufficient, he insisted, whereas the unions held out for forty-eight. So in May, after a little over four months, it closed. 'The fools were not capable of exploiting its huge success', Weill wrote to his brother. 'I didn't earn a cent.'

Weill was the last person on whom the closure could be blamed, and as he put it to Dr Kalmus of Universal Edition, in a piece of delicate understatement, although *The Eternal Road* 'had not been the financial hit people had been hoping for, it was a resounding success for me personally.' For a few weeks, indeed, he had two shows running simultaneously in New York – and this only a little over a year after arriving in the country.

As an achievement in assimilation, it would be hard to better. There was nothing fortuitous about it. On an NBC radio programme some years later he said that he and Lenya had made a resolve

> to speak nothing but English when we arrived. So many foreign-born use their native language in their homes and among their friends. I used to ask my German friends: 'How can you ever become Americans if you still cling to the language and customs of a country that has become the most un-American country in the world?'

Perhaps it expressed the centripetal influence of a shared exile which was becoming a shared adventure and a shared stimulus. Perhaps it represented the final, official dawn of the reality that, for complex and divergent reasons, and despite the corrosive strains under which their relationship laboured, he needed her and she needed him. Perhaps, given the circumstances in which they found themselves, it simply seemed the 'right' thing to do. Whatever... On January 19, 1937, before Justice of the Peace Julius A. Raven at North Castle, Westchester County, New York, Kurt Julian Weill of New York City and 'Charlotte Blamauer Weill of Paris, France' were remarried.

It was a symbolic act, a reflection of the way they wanted things to be. It changed nothing, nor did it impose any new conditions or responsibilities. Lenya's restless craving for other men – and, be it said, their eagerness to reciprocate – was not to be quenched by a signature on a piece of paper. But that piece of paper gave her a sense of assurance in the face of her inner insecurities, insecurities made the more disturbing by the pressures of a new environment and a new language, and especially by the implication that her prospects for an independent career in the American theatre at that moment were near zero.

He, for his part, knew that the woman he was remarrying in 1937 was the same woman, emotionally and psychologically, as he had married in 1926. Her needs for human company were doubtless greater than his. Yet in his gentle, tolerant way he enjoyed being needed – and there was no one, male or female, to whom he was so close. As for *his* freedom of association, as one might euphemistically call it, on the many occasions when his work was to take him to Hollywood, he was happy to follow the customs of the theatrical and film world and accept the favours offered to him, as a man of influence and importance, by aspiring young starlets. He may not have been the director but he did have a couch.

The second wedding of Weill and Lenya, like the first in Berlin, had something casual, incidental about it. There was no formal reception, no fanfare of trumpets – few, indeed, would have doubted that they were married when they arrived in America. And hardly had they made their solemn commitment to each other than they parted company. Lenya went back the same evening to the Manhattan Opera House and her roles in *The Eternal Road*. Weill set out for Los Angeles on his first excursion into films.

Whether serving the world of 'light entertainment' or writing primarily for opera house and concert hall, many composers cast an occasional, sometimes more than occasional eye in the direction of Hollywood, as the movie industry continued its triumphant march through the 1930s. Specialists emerged to service the romances and adventure stories that formed the staple diet of the studios, but there were also producers who thought to lend a special cachet to a film by commissioning a score from a 'serious' composer. Native American composers such as Aaron Copland, Virgil Thomson and George Antheil were among those approached, to be joined by distinguished Europeans who were to make their home in America during the years leading up to the Second World War – Stravinsky, Milhaud, Schoenberg, Hanns Eisler, Ernst Toch, Paul Dessau and others. From the opposite end of the musical spectrum came émigrés like Friedrich Holländer, of *Blue Angel* fame, and Emmerich Kálmán, composer of numerous Austro-Hungarian operettas and a masterly orchestrator, whose wares found a ready market in their new environment.

While a large proportion of the European emigrants stayed in New York, where most of them had landed, a substantial colony grew up in Southern California. By the time the United States entered the war Thomas Mann and his brother Heinrich, Brecht, Lion Feuchtwanger, Franz Werfel, Alfred Döblin, Walter Mehring and many lesser writers were established in the Los Angeles area, often directly attracted there by the prospect of writing film scripts. The problems of language often proved difficult to surmount, and the famous weekly 100-dollar cheques paid to emigré writers by Warner Brothers, Metro-Goldwyn-Mayer and other companies had the character of largesse rather than of a commercially-earned fee. Designers, composers and even directors, whose fields of activity were not based, in a narrow sense, on language, found it easier to become absorbed into the film world. Fritz Lang, with famous German films of the 1920s like *Metropolis* and *The Testament of Dr Mabuse* to his name, had been in America since 1934. Josef von Sternberg had come as early as 1927, returning to Berlin in 1930 to make *The Blue Angel* with Emil Jannings, and bringing back with him to Hollywood his European 'discovery', Marlene Dietrich. Billy Wilder arrived in 1934, Max Reinhardt had had a workshop in Hollywood since he made his permanent home there in 1938, while among the ranks of the actors Peter Lorre, a favourite of Brecht's, had been there since the early 1930s, soon to be joined by Curt Bois, Elisabeth Bergner, Oscar Homolka, Lilian Harvey and others who succeeded in overcoming the language barrier.

Although his foray into the world of Hollywood was no less speculative than that of most others, Weill did at least have the advantage of not being made to start from scratch. He had had a year in which to acclimatise himself to the American atmosphere, both materially and spiritually, and he had got his foot inside the theatrical door. Nor was he going to Hollywood unannounced. The producer Walter Wanger had arranged with the Group Theatre to have the services of a number of their members – Franchot Tone, then married to Joan Crawford, was one of them – who could be spared from their work in New York. On the one hand this gave employment to actors who, as the Group's affairs stood, were not exactly suffering from a surfeit of successful work; on the other, it gave Harold Clurman the opportunity to extend the name and influence of the Group to the film world, proposing, to ears more often deaf than receptive, that film versions be made of their productions and also, with rather greater success, that some of their authors be engaged as script-writers.

So when Weill arrived in Hollywood to find Clifford Odets, remuneratively relaxing from the class struggle on Broadway, and the director Lewis Milestone at work together on a screenplay, with Clurman assisting in the production and a contract for the music awaiting his signature, he looked, as the expression goes, to 'have it made'. The Odets-Milestone plan was for an adaptation of Ilya Ehrenburg's *The Love of Jeanne Ney*. Ehrenburg's novel is set in the time of the Russian Revolution and tells of the love between a Soviet agent in Paris and a young French girl. Odets and Milestone had the idea of bringing the action forward by twenty years and locating it in present-day Spain, where Fascists and anti-Fascists were at each other's throats in the Civil War. Here, it seemed, Weill had a firm base from which to win himself a part of the Hollywood action.

Then there was the prospect of working with Max Reinhardt again. Reinhardt's production of *Everyman*, Hugo von Hofmannsthal's version of the English medieval morality play, had acquired institutional status in Europe since its regular performance in the cathedral square at the Salzburg Festival. Still attracted by the subject and by the possibility of repeating an open-air staging, Reinhardt turned his mind to a new American *Everyman*, either as drama or as film, or both, the text to be written by that very American apostle of outdoor theatre, Paul Green, and the music to be composed by Weill.

Lastly, a plan for another musical emerged from a chance encounter at one of the Gershwins' Saturday night parties in Beverly Hills. The Gershwins were at work on *Shall We Dance?*, with Fred Astaire and Ginger Rogers, George having decided the previous year that he needed a lucrative Hollywood contract or two in order to finance his extravagant bachelor life-style. In the large house on North Roxbury Drive Weill was introduced to the husband-and-wife team of Samuel and Bella Spewack – witty authors of the Hollywood spoof *Boy Meets Girl* and later of the Cole Porter musical *Kiss Me, Kate* – and to E. Y. Harburg, the socially critical lyricist who had written the pop-music theme-song of the Depression, 'Brother, Can You Spare A Dime?'. Weill quickly found common ground with Harburg and the Spewacks, and over the following months they put together a storyline, while Harburg tossed off a handful of lyrics and Weill sketched a few musical numbers. They then went in search of backers for a Broadway production later in the year.

Alas, none of these projects saw the light of day. The Reinhardt *Everyman* got nowhere. An interesting sign of the times – though it brought the realisation of the idea no closer – had been Green's proposal to mount it with an all-black cast. Maybe *Porgy and Bess* had something to do with it. There was also talk of a negro *Johnny Johnson* for the Federal Theatre Project in Chicago.

But in an animated theatrical environment earnest propositions could easily be confused with casual enthusiasms. Weill's letters and private memoranda contain a bewildering wealth of names and works which were thrown up at one time or another in the tireless search for material, works which often clustered around certain focal areas of interest – the Old Testament (Naboth's Vineyard, Job, Susanne and the Elders), French literature (Zola, *Candide*, André Maurois, Froissart), America (the Revolution, Davy Crockett, O. Henry, Mark Twain, Poe), Kipling, Kleist, The Arabian Nights, Julius Caesar etc.

The musical play with the Spewacks and Harburg, like the Reinhardt *Everyman* and the *Johnny Johnson* film, fell by the wayside in the course of the year. The collapse of Weill's participation in the Walter Wanger film that had taken him to Hollywood in the first place came even more abruptly. For some reason Wanger, an independent, progressive producer, fell out with his director, Lewis Milestone – remembered today particularly for *All Quiet on the Western Front*. Then Odets, on the basis of whose script Weill had already gone to work, lost interest in the idea. Wanger commissioned a new script from John Howard Lawson, a resident left-wing screenwriter, and Weill completed his substantial score – forty items in all – as contracted. But Wanger turned it down and commissioned a new one from the prolific Werner Janssen, then conductor of the New York Philharmonic Orchestra. During Weill's involvement in it the film had been called first *Castles in Spain*, then *The River is Blue* and finally reached the screen in 1938 as *Blockade*, starring Madeleine Carroll and Henry Fonda. It was the sort of arbitrariness and confusion which, he was to find, was only too typical of the motion picture industry. He received the contracted fee for his unused music but his protests at the loss of publicity fell on deaf ears.

Hollywood, its ways of working, its ambience, its values, did not appeal to him – yet. That the ambitious writers, composers, designers, actors and actresses who had been streaming excitedly west since the invention of the talkies should have created the atmosphere of a gold rush, was only to be expected. The cinema was now *the* medium of mass entertainment, cheap, available nationwide, depending for its success on popular appeal and reflecting with an inescapable directness the psychology of the society to which it belonged.

The concept of an art in immediate contact with the community met a criterion firmly embedded in Weill's aesthetic since the days of the Novembergruppe in Berlin at the end of the Great War. Hence the enthusiasm with which now, in his new American homeland, he greeted the activities of the young spirits at work in the Federal Theatre Project, who faced the challenge, like Offenbach, Gilbert and Sullivan, and Johann Strauss before them, in their individual social milieux, of producing a new culture of musical theatre based on 'light' popular music. 'This young organisation,' he wrote,

> which has raised itself in a short period to become one of the most significant and promising forces in theatre and music in the entire country, possesses not only the physical resources but also the inner urge to tackle this task. . . . It has the great advantage of being represented over the whole country and of possessing the practical facilities for drawing together playwrights, composers, actors, singers, choirs and orchestras to create a single, unified great work of art.

At the end, as he sat in the Mecca of the film industry, reflecting on the forms that musical theatre might take in this country with no native tradition of opera, his thoughts settled on the speculation that in a new nation it might be to the new popular medium in which that nation excelled that one should look for the theatrical music of the future. 'Nowhere more than here,' he concluded, 'has film attained such a level of technical perfection and such popularity that it can pave the way for a new form of art.' In a sense it already had, if by 'a new form of art' he meant the Hollywood musical, part of a context of American entertainment to which he was to make his own contribution.

What particularly unsettled Weill about the workings of the film business was the demeaning quality of the expectations and the lack of continuity. It resembled a badly organised production line: there would be extended periods of inactivity while other parts of the product were assembled, followed by a hectic rush to supply his own contributions, then more sitting around, and so on. The compartmentalisation of the whole enterprise made for a soulless efficiency, each man seeing no further than his own specialism, creating what Weill called 'a strange mixture of organisation and confusion'. 'It is the craziest place in the world,' he wrote in a letter, 'and I have never seen so many worried and unhappy people together.'

Weill may have seen things in this jaundiced way but not all 'serious' composers did. George Antheil, for one, thoroughly enjoyed Hollywood and claimed that scores such as his had raised the whole level of studio music. 'Oscar Levant tells the amusing story,' wrote Antheil in his autobiography, 'of how most of the old stuffy routine composers of Hollywood suddenly ran out to Arnold Schoenberg in order to take "a few lessons in discords", this presumably to "modernise" their work, to make it as "up to date" as ours.' Not that there was much doubt about how the incompatibility of the 'stuffy routine composers' and the 'serious' invaders would be resolved. 'There were more of them than there were of us,' Antheil drily concluded, 'so it is redundant to observe that, mostly, they won.'

For Weill the compensations were climatic, social – and financial. He had rented a cottage on Whitley Terrace in Hollywood and acquired a car, which gave him the freedom to tour the surrounding countryside, especially the coast. He had always had a love of the sea. In what were now already the 'old days' he used to take vacations in the dune landscape of the Baltic Sea, and holidays by the Mediterranean had been regular features – necessities, almost – of his last years in Germany. Sport had little part in his scheme of things but he did play tennis after settling a few years later in New City, outside New York. If he already took up the game during this first stay in Hollywood, he might, just might, have been seen on court with George Gershwin and Arnold Schoenberg, who played regularly together after Schoenberg joined the faculty of the University of California at Los Angeles in 1936. It makes a pleasant thought – as it does to speculate on who might have joined the discrepant trio for doubles.

In practical terms, the only firm commitment Weill came away with from Hollywood was to do the music for a film, *You and Me*, by Fritz Lang. He returned to New York in July, shortly after the death of George Gershwin. Gershwin's unpredictable and sometimes unpleasant behaviour had long been put down to neuroses of one kind or another, and such was the reaction when he began to suffer excruciating headaches and fits of vertigo. On July 9 he lapsed into a coma; only then, when he was taken to hospital, did the doctors diagnose a tumour on the brain. Two days later he died. He was thirty-eight – one year older than Kurt Weill.

Almost two years had gone by since Weill and Lenya arrived in New York from Europe. With every day that passed, the finality of that step became more and more evident. He had rapidly grown to feel American; now he needed to actually become American. As he had entered the United States only as a visitor with a work permit, he needed to leave the country and re-enter on an immigrant visa before being able to file an application for citizenship. This he did, like so many at the time, by crossing from New York State into Canada and returning almost immediately on an immigrant visa. This made the whole procedure short and painless. Had he been arriving directly from Germany, or had it been a few years later, the difficulties could have been enormous. The files are bulging with near-horror stories of the lengths to which European would-be immigrants, above all refugees from Nazi Germany, had to go before they were allowed to hold the precious visa in their hands.

Perhaps Weill was luckier than he knew. The German passport on which he had travelled from France to America in 1935 expired the following year. On September 15, 1935 Hitler announced the introduction of the anti-Semitic Nuremberg Laws. As well as making Jews wear the yellow Star of David, forbidding sexual relations between Jews and 'Aryans', and enacting other degrading measures, these Laws deprived all German Jews of their citizenship. Yet when Weill presented himself at the German Consulate in New York City on February 25, 1936, he received a new passport without further ado. It bears a single endorsement: that he entered the United States at Buffalo, New York from Canada as an immigrant on August 27, 1937.

After returning to New York from California that summer he wrote from his 51st Street apartment to Dr Alfred Kalmus of Universal Edition in Vienna, asking to be sent scores of whatever works of his they still had:

> My position in America has become so secure that I am now able to contemplate making my earlier works better known here than they have been up to now. . . . I have been receiving enquiries from many different quarters about my earlier orchestral and stage works. . . . I have now

completely settled down and feel absolutely at home. As you know, it is heavy going in America, especially for someone who speaks his own musical language, but in the theatre the situation is still better and more favourable here than anywhere else, and I am sure I shall reach the point where I can carry forward here what I began in Europe.

For Schoenberg, Milhaud, Eisler and others America meant exile. For Weill it spelt future, promise – *Das Land der Verheissung*.

In personal relationships the open-heartedness of his new hosts had already brought him friendships of a sincerity to equal anything he had left behind in Europe. By 1938 all his immediate family – his parents, his sister, his two brothers – had emigrated; some of his longest-standing friends from Berlin days had found their own way to America, like Felix Joachimson (now Felix Jackson) and Maurice Abravanel. Darius Milhaud and his wife Madeleine, who had befriended him in Paris, now cleared his rooms in Louveciennes when it was clear that he would never come back, and shipped what they could of his belongings over to him. They themselves were to follow his path to New York after the fall of France in 1940, after which time a Jew could hardly expect to find a safe hiding-place anywhere in Europe. Weill was instrumental in organising their escape to the United States via Portugal.

Perhaps the saddest relationship he left behind, the sadder for its one-sidedness, was that with Erika Neher. Ever since he had arrived in America she had sent letter after despairing letter imploring him to return. He replied in his gentle way, but from the undisguisedly elated accounts he gave her of his musical successes in the New World she can only have sensed that he was slipping further and further away from her. 'Cas' knew what was going on, she told him, and it made no difference to either Cas's affection for him or his admiration for his music; and there would be the occasional scrap of interesting information, such as her delight that, as he told her, he had taken to playing Bach. For the rest her letters are the expression of an intimate world of grief in which outsiders have no rightful place. For her thirty-fourth birthday in November 1937 he sent her what he inscribed as 'Albumblatt für Erika', a piano transcription of an orchestral number from *The Eternal Road*, taken from the scene of Jacob and Rachel. The symbolism needs no labouring.

Having started the bureaucracy moving that would eventually lead him and Lenya to citizenship, and with at least a financial compensation for his rejected film score in Hollywood, he left the apartment shared with Cheryl Crawford and Dorothy Patten and moved with Lenya up-market to a duplex at 231 East 62nd Street, with terraces and a roof garden. New York had become 'his kind of town'.

But not only in the material, 'American-way-of-life' sense. Already at the time of *Johnny Johnson*, after being in the country only a few months, he had told Cheryl Crawford that he wanted to tackle 'a very American subject'. The American *Everyman* that had interested Max Reinhardt was now forgotten but Paul Green, who had been involved in the *Everyman* proposal, was a very American dramatist and an obvious source of further very American ideas. He was also on the board of directors of the Federal Theatre Project. True to the concern that he had always had with the social pressures of history, the ways in which the aspirations of the common people asserted themselves against the entrenched forces of reaction and obscurantism, Weill could conceive of no more American subject than the Revolution and the achievement of independence, and no more suitable writer to dramatise it than Green. In a letter to him Weill envisioned their musico-dramatic task as being to interpret these events in terms of 'the socialist idea in early America, its fight against the followers of European feudalism, and its final triumph in the Constitution'. He conceived the whole thing on a huge scale, a pageant with a mass appeal like that of *The Eternal Road*, a drama of invincible convictions and ineluctable destinies, requiring musical forces of comparable grandeur.

Theoretically all this appealed to Green, whose ideal of drama presupposed the proverbial cast of thousands for its realisation. But he found it impossible to 'centralise' the action in the manner that Weill required for his musical purposes, especially under the six-month deadline that the Federal Theatre had set for its production. So the Green-Weill *The Common Glory*, as it was to be called, remained a dream. Only a scrap of music has survived, though since the plan occupied his mind for a number of months, it seems unlikely that Weill should not have sketched some coherent sections of the work. Green went on to complete *The Common Glory* alone as what he subtitled 'A Symphonic Drama of American History'.

Also abandoned, after Weill had got a long way into its composition, was a musical version of Hoffman R. Hays's play *The Ballad of Davy Crockett*, which again the Federal Theatre wanted to take under its wing. Where *The Common Glory* had been chronicle history, a solemn evocation of the birth of the nation, *Davy Crockett* reached down into the realm of the popular consciousness through the story of the folk hero whose all-American life took him from a cabin in the backwoods of Tennessee to the heroic defence of the Alamo.

Unlike *The Common Glory* there was for the Davy Crockett project a finished and already performed dramatic text to work from, in need only of adaptation to the new musical format. The rest lay in the hands of the composer. Weill made his usual rapid progress, laying out a sequence of twenty-one vocal and orchestral numbers culminating in the Battle of the Alamo (Weill was always good at battle music).

He reached the stage of a substantial but incomplete voice and piano score for rehearsal purposes before breaking off in the early months of 1938. Quite why it got no further – and for all his attraction to the subject he never returned to it – remains uncertain. The actor Burgess Meredith and Charles Alan, a member of Max Reinhardt's production team for *The Eternal Road*, were the driving forces behind its promotion but as so often, the difficulties in finding sponsorship proved insurmountable. On Weill's side, at a time when thoughts of continuing with *The Common Glory* had not entirely evaporated, when Fritz Lang would soon require his presence in Hollywood for the film they had agreed, and when – an event of great moment in Weill's life – the figure of Maxwell Anderson had just appeared on the scene, the sheer pressure of commitments was bound to claim its victims.

The Common Glory had come to nothing. Cooperation with Maxwell Anderson was to become a triumph. Work with Fritz Lang fell somewhere in between – 'fell' being perhaps the operative word, for the form in which his work eventually reached the public turned out to be a travesty of the music he had actually written. In response to Lang's call he drove from New York to California shortly before Christmas, this time accompanied by Lenya, and rented a cottage by the ocean at Santa Monica.

Fritz Lang, now forty-seven, one of Germany's leading film directors of the 1920s, had left in 1933 after refusing an offer from Goebbels of a senior position in the Nazi film industry. He made a film version of Ferenc Molnár's *Liliom* in Paris the following year with Charles Boyer, then signed a contract with Metro-Goldwyn-Mayer and emigrated to Hollywood. Like Weill he felt at home in America from the moment he landed, and refused to speak German even with his fellow-exiles, deeply ashamed, as he was, of his native country. Interested only in making films with a social content, he had struck a profitable vein of subject matter in the injustice suffered by those falsely accused of committing a crime and by ex-criminals whose efforts to go straight are frustrated by the prejudices and lingering suspicions of society. He had found his ideal actress in Sylvia Sidney, whom he paired first with Spencer Tracy (*Fury*), then with Henry Fonda (*You Only Live Once*) and now with George Raft in *You and Me* for Paramount.

Lang's social commitment struck a chord of sympathy in Weill. From the beginning, moreover, *You and Me* was intended to have an integrated musical component along the lines of the *Dreigroschenoper*, which Lang knew from Berlin, just as Weill knew Lang's expressionist films of the same era. But to treat the theme of criminality and rehabilitation with didactic intent in the format of musical comedy proved disastrous, 'a curious comedy drama which never has a hope of coming off', as it was described. Lang called it his worst film.

Weill bore no responsibility for this conceptual failure and had his own disappointment and disillusionment to bear. He worked on the score at Santa Monica through the winter, went back to New York with Lenya for a few weeks early in the New Year, then returned alone to Hollywood at the beginning of April for the dubbing. His numbers were dropped, curtailed, 'adapted' and otherwise mauled by the studio music staff, and the names of a team of arrangers and orchestrators familiar with the conventional needs of the movie industry entered the list of credits. There was no ill-will, no disapproval of what he had written, no apology – it was just the way Hollywood did things.

While her husband was away working on *You and Me*, Lenya made a modest foray into show business on her own account. She was offered a four-week engagement at 'Le Ruban Bleu' supper club, where she sang selections from *Mahagonny* and the *Dreigroschenoper*, together with 'The Right Guy for Me', a number from *You and Me*. The opportunity gave her a psychological boost at a time when the prospects of starting a new career in their new surroundings seemed to be slowly but surely ebbing away. It was not a matter of language – Maurice Chevalier was only one of those whose foreign accent only served to enhance the charm of their singing. Rather, she came from a tradition of entertainment unknown in America and difficult to assimilate – 'she wasn't easy to cast', as Burgess Meredith put it.

But her show went down well. Marlene Dietrich came one evening, so did Cole Porter and her old friend and *alter ego* from *The Seven Deadly Sins*, Tilly Losch. She sent a succession of happy letters back to Weill in Hollywood – in German, despite their resolve to adopt the language of their new home – insisting that, frightened as she had felt to start with, she was gradually learning how to handle her audiences. 'I sing "The Right Guy" very softly now and it is a great success every time,' she wrote. 'They were really mad about me last night.'

Towards the end of May 1938 Weill left California and drove back east. The negative forces were in themselves strong enough to make him realise the futility of staying in Hollywood any longer. But there were also positive pressures at work. *The Eternal Road* had been a one-off extravaganza with its roots in Europe; *Johnny Johnson* represented a step, or half a step, towards a form expressive of the new world he had decided to join. Now he was poised to make his first full, successful entry into that world in the company of one of the most respected dramatists of the day, a man with whom he established a working relationship of a rare harmony and who was to remain to the end one of his most cherished friends.

CHAPTER XIV

Broadway I

———

At the time Weill came to know him, in the latter 1930s, James Maxwell Anderson had just reached fifty. Born in Pennsylvania in 1888, he was the son of a small-town Baptist preacher who stood for a dogmatism which his gentle son partly envied, because it represented conviction in a set of unshakeable moral values, but partly rejected, because it denied the individual's right to arrive at his decisions by his own route. He became a village schoolteacher in the Dakota wheat lands, was dismissed for his pacifist views during the Great War, then took up journalism and in 1923 turned out, in a matter of weeks, the play that made him famous – *What Price Glory*. Set among American soldiers in France in 1918, calculatedly crude in theme and profane in language, this bitter denunciation of war ran for almost three hundred performances in New York from September 1924 and made Anderson rich overnight. With this money he bought an old farmstead in New City, Rockland County, some thirty miles upstate from Manhattan, an unspoilt area of rolling woodland which over the coming years drew writers, artists and actors to its rural seclusion from the grime and bustle of the city. Kurt Weill was to become one of them.

Through the 1930s Anderson moved from one success to another – historical drama in blank verse, political satire, poetic tragedy. In between he made lucrative excursions to Hollywood, co-writing the screenplay for such classics as *All Quiet On The Western Front*, *Death Takes A Holiday* and *We Live Again*. Many of his own plays were also turned into films. The 1940s brought *Key Largo* (starring Paul Muni), *Joan Of Lorraine* (with Ingrid Bergmann) and *Anne Of The Thousand Days*, all made into successful movies. It was a spectacle of triumph for a withdrawn, humane, generous man with not only a gift of theatre but also a sense of poetic language unique in its place and its time.

During the Second World War Anderson traded in his old-style liberalism for a powerful anti-Fascist line and put his skills as a writer at the disposal of the war effort. In the practical guise of a near-combatant he appears on a highly posed wartime photograph as an airplane spotter, with his friend Kurt Weill standing beside him and peering earnestly through binoculars in improbable search of enemy aircraft. But after the war his activity fell into decline and he died in 1959 at the age of seventy, two days after suffering a stroke. Many at the time saw him as second only to Eugene O'Neill in the hierarchy of American playwrights.

In the spring of 1938, after the success of The Star Wagon, Maxwell Anderson asked his leading man Burgess Meredith, star of his last three Broadway shows, what he should write next. 'I said a musical, with Kurt Weill,' replied Meredith, as he recalled in conversation with Lenya's biographer Donald Spoto. 'Anderson wasn't opposed to the idea, so I brought Kurt, whom I'd met through Lee Strasberg, up to Rockland County to introduce him to Max at his home in New City.' Weill had been deeply moved by the open-heartedness and poetic charm of The Star Wagon, so when the two men came together in Anderson's converted farmhouse, it was against a backdrop of mutual sympathy and keen anticipation.

Little was happening in Weill's life at this moment – little of creative substance or promise, that is. The Common Glory and Davy Crockett had come and more or less gone; Hollywood, like many of the relationships it incubated, offered prospects only of a casual attachment of the one-night-stand variety. Moreover, although he had been sympathetically received and had rapidly acquired a circle of well-wishers, no compulsive new challenge had yet thrust itself before his creative imagination – no Georg Kaiser or Bertolt Brecht to dangle new projects before his eyes. A few years later he wrote music for a film called Where Do We Go From Here? Good question, he might have returned at this moment. Even 'Here' might have not been all that easy to define.

At all events he and Anderson got on well from the start, a relationship between respecting and tolerant equals, neither of whom harboured the thought of imposing his will on the other. Lenya too was welcomed into the family and not only became a close friend of Anderson's second wife Mab and her daughter but also won the affection of Anderson's three sons from his first marriage.

When the Weills drove out to New City with Burgess Meredith that April weekend, Anderson already had a proposition in mind. 'Kurt,' he is reported to have asked, 'do you think we can make a musical comedy out of Washington Irving's Knickerbocker History of New York?' Weill may or may not have been in a position to say Yes or No on the spot. Maybe Anderson needed first to tell him about Irving and this gloriously witty piece of satirical writing – an account of the New Netherlands of the seventeenth century before Nieuw Amsterdam became New York, ascribed to a fictitious elderly bachelor named Diedrich Knickerbocker, of whom Irving delicately observed that 'there are some reasons for believing he is not entirely in his right mind'.

Weill, the new American in love with his adopted country, could not resist such a blend of history and folklore, reality and poetry. Nor could he feel other than flattered that it was to him that the most prominent dramatist of the moment had put his question. So before he left again for Hollywood to make his final thankless contributions to *You and Me*, they agreed on an outline plot that would lay out a panorama of events in New York in 1647 under the governorship of Peter Stuyvesant and weave into the events the strand of a love story. Anderson had had no experience of the requirements and conventions of a text that passed from his hands, not straight to those of his actors but first into those of a composer – no experience, so to speak, of playing Gilbert to Weill's Sullivan. 'I had to follow *The Mikado* as I would a cookbook to find any kind of form,' he said. In the event the *Mikado* cookbook provided him with Gilbertian recipes for a few side dishes as well as the form. He undertook to have a text ready by the time Weill got back from Hollywood.

And he did. Using a framework form, he first showed Irving himself in his study at work on *The History of New York by Diedrich Knickerbocker*. Members of the corrupt town council are awaiting the arrival of their new peg-leg Governor Peter Stuyvesant, who announces that he is going to take over personal 'democratic' control of the people's affairs; the bribery and corruption of the past will continue as before but become hallowed under gubernatorial authority. He appoints the villainous Councilman Tienhoven as his 'fixer' who, in return, offers him his daughter Tina in marriage. But Tina loves Brom Broeck, a poor knife-grinder and believer in honest, democratic ideals who is thrown into jail when he dares to challenge Stuyvesant's tyrannical new order.

As preparations are being made for the wedding of Stuyvesant and Tina, a band of Indians attacks the town, burning down the jail and allowing Brom to escape; Brom joins in the fighting and at one point saves Stuyvesant from being captured. The Governor persists in his intention to have Brom hanged for treason until Irving steps back on to the stage and urges him, in the interests of acquiring a benevolent image for posterity, to desist and allow Brom and Tina to marry. Smirking at the prospect of becoming 'a sort of Manhattan Saint Nicholas', Stuyvesant is persuaded, and the proceedings are concluded by the entire cast singing the song in praise of the qualities of integrity and rugged independence which answers the question 'How Can You Tell an American?'.

With the text of the play before him, Weill wrote to Anderson:

> I have started to work out a style which would give a feeling of the period and yet be a very up-to-date music. This combination of old and new gives great opportunity for humour in music, and my idea is that the music in this play should take an active part in the humorous as well as in the sentimental parts, because the more we can say in fun, the better it is. For instance if we have the fight between the flute and the trumpet, I want the audience to laugh as much about the music itself as they'll laugh about the situation and the dialogue.

And the laughter starts at the very beginning, with the fat, corrupt little Dutch Councilmen talking a grotesque broken English in an 'inch-thick accent', as the Broadway producer Joshua Logan none too gently described Weill's own linguistic facility.

More seriously comic, however, and the source of some unease among Anderson's colleagues of The Playwrights Company, which had taken the work aboard, was the political satire. Irving had allowed himself a few swipes at Thomas Jefferson in his *History*, and Anderson's equivalent target was Franklin D. Roosevelt and the New Deal. Anderson found the latter suspect because, starting as a national necessity, it had spawned a proliferation of governmental agencies that now threatened personal liberties and usurped the right of the individual to make his own decisions. Hence his quip in the preface that 'the gravest and most constant danger to a man's life, liberty and happiness is the government under which he lives'. But Anderson's fellow-Playwrights were pro-Roosevelt to a man — as, indeed, was Weill — and over the months of preparation that followed, he was persuaded, against his better dramatic judgement, to soften some of his more prickly political jabs.

The Playwrights Company, a five-man body consisting of Anderson, Elmer Rice, Robert E. Sherwood, Sidney Howard and S. N. Behrman, had constituted itself earlier in 1938 in order that its members, who all had a keen sense of the social relevance and responsibility of art, could produce their own plays without the irritating interference of commercially motivated Broadway moguls. Each member made his financial contribution to the running costs of the Company, which was responsible for many outstanding productions, including a number of Weill's works, over the thirty years of its existence.

Anderson's entertaining text lay waiting for Weill's attention when he got back from Hollywood in the summer. Ever since his days with Brecht he had insisted on being involved at an early stage in the construction of the storyline to which he was to set his music, and although Anderson had written to tell him how things were going, ideally he would have liked to be personally on hand. However, in his accommodating way he accepted what he found, put some of his new Paramount money into renting a cottage in the countryside near Suffern, Rockland County, within comfortable reach of Anderson in New City, and set to work on his score. Anderson was fascinated. 'The healthiest man I knew,' he called him,

> healthy in body, mind and humour. In this age of uncertainty and mental torment Kurt was almost alone in his irrepressible enjoyment of work, life, play and friendship. . . . As a composer he was like a magician. He would take a lyric from my hands, run upstairs to a piano, spend an hour or so alone, and reappear with three different musical settings for me to choose among.

Joshua Logan, who had been in Berlin at the time of *Dreigroschenoper* and now came fresh from his Broadway triumph with the Rodgers and Hart musical *I Married An Angel*, was invited to take charge of the production and described how Weill played them the results of his labours:

> Kurt sat at the piano, staring at his manuscript paper through the two hunks of thick glass he used for spectacles. He was a little musical juggernaut. Nothing stopped him once he launched into a song. He caterwauled the melody in a toneless tenor with an accent so thick it hurt him as much as it did us. Lenya just smiled her pearly bear-trap smile. Kurt banged insistently on the keyboard to emphasise the bass rhythms. He had created the songs himself out of Max's little verses which he could scarcely understand.

Nor could Logan quite understand, musically, what he was listening to, but he knew quality when he saw it:

> It wasn't Dick Rodgers and Max wasn't Larry Hart, but everything about Kurt Weill was talent and enthusiasm.

Anderson had originally thought of casting Burgess Meredith as Brom Broeck but after first appearing keen, Meredith lost interest. The focus of attention now switched to the figure of Stuyvesant and to the suggestion that the popular Walter Huston be approached. Two difficulties had to be faced. Firstly Huston had never appeared in a musical and would have to fall back on an experience in vauderville which belonged to a time now many years in the past. Secondly, even if he were to accept, his image, on stage and screen, was that of a player of kind, likeable characters quite at odds with the tyrannical Stuyvesant. Huston told Logan he would take the part, asking only to be given a song of his own, a sentimental song with which to woo Tina. Maxwell Anderson sat down for an hour and produced the lyrics, Kurt Weill set them to music the same evening, and they presented Walter Huston with his 'September Song', the best loved number in the show and still the best known of all Weill's Broadway melodies.

Anderson had had to surrender much of the political import of his central figure to the personality of the actor who was to play that figure and to the pressures of Broadway. But compromise, as they say, is the name of the theatrical game. And as to 'September Song', supreme symbol of that compromise, it brought its compensations, as Anderson's biographer Alfred S. Shivers observed: 'Of Max's many accomplishments this one hauntingly lovely song about a man's autumnal love for a girl would earn him, surprisingly enough, the most money of all through sales of records, sheet music, and other rights, and it still gives tidy royalties to his estate and Weill's.'

Weill's music for *Knickerbocker Holiday* – tuneful, bouncy, attractive – is at times Broadway-ish, calling on the blues, subscribing to the conventions of form and the sentimentalities of contemporary popular music. At other times – on the direct invitation of the text – it draws on Gilbert and Sullivan and on the general stock-in-trade of the operetta/musical comedy industry. His perceived mannerisms are also well in evidence but the new surroundings have softened their impact. The refrain of the 'September Song', for instance, has his familiar oscillation between major and minor and settles on the added-sixth chord with minor third:

But it's a long, long while ____

– which says the same thing as the refrain of 'Surabaya-Johnny' from *Happy End*:

Su - ra - ba - ya John-ny,

– which, in its turn, is the minor counterpart of the opening of the 'Mackie Messer Song':

Und   der   Hai - fisch,

But *Knickerbocker Holiday* belongs to a different world. Maxwell Anderson's text may be political satire but Weill's musical aggression of the 1920s has slackened. In Berlin he could mock and parody, in a variety of styles, because the objects of the mockery and the parody had their own recognisable identity. Now everything has found its way to a single level, a level of attractive eclecticism where tensions are minimised and charm has both the first and the last word. Barely three years in America, he already has his new audience in his pocket. 'Here in America is the best audience to write music for,' he told a reporter some years later. 'They are remarkably quick to catch what you are trying to put over. . . . I find I can switch them over from laughter to tenderness or any other kind of response in a few bars.'

One of the tryout performances of *Knickerbocker Holiday* was scheduled for Washington D.C. A few minutes before the curtain went up, the audience were joined, to their surprise and delight, by Franklin D. Roosevelt himself, a friend of Walter Huston's but a rare theatregoer. This was a tense moment in the history of the world. A few days earlier Neville Chamberlain had returned from Munich with his celebrated piece of paper guaranteeing 'peace in our time'. Roosevelt's recent telegram to Hitler over Czechoslovakia even makes a disguised appearance in Anderson's text, and Roosevelt already knew, as he told the cast when he met them after the show, that war was inevitable.

It was also a tense moment for the actors and the production team, since nobody could be sure how the President would react to Anderson's digs, softened but still obvious, at the Roosevelt administration and the New Deal. When the jokes began to arrive, people looked furtively up at the President's box to see how the great man reacted. They need not have worried. 'Since he howled at every joke,' wrote the elated Joshua Logan, 'they didn't have time to follow suit, so they turned silently back to the stage. To a blind man it must have seemed like an empty auditorium except for one crazy, laughing fool.'

With Walter Huston as Stuyvesant, Ray Middleton, a popular actor-singer in movies of the 1940s, as Washington Irving, and Richard Kollmar as Brom, and with Maurice Abravanel conducting, *Knicker-bocker Holiday* came to the Ethel Barrymore Theatre in New York in November 1938 and ran for 168 performances. This did not lift it to the rank of a smash hit, but with competition from Cole Porter's *Leave it to Me!* and the Rodgers and Hart *The Boys from Syracuse*, both of which opened that same month, it had to be rated a considerable success, on artistic if not on financial grounds. The critics, in the familiar predicament of not being quite sure what kind of creature they were looking at – play with music, light opera, musical comedy – gave it a mixed reception. Some took Anderson to task for an overly ponderous book, others clapped Weill on the shoulder with a few perfunctory words of approval for his music. There was a general consensus of welcome, however, for the ever-popular Mr Walter Huston, and when it finished on Broadway, the show was taken on an equally successful tour around the country. The career of Kurt Weill the composer of musicals was well and truly on the road.

A growing warmth was surrounding his life, an enrichment of spirit, nurtured from both personal and professional sources. His immediate pleasure came from the success of *Knickerbocker Holiday* but he had already earned the goodwill of the Group Theatre people and now, through his association with Anderson, of The Playwrights Company. He had made a start in films; even his involvement in *The Eternal Road*, as he was shortly to see, had not been forgotten. And since he was a man of modest tastes, the money that he had earned had proven well sufficient to support his chosen life-style.

Some of that money at once found its way to a cause that could not have given him greater joy. Armed with Kurt's affidavit of sponsorship, the attestation without which such things were not possible, Hanns Weill, his wife Rita and daughter Hanne arrived in New York from Europe, the last of the family to flee, eleventh-hour fugitives from the holocaust. With a gift of 10,000 dollars from his brother, Hanns set up a scrap metal business on the Lower East Side, and during the years until Hanns' death in 1947 the two brothers and their families spent many weekends together in the woodlands of Rockland County. Here, Hanne remembered, her father could lay aside the worries of business life and 'be himself'.

When Hanns and his family crossed the Atlantic, they brought with them a substantial body of letters from Kurt to Hanns and to his parents, as well as a dozen or so of his earliest compositions from his schoolboy and student days. After Hanns' death Rita kept all this material to herself until shortly before her own death in 1983; before that its existence, leave alone its nature, had been a family secret. Only in recent years, since her daughter Hanne made this music and correspondence available to the Kurt

Weill Foundation, have we been able to form a picture of Weill the teenage composer, or had more than a partial view of his relationship to his family and his outlook on life, especially during his years of early manhood.

Weill's choice to live in the country and travel into the city for discussions and rehearsals was one which Lenya became increasingly ready to share. She had never known a settled family life. Her upbringing in a Viennese slum at the hands of an abusive father and a browbeaten mother had been as far removed as one could imagine from the comfortable reassurance that had pervaded the home of Cantor Albert Weill in Dessau, and her marriage to Kurt in 1926 could not check the potentially destructive tendency of her congenital promiscuity. But since their remarriage she had become more receptive to the values of conventional, old-fashioned friendship, starting with that of her husband. The arrival in their lives of welcoming literary and artistic couples from Rockland County, led by the Maxwell Andersons, encouraged the process of integration, and first in Suffern, then in New City, where they moved three years later, Lenya began to lose some of her insecurity to the process of domestication.

If the conditions of Weill's American situation seemed to stand near 'Set Fair', the world he had left behind on the other side of the Atlantic was registering 'Storm'. It was not a world he could ever forget or would ever deny – he owed it too much for that. But it was already a long way away, physically and spiritually, and receding by the minute. And while Hitler's onward march through Europe, in the wake of the persecution of the Jews and the consolidation of totalitarianism in Italy and Spain, was seen by perceptive observers in America for the threat to world peace that it was, the majority preferred to look the other way. Those who had recently escaped, and those who were in growing numbers still escaping, knew the horrors they had left behind; those who had already settled pretended they did not want to know and held to the conservative anti-interventionism which said that Europe should be left to fight its own wars. For all that Franklin D. Roosevelt warned his countrymen of what the spread of Fascism meant and of the inevitability of the war that would follow, it was not events in Europe that brought America into the Second World War but the Japanese attack on Pearl Harbor. From another point of departure the left-wing pacifist movement opposed war for its own reasons, while the prominence of Jews in the stream of newly-arriving émigrés fanned the flames of latent anti-Semitism.

Hailing the refugees from Hitler's Thousand-Year Reich, Romain Rolland wrote: 'You have brought with you everything of that Germany which we love and respect. You bring the spirit of Goethe and Beethoven, Lessing and Marx.' When Weill looked back at that Germany, his Germany, the Weimar Republic in which Goethe and Beethoven, Lessing

14. Bertolt Brecht, 1926. Portrait by Rudolf Schlichter.

15.   Macheath on the gallows, from the orginal production of the
Dreigroschenoper. From left to right: Kurt Gerron as Tiger Brown, Roma
Bahn as Polly, Harald Paulsen as Macheath and Erich Ponto as Peachum.

16.   Weill's manuscript of the 'Mackie Messer Song'.

17.   The house in the Berlin suburb of Kleinmachnow (Wissmannstrasse 7, now Käthe-Kollwitz-Strasse) which Weill bought in 1932 from the proceeds of the *Dreigroschenoper*. The plaque on the left side of the door states (inaccurately): 'The composer Kurt Weill lived in this house from 1929 to 1933'.

18.   Brook House, South Mountain Road, New City, New York, the Weills' home from 1941 onwards. Lenya continued to live there until her death in 1981.

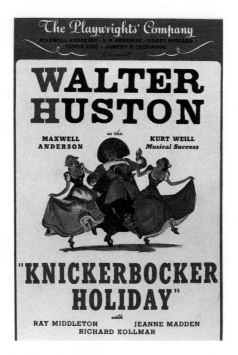

19.   Playbill of *Knickerbocker Holiday*, 1938.

20.   Weill and Ira Gershwin, 1941.

21. Weill and Lenya with 'Woolly' in Brook House, 1942.

22. Weill rehearsing the principals of *One Touch of Venus*, 1943. From left to right: Mary Martin, John Bowles, Paula Laurence and Kenny Baker.

23.   Weill in discussion of *Lost in the Stars* with Alan Paton (left) and Maxwell Anderson (right), 1949.

24.   Weill's gravestone in Mount Repose Cemetery, Haverstraw, New York. The words and music are from *Lost in the Stars*, the last work he completed (see p.331).

and Marx had held sway, there was scarcely a familiar face to be seen. The theatrical and musical world of Berlin had been drained of its life blood. Max Reinhardt, Piscator, Fritz Kortner, Elisabeth Bergner, Brecht, Feuchtwanger, Ernst Toller, Alfred Kerr were all gone, so were Schoenberg, Hindemith, Klemperer, Kleiber and Bruno Walter. Not to speak of the writers and poets, Jews and Gentiles alike. Only a few years ago he too, Kurt Weill, had had his place in that scene. But the scene could never be restored, and although some went back after the nightmare had passed, by then he had long found himself a new audience to address and had no intention of deserting it.

He was fortunate, also, in not having to worry about the fate of his immediate family, all of whom he had left behind in Germany when he fled to Paris in 1933. His sister Ruth and her husband, both ardent Zionists, emigrated to Palestine the year after, and later to the United States; Cantor Albert Weill and his wife had left for Palestine in 1935 and made themselves a new home in Nahariya, a coastal town north of Acre, where their eldest son Nathan and his family also settled. And Hanns, Kurt's dearly-loved Hanns, had just joined him in America. It was a family diaspora, a tragic reality of sadness and anxiety. Yet wherever they found themselves at this moment, on the threshold of the Second World War, the Weills were united in the privileged victory of survival. Which was more than a lot of Jewish families could say.

Public acknowledgement that Weill's star was in the ascendant now came from a prominent and totally unexpected quarter. 1939 was the year of the New York World's Fair, an occasion for the ostentatious flag-waving display by nations, American states, industries and corporations of their priceless contributions to the glories of modern civilisation. As well as through the exhibitions on permanent display, some of the wealthier participants aimed to make a particularly grand splash – often literally, since the erection of spectacular fountains seemed to obsess the minds of the Fair's designers – by commissioning pageants and dramatic scenes to publicise their wares. Hanns Eisler had been engaged to write the music for a film being shown at the oil companies' Petroleum exhibit, while Aaron Copland had provided one score for a film and another for a marionette show (The British pavilion ran only to the band of the Coldstream Guards playing jolly military music.)

The largest building on the site was the Railroad Exhibit, devoted to the achievements of the railroad companies in driving the iron horse across the country from coast to coast. To supplement the standing exhibit, the organisers commissioned from one Edward Hungerford, a well-known writer on railways and the urban scene, an historical pageant unfurling the development of the railroads from the days of the earliest steam locomotives, through the opening up of the West in the nineteenth century to the New York commuter trains of the 1930s. The locomotives themselves, old and new, were the real heroes of the occasion but Hungerford also supplied texts to be declaimed by narrators and lyrics to be sung by soloists and choruses. Charles Alan, who knew the problems of such mammoth productions from *The Eternal Road*, was appointed to direct the spectacle in an outdoor theatre to hold 4,000 people, with Isaac Van Grove again to conduct. Weill was invited to write the music – songs, choruses, orchestral interludes, incidental music in general. The whole event lasted something over an hour, including three-quarters-of-an-hour's music, and there were four performances daily. Someone irreverently suggested calling it *The Eternal Railroad*. The official programme gave it the title *Railroads on Parade*.

As the circumstances required, Weill applied his music to these scenes with broad strokes, in a cheerful, extrovert spirit. It was no occasion for subtlety but nor was there any disguising the confidence and craftsmanship that the music, page after page, exuded – unlike the text, which is painfully corny. Weill could sometimes be trite but he was never vulgar. Chorus and orchestra, the latter liberally laced with saxophones and including novachord and Hammond organ as well as piano, were located below stage, where they performed into microphones; amplifiers then piped the music to the audience, who would otherwise have barely heard it against the jubilant puffing and whistling of the locomotives.

It may be little more than a lighthearted frolic but it did give Weill a chance to indulge himself with the American folk tunes that he had picked up along the way. 'The pageant has loads of charm,' said Elliott Carter, reviewing the music on offer at the Fair and praising Weill's 'most excellent score',

> with real steaming and smoking locomotives playing the prima-donnas' roles. When the famous halves of the Union Pacific meet, the iron horses sing little songs with toots between phrases. Weill has appropriately used all kinds of American tunes, including one of my favourites, 'Fifteen Years on the Erie Canal', with fine taste, intelligence and showmanship.

Weill returned to this piece of fun for the Fair of 1940, cutting bits here, adding bits there, but by its nature it could only be a diversion from more serious concerns, in particular the urge to explore with Maxwell Anderson the paths that their new partnership opened up. Such paths did not always lead anywhere. For one thing, where Weill was committed to musical theatre, Anderson was not: *Knickerbocker Holiday* had taken him into new territory, and with the blood of 'straight' poetic drama coursing through his veins, he felt unsure, as an Alan Jay Lerner or a Moss Hart would not, as to what the script should look like which he handed to his composer. On the other hand *Knickerbocker Holiday* had been both a pleasure and a success, and collaboration with Weill was a delight.

So with the Broadway run of *Knickerbocker Holiday* coming to an end, they looked around for a new subject and lighted upon a Civil War story set in Georgia at the time of General William T. Sherman's famous march to the sea in 1864. Written in 1919 by a well-known Georgia newspaper editor called Harry Stillwell Edwards, it had the title *Eneas Africanus*. It tells of a slave who is entrusted with his employers' valuable silver in the confusion of war, cannot find his way back to their plantation when peace returns, and wanders the Southern countryside for eight years before his odyssey finally takes him back to his homeland, where he returns the silver that he has been guarding all this time. Anderson described it as a story about 'a man in a chaotic world in search of his own manhood'.

Edwards' little tale is written in epistolary form, that is, as a succession of detached episodes, like snapshots, from the years of Eneas' wanderings. As such it is ready-made for treatment as a series of individual musical numbers, each number focusing on a scene, an experience, a character encountered along the way, and unity being achieved through dramatic dialogue and a framework of historical events. The story itself also had a moral appeal, centring on the hero's steadfast honesty of purpose in the confusion of his dealings with the world of whites and blacks.

There was at this moment, as it happened, a surge of that interest in shows with all-black casts which goes back to Lew Leslie's *Blackbirds of 1928*. *The Swing Mikado*, a child of the Federal Theatre, and its more lavish successor *The Hot Mikado* were both running on Broadway; so too was Leslie's *Blackbirds of 1939*, the last of its avian line. All these shows, like *Porgy and Bess* of 1935, were all-white creations for all-black performers, and in financial terms they all turned out to be either flops or barely successful. Even *Porgy and Bess* did not recoup its initial 50,000-dollar investment.

But the thought did not go away. In 1942 Paul Robeson's wife wrote to Weill on her husband's behalf, telling him of plans to form a Negro Cultural Foundation on the West Coast and of their wish to launch its activities with a *Threepenny Opera*. Weill had every sympathy with the idea of such a Foundation but was appalled at their attitude towards his score, which they demanded to be allowed to cut, supplement and generally manipulate as the spirit took them, totally destroying the conceptual unity of the work. The contract they proposed, he told Eslande Robeson, was 'the most shameful proposition that has ever been made to me'.

Anderson now drew his own blank with Robeson. As he had seen with *Knickerbocker Holiday*, success in a musical was tied, more firmly than in a play, to a dominant personality whom people would flock to see in whatever he chose to do. He therefore sent Robeson a lengthy account of *Ulysses Africanus*, as they were now calling their project, in the hope of rousing his interest. Robeson turned a deaf ear. As his wife explained in her reply, he had no wish to play a stereotyped Uncle Tom of the kind that no longer existed – or rather, that existed only in order to encourage the white man's patronising prejudices. 'We feel Mr Robeson must play a Negro who does exist', wrote Essie Robeson, 'who has something to do with reality. That's all he asks.'

None of Weill's hopes, kindled in the 1930s, of seeing Robeson appear in one of his shows ever materialised. Nor, it seems, did Robeson ever perform the fine Walt Whitman songs which Weill composed in 1942 with Robeson's voice in mind. At least he could console himself with the knowledge that he was in good company. Among the many offers that Robeson turned down were those of Porgy – although Gershwin said he was 'bearing in mind Paul's voice in writing it' – and of Mephistopheles in G. W. Pabst's film of Gounod's *Faust*.

But Anderson and Weill had grown too attached to *Ulysses Africanus* to give up so soon, and when Anderson went to California in June for a festival of his plays, Weill drove out with Lenya in their used – very used – Oldsmobile to join him. Near Pittsburgh the car broke down and was diagnosed as unfit for an immediate onward journey of over 2,000 miles. A dealer offered 300 dollars in part-exchange, which, since it had only cost him 400 dollars in the first place, seemed to Weill a fair deal, as he related with no hard feelings. So they bought another car from the dealer on the spot and continued their journey westwards. Swimming in the ocean, working on *Ulysses* and watching the festival productions take shape, he spent two delightful months in Malibu.

Since they could not get Robeson for their scheme, Weill and Anderson set their sights on Bill Robinson, the song-and-dance man then appearing in *The Hot Mikado*. Alas, Robinson did not accept either and Anderson's play was never published. Some of the music Weill had already written was to resurface ten years later in *Lost in the Stars*.

They did, however, complete shortly afterwards an entertaining little piece of commissioned *Gebrauchsmusik*. This was *The Ballad of Magna Carta*, a cantata for soloists, chorus and orchestra, 'arranged for presentation by glee clubs and choral societies in schools and colleges', as the vocal score describes it. Formally and functionally it is an American counterpart of *Der Lindberghflug* and *Der Jasager* – American, despite its subject matter, because the principles of responsible government and a refusal to submit to tyranny are seen as equally characteristic of the young America as of the England of seven hundred years ago. A narrator, sometimes in speech, sometimes in song, describes how the despotism of

King John has finally brought the nobles to the point of rebellion, and how they force the King to sign the charter guaranteeing the laws basic to the just government of the country.

Vocally *The Ballad of Magna Carta* is straightforward, diatonic, sometimes rather naive, whereas the orchestral accompaniment shows some of the rhythmic, harmonic and even contrapuntal variety which characterised the European Weill of old. Anderson's familiar moral and political stances are also on display, didactically couched in a tabloid poetic manner which could not but circumscribe Weill's musical response from the outset. This could hardly be separated from the occasion, for *The Ballad of Magna Carta* was the product of a commission from CBS for a work to be included in a radio series called 'The Pursuit of Happiness', and as such needed to strike a suitably elevated moral note. On its transmission in February 1940 Burgess Meredith took the role of the Narrator. The modest format and its practical requirements attracted Weill to the notion of doing a series of such cantatas with Maxwell Anderson, focused on great individual moments in American history and executed in the socio-educational spirit of the *Gebrauchsmusik* of the German 1920s. But *Magna Carta* had no successors.

Intellectual and articulate musician that he was, and increasingly sure of the base on which he was building the successes of his new career, Weill now took the opportunity offered by a newspaper interview to tell the world where he stood in the debate on the function of music and the composer's craft. 'I'm convinced,' he told *The New York Sun* in February 1940,

> that many modern composers have a feeling of superiority towards their audiences. Schoenberg, for example, has said that he is writing for a time fifty years after his death. But the great 'classic' composers wrote for their contemporary audiences. They wanted those who heard their music to understand it, and they did. As for myself, I write for today. I don't give a damn about writing for posterity.

Newspaper attributions can be perversely misleading, and these may not have been Weill's precise words. Even if they were, it is not hard to detect a gently provocative note of irony in his voice as he speaks, and to see a mischievous twinkle in his eye as he submits to the earnest journalist's probing. But the sentiments ring true. The philosophy of 'writing for today' had underlain his passage from the dissonant manner of the early and mid-1920s to the direct, immediately accessible song-style of the *Mahagonny Songspiel* and its successors. The new style, moreover, had not evolved in an aesthetic vacuum but accompanied a shift in sociological rationale towards a music directed at a wider market than that constituted by the bourgeois 'concert- and opera-going public' as conventionally understood. 'Music is seeking to enter the consciousness of wider audiences,' he had written in an essay of 1927, 'for only in that way can it maintain its viability'. His attitude had not changed. 'I wrote ten operas in Germany,' he told his interlocutor from *The New York Sun*:

> Several of them were very popular. But I got tired of composing for so limited an audience, limited not only numerically but emotionally and intellectually. I wanted to reach the real people, a more representative public than any opera house attracts.

Similar sentiments inform a typescript article (in German), apparently never published, that he dated May 1937, i.e. the time when *The Eternal Road* was closing. Surveying the possibilities for music in theatre and film in his then still comparatively new environment, he wrote:

> What one calls artistic freedom is a strange thing. Creative artists look for independence, for the freedom to engender their works without external constraints. On the other hand they need restraints to prevent them from going astray and getting into areas of abstraction. They have to know for whose benefit they are working, because it is only by bearing in mind the target at which their works are directed that they can discover the spiritual foundation without which any art is merely an empty play with forms. Only in this way can we understand why the majority of the world's great works of art are the result of commissions, i.e. were intended for a specific purpose and for a specific circle of people, works created in the area of friction where external pressure interacts with inner freedom, compulsion with desire.

In a sense Weill's distinction between writing for today and writing for posterity is a formal contrivance, invented for the purpose of identifying with a particular contemporary cause or of declaring a commitment to a particular philosophy of the artist's activity. Any artist is concerned to affect his immediate environment by the works that he makes public. He cannot know how they will be received in fifty years' time, or even whether the world will still know of their existence, but he can and must witness their impact on the present.

This is specially evident in the performing arts. A poet or a novelist will not know, unless he goes out of his way to investigate or is told by others, how his words on the printed page are received, since reading is a silent, private activity. What the composer has to communicate requires the performer as intermediary, and performance presupposes an occasion, however intimate, at which the composer's thoughts are conveyed to those who wish to hear them. His music may be ill-received and rejected, and he may conclude, sullenly or defiantly, that only future generations will understand its true meaning. History is not poor in examples of works now enshrined in the canon of universal masterpieces which were hissed off the stage at the time of their composition. Composers may wax scornful over the public's response, even if it be favourable, but few will be so perverse as to deliberately cultivate public rejection.

So when Weill declares 'I write for today', he is stating a truism. One cannot escape belonging to today, and one cannot write for tomorrow because one does not know what tomorrow will look like or what it will need. If what one writes for today is also listened to tomorrow, that will be the judgement of history. But one will not be around to enjoy it. In 'not giving a damn' about posterity, Weill is drawing the conclusion that follows from a second, complementary truism.

Nor has 'today' only a temporal connotation. 'You hear a lot of talk about the "American opera" that's going to come along some day,' Weill continued his *credo*:

> It's my opinion that we can and will develop a musical-dramatic form in this country but I don't think it will be called 'opera', or that it will grow out of the opera which has become a thing separate from the commercial theater, dependent upon other means than box-office appeal for its continuance. It will develop from and remain a part of the American theater – 'Broadway' theater, if you like. More than anything else, I want to have a part in that development.

Weill's 'today', in other words, the present of which he is an enthusiastic and fully paid-up member, means not just '1940' but 'America 1940'. He remains the man of the musical theatre that he always was but his parameters are now those of Broadway, not of Berlin or Leipzig; his literary and dramatic points of reference have become Maxwell Anderson and Ira Gershwin, no longer Georg Kaiser and Bertolt Brecht. So that, although in linear biographical terms chronology compels us to trace a twelve-year journey from *Mahagonny* and *Dreigroschenoper*, through *Die Bürgschaft* and *Marie Galante* to *Johnny Johnson* and *Knickerbocker Holiday*, each work, or cluster of works, receives its immediate meaning from within the circumstantial world to which it is a response.

Thus while judgements based on the internal criteria of Weill's development will inevitably be passed on the relative merits of the *Dreigroschenoper* of 1928 and *Lady in the Dark* of 1941, or of the *Mahagonny* opera of 1930 and the 'Broadway Opera' *Street Scene* of 1946, the proper context of *Dreigroschendoper and Mahagonny* is music theatre in Berlin in the years of the Weimar Republic, while that of *Lady in the Dark* and *Street Scene* is the world of *Porgy and Bess*, Jerome Kern's *Roberta* and Rodgers' and Hammerstein's *Oklahoma!*. Weill identified himself frankly and constructively with successive worlds, improvising and adapting with a skill that few were able to emulate. Many, no doubt, did not wish to. But these are the terms that he consistently accepted, and the path to a fair understanding must follow that path for some distance, even if one may later choose to survey the scene from a different vantage-point.

This, like any other of Weill's statements of principle and procedure, presupposes the assumption that he makes, and always made, about the centrality of art to the spiritual experience of man. Much else may be subject to negotiation and interpretation, but not this. As he wrote in a short unpublished and undated article, in English:

> In the arts, the human race makes its claim to eternity, because the eternal search for the secret of the 'great beyond' which is inherent to the human race, finds its fulfilment in the imagination of the creative artist. Beethoven and Michelangelo have reached deeper into the Universe than the rocket ship ever will do.

Finally in his interview for *The New York Sun*, Weill unburdens himself of a fashionably provocative article of faith. 'I have never acknowledged the difference,' he declares, 'between "serious" music and "light" music. There is only good music and bad music.'

Only good music and bad music? Does accepting the obvious, that there is good music and bad music, remove the validity of our experience that there is a basic difference of intent, and ultimately of level, between, say, *The Magic Flute* and *The Mikado*, both pieces of undoubtedly 'good' music? To be sure, there is much bad 'serious' music around but its seriousness is as intrinsic as its badness, and the one term does not make the other superfluous. A skilfully designed advertising poster may be 'good' art, but it remains a poster and will not be discussed in the same breath as a still life by Cézanne. Eric Coates' *Knightsbridge* or *Dam Busters* march, or the marches of John Philip Sousa, are undeniably 'good' music but do they breathe the same air as the Prelude to *The Mastersingers of Nuremberg*? Difficult as it may be to define, the distinction between 'serious' and 'light' music is an unspoken reality to anyone who feels the difference in spiritual demand between *Fidelio* and *Die Fledermaus*.

Behind Weill's words lay a wholesome dislike, central to his personality, of the pretentiousness that so often attended the composition of 'serious' music, and his accompanying resentment of the implication that 'light' music did not need or deserve to have such care and attention lavished upon it. Art, all art, was the property of society, and society was constituted by all the art within it, not just by arbitrarily selected manifestations of that art. The music of cabaret and dance-hall is as much the music of the culture in which it flourishes as the music of the concert-hall and the recital room, and Weill, punctilious craftsman that he was, devoted as much attention to the detail of the 'school' opera *Der Jasager* as to that of the 'opera-house' opera *Die Bürgschaft*.

This holistic conception, moreover, enables him to rationalise the nature of his own activity in its new cultural home. For where musical theatre can claim a validity in a culture equal to that enjoyed by, say, the symphony and the string quartet, there is no call to apologise for working on a less 'elevated', less 'serious' level, or to pre-empt criticism that one is thereby denying oneself access to the highest reaches of that culture. Parallel to this runs the sociological view of literature as comprising not only the dramas, the poetry, the novels and the other conventionally accepted genres of 'serious' artistic intent but also journalism, official documents, comic strips, graffiti and any other public sources of the written word. It was a conception that made it easy for Weill to feel part of the society in whose midst he found himself, and natural for him to compose music for it.

And no less natural to pledge himself to its defence. For what purpose would it serve to create works of art for a society which no longer existed, which did not want to hear, or was perhaps forcibly prevented from hearing, what he had to say? He knew it all from his heyday in Germany, when gangs of brown-shirted thugs had been sent to disrupt performances of his works, and when hysterical outbursts in the Nazi press had made it clear that his days as a composer were numbered. Now, with Europe at Hitler's feet and only Britain still resisting, he was determined to play his part in mobilising the minds of the Americans to realise the inevitability – more, the propriety – of war and pointing to the contribution that the European refugees could make both to the prosecution of that war and to the social and cultural life of the United States in general.

1940 saw the establishment of William Allen White's 'Committee to Defend America by Aiding the Allies', a name whose formulation made explicit the terms in which a growing number of people saw the future of their country. In June of that year, impelled by just such motives but with his mind particularly on the position of his fellow-émigrés, Weill wrote a letter in impeccable English to Erika Mann, Thomas Mann's daughter, who, like her father, had been in America since 1938. 'What can we do to help America in her inevitable fight against Nazism?' he asked:

> My idea is to form immediately an organisation called something like 'Alliance of Loyal-Alien Americans', with the purpose of convincing the authorities and the public opinion in this country that we are strongly anti-Nazi, that they can count on us in every effort to save American democracy and that they can consider us in every way as faithful American citizens. . . . We could provide the press with material about the contributions of our friends to the economic, cultural and educational life in the U.S.A.
>
> In order to do all this and much more it would be necessary to create an organisation of a very high reputation. . . . We should start out with a relatively small, carefully selected group of more or less well known members of the German, Austrian, Czech, Scandinavian, Spanish and

Italian immigration under the leadership of your father. . . . I talked to
some American friends about this project. They all think it is a very good
idea but they all agree that it has to be done without delay, before it is too
late.

Erika Mann welcomed Weill's initiative, which, along with other
similar pressures, led to the formation of the 'Emergency Rescue
Committee', chaired by Frank Kingdom, President of the University
of Newark, and including influential liberals like the columnist Dorothy
Thompson, wife of Sinclair Lewis, the radio commentator Raymond
Gram Swing and Robert Hutchins, President of the University of
Chicago. Through the Committee's activities in various European
countries many well-known fugitives from Nazism found their way
to the safety of the United States, among them Thomas Mann's
brother Heinrich and son Golo, Lion Feuchtwanger, Alfred Döblin
and Franz Werfel. When Franklin D. Roosevelt set up his 'Presidential
Advisory Committee on Political Refugees' in July 1940 to expedite
the granting of entry visas to those whose lives were threatened by the
Nazis, the 'Emergency Rescue Committee' had an important advisory
role in the process of ruling on the bona fides of the thousands
of applicants. It was a time not only of widespread suspicion of
aliens as such – a hangover from the days of the Depression –
but of a growing fear that hidden among the genuine victims of
persecution, foreign agents and agitators might be smuggled into the
country.

But the need to oppose Nazism remained paramount, and the
realisation of that need was strengthening. A week before Weill wrote
his letter to Erika Mann, The Playwrights Company, on the initiative
of Maxwell Anderson and Robert E. Sherwood – who was, as it
happened, a member of the 'Defend America' Committee – placed a
full-page advertisement in newspapers throughout the country, headed
'Stop Hitler Now!'. They demanded an unequivocal commitment from
the government to send armaments, warplanes, food and other supplies
to Europe before it was too late – indeed, after the traumatic experiences
of Dunkirk and the fall of France maybe it was already too late. It was
not the first time that artists and intellectuals saw further than many of
the politicians.

Such efforts mattered deeply to Weill, and he became increasingly
involved, more particularly after the United States entered the war, in
cultural and political activities to support the war effort. Nor did he
hesitate to put his money where his mouth was. As well as signing
affidavits for his parents and his brother Nathan to come to America,
he unhesitatingly performed the same service for his old associate Ernst
Josef Aufricht, and joined with Fritz Lang, Dorothy Thompson, Fritz

Kortner and others to help Brecht when he arrived penniless in California in 1941. A generation later a challenge was to ring out from the White House: 'Ask not what your country can do for you – ask what you can do for your country.' Kurt Weill would have been very much John F. Kennedy's man.

The Ballad of Magna Carta, written in January 1940, marked the end, for the time being, of Weill's professional collaboration with Maxwell Anderson. Under the pressure of the events in Europe Anderson was becoming preoccupied with the theme of spiritual faith confronted by the powers of evil, a theme which carried his thoughts away from the play-with-music format and back into the realm of 'straight' theatre. Weill, as far as substantial projects were concerned, was in a kind of limbo. Since *Knickerbocker Holiday* he had nothing to show beyond a few items of light relief – *Railroads on Parade*, *The Ballad of Magna Carta*, some folksong arrangements and incidental novachord music for Elmer Rice's comedy *Two on an Island*, a handful of songs. The only deadline in his diary was April 30, the day of the reopening of the New York World's Fair, by which time he needed to submit new material for a revised production of *Railroads on Parade*.

In the random manner in which so many unpredictable, later highly productive relationships come about, Weill found himself one day in conversation with Hassard Short, designer and stage producer of a number of recent successful musicals, among them Irving Berlin's *Face the Music*. This, and others that Short had produced, had a book by Moss Hart, known not only as one of the wittiest writers on Broadway but, before this, as co-author with the great George S. Kaufman of the priceless Hollywood spoof *Once in a Lifetime*. After doing *Jubilee* for Cole Porter in 1935, Hart had left the musical to do a succession of brilliant comedies with Kaufman over the following four years, starting with the Pulitzer Prizewinner *You Can't Take It With You* in 1936 and ending with *The Man Who Came To Dinner*, starring Monty Woolley, in 1939.

Weill had in his hands a musical comedy script that he had just been sent, based on comic strip characters and called *The Funnies*. Short saw possibilities in the script, thought Moss Hart might be induced to polish it up for Weill's use, and arranged for Hart and Weill to meet. A year later Hart described in his quizzical way what came out of that meeting:

> One rainy afternoon a year ago Kurt Weill and myself sat at a table in a little midtown restaurant and told each other vehemently why we would not write a musical comedy: Kurt Weill because he would not write the music for the regulation musical comedy book, and myself because I

would not write the book for the regulation musical comedy music.

We parted in complete agreement though it was a far cry from the purpose of the meeting. We had arranged to meet to see if we could not do a show together and had thoroughly succeeded in discovering that we couldn't. . . .

We met again the following week, and after another luncheon, that lasted well into the evening, we discovered the kind of show we both definitely *did* want to do. It was, we decided, a show in which the music carried forward the essential story and was not imposed on the architecture of the play as a rather melodious but useless addendum.

This is an easy phrase to write but to achieve that end it was necessary to create both a new technique and a new musical form. I say this at the risk of sounding a little pompous, but it seems to me that in *Lady in the Dark* this has in some measure been successfully accomplished.

Lady in the Dark, written in the course of 1940 and first performed at the Alvin Theatre in January 1942, marks perhaps the most radical turning-point – ideologically, musically, financially – in a career with its fair share of turning-points. The Americanisation of Kurt Weill had been under way for some time. This was now the consummate American Weill, the genuine article, culturally naturalised, rubbing shoulders with the great names of Broadway and revelling in the bright lights. Not only were the days of *Der Protagonist*, of *Dreigroschenoper*, of *Mahagonny*, of the Second Symphony all but invisible behind banks of European cloud: even the socially and politically conscious world of Federal Theatre Project and Group Theatre suddenly seemed remote. He was surrounded by men who knew exactly what the production of a musical show on Broadway demanded, and he submitted wholeheartedly to those demands. It was in any case not in his nature to do anything less than wholeheartedly, including the enjoyment of success.

And the success of *Lady in the Dark* was overwhelming. It had a continuous run of 467 performances, with its most popular songs available as sheet music and on gramophone records; and at the financial summit, Paramount Pictures paid the highest sum ever heard of – 283,000 dollars – for the film rights. 'This quiet and affable and cooperative classically-trained musician,' as Ira Gershwin affectionately described him, who had been able 'to adjust his great talent to the lighter and more melodious requirements of Broadway', had every reason to smile all the way to the bank – it would have been too vulgar to laugh.

The feeble film that Paramount eventually released in 1944 – the same year as *Knickerbocker Holiday* from United Artists – starred Ginger Rogers as Liza Elliott and Ray Milland as Charley Johnson. The show's basic plot survived – just – but little else. Weill's score was butchered. Disembodied fragments of 'My Ship' float past from time to time but the song as a whole is never heard, and only 'Jenny' is salvaged more or less intact from the wreck. Numbers by other composers and lyric writers were inserted, and smarmy background music by 'arrangers' agglutinated the whole sorry hash. Such was the Hollywood way. For 283,000 dollars you could do what you liked.

When Weill and Moss Hart left the midtown restaurant that dark January evening in 1940, they took nothing with them but a pleasant feeling that, with Hart seeking a liberation from his father figure George Kaufman, and Weill momentarily in a trough of uncertainty, becoming known as a composer but not yet known well enough, their roving thoughts on a joint exercise in words and music might – just might – lead somewhere. Though wherever that somewhere might be, Hart made it clear it would not be *The Funnies*.

Born into the slums of the Upper Bronx, his heart and eyes always set on Broadway, Hart was at this time in the grip of psychoanalysis, both as a patient on the analyst's couch and as one fascinated intellectually by the hidden mysteries that analysis brings into the open. So, he mused, why not put psychoanalysis itself on the couch? Or, as he explained in the theatre programme: 'Why not show someone in the process of being psychoanalysed and dramatise the dreams? And what more natural than that the dreams be conveyed by music and lyrics so that the plane of reality and that of the dreams would be distinct?'

Here, in a nutshell, are both the substance and the form of the work that began, in the spirit of the analyst's welcome to his patient, as *I Am Listening* and ended, with gently mocking overtones of the patient's predicament, as *Lady in the Dark*. After much chopping and changing, cutting and adding, what emerged was a two-act play centred on the duality of the real and the fantasy worlds of Liza Elliott, a successful middle-aged editor of a fashion magazine; step by step the analysis of her psychotic state reveals the sources of her fantasies and makes her realise what she really wants.

The dramatic outline, the spoken dialogue, encompasses a serious problem – a disturbed person's struggle to discover her true personality. The three men in her life are Kendall Nesbit, her married lover and the magazine's publisher; Charley Johnson, her advertising manager; and, in her imagination, the film star Randy Curtis. Set into this framework is a musical-comedy sequence of dream scenes in which the bizarre events of Liza's fantasies are played out. Each of these three dream scenes is a through-composed entity with individual solo and choral numbers within it. The 'Glamour Dream' envisions her as a *grande dame*, centre of admiration and attraction, the dedicatee of works by Aldous Huxley and Stravinsky. When Kendall Nesbit tells her that his wife is going to divorce him, she luxuriates in her 'Wedding Dream', imagining that Curtis has fallen in love with her and acting out a surrealistic wedding scene which culminates in a deafening bolero described in the stage directions as 'a cacophonous musical nightmare'. Liza's equally surrealistic third experience, the 'Circus Dream', turns the scene of the big top into a court of law in which she is arraigned for failing to make up her mind about what sort of woman she wants to be.

In her final session on the couch Liza is persuaded to reveal the childhood circumstances that lie at the root of her neuroses. She now realises that she loves not the exciting Randy Curtis or her long-standing lover Kendall Nesbit but her modest colleague Charley Johnson. And at this moment she recalls a song called 'My Ship', which she used to sing with her father. She had hummed the opening bars at the beginning of her 'Glamour Dream', and snatches of it had been bandied around like a Leitmotiv in the course of the play. But only now, in a final sequence called 'Childhood Dream', is she able to sing it in its full sentimental glory to symbolise her recognition of the true love she had at last found.

For the songs in *Knickerbocker Holiday* Maxwell Anderson had written his own lyrics; so had Paul Green for *Johnny Johnson*. But Moss Hart, for all his wit and verbal agility, could not. And because Weill always needed, and rose to, the challenge of the words before him, the choice of lyricist for the items in the dream scenes was crucial. Whose inspired idea it was to approach Ira Gershwin, we do not know. But inspired it was.

Since his brother George's death there in 1937 Ira Gershwin had made his home in Beverly Hills, having, as Benjamin Welles put it in *The New York Times*, 'figuratively closed his front door on the world. Ira Gershwin is probably the only man in Hollywood who underacts his life. He lives with and moves among showmen yet exhibits no overtones of the movie colony. He is so normal in his appearance and deportment that one suspects he lets off steam in his lyrics – and he does.' When, with the European mud still fresh on his boots, Weill had met the two brothers at one of his first parties in New York and told Ira he would like to collaborate with him, Ira had hardly taken it seriously. A lot had changed since then.

Welles picked up the threads of his story:

> Through the lazy round of afternoon tennis games and evening poker parties with a few intimate friends in Beverly Hills came the tinkling of a long distance phone. Moss Hart on the wire in New York. He was writing a new show about a brilliant editor of a fashion magazine, a woman admired and envied yet unhappy and alone. The action would revolve around her psychoanalysis. Kurt Weill had agreed to do the score. They both wanted him for the lyrics. Would he consider it?
>
> Gershwin didn't consider it. He said yes, and hung up. Then he thought about the blissful, sun-drenched ease of Beverly Hills. He feared that his

wife might not take too kindly to the winds and stone chasms of New York in the fall. But as the days passed, he knew he was going back to work and when Moss Hart arrived later in Hollywood to confer on the filming of *The Man Who Came To Dinner*, the deal was set. Ira Gershwin was ready for the wars.

In May Gershwin came to New York and over the following four months the three men knocked their material into shape. 'Kurt and I worked in my hotel suite at the Essex House for sixteen weeks during the hottest summer I'd ever known (and no air-conditioning either),' wrote Ira:

> Frequently we were at the piano after dinner till 11 or 12, when he would leave for the country, while I then would go on working till 4 or 5 in the morning on the lyrics for the tunes he had left me. . . . Kurt was receptive and responsive to almost any notion. And there were several times when he came up with excellent suggestions for lyrics.

Sometimes they adjourned to Hart's country house:

> The food was excellent, the guestrooms cozy; there were a swimming pool and thousands of trees and any amount of huge and overwhelmingly friendly, woolly dogs; there was even a rarity for those days (1940), a TV set; but the show was ever on our minds and mostly we were at it, discussing the score in progress and what lay ahead.

Weill had the position he wanted – to have a say in the assembling of the work as a whole. And in true Broadway manner – Ira Gershwin described it as the way he used to work with George – Weill would sketch tunes, or just catchy openings of tunes, and leave Ira to add his catchy lyrics. 'What we want to do,' wrote Ira to Weill, as they were getting down to work, 'is turn out one hell of a score with at least four or five publishable numbers.' It turned out to have seven.

But what mattered more than Ira Gershwin's witticisms and sometimes outrageous puns was his sheer professionalism, his knowledge of what went into the recipe for a successful Broadway musical. He had no lofty intellectual pretensions. He was an adroit, quick-witted manipulator of words in a context whose limits he cheerfully accepted. Nothing reveals his nature more delightfully than his prefatory inscription to *Lyrics on Several Occasions*, the nearest he came to writing his memoirs: 'Since most of the lyrics in this lodgment were arrived at by adding words mosaically to music already composed, any resemblance to actual poetry, living or dead, is highly improbable.'

Lady in the Dark is described on its title page as a 'Musical Play' – something different, in the eyes of its creators, from a 'musical', like *Show Boat* or *Lady Be Good*, and a 'play with music', which is what, in their different ways, *Dreigroschenoper*, *Der Silbersee* and *Johnny Johnson* are.

'I think for the first time,' said Moss Hart, 'at least so far as my memory serves, the music and lyrics of a musical "show" are part and parcel of the basic structure of the play. One cannot separate the play from the music or vice versa.' But can one not? 'More than that, the music and lyrics carry the story forward dramatically and psychologically.' But do they?

Ira Gershwin's texts are not narrative. We may know more about a character's feelings and state of mind by the end of his or her song but the story itself has not advanced, and when the song is over, we have to return to the spoken dialogue to pick up the threads of the action. When Gershwin told Weill that what they wanted was 'one hell of a score with at least four or five publishable numbers,' he was talking the language of the musical, the language of which he was a master. And 'one hell of a score' is what he and Weill give us. But in formal function and effect their songs occupy a position no different from that of the songs in *Dreigroschenoper*, which, as Brecht had explained at the time, took over the psychological action at moments when the talking stopped.

Every work of art is unique, and every artist seeks as high a degree of originality as his creative personality can achieve. Like Randy Curtis, he has to be able to sing 'This is New', even if the novelty is not all that evident. But in Weill, who saw almost every successive work as a step in a new and original direction, there was an unremitting urge to go further and create within the broad context of musical theatre new forms, even new genres.

Indeed, he constantly maintained that he had done just that. Back in 1929, discussing the philosophy behind his *Dreigroschenoper*, he claimed that he had succeeded in creating 'a new type of musical theatre'. In *Street Scene*, written in 1946, he was to maintain that he had created 'an American opera . . . a special brand of musical theatre which would completely integrate drama and music, spoken word, song and movement'. And although they are not his words but Moss Hart's, in the introductory remarks to the vocal score of *Lady in the Dark*, Weill will not have objected to finding himself and Ira Gershwin credited with having 'created a new musical and lyrical pattern in the American Theatre'.

But novelty, however striking, is no alibi for quality, nor will theory about a work's historical importance render that work better or worse *qua* work. *Vice versa* triumphant practice may show the theoretical statement to be mistaken, or valueless, which is not a situation to weep over. *Lady in the Dark* is not an occasion for tears, or for strained intellectualisations on structure and classification, but one for the uncomplicated enjoyment of a piece of wit and sophistication inseparable from the ethos of the time and the place to which it belongs. With the occasional moment of exception, like the pungent harmonic accompaniment of 'The Princess of Pure Delight' and the splendid 'Dance of the Tumblers' – both bearing the signature of the Weill of the 1920s – it speaks the common language, including the clichés, of the American popular song. It is only from within the context of this language that it can be judged.

To star in the show as Liza Elliott Moss Hart had captured with gratifying ease, the temperamental British actress Gertrude Lawrence, Noël Coward's leading lady of the 1930s, still affectionately remembered on Broadway as the star of Gershwin's *Oh, Kay!* in 1926. Weill's music lay within her scope but her act rested on personality rather than on musical accuracy. ('She had the greatest range between C and C sharp of anyone I ever knew,' Weill once said to Alan Jay Lerner.)

For the role of the fashion photographer Russell Paxton, who reappears in Liza's 'Circus Dream' as the ringmaster, the producers engaged an up-and-coming young comedian who called himself Danny Kaye. More problematical was the casting of Victor Mature as Randy Curtis, the film-star lover who has to woo Liza with the song 'This is New'. He looked the part perfectly but there was a snag. 'When handsome "hunk of man" Victor Mature sang,' said Ira Gershwin, 'his heart and the correct key weren't in it.' So Gershwin altered a word here and there for Gertrude Lawrence to sing the whole song alone, leaving the literally dumbstruck Mature to do nothing but look suitably film-starry.

A change of this kind cost the old pro Gershwin only a few minutes, and as it happened, it did not affect the music. Extension, truncation, deletion and substitution of material, even of whole sequences, was the order of the day as a musical took shape during rehearsals, and the composer had to be prepared to supply tracts of new music at a moment's notice.

For almost all composers, including the Big Five – Gershwin alone excepted – this would entail writing a new melody or two and perhaps (but not necessarily) blocking out the basic harmony, then passing it to a professional arranger to give it its final, orchestral form. But for Weill, conservatoire student of harmony and counterpoint, one-time composer of classical works for the concert hall, the task of composition entailed doing all these things. There was nothing he would delegate. If the producer, or perhaps one of the stars, decided at the eleventh hour that a certain number was not to his liking, or insisted that he needed a new sequence in order to show off his talents, Weill would sit down on the spot and work on until the job was done. And from the 'Mackie Messer Song' in *Dreigroschenoper*, through Walter Huston's 'September Song' in *Knickerbocker Holiday*, now to Gertrude Lawrence's 'Saga of Jenny' in *Lady in the Dark* – a distant cousin of the *Dreigroschenoper* 'Pirate Jenny' – the latecomer could turn out to be a winner.

Not that the whole musical world was falling over itself with admiration. Voices were already raised in caustic regret at the sacrifice of a European talent on the altar of American commercialism. By avoiding 'all contact with what our Leftist friends used to call "social significance",' wrote Virgil Thomson, 'his music has suffered on both counts, it seems to me. It is just as banal as before; but its banality expresses nothing.' 'Since no producer wants his best stuff here,' said the critic Samuel Barlow, more in sorrow than in anger, 'Weill has attempted to tune himself to our ears. The results have been tragic:

> There is a constant, thick soup of music going on; and you wait for just one touch of the old salt. In this long score there are not three minutes of the true Weill. . . . This is sad, and no joking matter. Something first-rate has gone third-rate, which is a loss for everyone who cares deeply about an art, beyond any prejudice or timeliness or mode.

Barlow was only one of many to find himself in this dilemma.

Before it arrived on Broadway in January 1941, *Lady in the Dark* was given a run of tryouts at the Colonial Theatre in Boston. Maurice Abravanel conducted and the piece was produced by the veteran Sam H. Harris – the last show he did. The opening night sold out and the audience's enthusiasm was undisguised from the beginning. They rose to the bounciness and tunefulness of the music and guffawed their way through Ira Gershwin's monstrous couplets:

> It's never too late to Mendelssohn,
> Two hearts are at Journey's Endelssohn,
> Whate'er their future, they must share it.
> I trust they Lohengrin and bear it.

And few will have missed the point when the Ringmaster, in the circus dream, sings a suspiciously familiar snippet of melody to the words,

> Our object all sublime
> We shall achieve in time:
> To let the melody fit the rhyme,
> The melody fit the rhyme.

But just in case some did, Gershwin adds:

> This is all immaterial and irrelevant!
> What do you think this is – Gilbert and Sellivant?'

Suddenly, with the circus dream almost over, there came a moment of panic. 'We were playing to a packed house,' Gershwin recalled,

> and the show was holding the audience tensely. It was working out. I was among the standees at the back of the house; next to me was one of the Sam Harris staff. In the circus scene when Danny Kaye completed

the last note of "Tchaikovsky", thunderous applause rocked the theatre for at least a solid minute. The staff member clutched my arm, muttered: "Christ, we've lost our star!", couldn't take it, and rushed for the lobby. Obviously he felt that nothing could top Danny's rendition and that either Miss Lawrence would leave the show or that Danny Kaye would have to be cut down to size.

A few moments later everything looked different. Revealing nuances of interpretation never heard in rehearsals, the haughty, elegant Gertrude Lawrence came on stage and launched into her 'Saga of Jenny' – as Ira Gershwin put it, 'to the complete devastation of the audience':

> At the conclusion, there was an ovation which lasted twice as long as that for "Tchaikovsky". "Tchaikovsky" had shown us the emergence of a new star in Danny Kaye. But "Jenny" revealed to us that we didn't have to worry about losing our brighter-than-ever star.

The 'Tchaikovsky' *tour de force* that shot Danny Kaye to fame is an 'Allegro barbaro' consisting of a breathless catalogue of 49 names of Russian composers which he rattled off in 39 seconds. It became one of the staple items in his variety performances the whole world over, and it was his lasting ambition to clip more and more off his time. On one of his tours for UNICEF in the 1950s he clocked in with 36 breakneck seconds in Barcelona and 31 in Madrid.

'Tchaikovsky' and Liza's following number on the fate of Jenny, who suffered the penalties for always making up her mind, are the biggest show-stoppers in *Lady in the Dark*. Both were afterthoughts, and neither, whatever Moss Hart claimed to the contrary, is 'part and parcel of the basic structure of the play'. But who cares?

At the end of the work Liza discovers the song that has haunted her throughout her dreams and experiences – 'My Ship', perhaps the most beautiful Broadway melody Weill wrote. 'My ship has sails that are made of silk, The decks are trimmed with gold,' she sings. After the triumphant opening in New York George Kaufman sent Weill a telegram: 'Your ship has sails that are made of gold. Relax.' A Good Luck message from Richard Rodgers conveyed the admiration of his fellow-professionals: 'If you have any second endings left over, please let us know.'

One winter's day in 1928, almost exactly eleven years earlier, Weill had been walking through the streets of Berlin when he met Max Butting, his old revolutionary friend of Novembergruppe days. Butting had just been to see *Dreigroschenoper*. 'Well?' Weill greeted him: 'What do you say? Is *Dreigroschenoper* my new path or not?' He did not need to wait for the answer. 'The question of how he should write had been quickly resolved,' Butting observed, 'because he believed he had found his public,' In 1941 he had too.

CHAPTER XV

'I'm an American!'

On the surface it looked as though *Lady in the Dark* might herald a triumphant succession of musical collaborations to rival those between the Gershwins, between Richard Rodgers and Lorenz Hart, and later between Rodgers and Oscar Hammerstein II. The ingredients were there, a congenial *modus operandi* had been found, and the public had delivered its approval. And if Moss Hart's claim for its originality in the context of American musical theatre were to be believed, there would be every reason to investigate the possibilities of the 'musical play' further.

But although he was to join forces with Ira Gershwin again, Weill never did another piece with Moss Hart. A frustrating period of false starts, dashed hopes and minor occasional pieces set in, and it was to be two years before another collaboration produced substantial results. On the one side was his urge to constant experimentation, to extend the frontiers of expression of musical theatre, along with an unwillingness to settle for a formula, however successful. On the other were the advantages of a certain continuity, of building on a base established with a partner whose ways he understood and whose broad aims he shared, which implied that the relationship would yield more than one harvest as it had done with Georg Kaiser and Brecht, and as it was to do with Maxwell Anderson.

The first of these options presumes the appearance at that self-same moment of a kindred spirit from the world of literature prepared to submit, if only in passing, to the conditions of the musico-dramatic world; the second demands a sustained commitment from that spirit to the principles of some kind of *Gesamtkunstwerk*. Both require from the poet-dramatist a willingness to withdraw the absolute autonomy of his art in deference to the demands of the other art with which his literature is, quite literally, sharing the stage. The dramatic text would not have the form it has if the playwright did not know from the outset that music was going to be written to it. On the other hand a dramatist might, in a spirit of adventure, cooperate with a composer to see what opportunities it threw up, 'what there was in it for him', so to speak. That was Brecht's attitude. Let us have music by all means, he would say, if it enhances the effectiveness of my play, but the words – my words – come first. A dramatist is not a librettist – although a librettist may be a dramatist.

The composer starts from a position of dependence: he needs the dramatist, otherwise – unless he can write his own texts – he cannot compose his music. Had Weill been content to use the products of a conventional musical-comedy writer, he would no doubt have made life a lot easier for himself – and earned a lot more money. On the contrary, he sought out the Paul Greens, the Maxwell Andersons and the Elmer Rices – the real dramatists, who would find time for him when it suited them but whose horizons were not bound by the terms of musical theatre. Moreover he wanted to be involved in the planning of the whole musico-dramatic enterprise from the outset. He was not in the business of prospecting for soft options.

Nevertheless, as he wrote to Ira Gershwin: 'It is lots of fun to have a smash hit. The show is doing wonderful business (as you know from your statements). We have between 20 and 100 standees in every performance and the audience reaction is wonderful.' 'We bought a Buick convertible today,' he added.

In May, in the full flush of this fun, he celebrated by making the supreme symbolic gesture of a man at one with his physical and spiritual environment. For 16,000 dollars, taken from his share of the film rights for *Lady in the Dark*, he bought a house, a converted nine-room farm building, some hundred and fifty years old, on South Mountain Road in New City, Rockland County, which had been modernised by its former owner, the actor Rollo Peters. Surrounding the house were fourteen acres of woods and grassland through which flowed a trout stream that gave the place its name – Brook House.

Less than an hour's drive from Manhattan, nestling among the tree-covered hills to the west of the Hudson River, Brook House was to become a real home for Weill and Lenya, far more so, for a variety of unhappy reasons, than Kleinmachnow in the 1930s could ever have been. A short walk from the Andersons, with artists, writers and actors as their immediate neighbours, Brook House offered what had first attracted them to Rockland County – the tranquillity of the wooded countryside combined with the proximity of the city.

Resident in New City at one time or another during these years were Burgess Meredith and his wife Paulette Goddard (formerly wife of Charlie Chaplin), the painter Henry Varnum Poor, the cartoonist Milton Caniff (creator of 'Terry and the Pirates' and 'Steve Canyon'), Alan Jay Lerner and the actress Helen Hayes. Friendships blossomed, Maxwell Anderson, strong of personality and conviction, a magnet of intellectual attraction, was now even closer at hand, and Lenya, perhaps now truly aware of the value of security and companionship, was making peace with herself. 'Lenya is dashing around all day and we are having lots of fun buying furniture etc. and I think it will be very nice,' wrote Weill to Ira Gershwin. She was also able to indulge again in her passion for playing cards, and found in Mab, Anderson's wife, an equally indefatigable partner. Lenya, in fact, made a more easy-going, more relaxed impression on their friends than did her husband; she had more time on her hands, whereas he seemed to sense that it was already September and that, as Peter Stuyvesant felt, the days were growing short.

Their relationship as husband and wife in the notoriously volatile world of show-biz liaisons had for one observer in the New City community a curiously neutral, matter-of-fact quality. 'I wasn't conscious either of a division between them or of affection between them,' Quentin Anderson, Maxwell's eldest son, told Donald Spoto:

> It was as if they were by now partners who knew each other so well and relied on each other. But as a marriage I could never quite take it in.

Still, this was the life they had chosen, in the place they had chosen, and they set about making Brook House a real home. Faithful to the origins of the place, they furnished it to a large extent in the old American style, and some of these pieces, together with the upright Steinway that stood in Weill's study, have since found a safe haven in the rooms of the Kurt Weill Foundation.

To complete their rustic idyll Moss Hart presented them with one of his own sheepdogs, to whom they gave the name 'Woolly' – though, given Weill's 'inch-thick' accent, as Joshua Logan had called it, outsiders could be forgiven for thinking he was called 'Voolly'. He took the place in Weill's affections of his beloved Harras, whom he had had to leave behind in Paris.

Before moving from Suffern to New City, Weill had written to his parents in Palestine, anxious that they and his brother Nathan should join him in America; he has lodged affidavits on their behalf, he says, and the financial rewards from *Lady in the Dark* would alone enable him to support them. But Albert Weill was now seventy-four. He had been in poor health for some while and remained so for the rest of his life, and did not wish to uproot himself a second time.

From his letters to his parents, full of news about his home life and his musical success, there emerges an unmistakeable sense of contentment and well-being. He has planted his own vegetables, he tells them, and feels a lot healthier for working in the large garden where the blossoming trees are his special joy when spring approaches and the snow has melted.

1941–2 was a severe winter: 'I have to shuffle [sic!] the snow for several hours to get my car out of the garage.' Of course, he adds, 'as you can imagine, I have to pay a lot in income tax. But anyone who is lucky enough to live in this wonderful country is only too willing to pay.' He had in the past given them sums of money for various items, sometimes personal, sometimes for the local Jewish community and its temple, and from 1942 onwards sent them a regular allowance of 125 dollars a month.

During the time Weill and Lenya were putting down roots in Brook House, three voices hailed them from the past – a past which, after the dazzling success of *Lady in the Dark*, must have looked more remote than ever. The first was that of Ernst Josef Aufricht, who had recently landed in New York with his wife and son, after an uncomfortable journey across the Atlantic in the converted cargo hold of a Spanish freighter. Back in Berlin Aufricht had been a young man with money to burn – more money than sense, said the scoffing wiseacres who watched him sink his fortune in the hopelessly unpromising *Dreigroschenoper* in 1928. Now, no longer young, his days of unquestioned prosperity behind him, he was just one more Jewish refugee, known, if at all, only as a man with a knack for backing the right theatrical horse.

With the help of one of the many charitable bodies, some Jewish, some Christian, some secular, that had come into being to help the refugees over their first few weeks, Aufricht and his family established themselves in an apartment on the Upper West Side. A few evenings later Weill called by in his big new car to take him to see *Lady in the Dark*. There was no disguising who had the money now. 'I was full of admiration for his Buick convertible,' said Aufricht, not without envy. 'He could raise and lower the top just by pressing a button.' Weill took him home after the show and was about to drive off when Aufricht called out: 'I shall need a little money.' 'Of course,' replied Weill. 'I'll send you a cheque tomorrow.' The cheque that arrived was for 100 dollars. 'I found that a bit tight-fisted,' grumbled Aufricht, 'but Vambery [now a teacher of drama at the Brander Matthews Theatre of Columbia University] pointed out to me that in America it was not done to ask for money personally, or to give any. If one has financial problems, one takes on any sort of job and sticks at it until one is in a position to carry out one's own schemes.'

In any case, as Aufricht's wife Margot found, Weill's helpfulness and generosity had not changed. 'He always was the gentle, good friend,' she said, 'well-balanced and easily accommodating himself to his surroundings.' With Margot Aufricht helping to run a health studio in New Jersey, and their son working for the NBC network, the Aufrichts soon hoisted themselves back to something like the standard of living they used to know. But Aufricht himself never fully took to his new circumstances and returned to Germany in 1949.

Weill's second voice from the past, a still, small voice muffled further by transmission through an intermediary, came from Engelberg, in Switzerland. The intermediary was Paul Gordon, literary adviser to the Shubert Theatre; the voice was that of Georg Kaiser – lonely, forgotten, impoverished, looking pessimistically for some kind of recognition from the world outside. 'Some time ago,' Kaiser wrote to Gordon,

> you asked whether I would be willing to produce something together with Kurt Weill. Well, the novel of Billy Budd ends with a ballad. After I had read this ballad, the style of the play became clear to me. It would have to be a play with music. This music should be written by Kurt Weill. May I therefore ask you to read Melville's novel and then try to have a personal discussion with Kurt Weill.

Among titles of works and ideas for further projects that Weill jotted down in his early American years had indeed been plays of Kaiser's, and in the late 1920s Kaiser, with *Mississippi* and a number of comedies, had joined the current fashion for plays set in America. But the Weill Kaiser knew was the Weill of *Der Silbersee*, and before that of *Der Protagonist* and *Der Zar lässt sich photographieren*. He would have walked past the composer of *Lady in the Dark* without recognising him. The *Billy Budd* idea came to nothing, so whether that composer could have done in the 1940s what Benjamin Britten did in 1951 must remain an open question though many might not have great difficulty in closing it. Silence also greeted Gordon's idea that Weill might write music for Kaiser's *Soldat Tanaka*, with Paul Muni in the leading role.

The tentative approaches from the unhappy Georg Kaiser were quickly swamped by insistent, sometimes rasping tones from closer at hand. They came from another recent late arrival from Europe, like Aufricht, a man who never came to terms with life in the land which gave him sanctuary and which he was to leave abruptly six years later, as abruptly as he had left Germany the day after the Reichstag fire. After travelling from Finland via the Trans-Siberian Railway across the entire Soviet Union to Vladivostok, then down to Manila and across the Pacific, Bertolt Brecht finally arrived in California with his family and his mistress Ruth Berlau in July 1941.

Brecht had been at his ease in the mercenary, cheating, whoring, boozing America of his anti-capitalist imagination of the 1920s, and still professed a commitment to the joys of Soviet Communism, though they were apparently not joyful enough to induce him to stay. In the America of his real experience he did not get much beyond a sense of cynical confusion. That confusion, based on a refusal to grasp the political realities of a liberal democratic system to which he, like thousands of others, had reason to be profoundly grateful, became the more irritating when he saw around him friends and former colleagues from Europe who had fallen on their feet. Weill, who had sent him a contribution towards the formidable cost of his journey, was a spectacular newcomer to the ranks of these success stories but others had also found niches for themselves. Hanns Eisler, whose Communist past had caused him considerable difficulties when he first arrived in 1938, had been appointed to a post at the New School for Social Research in New York in 1940, moving in 1942 to California, where he joined both the faculty of UCLA and the Hollywood film-music industry. Paul Dessau had settled into a teaching job in New York, while Leo Lania had joined the hundred-dollars-a-week 'scriptwriters' subsidised by Hollywood.

There was also Erwin Piscator, who had been in New York since 1933 and for whose benefit the Dramatic Workshop was founded in 1939 under the aegis of the New School for Social Research. Starting with a mere twenty students, the Workshop became during the twelve years of its existence a powerful magnet for dramatic talent, and among its students were Walter Matthau, Marlon Brando, Rod Steiger and Tony Curtis. Weill was to serve on the Workshop's board of trustees from 1947 until his death.

But no flags were put out to welcome Bertolt Brecht. Until Fritz Lang's film *Hangmen Also Die* put a respectable sum of money in his pocket a year later, he had to make do with his weekly 100 dollars from the film industry, supplemented by hand-outs from established émigrés and American defenders of the anti-Fascist cause, like Sinclair Lewis and his wife, Dorothy Thompson.

While still in Finland Brecht had sent Weill his play *Der gute Mensch von Sezuan* in the thought that he would provide song-settings and incidental music – a project which had a tortuous and unhappy history over the following years and was finally written off in 1944. The Broadway Weill was not the Berlin Weill, but Brecht seemed to think he was, or must be, or in any case ought to be.

With *Dreigroschenoper*, the obvious other hope that Brecht now raised, the outcome should have been different. But again the divergent development of their thoughts and careers was of itself almost a guarantee of frustration. Writing to Weill from California, Brecht suggested he direct an all-black *Dreigroschenoper* – the idea already associated with Paul Robeson and a Negro Cultural Foundation. Weill, who held both the performing rights and the music reproduction rights for the United States, had had the same idea some years earlier and found it unworkable. He knew his man, and could feel that Brecht's motives were largely financial; he refused, however, to prejudice a future success with *Dreigroschenoper* on Broadway by permitting a second-rate production on the West Coast, especially as the memory of its flop in the Empire Theatre in 1933 still lingered in the commercial mind.

In fact, whereas Brecht still saw his play much as he had seen it in 1928, Weill realised that the American market would not possibly accept it in that form. What was needed, he said in his reply, was 'not a translation but an adaptation for the American theatre'. 'The sort of production I have in mind,' he went on, 'would not only bring you real financial benefits but would establish you as a writer for the theatre in America.' In other words, what he envisioned was not a translation of the Schiffbauerdamm to Broadway but the creation of a Broadway *Dreigroschenoper* on the spot, with the help of a writer like Moss Hart.

Reading between the lines, one senses that Weill was actually far from keen on pursuing the *Dreigroschenoper* idea, whatever the skin colour of the performers. It *is* a difficult work to revive, more problematical than *The Beggar's Opera*, whose tunes remain less dated in their simple, universal appeal than Weill's intellectual sophistications, and whose text, as honest-to-goodness historical satire and romance, is still an uncomplicated delight. Weill insisted that any later version of his music should be heard only in his own instrumentation, and he took sharp exception to a proposal from Adorno that a black *Threepenny Opera* should be based on the principle of jazz improvisation, since, said Adorno, that was the natural music idiom of the American negroes. At the same time he accepted that it would be impossible to return to the literal musical score of 1928 and the now hopelessly out-of-date style of Mackeben and his band, which would only produce hilarity in America. With so many incompatibles to accommodate, the only predictable outcome was defeat.

Also doomed to a life on paper were assorted plans for new works – an adaptation from William Saroyan or of S. N. Behrman's *The Pirate* (for which Cole Porter later did a movie score), to something based on *Pygmalion, Caesar and Cleopatra* or another of Shaw's plays, a musical on James Bridie's *Tobias and the Angel*, on a novel by Herman Wouk and so on. In long letters to Ira Gershwin he put up whole rows of proposals for collaboration on this and that, most of which the canny Ira took with a goodly number of grains of salt. 'I didn't answer you about all those ideas you wrote me because you intimated (and I felt) that they were tentative and probably merely possibilities,' he replied (one can see the gentle grin). 'I was waiting to hear something of a more definite nature.' He was to hear that something in a few years' time.

The letters of the genial Gershwin are as one would expect them to be – natural and easy-going, chatty in tone, light in intellectual argument, substantial in detail on passing trivia. Even in early 1942, describing the appearance of soldiers on the streets of Los Angeles, the erection of searchlights, the temporary closing of Hollywood night clubs and other signs that America was preparing to take the war seriously, he manages to sound unruffled, almost detached. Weill felt the war as a European. Yet – and it is an experience as startling as it is amusing – the style of his letters to Ira Gershwin, written in idiomatic English, mimics that of Ira's letters to him with an uncanny accuracy – the same conversational, almost playful tone, the same lingering over matters of slight import, the same avoidance of heavy argument. To Brecht, on the other hand, he writes briskly and to the point – sober, practical letters with a minimum of sentiment. It is as though he were assuming his partner's persona, addressing him in his own style and language.

So it was with his music. He had made the decision to address the American public in the language of the American musical. The roots of *Lady in the Dark* lie not in the German past that Weill brought with him but in the American present that enveloped him on his arrival. Yet he could readily revive the idioms of that past – that is, could address the imagined audience of those days – if its associations were reactivated. When, in March 1942, Brecht sent him a copy of a sardonic anti-war ballad he had just published called 'The Song of the Nazi Soldier's Wife', he reverted to an ironical tone of voice reminiscent of the acidic 'Brecht style' with which he had wooed audiences in pre-Nazi Berlin. With its mocking message directed at undermining the morale of the German population as the disasters of the Russian campaign mounted, it was used by the Office of War Information in its behind-the-lines propaganda broadcasts to Germany – the second of Weill's songs, after 'J'attends un navire', to acquire a direct political function.

Most of his other songs from 1942 – in compositional terms a year of bits and pieces – are concentrated around his activities on behalf of the American war effort, to which he devoted much energy in the months after Pearl Harbor. Isolationism died hard and there was a job of education to be done. Even before Pearl Harbor he had joined in a typical one-off show called *Fun To Be Free*, put on by a pressure group of show-business liberals calling itself 'Fight For Freedom'. *Fun To Be Free*, written by the fiery journalist and scriptwriter Ben Hecht and the playwright Charles MacArthur, was an historical pageant with incidental music in praise of American democracy, reminiscent in conception of *The Common Glory* and *The Eternal Road*. Weill's score, for chorus and orchestra, has not survived but 'Fight for Freedom' had sufficient kudos to attract for the single performance at Madison Square Garden the services of Melvyn Douglas, Burgess Meredith, Franchot Tone and Tallulah Bankhead as the four narrators in the work.

Spurred by this challenge, Weill now looked for further opportunities to put his music to the service of the war effort. The titles of some of the patriotic songs he wrote tell their own story – 'Schickelgruber', 'Buddy on the Night Shift', 'Toughen Up, Buckle Down, Carry On'. No doubt they served a purpose. But they are the work of an intellectual writing down to his assumed public, which is a recipe for embarrassment. Closer to his intellectual homeland were the activities of the German-American community in New York, in particular the work of the German-Jewish weekly *Aufbau* ('Reconstruction') and its associated radio programme 'We Fight Back', in which Aufricht found himself a niche.

The target of these programmes was those elements in the German-American population which had yet to be convinced of the need to fight Hitler and support the United States war effort. Some of those who had been in the country from pre-Nazi times retained a pride in their national heritage which made it hard for them to accept that in the physical and moral destruction of their native land, as it then confronted the world, lay the only way to save freedom and human dignity in the civilised world. Others were unrepentant Nazis or opponents of the war for other reasons, while yet others considered the appropriate stance to be one of neutrality, a stance which large sectors of the American population as a whole had adopted before the trauma of Pearl Harbor. And in 1941 and 1942 one could not be certain which way the war in Europe would go.

In its daily one-hour broadcasts, 'We Fight Back' transmitted scenes from the German classics, radio plays and serials, music by German composers in exile, including Weill, Eisler and Dessau, and political commentaries by prominent members of the German émigré community, such as Thomas Mann, Franz Werfel and the theologian Paul Tillich. It was under the auspices of this programme that a year later, in April 1943, to mark the tenth anniversary of the Nazi book-burning demonstrations, a well-publicised and long-remembered cultural event, arranged by Aufricht and Manfred George, editor of *Aufbau*, took place at Hunter College in New York. Fritz von Unruh read from his own works, dramatised scenes and sketches were performed, including Stephen Vincent Benét's radio play *They Burned the Books*, and Lotte Lenya, accompanied by her husband, sang three numbers from *Dreigroschenoper* and gave the first performance of 'The Song of the Nazi Soldier's Wife'. Brecht attended, as did Elisabeth Bergner and other émigré actors and actresses, and to raise money for the War Bond Drive original manuscripts and drawings were auctioned. A poem of Brecht's raised 500 dollars; the script of a radio broadcast by Thomas Mann made 1,500 dollars, while the manuscript of Einstein's address to commemorate the twenty-fifth anniversary of the Red Army went for 2,000 dollars.

Weill derived a great deal of pleasure and satisfaction from being part of such activities. Even more rewarding, he found, because of the sustained commitment it required, was an invitation early in 1942 to become involved in entertaining the workers in shipyards and factories on whom war production depended. A group of theatre people, among them Moss Hart, had observed the activities of ENSA (Entertainments National Service Association) in Britain, which, under government direction, organised a broad spectrum of events for servicemen and factory workers. ENSA had shown that even the most modest of shows could work wonders for morale. Impressed, Hart saw that here was a way in which American show business could make a direct contribution to the war effort, and he invited Weill to join in organising a pilot show at the Wheeler shipyard in Brooklyn. Weill described the scene in a little essay called 'A Coke, A Sandwich and Us!':

> We arrived at the shipyard with a group of about ten performers. The workers had built a little outdoor stage in a square overlooking the sound, against the background of a victory ship which was just ready to be launched. It was one of the most exciting moments of my theatrical life when at noon, with the sound of the lunch whistle, some 1,400 men rushed into the square and watched the show while they were eating lunch. The show consisted of some singing and dancing, with the Kaufman and Hart sketch 'The Man Who Came to Russia' as the centre piece. We felt immediately that the idea was what Broadway would call 'a natural'. It had the informality, the genuine popularity, the immediate contact between audience and performers which you find when a wandering circus comes into a small town. Strangely enough, ever since, whenever I went out with our shows, I experienced the same excitement at the sound of the whistle, the same feeling that this was theatre in the oldest and best sense, comparable to the Greek theatre, the Chinese theatre or the miracle plays of the Middle Ages.

Out of this beginning, launched in a spirit of bubbling enthusiasm, grew the 'Lunch Time Follies', a kind of American 'Workers' Playtime', and under Weill's guidance, as Chairman of the Program Committee, half-hour shows were put on in factories up and down the East Coast.

With Weill engrossed in his 'Lunch Time Follies', Lenya spent the first half of 1942 on tour in Maxwell Anderson's play *Candle in the Wind*, in which Anderson, aware of her frustration at no longer having a career of her own, had written a small part for her. She took up with a young air-force pilot from Texas, an affair as unconcealed from her husband as any of its predecessors, but her chatty, affectionate letters to New City from Pittsburgh, Philadelphia, Dallas and other stops along the route convey no sense of fulfilment at treading the boards again.

In the summer came the first glimmerings of hope that a substantial new collaboration might be in the offing. The idea of a work on the subject of Pygmalion had occurred to Weill more than once, and included in one of his project lists from this time is the name *The Tinted Venus*. This is the title of a charming little story by the humorous Victorian writer F. Anstey, which he had recently read. It tells the tale of Leander Tweddle, proprietor of a barber shop in Bloomsbury, who, on his way with his fiancée Matilda to a garden party one evening, passes a statue of Venus. He has with him the engagement ring he intends to give Matilda but the sight of the Venus induces him to slip the ring over one of the statue's fingers in jest. The statue thereupon comes to life, and to Leander's embarrassment she attaches herself to him like a limpet. When he finally succeeds in getting the ring off her finger, she resumes her existence as a statue and leaves him free to return to the long-suffering Matilda. Out of this story, as Weill wrote to Ira Gershwin, he could see his way to producing 'a very entertaining and yet original kind of *opéra comique* along the lines of Offenbach'.

At this moment Cheryl Crawford reappeared on the scene. Since the disbandment of the Group Theatre the previous year she had gone into business as an independent producer – a special feather in her cap was a recent revival (minus its recitatives) of *Porgy and Bess*, which Weill called 'a wonderful thing for the American theatre'. Visiting Weill after the success of *Lady in the Dark* and learning of his attraction to this Venus story, she invited Sam and Bella Spewack to prepare a script, and the mildly mad versifier Ogden Nash to supply lyrics. As the plot began to take shape, they agreed that the role of Venus was tailor-made for Marlene Dietrich. So after Weill, who knew her from Berlin days, had written to explain what they had in mind, he and Cheryl Crawford set off for Hollywood with the first pages of the script and a few songs to try and capture her for the part.

She had taken to playing a five-foot-long musical saw, Cheryl Crawford remembered:

> I was accustomed to many varieties of eccentric behavior from stars but I must confess that when Marlene placed that huge saw securely between her elegant legs and began to play, I was more than a little startled. . . . We would talk about the show for a while, then Marlene would take up the musical saw and begin to play. That, we soon found out, was the cue that talk was finished for the evening.

Dietrich was romantically involved with Jean Gabin at the time, and unlike Jenny in *Lady in the Dark*, would *not* make up her mind. The attraction of the idea persisted, however, and when she visited New York a few weeks later, she was to be found inspecting the various Venuses in the Metropolitan Museum of Art. She bought a number of reproduction statues, then ordered yards and yards of grey chiffon, draping herself in it in the various poses of the statues. 'We were summoned to view her, while she would model her latest discovery,' wrote Cheryl Crawford. Finally she settled for the so-called Callipygian Venus – 'Venus of the Beautiful Buttocks' – and signed a contract without further hesitation.

Then things started to go wrong. Work on the book became sluggish and finally ground to a halt. Despairing of the Spewacks, Cheryl Crawford turned to the humorist S. J. Perelman, who wrote a totally new script, with Ogden Nash supplying the lyrics as before. Shown Perelman's altogether brasher, more *risqué* book – what would one expect from the scriptwriter of the Marx Brothers' *Monkey Business*? – Marlene Dietrich threw up her elegant hands in horror. In a telephone conversation with Weill that Perelman overheard she became very agitated and exclaimed, to Weill's unconcealed annoyance: 'It really is impossible for me to play it. You know, Kurt, I have a daughter who is nineteen years old, and for me to get up on the stage and exhibit my legs is now impossible. . . . It is too sexy and profane.'

And there, as far as Dietrich was concerned, the matter ended. For months they had had a star but no play; now they were left with a play but no star. Gertrude Lawrence also turned the offer down. Eventually the part of Venus was taken by Mary Martin, and the show that went on the stage was called *One Touch of Venus*. But that was still many months away, and until he knew that a production would definitely go ahead, Weill saw little purpose in becoming involved beyond the point he had already reached – that of having sketched a few songs for a show, scripted by Bella Spewack, which was never going to be finished. And more serious matters were to claim his attention.

Never even to be started, but allowing delightful speculation on what might have been, was a project for Weill to revamp and reorchestrate Offenbach's *La belle Hélène* for a Broadway production starring Grace Moore. Back in the 1920s he had ranged Offenbach alongside Johann Strauss and Gilbert and Sullivan as triumphant proof that so-called 'light' music could embody high artistic values, and had expressed his indignation that an 'inspired' work like *La Grande Duchesse de Gérolstein*, 'bubbling over with brilliant ideas', should be so neglected. But now his view had changed. 'I saw *La Vie Parisienne*,' he wrote to Russell Lewis, who was to produce the new *Belle Hélène*, 'and was quite shocked how stale and how dated the Offenbach music sounded.'

Moreover, the moral and spiritual needs of the times impressed themselves increasingly upon him, making Offenbachian trivialities look irrelevant. These needs he felt not only in the national political arena of the war effort but also in his exposed personal position as a German Jew. By the end of 1942, at the latest, the evidence of the policy of extermination that constituted Hitler's 'Final Solution' to the 'Jewish question' had become public knowledge. Yet anti-Semitic feeling, hand-in-hand with its natural ally, opposition to immigration, induced a psychological conspiracy of inaction. Until the establishment of the War Refugee Board over a year later, Roosevelt did nothing. The Churches remained almost completely silent. Only Jewish organisations themselves were left to defend their own cause, often squabbling among themselves over the best way to do so, or even over the wisdom of doing anything at all. 'It's the same old story,' said Peter Bergson, a prominent Zionist. 'Jews must always battle Jews. It's the only politics open to a stateless people. The only victories they can hope to enjoy are victories over each other.'

Ben Hecht organised a dinner party to which he invited thirty prominent Jewish writers and intellectuals in the hope of stimulating some form of public activity that would draw attention to the Jewish tragedy. Only two of the thirty offered their support. One of them was Moss Hart. 'I thought I'd tell you,' he said to Hecht, 'that if I can do anything definite in the way of Jewish propaganda, call on me.' The other was Weill. Hecht recalled the moment in his autobiography: 'Kurt Weill, the lone composer present, looked at me with misty eyes. A radiance was in his strong face. "Please count on me for everything," Kurt said.'

Born of this cooperation was *We Will Never Die*, a pageant in the line of *The Eternal Road* and *Fun To Be Free*, written by Hecht, directed by Moss Hart, music by Weill. Backed by Ernst Lubitsch and Billy Rose, among others, it played two performances in its one night at Madison Square Garden in March 1943. The cast of narrators and actors included Paul Muni, Ralph Bellamy, Frank Sinatra, Edward G. Robinson and Sylvia Sidney, accompanied by full orchestra and chorus – a huge celebration of the Jewish contribution to civilisation and a chilling reminder of the massacre taking place at that very moment in the concentration camps of Europe. The climax came with fifty rabbis reciting in unison the Mourner's Kaddish, the Hebrew prayer for the departed.

Thousands in New York and other cities saw the 'Memorial: Dedicated to the Two Million Jewish Dead of Europe', as Hecht called it. Senator, later President, Lyndon B. Johnson sent Weill a telegram of congratulation after the first performance and invited him to a dinner in his honour at the Waldorf Astoria Hotel a few days later. But in effect it preached only to the converted, and Weill, for one, had no illusions about its influence on the American public at large. As he and Hecht were walking down a wintry Fifth Avenue late one night, Hecht recalled that he turned and said, 'The pageant has accomplished nothing. I know Bergson calls it a turning-point in Jewish history but he is stage-struck. Actually all we have done is make a lot of Jews cry, which is not a unique accomplishment.'

A few weeks after the evening of *We Will Never Die* Brecht made a trip from California to New York, in the course of which he and Ruth Berlau spent a week with the Weills at Brook House. He brought two proposals with him, neither of them new. One concerned a musical version of *Der gute Mensch von Sezuan*, in which he had tried to interest Weill before leaving Europe and which he now thought might launch his career on Broadway. Discussions dragged on until late the following year but no one interested or competent enough to prepare an English text ever appeared, and the plan died of natural causes.

The other project proved more obdurate, and eventually died not so much a natural death as the death of a thousand cuts. This was for a stage version, with music, of Jaroslav Hašek's famous picaresque anti-war novel *The Good Soldier Schweyk*.

The history of this stop-go epic of collaborative non-fulfilment goes back to Piscator's famous 'collective' dramatisation of Hašek's book at the Theater am Nollendorfplatz in Berlin in 1928. Brecht had had a hand in this, and Weill, for whom Hašek's tragi-comical story had an attraction that stayed with him all his life, hoped that he and Brecht might tackle the subject after they had finished the *Mahagonny* opera. But there had been problems with the Hašek estate over the rights – Hašek had died in 1923 – and Brecht moved into a phase of rigorous ideological didacticism which turned issues of common humanity and moral decision such as *Schweyk* presented into matters of weak irrelevance. So the plan went no further.

Now, twelve years later, there was a sudden resurgence of interest in the *Schweyk* story. Piscator commissioned an English translation of his old Berlin version from H.R. Hays (with whom Weill was to have done *Davy Crockett*) and offered it to the Theatre Guild. At the very same time Brecht, his interest rekindled after his stay in Brook House, set about doing a new text of his own, obviously and characteristically behind Piscator's back. The intention was that Weill would provide the music and that Aufricht, rejoining the *Dreigroschenoper* team of happy memory, would look after the production.

Considerable suspicion and acrimony was generated, not surprisingly, when it became known that two *Schweyk*s were being prepared in parallel, Brecht apparently having a finger in both pies. In the event neither version reached the stage. Weill had always had reservations about the sort of script Brecht was producing and, as the year progressed, he found himself occupied with other things. Aufricht, too, saw no future in the project and handed back to his sponsors the 85,000 dollars he had already raised. Brecht, on the other hand, persisted in trying to attract a prominent Hollywood actor to the title role – first Peter Lorre, then Charles Laughton – but no Broadway backers could be found. The first performance of his *Schwejk im zweiten Weltkrieg* ('Schweyk in the Second World War'), as it came to be called, did not take place until 1957, a year after Brecht's death, with music by Hanns Eisler.

From midsummer 1943, with Bella Spewack's script abandoned, Perelman's book and Ogden Nash's lyrics firmly in place, and Mary Martin, fresh from *The Birth of the Blues* and other film roles, capering about delightedly in her role as leading lady, Weill concentrated his efforts on *One Touch of Venus*. Like all archetypal mythological subjects, the Pygmalion story lends itself to interpretation and reinterpretation according to the psychological and social pressures of successive times and places. So the gentle, whimsical humour of the situation in Anstey's Victorian London gives way to the pungent, wisecracking wit of the caustic Perelman as he looks out at society, his society, in World War Two Manhattan.

In Perelman's racy storyline the name of the barber hero has been changed to Rodney Hatch. A young man of no great distinction, Rodney has recently become engaged to Gloria Kramer. One day he goes to attend to a client, the director of an art foundation, and as he waits in the gallery for the director to appear, his eyes light on a statue of Venus. Idly taking from his pocket the wedding ring he has just bought for Gloria, he slips it over Venus' finger. Venus thereupon comes to life and displays a passionate desire for her liberator, pursuing him through the city until finally chasing him into a hotel, where they spend the night. She drives the thought of Gloria from his mind – 'A girl on the couch is worth two on the mind', quips Perelman – and sets up a *ménage* with Rodney, only to be made aware, in a ballet sequence, how boring the life of a suburban housewife will be. A bacchanale, also choreographed, then restores her to Olympus, her natural habitat, leaving poor Rodney back in the art gallery gazing at her statue. At that moment a girl resembling Venus comes into the gallery – 'she might be Venus's country cousin,' says the script – and the two go off hand-in-hand.

To this piece of wit, satire and romantic parody, with the touches of monumental absurdity without which Perelman would not be Perelman, Weill wrote an attractive, romantic score of the kind that could not fail to capture the affection of the Broadway audience. It had its fair share of winsome hit numbers which acquired a life of their own – 'That's Him' and the waltz 'Foolish Heart' for Venus, the duet 'Speak Low' for the goddess and her tonsorial lover. It also had its private jokes: the male quartet complaining of 'The Trouble With Women' in Rodney's barber shop is singing the satirical whining tune of the Salvation Army song 'In der Jugend gold'nem Schimmer' from *Happy End*, which had already reappeared in Weill's Parisian days as 'Les filles de Bordeaux' in the seedy *Marie Galante*.

Production matters lay in the familiar hands of Cheryl Crawford, and Maurice Abravanel was to conduct. For the Perelman-Nash-Weill team, however, it was a first and last time together. Nash was not a theatre lyricist like Ira Gershwin, and his friend Perelman was more at home in the pages of *The New Yorker*, as Anstey had been in his element writing for *Punch*. Only Weill had the blood of theatre in his veins, though where the music came from, Nash later mused in a characteristic piece for *The New York Times*, he never found out:

> He has a piano but he does not sit at it picking out melodies with one finger; he uses it for laying his pipe on before going out to chuck pebbles at the trout in the brook that runs past his window. He does not pace the floor in a brown study humming tum-ti-tum, tum-ti-tum until suddenly he claps his brow and his face is transfigured as another ballad is born. Nor is he ever to be found curled up in his favorite armchair poring over a dog-eared copy of Tchaikovsky. He simply puts in a full day at the OWI [Office of War Information, for whom Weill did some propaganda music], gets on the Weehawken ferry, rides for an hour in a non-air-conditioned smoking car, gets home, goes to his desk and writes 'That's Him'.

With the success of *Lady in the Dark* still ringing in his ears, with a spicy text and sparkling lyrics at his disposal, and fully aware of what was needed to ensure a second conquest of Broadway, Weill was determined to make *One Touch of Venus* a comparable triumph. The demands of the medium, not the creative urges of the artist, were paramount, and whatever his attachment to a particular sequence, he would cut it ruthlessly if the show so required. For the final ballet section, choreographed by Agnes de Mille, as Venus is wafted from the torpidity of American suburbia back to her rightful place among the deities, he had composed an elaborate orchestral score which he described, according to Cheryl Crawford, as 'the finest piece of orchestral music he had ever written'. But *One Touch of Venus* was not a piece of orchestral music, and he had no compunction about sacrificing his ballet music – or, for that matter, the notion of an Offenbachian *opéra comique* which had occurred to him at the beginning – on the altar of the Broadway musical. 'He was ruthless about such things,' said Agnes de Mille; 'he wanted a success. He was predominantly a theatre man.' 'Kurt used to say,' added Cheryl Crawford: '"To hell with posterity. I want to hear my music now, while I'm alive. I want my things performed and I want them to be a success."'

He need not have worried. After tryouts in Boston *One Touch of Venus* opened at the Imperial Theatre, New York in October 1943 and ran for 567 performances, netting over 35,000 dollars a week. In the awards for Best Musical Play of the Season it came second to Rodgers' and Hammerstein's *Oklahoma!*; Elia Kazan was named Best Musical Producer, Kenny Baker, as Rodney Hatch, Best Male Supporting Actor, and the star, Mary Martin, Best Female Lead. The part fitted her like a glove. To be sure, she had at the beginning jibbed over speaking one of Perelman's particularly *outré* lines: 'Love is not the moaning of distant violins; it's the triumphant twang of a bedspring.' But the hoot of laughter that greeted her embarrassed delivery of this definitive wisdom quickly overcame her qualms. She was required to appear in fourteen different gowns, all designed by Mainbocher, costing between 15,000 and 20,000 dollars each, and wild applause greeted her every appearance. United Artists bought the film rights for 310,000 dollars plus a percentage of the grosses. Weill's income for that year came close to 100,000 dollars.

Critical opinion divided, as so often with Weill's works, into those who saw it as theatre and those who heard it as music. The stage journal *Variety* hailed it as 'Broadway's first musical smash of the season'. Somewhat more cagey, the *New York Herald Tribune*'s drama critic Howard Barnes thought it 'a cunning combination' of fantasy, music and ballet. The composer Elliott Carter, representative of those who saw the dichotomy of Weill's career, admired the skill with which he had adapted his talents to his new market but lamented that it should have come to this:

> Where in pre-Hitler days his music underlined the bold and disillusioned bitterness of economic injustice, now, reflecting his new environment and the New York audiences to which he appeals, his social scene has shrunk to the bedroom and he has become the composer of 'sophisticated' scores.

And only in its immediate context can his craftsmanship carry the day:

> In the atmosphere of Broadway, where so much music is unconvincing and dead, Weill's workmanlike care and his refined sense of style make up for whatever spontaneity and freshness his music lacks.

The box office will have been grateful that the musical-theatre-going public was not so intellectually fastidious.

That sensitivity to the feelings of others which so endeared Weill to those around him was affectionately recalled by Maxwell Anderson in a little story from the time of the tryouts of *One Touch of Venus*:

Once when Kurt was in Boston with the tryout of a musical he came downstairs to have breakfast with the producers, the lyric writer and the man who wrote the book for the show. He found them all sitting about the table over black coffee discussing the problems of the play and the sleepless night they had spent. Each one described the sleeping pills or prescription which he had tried and which had failed, and then turned to Kurt and asked wearily how he slept.

'Oh, fine,' Kurt said, because he had slept well and always did. Then he realised that they all hated him for that answer, and he added gloomily: 'But I had bad dreams.'

On August 28, 1943, when Weill was in the middle of work on *One Touch of Venus*, *The New York Times* carried an item of domestic news on an inside page:

> Three prominent contributors to the theatre arts were among two hundred and fifty persons who took the oath of citizenship yesterday morning at the Naturalization Bureau, 641 Washington Street, before Federal Judge Gaston L. Porterie.
>
> The new citizens are Kurt Weill, well-known composer of operatic and musical comedy scores; Otto L. Preminger, producer, writer, actor, director and communicator, and Dr Saul S. Colin, agent and personal representative of artists and authors. The men had no foreknowledge of one another's presence at the ceremony.

It was one of the proudest moments in his life.

CHAPTER XVI

Broadway II

One Touch of Venus had put a great strain on Weill. Not just the 'normal' strain of the sketching and composition of the score to meet the producer's deadline, aggravated by the false start with the abortive libretto of the Spewacks, but also the pressure of cutting, adding, transposing, re-orchestrating and so on, once rehearsals started and opening night edged closer. 'You sleep about two hours a night for the four weeks that it [the orchestration] takes, but it's fun,' he explained. 'Not until the rehearsals get under way can you start your orchestrating, since until you know who the singers are going to be you can't tell what key to put each number in.'

But already the previous year, when he was working to get the 'Lunch Time Follies' off the ground, a medical check-up had revealed high blood pressure and an uneven heart beat. The symptoms now returned, with no chance, being the man he was, that he would take heed of medical advice to slow down. The composure and quiet reasonableness that he showed to the outside world impressed only to deceive.

Hypertension ran in the Weill family. Cantor Albert Weill and his wife both suffered from it, and it caused the death of Kurt's brother Hanns in 1947, before claiming Kurt himself three years later. That hereditary factors played a major part in the transmission of the condition was only just beginning to become clear, and none of the Weill children, not even Nathan, the physician, had been aware of it. Explaining the nature of coronary thrombosis in a letter to Lenya after Kurt's death, Nathan wrote: 'It is something we did not know before – that high blood pressure runs in our family and we *all* suffer from it, not excepting our parents.'

However, the doctor whom Weill had consulted in Rockland County apparently did more than just produce an ominous diagnosis. A change of diet seems to have been one of his recommendations. Weill tells his parents that both he and Lenya have 'almost become vegetarians' – in Lenya's case this was a response to anaemia, for which the doctor had prescribed a régime of vegetables, no cigarettes or alcohol (a considerable sacrifice), and no meat except liver. 'It does her a world of good,' he writes, 'and I have a good mind to follow suit' – adding, roguishly, 'when I can find the time.' To offset the effects of a sedentary life he was also advised to take up physical training. 'At seven o'clock every morning,' he says, with almost audible pride, 'I go cycling for half-an-hour so as to get some exercise.' Given the hilly countryside around Brook House, that half-an-hour will not have gone unfelt.

In November 1943, a month after *One Touch of Venus* opened on Broadway, he took off for Hollywood with Lenya for what was to be his most substantial piece of work for motion pictures. Before accepting the approach from Twentieth Century Fox, however, he assured himself of two things: first, that his partner, as far as the song texts went, would be Ira Gershwin; and second, that his contract would allow him a measure of artistic control over the use made of his music and prevent his score from being 'arranged' by others, i.e. mangled beyond recognition.

He had good cause for suspicion of the film industry. In 1930 he had successfully sued the Tobis-Warner company over their abuse of his music in the *Dreigroschenoper* film, and had established the twin principles of the inviolability of the work of art and the inalienable rights of the artist over his own work. Hollywood knew nothing of such principles. What its principles, or lack of them, were, had already been made clear from its treatment of two of his musicals. *Knickerbocker Holiday* had been castrated by United Artists, with the connivance of Nelson Eddy as Brom Broeck and Charles Coburn as Peter Stuyvesant; 'September Song' survived but the credits put the film's music down to a studio collective, and when the music was nominated for an Academy Award, it was in the name of Werner R. Heymann, the head of the collective. In *Lady in the Dark*, from Paramount, with Ginger Rogers and Ray Milland, Weill's score fared no better. Again outsiders were employed to provide new songs, and again a resident studio composer was credited with assembling the music.

This time the situation was different in that he had been invited to provide music for what was a film from the beginning – a lightweight comedy with a wartime background called *Where Do We Go From Here?*, written by Morrie Ryskind (author of the Marx Brothers' classics *A Night at the Opera* and *Animal Crackers*) and starring Fred MacMurray, Joan Leslie and June Haver. He wrote a handful of songs to Ira Gershwin's lyrics, and a superb extended *scena*, like a miniature comic operetta, known as the Columbus Sequence, or 'The Niña, The Pinta, The Santa Maria', in which the hero is transported back in time to find himself sailing across the Atlantic with Columbus' three ships in order to bestow upon the world the greatest blessing it has ever received – the discovery of

America. But Weill's contributions to the film are swamped by those of a posse of studio professionals recruited into the exercise. Snippets of his melodies are scattered throughout the score, 'developed' and manipulated by these *maestri* as they saw fit and mixed in with material of their own invention. Even the 'Columbus Sequence' ended up in a staff arranger's orchestration. So not much had really changed, though Ira Gershwin's entertaining lyrics did enable him to 'have fun', as he put it.

He also 'had fun' pocketing a cheque for 2,500 dollars a week. This was the principal compensation for a mode of living and working that he found little more congenial now than when he had made his first sortie into the movie world in 1937. 'I am looking forward to soon being able to leave these verdant pastures,' he wrote sarcastically to Brecht. Ordeal by New Year Party was particularly painful. 'We are glad the holidays are over,' he wrote to his brother Hanns (in English), 'because they are a real ordeal out here. We had to go to two of those awful parties. I just cannot have any fun when sixty or eighty people get together in a room and command you to have fun.' 'Well, anyway,' he graciously concluded, 'they mean well.' At one party they found his old Berlin friend Felix Joachimson, librettist of their abortive *Na und?* back in 1926, now a screenwriter and producer calling himself Felix Jackson, who was devoting himself to the career of the singing star Deanna Durbin ('very pretty, extremely dull', according to Lenya), whom he later married.

A winter spent in Los Angeles rather than in New York did, however, have advantages for his and Lenya's health. 'Lenya is now feeling a lot better,' he wrote in January 1944 to his parents from his temporary home on Hollywood's Moraga Drive,

> and alongside my work I have been busy doing something for my health as well. I spend around two hours every day in the garden, playing badminton (a kind of tennis) and table-tennis, lying in the sun, then going into the ice-cold swimming pool for a few moments. My body has a good tan and I feel in the best of health and full of energy for new activities.

'Speak Low' from *One Touch of Venus*, he goes on cheerfully in his long letter, has twice been in the Top Ten in recent weeks and Bing Crosby has just made a recording of 'September Song', with the release of the films of *Lady in the Dark* and *Knickerbocker Holiday* expected later in the year. All this has made him a lot of new friends, but also, he adds darkly, 'a lot of new and old enemies'. Not everybody was prepared to drink to the success of this Jewish émigré intruder. And those who said he had just been lucky ignored how much anxiety, disappointment and intrigue he had to overcome, as well as how much sheer hard work and sweat was involved. Neither he nor they could have known that a bitter setback was lurking just around the corner.

Yet he never lost sight of the needs of others, the world outside, the world still at war. In a letter to Brecht dealing mainly with their *Schweyk* project he says he has looked into the possibility of selling the film rights of *Mahagonny*, principally as a way of helping him, Brecht, out of his miserable financial condition. Asked by his parents whether he would contribute to a musicians' rest home in Nahariya, he explains that he already gives donations to so many charities that he could afford only a small contribution, and that moreover 'the major part of my income goes on helping to bring this war to a speedy and victorious conclusion – which is the finest cause to which a man can give his money today'. Weill was the one, we recall, who gladly paid his high income tax for being 'lucky enough to live in this wonderful country'. Another contribution to the war effort of that 'wonderful country' was to write the music, at the direct behest of the Office of War Information, for *Salute to France*, a propaganda 'short' scripted by Maxwell Anderson and directed by Jean Renoir.

Before he left for New York in the spring – he became a constant traveller between the East and West Coast in this and the following year – the seeds of another musical had already been sown in his mind. The idea again involved Ira Gershwin, who was in a sense responsible for Weill being in Hollywood at all, together with Gershwin's friend Edwin Justus Mayer, scriptwriter and author of a one-off Broadway success of the 1920s called *The Firebrand*.

It was not the first time the three men had come together. Two years earlier, when Weill had been in Hollywood to try and persuade Marlene Dietrich to take the lead in *One Touch of Venus*, they had agreed in principle to do a musical play on Nell Gwynn. The project never left the ground. But coming, as it did, at a time when talk of a revamp of Offenbach was in the air, it fitted into a context of thoughts on operetta, European-style, which was still open-ended when Weill found himself back in Hollywood in the spring of 1944.

Initially the idea of a musical on Mayer's *Firebrand* did not appeal to him. 'I was very unenthusiastic,' he wrote to Gershwin, 'but they finally asked me if I would be interested in case you would do the lyrics – and I said yes.' One prospect that attracted them, each in his own way, was that which had drawn them to the subject of Nell Gwynn – the opportunity to compose a costume musical with the scope offered by a setting in the European past. Weill described his idea as being 'more for a comic opera than a musical comedy, which means it would have a great deal of music of all types: songs, duets, quartets and sextets, recitative, underscored dialogue and some dancing.' To Gershwin he said it would be 'an intelligent, intimate operetta based on charm, humor and warmth'.

But more vital to him than a definition of terms – which he had a tendency, like Brecht, to invest with an individual and sometimes idiosyncratic set of associations – was an urgent personal pressure. Lenya's dissatisfaction with her professional inactivity, after the first flush of pleasure at settling into Brook House and being received into a sympathetic community, had begun to smoulder. A housebound routine was not her idea of fulfilment. As a 'straight' actress, now forty-six years old, reared in a Central European environment and with an accent to match, she was not easy to cast. Her Berlin-based song repertoire had limited appeal, and her engagement at the Ruban Bleu club had had no successors. Émigré actors and actresses with linguistic and cultural adaptability – Conrad Veidt, Peter Lorre, Oscar Homolka, Elisabeth Bergner, Marlene Dietrich – had found niches for themselves in the United States but Lenya was not of this company, and a theatrical future could hardly be founded on her little role as an Austrian maid in Maxwell Anderson's *Candle in the Wind*.

Weill felt an obligation, both towards Lenya herself and in the interests of their life together, to try and offset this frustration. Maurice Abravanel tells how he repeatedly tried to get him to write an opera – opera, that is, in the new context of Broadway, not the old context of Berlin. Yes, yes, Weill would reply, 'but first I must write something for Lenya'. So woven into the emerging fabric of the musical version of Mayer's play was the firm intention that whatever direction the work took in musical terms, it should have a part, a proper part, for her.

Mayer's 'Firebrand' is the adventurer, murderer, fornicator and jail-bird Benvenuto Cellini, also known as the greatest gold- and silver-smith of the Italian Renaissance. And the source of his 'Comedy in the Romantic Spirit', as Mayer called his play, is the splendidly outrageous autobiography in which Cellini revels in his extravagant crimes.

Inspired by the extravagant improbability of Cellini's revelations, Mayer concocted a riotous three-act comedy-cum-farce of love, licenti-ousness, crime and confusion with a lightness of touch which made it an instant success on its appearance in 1924. Its episodic plot consists of a series of amorous escapades interspersed with scenes depicting the misdeeds, the arrest and the threatened execution of Cellini. Cellini wants Angela, his model, for himself; the Duke of Florence also wants her, while the Duchess wants Cellini. Sometimes these desires are public knowledge, sometimes they are half-concealed, leaving manifold permutations of subterfuge, accusation and deception, and equally lavish opportunities for the situations of bedroom farce. In the end Cellini talks his way out of the hangman's noose – thereby joining his fellow-escapees Mackie Messer from *Dreigroschenoper* and Brom Broeck from *Knickerbocker Holiday* – and graciously cedes his Angela to the Duke, while the hanky-panky between Cellini and the Duchess, the end of the play implies, can look forward to a robust future.

Weill's last two Broadway works, *Lady in the Dark* and *One Touch of Venus*, had both been heroine-oriented, with the portrayal of the surrounding figures appearing as a series of character studies, like cameos. In *The Firebrand of Florence*, as the new piece, with a new libretto by Mayer, lyrics by Ira Gershwin and music by Weill came to be called, things are more closely integrated, with more direct interplay between the principal players *en groupe*. It thus mattered more, perhaps, than in the two earlier works that in the many duets and ensembles the singers should be attuned to each other's style and view their interacting roles with the same eyes, particularly in the situations of comedy and farce.

From the moment the cast was assembled for the first rehearsals the absence of this rapport cast a jinx over the enterprise. Weill intended Lenya for the Duchess, the part he had promised he would write for her. It turned out to be a sad miscalculation, partly because of the demands of the role in itself, partly because Lenya found herself at odds with the personality of her Duke. It had been hoped that the role would be taken by Walter Slezak, son of the famous Leo, but he withdrew, to be replaced by Melville Cooper, the British-born comedy actor who had built his act on playing pompous upper-class idiots. With the part of Angela going to Beverly Tyler, attractive of aspect but small of voice, and a Cellini (Earl Wrightson, known from musical comedy recordings) not equipped to project the hero's complex personality, the pall of doubt and apprehension hanging over the occasion became even denser.

Percy Grainger once wrote a jolly little piece called 'Handel in the Strand' – the music, he explained, 'seemed to reflect both Handel and English musical comedy'. On this analogy Weill's *Firebrand of Florence* might be called 'Lehár on Broadway', for its set pieces, choreographed sequences and vocal and choral numbers have their spiritual antecedents in the idioms of operetta. The music has Weill's irrepressible sense of theatre and the song tunes can be charming but their simplicity borders on the obvious, with mechanical sequential repetitions and a heavy reliance on the melodic and harmonic commonplaces of contemporary dance music, as though Weill's mind were weary, not responding at its liveliest. Nor was Ira Gershwin always at his sharpest. His was a wit irresistible at its best but frighteningly vulnerable to falling short of that best.

At all events Broadway did not appreciate its Lehár in this guise. Neither did Boston, where, under the title *Much Ado About Love*, the tryouts opened in February 1945 under the musical direction of Maurice Abravanel. So unsatisfactory was the first night that the master playwright, George Kaufman, was hastily summoned to prescribe urgent remedies, like a doctor giving first aid to a stricken patient.

Nor did the gods look kindly on Lenya's return to the stage. 'Lotte Lenya . . . is hardly up to the comedy and the songs which have been given her,' said the *Boston Post*. 'Her ability is not in question, nor her personal charm. But someone else should be playing the Duchess, for the sake of all concerned.' After Kaufman had done what he could, the work transferred the following month to the Alvin Theatre. The verdict remained the same. Even the Duchess' opening song, 'Sing Me Not A Ballad', on which Weill had lavished so much care for Lenya's sake, could not rescue the occasion. 'The real disaster is Kurt Weill's music,' wrote the merciless S.L.M. Barlow in *Modern Music*. 'What was "the most arresting voice of young musical Germany, a voice with the grinning, pavement pathos of Villon", has become increasingly dreary and now finally clap-trap.'

After 43 performances *The Firebrand of Florence* was taken off and vanished into history. Some laid the lion's share of the blame on the libretto: what had been riotously successful as a straight comedy, it was said, did not work under the quite different exigencies of musical theatre. Others pointed to the shortcomings of Max Gordon's production: the director, John Murray Anderson, had not been able to weld his cast into a coherent force; the extravagancies of the piece had led him, it was said, to overload the production and slow it down, when what it needed was lightness of touch. Perhaps Weill himself was in two minds about what he wanted, so that what he had described as 'more a light opera than a musical comedy' failed in the end to crystallise as one or the other, or as a happy blend of the two.

'The blame probably may be distributed more or less evenly on all sides, save Mr Gordon's purse,' *The New York Times* concluded. That Weill uncharacteristically left much of the orchestration to a professional arranger also implies something profoundly negative – lack of confidence (hard to imagine), loss of interest (less hard to imagine), maybe even resignation. It was a flop, his first and only out-and-out Broadway failure, the more distressing for its involvement of Lenya both as cause and effect.

He put a characteristically brave face on the situation. 'In a way,' he wrote to his parents, 'I am pleased not to get into the rut of writing one success after another':

> As long as I use each work to do something that is new and in many cases ahead of its age, I must put up with setbacks like this from time to time – which is all the easier, of course, because financially I can easily afford it. So let's forget it and strike out afresh.

Whether he is really as pleased at having written a flop as he makes out, we may wonder. And perhaps we may direct a gentle smile towards the man who a few years ago proclaimed 'I write for today. I don't give a damn about writing for posterity' but who now reacts to the public's thumbs-down by explaining that the failure at issue is 'ahead of its age'. The past fifty years have shown little sign that they have caught up with it.

Much of *The Firebrand of Florence* had been written during the late summer months of 1944 when Weill was back in Hollywood, this time alone, for the dubbing sessions of his music for *Where Do We Go From Here?* But not quite alone. For he had taken into his intimate affections a woman who shared much of his life in the house he rented in Bel Air for the duration of his film work. Weill made no attempt to conceal the affair, and when Lenya visited him from New York, he took her to see the lady. Lenya, who had a volume of extra-marital experience with which her husband could not compete, waxed sarcastic over what she described to Rita Weill, Kurt's sister-in-law, as 'a little tragedy' with her husband's 'little mistress', but a sense of injured pride still lingered. The 'little mistress' continued to write to Weill over the following years. The fact that she has requested that her surviving letters not be made public gives a broad hint of their nature.

During these weeks in Los Angeles he renewed his contacts with a growing number of friends and acquaintances in celluloid city. He also saw Brecht again, who had still not abandoned hope that Charles Laughton might adopt his *Schweyk* play and who had taken heart over the recent interest shown in his *Caucasian Chalk Circle* by Luise Rainer, the German émigrée actress married to Clifford Odets. But again these visions turned out to be phantoms, and it was at this time too that the plan for a version of *Der gute Mensch von Sezuan* with Weill's music was finally laid to rest.

In the colony of émigrés that had formed in California a special welcome always awaited him at the home of Lion and Martha Feucht-wanger in Pacific Palisades. Their friendship went back to Berlin days, the days of *Dreigroschenoper* and Weill's songs for Feuchtwanger's play *Petroleuminseln*; with Franz Werfel, on the other hand, who was equally well established in Los Angeles, Weill seems to have had little or no contact. And in view of what Schoenberg thought of his music he will have given the Schoenberg house in Brentwood Park a wide berth.

A valued acquaintanceship that went back to Berlin, had been revived in Paris and now again in America, was that with Igor Stravinsky. Stravinsky, resident in Hollywood since 1940, had been in the audience at the house of the Vicomtesse de Noailles in 1932 when *Jasager* and

Mahagonny had been performed – 'both of which I admired,' he later said. His admiration had returned to greet the new Weill of Broadway, when, as he recalled, he 'went on stage to congratulate him after the première of *Lady in the Dark*'.

Back in the spring of 1944 Weill had received an invitation from the impresario Billy Rose to write, for 5,000 dollars, a short ballet score for a Broadway extravaganza to be called *The Seven Lively Arts*; the ballet was to be choreographed and danced by Anton Dolin. Weill's mind was on other things, and he suggested that Rose ask Stravinsky. The result was the *Scènes de Ballet*, described by Stravinsky as 'a portrait of Broadway during the last years of the war'. After the tryout in Philadelphia he received a telegram from the producer: 'Your music great success. Could be sensational success if you would authorize Robert Russell Bennett retouch orchestration. Bennett orchestrates even the works of Cole Porter.'

'I telegraphed back,' said Stravinsky: '"Satisfied with great success."'

Not long after the débâcle of *The Firebrand of Florence* in the spring of 1945 Weill found himself again in Hollywood, this time for work on a film version of *One Touch of Venus*. His dislike of the movie world, its pretensions and its self-glorification, receded from time to time, not least under the near-irresistible allure of the money it dangled in front of his eyes. Apart from this, he had always enjoyed working under pressure. What he liked less were the unpredictable periods of inactivity, though without them his hypertension might have killed him even sooner. His letters to Lenya leave no doubt that he sees himself as an East Coast, not a West Coast man. His eye constantly roams the field in search of a subject for the next Broadway show, and once the book lies before him and the composition is begun, he looks forward to nothing so much as working undisturbed on the orchestration of his score in the tranquillity of Brook House.

With *One Touch of Venus* he seemed to have better prospects than with *Knickerbocker Holiday* and *Lady in the Dark* – it would be difficult to have worse – of a film that retained some degree of fidelity to his original stage show. But Hollywood had not changed its spots. Universal could not make up its mind what sort of film it wanted, and after weeks spent writing new material to the studio's specifications, with no prospect of a satisfactory finished product in sight, he left and went back east.

It took the company over two more years to admit that, with Ava Gardner now in the role of Venus and Robert Walker as Eddie Hatch (his change of name from Rodney to Eddie says it all), what they were looking at was no longer a satirical musical comedy but a sentimental romance with incidental music, which was much cheaper to make. And such is the film that was eventually released, to Weill's considerable displeasure, in 1948, pillaging his tunes in the interest of supplying what the public was deemed to want.

During these weeks in Hollywood the war in Europe ended. He was an American, and felt as an American. As the Red Army was fighting its way into the heart of his Berlin, he was relaxing in Southern California, swimming, sunbathing, playing tennis among the palm trees of paradise. But what was happening in Europe made him a European again, even a German, as he contemplated the death and destruction that the country of his birth had wrought upon the world and the retribution that must follow. 'Never, I believe, in the history of mankind,' he wrote to his parents (in German),

> has a nation suffered such a terrible defeat as Germany, and never has a people deserved such a humiliation as these barbarians who insolently claimed the right to destroy all the good and decent things that man had built up over centuries. When one thinks of the pride and courage with which the British, the Dutch, the French, the Russians, the Jugoslavs and above all the Jews bore their tragedies, there wells up a feeling of repulsion at the cowardice, the degradation and the pathological orgy of self-destruction being indulged in by the so-called Master Race at this moment of its defeat. What the allied armies have achieved in four short years borders on the miraculous and was made possible only by the fact that it was so obviously a war of good against evil.

The world can now look forward to an era of spiritual renewal:

> To be permitted to share in this victory of right over wrong, and to see, after so short a time, how evil was punished and goodness triumphed, is to be filled with hope and confidence.

Yet only a few weeks later, still in Hollywood, he wrote to his brother Hanns and his wife (in his own English) of a disturbing sense of anticlimax:

> It is strange how depressed everybody has been since the end of the war in Europe. It is appalling to think that not the slightest attempt is being made to solve any of the world problems, and it looks as if the world will be in a worse condition after this war than after the last one.

What underlay this pessimism, one can only surmise. The aftermath of the holocaust, the uncertainty of the situation in Palestine, both for his family there and for the future of the Jewish homeland, the physical and moral annihilation of the country in which he had been born and in which the name Kurt Weill had once stood for brilliance and success, the incipient antagonism and incompatibility of the superpowers of East and West – thoughts like these would easily induce a mood of dark uncertainty in one forced to watch events from a distance. He was fearful of what the future held. 'Only the wisest and most inspired statesmanship can save us from fresh disasters,' he told his parents.

Nor had Europe forgotten him. Towards the end of the year he learned that the Hebbel-Theater, the only theatre in Berlin left undamaged at the end of the war in 1945, had reopened its doors with *Dreigroschenoper*, directed by Karlheinz Martin, and was playing to packed houses. Brecht tried, unsuccessfully, to get the performances stopped because he considered the chaotic conditions in a shattered, starving, demoralised Berlin unconducive to a proper understanding of the work. 'In the absence of a revolutionary movement,' he complained, 'the "message" is pure anarchy.' It always was. In any case Weill saw no reason to be so squeamish. Conversely, when Brecht, a few years later, wanted to put on an 'up-to-date' version of his text for a production in Munich starring Hans Albers, it was Weill who hedged, pointing out that his music was wedded to the letter and the spirit of words written in 1928, not 1949.

Universal Edition, his old publishers in Vienna, also began to correspond with him again. Much of the 'degenerate' music they had published before the war, including his *Mahagonny*, had been confiscated or destroyed by the Nazis, and learning of his American success, they wrote to inquire whether he had any material from which they could reprint. 'During the Nazi period,' they told him, 'the songs of the *Dreigroschenoper* were like a national anthem in certain circles and helped to raise the spirits of many a dejected soul. You have no idea how loved and honoured you were.'

The Jewish consciousness that Weill had brought with him from Europe as part of his spiritual heritage was to manifest itself on three public occasions over the next two years, each time with its own practical demands. For the seventy-fifth anniversary of the Park Avenue Synagogue in New York in March 1946 he made a setting of the *Kiddush*, the benediction of the bread and wine on the Sabbath, for tenor, mixed choir and organ – one of a number of pieces commissioned by the synagogue's cantor and bearing a dedication 'To my father'. Also made for a ceremonial occasion was an arrangement for full orchestra of 'Hatikvah', the Israeli national anthem, performed at the celebration of Chaim Weizmann's seventy-third birthday in New York in November 1947.

More substantial, in terms both of his investment of emotional energy and of the amount of music he was called upon to write, was his contribution in September 1946 to a Jewish pageant called *A Flag Is Born*. The third in racial line of descent from *The Eternal Road* and *We Will Never Die*, but also in the same dramatic mould as *Railroads on Parade* and *Fun To Be Free*, *A Flag Is Born* was the brain-child of the irrepressible Ben Hecht.

Bohemian by temperament and a born demagogue, seven years older than Weill, Hecht had taken care not to be out of the headlines for long, starting with his days as a reporter in Berlin in 1918–19. Virulently anti-German since the rise of Hitler – 'a race of butchers', he called them – he now put his crusading zeal behind the struggle for a Jewish homeland, noisily embracing the cause of those whom he and his fellows, from the comfort of their American firesides, hailed as Zionist freedom fighters and most others branded as Jewish terrorists. He was addressing the largest community of Jews in the world, and under the auspices of the American League for a Free Palestine he wrote a drama built, in the manner of his earlier pageants, on the framework of an interplay between narrative action and reflective moments derived from the Scriptures and from a contemplation of the Jewish fate. Its motto was 'It is 1776 in Palestine'. The young hero, who has himself survived the holocaust, takes over the mantle of the cause from two elderly fellow-survivors, husband and wife, whom he has met. Tevya, the husband, dies. The young Jew takes his prayer shawl, fashions it into a battle flag and is finally seen tramping off to join the Irgun in the defiant liberation of the land of his fathers. 'The most virulently anti-British play ever staged in the USA', reported the London *Evening Standard* in disgust.

With Paul Muni as Tevya, Marlon Brando as the boy, and the radio correspondent Quentin Reynolds as the narrator, *A Flag Is Born* opened in New York in September 1946 and ran up 120 performances. Afterwards it was taken on tour around the country, eventually raking over a million dollars, both from box-office takings and from donations, into the coffers of the American League for a Free Palestine and the Committee for a Jewish Army of Stateless and Palestinian Jews. With part of the money these bodies bought an ocean liner, which, re-named the *S.S. Ben Hecht*, transported refugees to Palestine until captured by the British. Later it became for a while the flagship of the Israeli navy.

Some of the takings from the production was conscience money, some – not only from Jews – a spontaneous response to the horrors of the concentration camps which the Allies' victory had revealed. But nobody present at the première could have failed to have in his mind's eye the pictures of the King David Hotel in Jerusalem, blown up a few weeks earlier by the Irgun in their war to drive the British out of the mandated territory.

Quite what thoughts might have been going through Weill's mind when, in the immediate shadow of the King David Hotel attack, he sat down to compose his items of incidental music for Hecht's propaganda piece, is difficult to fathom. He was not a man of violence. He had jumped to support the Fight for Freedom organisation, to urge the Americans to see the war in Europe as their war too, and had unfalteringly seen the defeat of the Fascist powers of darkness by force of arms as the primary obligation of the civilised world. World War Two, in his eyes, had been not primarily a political but a moral struggle, a conflict of good against evil, totally different from the use of force to further a specific political, social or even national aim.

But nowhere in his surviving letters of the war and post-war years to his parents, to other members of his family or to his friends, does he talk of the holocaust or of the agonising problems attendant on the struggle for a Jewish homeland. Even after his visit to Palestine in 1947 the nearest he comes to a direct utterance on the Zionist cause and its belligerent adherents is to make mention in a letter to the Maxwell Andersons of 'Ben Hecht's silly one-man campaign against the English [sic!] empire'. The strong group consciousness characteristic of the ethnic cultures in the United States may also have helped, through its particularism, to preserve in him an awareness of origin and destiny which had been absorbed into the process of assimilation while he was still in Europe – where he had often been highly critical of the behaviour of the Jewish community and far from willing to be identified with it.

Maybe one should not press the matter too hard. Maybe Weill's involvement, if only by implication, with the policies of extremists at this moment only reflected his inability to say No to a cause whose principles, if not all its procedures, he supported. He was a Jew by culture rather than by politics, and from *The Eternal Road* to *Kiddush*, from *A Flag Is Born* to 'Hatikvah', he spread his offerings to his people over a gamut of activities and needs with the humanism and tireless liberality that were the hallmark of his personality.

In November 1946 Weill wrote from Brook House to his brother Hanns:

> I am working like never before in my life, and so far it looks awfully good. It is without doubt the most important piece I have written since *Bürgschaft*, and it might turn out to be the best of all my works.

He was talking of *Street Scene*.

The origins of this 'American Opera', as Weill called what is one of his biggest, most ambitious and most effective works, went back to 1936 and a rehearsal of *Johnny Johnson*, his first piece for the Broadway musical stage. Here he had met the dramatist Elmer Rice. Rice's career was an archetypal rags-to-riches story. Born in a rough area of New York in 1892 as Elmer L. Reizenstein, he was the son of an impoverished cigar maker of German-Jewish descent in whose house books were unknown and education a dream. From his work as a clerk in a law office he saved enough to attend night school and graduate in law, while reading all the literature he could lay his hands on and beginning to write his own plays.

In 1923 Rice had scored a hit with *The Adding Machine*, an expressionist fantasy on man as robot, and in 1929 he won the Pulitzer Prize with *Street Scene*, a powerful drama of love, jealousy and murder set in the kind of sordid, dehumanising tenement in which he had grown up. He became a utopian socialist and visited the Soviet Union and Germany; *Street Scene* was performed in Berlin in 1930, and his plays were among the books ceremonially burned by the Nazis in 1933. 'It was the highest honour that has ever been paid me,' he boasted. He helped to set up the Federal Theatre Project in the post-Depression years, was a co-founder of The Playwrights Company in 1937 and on the board of the American Civil Liberties Union, working indefatigably, often through litigation in the courts, for the right of self-expression and the abolition of censorship. A stocky, pugnacious figure in a crumpled suit, emanating no personal magnetism but giving himself no airs, Rice was the perfect radical, underprivileged antithesis in The Playwrights Company to the charismatic, humanitarian Maxwell Anderson. It is wholly characteristic of Weill that he should have been attracted in genuine friendship to both of them, and they to him.

Before he first met Weill, Rice had already been approached by several composers who had had their eyes on *Street Scene*. He declared it 'too early', however, for a show of that type. His play was a stark, naturalistic panorama of 24 hours in the life of a tenement community in a 'mean quarter' of New York City – Italians, Swedes, Jews, an unhappy marriage, a childbirth, a frustrated romance, a murder, intolerance and bigotry but also kindness and humour – all in the sweltering summer heat when spirits sag and tempers flare. An air of suffocation hangs over the scene, an atmosphere of fatalism and depression, clogging all hope that the street might some day see happier times.

A suitably sombre film version of the play, starring Sylvia Sidney, was made in 1931. But Rice's persistent reluctance to permit it to be converted into a piece of musical theatre expressed a legitimate fear – the fear of the lyricisation, and with it the de-dramatisation, of the play's naturalistic substance. Singing would slow down the dramatic momentum, and the text of an already long play would have to be cut to make room for the music. To be sure, music of a proper nature and quality would intensify the aesthetic experience as a whole – as Alban Berg's *Wozzeck*, for example, raises to an almost unbearable pitch the intensity that already threatens to blow apart the quivering framework of Büchner's tragedy. But this was hardly Elmer Rice's world. The only work in the immediate vicinity that could have overcome his reservations, or anybody else's, was *Porgy and Bess*, which shared the mean, urban setting of *Street Scene* and breathed the same atmosphere of smouldering human passions at their most primitive and most violent. And as *Porgy and Bess* also showed, in any aggregation of words and music, whether in the miniature mould of a song or in the wide open spaces of opera, the music is bound to predominate, and hence become the touchstone of critical judgement on the work of art as a whole.

By 1945 Rice was willing to change his mind. From Weill's collaborations with Paul Green, Maxwell Anderson and Moss Hart he had seen how playwrights of distinction were prepared to think in terms of musical theatre. So when, as they happened to be leaving a meeting of the Dramatists' Guild together, Weill raised the question of *Street Scene* again, Rice said why not. Weill had seen the play in Berlin in 1930; he had also done incidental novachord music for Rice's comedy *Two On An Island* in 1939. The two now decided to tackle *Street Scene*, in Weill's words, 'as a musical version of the play, to cast it entirely with singers, so that the emotional climax could be expressed in music, and to use spoken dialogue to further the realistic action.'

The basic format, in other words, was to be that of the *Singspiel*. The dialogue would be assembled by Rice from the text of his original play, parts of it left unaccompanied, other parts underscored by an orchestral accompaniment, leaving the musical high points to rest on the songs, duets, ensembles and dance numbers. To write the lyrics, which, as Weill put it, 'should attempt to lift the everyday language of the people into a simple, unsophisticated poetry', they chose the black poet and writer Langston Hughes, a controversial figure whose radical politics had already attracted the unwelcome attention of the Committee on Un-American Activities in Washington.

Collaboration between the three men took place in a genuine, if not always eye-to-eye spirit of collectivism. Weill, as was his wont, insisted on helping to shape the libretto and impressed on Hughes, a newcomer to musical theatre, what his music required of the lyrics; Hughes protested at what he saw as the imperialistic tendency of the music to encroach on territories where it had no business to be and to undermine the realism of the spoken dialogue; Rice, as a simple matter of principle, wanted to preserve as much of his original play as possible and resented the interruptions which music and dance were constantly forcing on the dynamic course of the drama.

Through the twenty-four-hour slice of city life that the play presents, run two interwoven strands of personal action. One carries the tragedy of the unhappy marriage of Frank and Anna Maurrant, Anna's affair with Steve Sanky and Frank's shooting of his wife and her lover *in flagranti delicto*; the other traces the emotional relationship between the Maurrants' daughter Rose and the young Jewish student Sam Kaplan, which Rose, her mother dead and her father in jail, gently closes by bidding him farewell and setting out to make her own way in the world. For those left in the house after the excitement and tragedy have passed life resumes its old pattern in the insufferable summer heat.

The score occupied Weill throughout almost the whole of 1946. Some of this time he spent on research in the field, visiting night-spots in Harlem with Hughes to feel his way into the atmosphere of the Blues, walking the streets in the run-down neighbourhood where the action takes place, then going back to the seclusion of the New City woods and working his experiences into his music. 'I had an opportunity,' he said,

> to use different forms of musical expression, from popular songs to operatic ensembles, music of mood and dramatic music, music of young love, music of passion and death – and, over all, the music of a hot summer evening in New York.

Street Scene has twenty-one musical numbers linked by spoken dialogue, and the range of the 'forms of musical expression', as Weill put it, is indeed wide. 'I discovered that the play lent itself to a great variety of music,' he said. But this very variety is centrifugal in tendency, constantly threatening the aesthetic unity of the work, and with it its dramatic intensity. The problem arises in the first quarter of an hour. There is a superb orchestral introduction: four bars of the incisive, sit-up-and-take-notice Weill of old –

followed by a 'Molto agitato' on a striding ostinato figure, also in the mould of the European Weill, which runs without interruption and without stylistic hiatus into the first sung number, 'Ain't it awful, the heat?' This number over, we are plunged without warning into the Blues – not a simple folksy Blues but a sophisticated, intellectuals' Blues over a hill-billy bass, a piece of pseudo-jazz from a mind that has learned the requirements of an idiom rather than absorbed it as his second nature. A little later Anna Maurrant's aria 'Somehow I never could believe' gives us a piece of jaded Puccini, and the high-kicking high-school chorus 'Wrapped in a Ribbon and Tied in a Bow' has us in smiling musical-comedy mood. By the time of the jitterbug sequence 'Moon Faced, Starry Eyed' – which invariably stops the show – all thought that this is an opera has evaporated. Such dance sequences cannot but tend, through their sheer entertainment value, both to disperse the dramatic concentration – of the work itself and of its audience – and to trivialise the events of the unfurling drama.

To compare *Street Scene* with *Porgy and Bess* is tempting, perhaps inevitable, especially in view of the elevated terms in which Weill discussed his work. But to do so is no service to Weill. Leaving the theatre after *Street Scene* is like leaving *West Side Story* rather than leaving *Porgy and Bess* – 'an American opera', if ever there was one. There are catchy tunes and vivacious ensembles in *Street Scene*, and 'Lonely House' – the motif, symbolically, with which the work opens – must be one of the most hauntingly beautiful melodies, firm, harmonically subtle, totally unsentimental, that Weill ever wrote. Yet before the lump in our throat has dissolved, we find ourselves in the middle of a nondescript patch of dialogue between Rose Maurrant and her would-be seducer Harry Easter, and the next music is that of the routinely syncopated jingle 'Wouldn't you like to be on Broadway'. There is a predictability about the melodic lines and the harmonic patterns, a feeling that the music, rather than being naturally sovereign, is often puffing itself up to try and hide the not infrequent banalities of the lyrics from view and raise the work to a higher plane.

After seeing a matinée performance of *Street Scene* in New York shortly after its opening, Noël Coward wrote in his diary: 'It is beautifully directed and staged. The music is fine and the singing quite superb. A really rich and lovely afternoon in the theatre.' Just so. Not a profound emotional experience at the opera but a piece of opulent, skilfully crafted theatrical entertainment, an original musical. Were it not for the fact that Weill made such claims for it, and gave it such a key position in his *oeuvre*, there would be little cause to think of it in any other terms.

The true context of *Street Scene* is that set by Rodgers and Hammerstein. *Oklahoma!* opened in New York in 1943 and was still in the middle of its 2,000–performance run when *Street Scene* came off; and *Carousel*, based on Ferenc Molnár's *Liliom* – which, by an unkind irony, Molnár had refused Weill permission to put to music some ten years earlier – followed in 1945. Oscar Hammerstein II viewed modern musical theatre in precisely the same integrated terms as Weill. 'It must be understood,' he wrote in his book *Lyrics*, that the musician is just as much an author as the man who writes the words. He expresses the story in his medium just as the librettist expresses the story in his. Or, more accurately, they weld their two crafts and two kinds of talent into a single expression. This is the great secret of the well-integrated musical play.

To which Weill would have said Amen – said so, moreover, with as much fervour in 1930 in Berlin as in 1947 in New York.

And after *Oklahoma!* Hammerstein's partner Richard Rodgers re-called in his autobiography, with the flicker of a smile, 'everyone suddenly became "integration"-conscious, as if the idea of welding together song, story and dance had never been thought of before.' They had stolen much of Weill's thunder, and he jealously admitted it. 'Rodgers has certainly won the first round in that race between him and me,' he wrote ruefully to Lenya after *Carousel*. 'But I suppose there will be a second and third round.' There were and they – with *South Pacific*, for example – went to Rodgers and Hammerstein as well. In the meantime, to Weill's no great pleasure, the Metropolitan Opera – to which Abravanel, conductor there from 1936 to 1938, had tried in vain to introduce his friend's music – had taken up Gian Carlo Menotti.

Street Scene, which, after Hanns' death the following year, Weill dedicated 'To the memory of my brother Hanns Weill', did not prove easy to produce. The Playwrights Company, of which, in a singular gesture to a non-playwright, Weill had been elected a member the previous year, were anxious to take it on but had no experience of musicals and were intimidated by the prospect of such a large cast – 26 singing roles plus non-singing actors and choruses, with a full symphony orchestra. An approach to the Rodgers and Hammerstein team about a possible co-production was quickly withdrawn when it became clear that the prospective co-producers had a virtual takeover in mind. In the end the rich Dwight Deere Wiman, with *I Married An Angel* and many other shows to his bow, stepped in to help the Playwrights, with the musical direction, as ever, in the hands of Maurice Abravanel.

The try-outs in Philadelphia just before Christmas 1946 were a disaster. 'The reviews were tepid, the audience pitiable,' recorded Elmer Rice, who put most of the blame on the intrusive dance routines for breaking up the dramatic unity of his play. Moss Hart, who attended one of the previews, agreed. 'For God's sake take out all that musical comedy stuff,' he urged the authors. So Weill, co-operative as ever, made the required revisions – though there is still plenty of 'musical comedy stuff' left. 'I was afraid he would crack up,' said Rice, 'but in spite of the apparent hopelessness of the whole venture he kept doggedly at it.'

It paid off. At its New York première in the Adelphi Theatre early in the New Year *Street Scene* received an enthusiastic welcome. 'The overture was warmly received,' wrote Elmer Rice in his autobiography, 'and when the curtain rose, the attention of the audience was engaged. Ten minutes later Polyna Stoska's beautiful rendition of her long tragic aria [as Anna Maurrant] evoked an ovation that literally stopped the show. From that moment on, success was unquestionable.'

But not unrivalled. The competition was fierce. Apart from *Oklahoma!* and *Carousel*, both wearing an aura of eternity, *Finian's Rainbow* arrived on Broadway the evening after *Street Scene*, followed a few weeks later by the Lerner-Loewe *Brigadoon*. And just after Christmas Duke Ellington's assault on John Gay, *The Beggar's Holiday*, had opened at the Broadway Theatre – which, if it was any consolation, ran a month less than *Street Scene*.

Nor had critical opinion always struck the note that would bring in the crowds. Olin Downes, music critic of *The New York Times*, lapsed into an intellectual rumination on the remarkable circumstance that it should be a once-avant-garde ex-European, a pupil of Busoni, who so enthusiastically pursued the cause of American music drama – which may give pause for thought but does not send the public rushing to the box office. Even Downes' assessment of the work as 'the most important step towards significantly American opera that the writer has yet encountered in the musical theatre', has a guarded, less than wholehearted tone. Likewise Downes' colleague Brooks Atkinson, always respectful and gentlemanly, wrote of an 'immense depth and scope in the score' and concluded: 'With his insight, modesty and humanity, Weill composed a work of art that did not evade the truth of a corrosive city but also retained a certain wistful beauty.' Hardly the voice of one who has been swept off his feet.

Street Scene made little or no money for its backers. After the first couple of months audiences began to dwindle and it was taken off in May after 148 performances. At least that was 24 more than *Porgy and Bess* achieved in 1935. But it was not what Broadway called a hit. And although he enjoyed having a hit as much as the next man, Weill seemed to want to distance himself from the process, and the people, that could achieve it. In his notes on a conversation with Alan Jay Lerner for a biography of Weill (never written), George Davis, Lenya's second husband, observed that although fascinated by the nature of Rodgers' and Hammerstein's success, Weill did not want to compete in the same market. When Lerner suggested *The King and I* to him, he replied: 'Leave that to somebody else.' The somebody else turned out to be Rodgers and Hammerstein – a year after Weill's death. Public acknowledgement of his achievement in its own right and on its own terms came a few weeks after *Street Scene* had closed, when he was honoured with a special Tony Award for his services to the theatre.

Not since the 1920s, the days of his regular contributions to *Der deutsche Rundfunk* and his statements on 'gestic' music and other principles of those Brechtian days, had Weill been so concerned as he was at the time of *Street Scene* to make the public aware of the infrastructure of theories and beliefs on which his music rested. He gave interviews, wrote to *The New York Times*, sent articles to professional journals, all in the interest of making clear, firstly his faith in a broadly-based American musical theatre, or American opera – his terms vary – based on Broadway, and secondly his conviction of having a central role to play in its evolution.

As in his writings from Berlin days, Weill takes his stand on the social function of art, art with a comprehensive responsibility, egalitarian in tendency. He writes of the 'markets' that art should serve, seeing art as a commodity that should be available, like any item of consumer goods, to whoever wants it, and with the implied condition that the artist has an obligation to produce what the consumer needs. In scenarios of this kind those needs are usually defined, then fulfilled, by the artist who claims to have identified them – or created them. But Weill seems not to have recognised the circularity of his argument.

Moreover he is still caught up in the wake of his attempt to abandon the distinction between 'serious' and 'light' music in favour of one between 'good' and 'bad' music. In a front-page contribution to *The Composer's News-Record*, written as the Broadway run of *Street Scene* was coming to an end, he declared:

> I never could see any reason why the 'educated' (not to say 'serious') composer should not be able to reach all available markets with his music.

But not all 'available markets' – a rather impersonal way of saying 'types of listener' – want to be reached, or are capable of being reached, by the music of 'serious' composers. The market for Paul McCartney is not coterminous with the market for Mozart, as the readers of Barbara Cartland are not usually the readers of Marcel Proust. Weill was only one of many in the twentieth century who have argued that art is for the people, not for an élite, and have quoted Haydn's work for Prince Nicholas Joseph Esterházy, or Mozart's commissions for the Archbishop of Salzburg, to show that art, great art, is properly of a community, not outside it – that it starts from, and returns to, its social context. And indeed, in an obvious sense a commissioned work, whatever its genre, must meet the requirements of the commissioner and serve the purposes that he had in mind.

But the crucial consideration remains the extent and nature of that social context, linked to the process of receptivity without which no communication between artist and public can take place, however that public be constituted. The music written by Mozart at the Archbishop of Salzburg's behest was no more intended for the peasants of the Salzkammergut than the *Dreigroschenoper* was aimed at the Berlin proletariat. Varying levels of appeal and response persist, and circles outside those being addressed remain untouched by the operation. This is not to say that the parameters of these circles are set in stone, fixed for all time. To return to Weill's imagery – the markets expand and contract. Tastes change. But the reality of differing needs and attractions will not go away, and in any context that accepts the premise of art as communication the artist has to decide whom he is addressing. Since Weill always knew whom he was addressing, it is all the stranger that he should have adopted a theoretical stance with which his musical practice could not be reconciled.

It is perhaps in terms of such a concept of differing contexts that the phenomenon of Weill the musical chameleon can most fairly be accommodated. From the moment he arrived in America, he deliberately turned his back on the context of his European past and elected to function within that of his Broadway present. In the first instance, therefore, he was asking to be set in the company, and judged by the musical standards, of the Big Five – Gershwin, Porter, Berlin, Kern and Rodgers. The judgement is not always flattering to Weill. And if challenged to explain, one would lodge a large share of the responsibility with the middle B-section of the symmetrical A A B A-refrain of the formulaic 32-bar popular song. Only in the best songs does this B-section have an independent musical interest: typically it amounts to little more than eight characterless bars of doodling until the principal theme returns. Unhappily few of Weill's tunes do better. The middle section of once popular numbers like 'Speak Low' and 'Foolish Heart' is so much perfunctory padding, and even that of the unforgotten 'September Song' merely shuffles repetitively to and fro waiting for the opening melody to come back. Weill's show tunes do not make the Big Five into the Big Six.

Maybe he was committing the unforgivable sin of 'writing down' to his new context, while George Gershwin – as a composer not only for musical theatre but also of orchestral and instrumental music – had been 'writing up'. This seems to be the sense of the admission he made to Ernst Křenek that, as Křenek wrote, 'he did what seemed necessary to comply with that natural, invincible urge of his to communicate via the musical theatre: he adapted this communication to the only vehicle at his disposal, namely the Broadway stage.' 'Adapted' hardly goes far enough – it is a whole new language that Weill chooses to learn. He said one or two fetching things in that language but the unforgettable utterances, 'evergreens' in abundance, were made by others.

In an interview with a New York journalist in 1940, looking for ways of warding off the disapproval of his American development from Brecht, Adorno, Ernst Bloch and others who prized his European works, Weill quoted a saying of his former teacher's. 'Busoni once said to me,' he told his interlocutor: ' "Don't be afraid of banality. After all, there are only twelve notes in the scale".' It is a perilously thin smoke screen behind which to hide.

Equally double-edged and question-begging is his declaration, in the same interview: 'Music can only express human sentiments. . . . I write only to express human emotions'. If the nature of those emotions is to be deduced from his Broadway music as it stands, it is difficult not to conclude that the emotions in question rarely go deep and are often banal. The libretto – of *Street Scene*, for instance – may leave no doubt about the intensity of the passions and anxieties that rack the characters. But rarely does the music rise – indeed, given the idiom of the piece, rarely *can* the music rise – to this intensity. The format, the context, ensures that it is so.

This, essentially, is what underlies the scorn for the American Weill affected by Otto Klemperer, who blurted out in his blunt way what many European intellectuals thought. Asked 'why Weill went to pieces as a composer in America', Klemperer replied: 'He was very interested in money, that's the reason. He got too involved in American show business and all the terrible people in it.' The gratuitous sneer does Klemperer no credit. Weill was the most selfless of men. He spent little on himself and much on others – the less fortunate members of his family above all. He courted success, not money. To be sure, the one may follow the other, and Weill did not complain if it did. But one must get the order right.

There remains in Klemperer's remark, however, the constantly recurring argument of the difference in level, the qualitative difference, first between the European and American contexts in which he worked, then between his works written in the one context and those written in the other. Philipp Jarnach, a fellow-member of the Busoni circle in the early 1920s who had recognised Weill's remarkable gifts and helped to cultivate them, acknowledged the originality of his works from *Dreigroschenoper* to *Mahagonny* and *Der Jasager* while regretting that 'his later development in no way lived up to the expectations which his talent had originally promised.' 'These later [i.e. American] works,' Jarnach concluded, some years after Weill's death, 'represent the utter denial of the serious goals that he had formerly pursued, and in my view it is quite unacceptable to allow oneself to be persuaded that they are of any stylistic consequence today.'

As Křenek put it, by embracing the 'sumptuousness' and 'mundane sentimentality' of the Broadway manner, Weill 'was probably hardly aware of the fact that in so doing he descended in our eyes below the level of his tradition and his earlier works'. But it is hardly credible that so socially and musically conscious – self-conscious – a composer, who went out of his way to make his attitudes public, did not know what he was doing. Weill never did anything by accident. From the time when he chose to study with Busoni in Berlin to the moment when he opted to become an American, roll up his sleeves and join in the hurly-burly of Broadway, he made his own decisions and accepted their consequences. In Berlin, moreover – and here one approaches the heart of the matter – he had created his own idiom, taken out a patent on a personal musical language. In America, despite his concern to attach his music to texts of a certain intellectual aspiration, he accepted the basic, ready-made form of musico-theatrical entertainment – the Broadway musical – as he found it and placed his talent at its disposal. In Europe he had been master of his forms. In America he became their servant.

Not that Broadway had killed off the old, the inimitable Weill altogether. The orchestral introduction to the first act of *Street Scene* and the Arioso 'Lonely House' are enough to show that. But he does not stay long. When he reappears in the introduction to the second act, *fortissimo*, it is for an even shorter time, as though he no longer enjoys speaking in that distinctive tone of voice and has decided to relinquish it in favour of blander, more conventional, ultimately less interesting utterances. To change the metaphor: it is as though he has decided to join a team that plays in a lower league.

Lys Symonette, Weill's rehearsal pianist, a close friend of Lenya's and today Musical Executive of the Kurt Weill Foundation for Music, tells a story of a performance of *Der Zar lässt sich photographieren* which was being prepared by students at a college in New York City. The conductor invited Weill to attend the dress rehearsal. Weill had no wish to go but when he learned how disappointed the students would be if he did not, he finally agreed. Sitting in the taxi with Lys Symonette, he said nothing – he was in any case a man of few words. After the performance he went backstage and thanked the cast. Then he turned to the conductor and said apologetically: 'I'm sorry I wrote that sort of thing.'

Many would be proud to have written 'that sort of thing'. For Weill, the American, it was something that recalled a past he had chosen to forget.

CHAPTER XVII

'And The Days Grow Short When You Reach September'

– 'September Song' from *Knickerbocker Holiday*

By 1947 Europe and the rest of the world, within the new post-war reality of two superpowers snarling at each other across the Iron Curtain, were showing signs of a return to normality – though 'normal' is a relative term, and much of pre-1939 could never be returned to. France and the other former occupied countries still had their own internal political battles to fight, Britain still had food rationing. Germany was staggering to its economic feet – the West optimistically, buoyed up by Marshall Aid, guided by a sense of purpose, the East sullenly, weighed down by ideological ballast, exploited and enslaved by new Russian masters. So for those Germans who had fled from Nazism in the 1930s and found refuge in America, there was now a choice between two Germanies, incompatible and growing politically and socially ever further apart, to which to return. Or not.

Sometimes the decision rested on politics. Brecht went back – though not as fast as he could – to the East, like his loyal servant Elisabeth Hauptmann, his composers Hanns Eisler and Paul Dessau (who had married Elisabeth Hauptmann in California), the philosopher Ernst Bloch; others of equally, or almost equally radical persuasion – Lion Feuchtwanger, Heinrich Mann – opted for the continued enjoyment of the Californian sunshine. The sociologist Theodor W. Adorno and his colleague Max Horkheimer took their neo-Hegelianism from New York back to the University of Frankfurt, while Alfred Döblin, who had been desperately unhappy throughout the years in Los Angeles, went to work as an education officer in the French zone of occupation. Piscator and Aufricht, men of the theatre, tried to pick up the threads of their earlier careers in West Berlin.

Thomas Mann, doyen of the German literary emigrés, became an American citizen and gave every indication of intending to stay. But in 1952, growing increasingly uneasy over political developments in the country, he returned to Europe and, unwilling to be judged as identifying himself with either one Germany or the other, spent the rest of his life in

Switzerland. Hindemith, who had been on the faculty of Yale University since 1940 and an American citizen since 1946, secured for himself the best of both worlds by moving to Zurich for one half of the academic year and continuing at Yale for the other half, until finally settling in Switzerland in 1955. Also back in Switzerland from very soon after the end of the war was Hans Curjel, Klemperer's dramaturge during the heyday of the Kroll Opera in Berlin and a friend of Weill's in those distant times.

Weill stayed. He had never gone out of his way to court friends among the émigrés, still less to join the cliques of aggressively homesick countrymen – ex-countrymen – who huddled together to relive an ambivalent past. But he was sad when the one or the other left. In particular he missed the Milhauds, Darius and his wife Madeleine. Weill and Milhaud had shared the 1920s as fellow-*avantgardistes* at the Baden-Baden Festival and elsewhere, and Milhaud had helped to promote the Paris performances of the *Mahagonny Songspiel* and *Der Jasager* in 1932. Madeleine Milhaud attended to the transportation of some of Weill's possessions to the United States after he and Lenya had left France, and he had met her and her husband off the boat when they arrived in New York from Lisbon in 1940. A teaching job was found for Milhaud at Mills College in Oakland, California, where his sometime colleagues included André Maurois and Fernand Léger and where he stayed throughout his exile.

Weill's emotional involvement with Madeleine persisted through the war years. 'I am very close to you,' she once wrote to him: 'you must often feel how close. It is so unbelievable, this life that we lead together in spite of being so far apart.' After the war Milhaud was offered an appointment at the Paris Conservatoire, and he and Madeleine returned to France in 1947. The following year the affection between the families came to embrace the next generation as well, when Hanns Weill's daughter Hanne, with financial assistance from her uncle, went to study at the Sorbonne and was helped by the Milhauds to find her feet in the French capital.

With travel to Europe now opening up again, with *Street Scene* still running – just – at the Adelphi Theatre, and experiencing the nearest thing to what he would have recognised as a pause in his creative output, Weill decided that this was the moment to satisfy a desire which had become the more insistent the longer it lay in his mind – the wish to visit his parents in Palestine.

Partly he was guided by a sense of duty. His father had turned eighty at the beginning of the year, his mother was seventy-five, and he had seen neither them, nor his elder brother Nathan, nor his sister Ruth for fourteen years. His father was in no state to travel far and would obviously never see

Europe again, leave alone America, so if father and son were ever to meet again, the onus of making the journey fell on Kurt. The previous year, perhaps feeling that he had not much time left in which to settle such matters, Albert Weill had sent Kurt the outlines of a will, dividing his possessions equally among his four children and asking Kurt to inform the others of certain valuables – rings, medallions, silverware – that he wished them to have. To Kurt he left the *mizrah* from the family home.

At the same time such a visit would have a public aspect. Weill was a man with a reputation – more properly, with two reputations, one European, one American. As a refugee from Germany he was a distinguished son of the race whose survivors were building the Holy Land he would come to see; as a successful composer in the New World he had brought credit to that race and, even more importantly, had rediscovered his religious origins and enlisted his energies in the Zionist cause with men like Meyer Weisgal and Ben Hecht. It was clear what kind of welcome would await such a man.

But his journey was to have a sad *envoi*. At the beginning of March his brother Hanns died of a cerebral embolism at the age of forty-eight. His congenital hypertension had been exacerbated by the unsettled course of his life. Kurt had helped to establish him in business in America but he never made more than a passable living for himself and his family. His death came after a period of deep depression following what his daughter described as a 'gruesome operation' in connection with his high blood pressure.

Kurt's attachment to his brother had been one of the deepest relationships of his life. As schoolboys in Dessau they had lived through the First World War together, and after Hanns was called up in 1917, Kurt's letters to him, written with a faithful regularity, are our most precious source of knowledge about Kurt's thoughts on the war and its aftermath, on Jewry, on music, on life. Highly musical, Hanns had been for Kurt the natural partner in whom to confide and the one in the family best placed to appreciate his achievement. It was to fall to Kurt, whose psoriasis broke out again under the nervous strain of Hanns' death, to tell his parents of his brother's last days.

At the beginning of May he sailed aboard the *Mauretania* to England and spent some days in London, staying at Claridge's. London had not treated his *Seven Deadly Sins* too kindly in 1933, or *A Kingdom for a Cow* two years later, but there were a few acquaintanceships from those days that he thought worth reviving, among them that with the film producer Alexander Korda. 'Very grim' was his verdict on life in London. 'They have very little to eat and drink and shelter,' he wrote to the Andersons, 'but the spirit is amazing – and more than anywhere else I have found a young intelligentsia of great determination and political wisdom.' Paris, on the other hand, the next stop on his journey, he found 'as corrupt as a Balkan city, without belief or morale, with plenty of excellent food for the rich but a very superficial philosophy, choking in tradition'.

So much the greater was his delight when he saw what his final destination had to offer. 'Palestine is like fresh air after Europe,' he wrote in his enthusiasm –

> one sees happy faces everywhere, youth, hope, and the general theme is construction. The most fascinating aspect for me here is the mixture of civilisations. It is all basically Oriental and very colorful but overimposed by the Christian civilisation of the last two thousand years and now a new Jewish civilisation which is very impressive.

His prime commitment was to his parents, living in the coastal town of Nahariya in the northern part of the country, but he also found time to visit some of the new settlements, to go swimming in Lake Genezareth and dine in the house of what he colourfully called 'an Arabian chief', a patient of his brother's. Nathan, a radiologist, also lived and worked in Nahariya and during Kurt's stay he checked his brother's health, with his eye above all on the hypertension that plagued the family. He seems to have discovered nothing alarming, and recommended only that Kurt keep to a low-cholesterol diet and avoid an overly hectic pattern of life. The former piece of advice Kurt accepted and had already been following for some time; as to the latter, Nathan might just as well have addressed a brick wall.

It was also a moment of reunion with his sister Ruth, confidante of his exploits and secrets during the years, two wars ago, when they had been the only children left in the family home alongside the Dessau synagogue. Ruth's husband, Leon Sohn, had started up a small film agency in Tel Aviv. They were both proud and militant Zionists, representatives, to this extent, of a rigid religious and political commitment which led in a very different direction from Kurt's secularised development. But family was family.

When word got around that he was in the country, the press came to interview him, anxious to learn his views on the prospects for a national Jewish music, and he was photographed addressing the assembled Palestine Symphony Orchestra. He also had an audience with Chaim Weizmann.

He stayed in Palestine some two weeks, then took a series of flights back to Paris and London again, this time with stopovers in Rome ('poor and shabby') and Geneva. Here, reliving a moment of a distant past, he spent a day in the company of Nelly Frank, the rich distant cousin with whom he had had a romantic liaison in the early 1920s and to whom he had dedicated – shades of another world – his song-cycle *Frauentanz* in 1923. Nelly remained the custodian of the secrets of this period in his life. When, after his death, Lenya was seeking information about his life in the years before she knew him, she asked Hanns' widow, Rita, who was a cousin of Nelly's, to find out what Nelly was willing to tell. (Whether Rita did so or not, we do not know. She and Lenya were in any case, to put it mildly, not the closest of friends.)

From London he flew directly to New York. 'Coming home to this country had some of the same emotion as arriving here twelve years ago,' he wrote from Brook House to the Andersons, who were in Hollywood at the time:

> With all its faults (and partly because of them), this is still the most decent place to live in, and strangely enough, wherever I found decency and humanity in the world, it reminded me of America, because to me Americanism is (or ought to be) the most advanced attempt to fill the gap between the individual [he writes '*individuum*', the German word] and the technical progress.

The proud voice of a two-hundred-per-cent American. Who – or where – is that German cantor's son who wrote *Mahagonny* and *Die Dreigroschenoper*? Certainly Kurt Weill did not know. When a review of *Street Scene* in *Life* magazine called him a 'German composer', he sent a sharp riposte for them to publish: 'I do not consider myself a "German composer". The Nazis obviously did not consider me as such either, and I left their country (an arrangement which suited both me and my rulers admirably) in 1933.' And to drive the point home in the most telling way he could, he listed the theatrical works he had composed since arriving in America: every one of them, with the single exception of *The Firebrand of Florence*, had an American background.

Lenya had been anxiously waiting for his return, realising in such moments of separation how much he meant to her. 'One forgets in time how much one has become a part of the person one loves,' she wrote to Mab Anderson, 'and to be left alone for a while gives you time to reassemble your feelings and thoughts and then you know again and sure, that you wouldn't like to live without him.'

Once back, he needed to be at work again. After only a week he was 'getting a little fed-up with doing nothing', as he put it to the Andersons, whose return from California he was eagerly looking forward to. One thought was for a musical with Anderson himself – 'possibly without Danny Kaye who is a lot of newsance [sic!]', he delicately added. In the event a challenge came from a new quarter.

The previous year Cheryl Crawford had had a hit with her production of *Brigadoon*, by Alan Jay Lerner and Frederick Loewe. This pair were to have their greatest success in 1956 with *My Fair Lady* but for the moment they had no plans for a successor to *Brigadoon*, and Cheryl Crawford intervened with the idea that Lerner might do something together with Weill. The result was a strange piece, ingenious, maybe over-ingenious, in intellectual conception, while at the same time emotionally tepid and formally not calculated to draw a sustained, warm musical response from a composer. Indeed, the storyline that Lerner laid out almost precluded a convincing coherence in a musical score, Weill's or anyone else's, and would rather have lent itself to the medium of film – time-splits, flash-backs, techniques part-realistic, part-surrealistic. The vaudeville that emerged was first called *A Dish for the Gods*. When it reached the New York stage, its title had become *Love Life*.

Alan Jay Lerner, Harvard-educated son of a wealthy New York family, a recent addition to the artists' and writers' colony in Rockland County, had a witty way with words, albeit a tendency also to overreach himself – the occupational hazard of lyric writers, not excluding the best, like Ira Gershwin. But the achievement of tension in a hard-faced dramatic plot of his own invention – as distinct from the exploitation of 'entertainment' material and comic fantasy – was not his forte. For his collaboration with Weill, Lerner conceived the idea of an historical portrait of a marriage, traced through a series of scenes representing key stages in the one-hundred-and-fifty-year chronicle of American society since the Revolution. On the one hand it was to be a study of the ways in which an American couple behave in response to the social pressures of successive ages: starting from the rural idyll of the eighteenth-century American dream, the action moves forward to the tensions of industrialisation, the obligation to mount the treadmill of ambition and success, the conflict between the sexes and the other strains inflicted on a family. In its other aspect it was an essay in social comment, an historical survey of social conditioning forces and their corrosive influence, not least on the institution of marriage itself.

The form of the show that emerged within this framework was one of pairs of scenes: each successive stage in the marriage of Sam and Susan Cooper is introduced by a vaudeville act in which a magician, a ventriloquist or a band of minstrels lead the way into the following scene from the Coopers' married life. Starting in 1791, the couple still at peace with themselves and their rural existence, the story leads forwards thirty years to a time when factory chimneys are beginning to sprout in the Garden of Eden, then on to the mid-nineteenth century, with Sam a railroad king who can no longer find time for his wife.

By the end of the century the roles have become reversed: Susan has joined the suffragette movement and found a satisfying life independent of her husband. On board a cruise liner in the 1920s they are seen indulging in extra-marital affairs, and back in their New York apartment in the present day all their frustrations come to the surface. The only solution is a spectacular divorce, and the work concludes with a large-scale minstrel show in which a motley collection of characters review the events of the story and the moral to be drawn from them. At the very end we are left with a faint hope that Sam and Susan, cast in the symbolic role of tight-rope walkers, might yet succeed in negotiating the precarious path that could bring them together again.

A revue in character and form, *Love Life* uses the resources of song, pantomime and ballet in the mixed manner that Weill had long favoured. Over the six months, the latter half of 1947, during which most of the music was written, the work assumed its final shape in a patchwork process, the patches being of unequal quality and interest, both textually and musically. The intellectual intention is clear enough: Lerner presents a heavily pessimistic panorama of the dehumanising economic and social forces that destroy the intimacy and integrity of the relationship between man and woman. But emotionally, dramatically, aesthetically the point is not made, a convincing experience not transmitted. ('In 1948 Alan had been married only twice,' observed Cheryl Crawford drily in 1977. 'Now, after six marriages, he would probably have more emotional material at his command.)'

Its form thus predetermined, Weill's score consists of a collection of cameos, some brilliant, some charming, others undistinguished. Lively ensembles like the bouncy 'Economics' for negro quartet and the clever 'Madrigal' for six-part *a cappella* choir show him at his inventive, parodistic best. Lyrical numbers like 'Love Song' and 'Is It Him Or Is It Me?', by contrast, with their harmonic flatness and reliance on contemporary clichés, lower the tone of the proceedings. And when Lerner's verbal exuberance leads him to supply a succession of witty strophes to a weak tune, the weakness receives a merciless exposure from which it cannot recover. In recording his 'feeling of general disappointment with the show', while conceding that 'most of the pleasures come out of Mr Weill's music-box', Brooks Atkinson chose his own image to present the score as a collection of unequal parts.

Cheryl Crawford herself was realistic enough to admit that *Love Life* did not really take off. In her autobiography she later reflected on the reasons why:

> Its theme was fresh, the form unusual, the cast exceptional, the settings by Boris Aronson delightful. But it had no heat, no passion. The audience couldn't get emotionally involved in the marital problems of the couple. And though it was satirical, it lacked penetrating wit for the most part.

Because Kurt's score served the style of the writing, it didn't have the warmth of his best ballads.

Largely due to difficulties in finding a leading lady – Gertrude Lawrence and Ginger Rogers figured among the names mentioned – *Love Life* was not ready for the stage until September 1948. After tryouts in Boston, it opened in the 46th Street Theatre (now the Rodgers Theatre) in New York the following month with the effervescent one-time child prodigy Nanette Fabray as Susan Cooper. Ray Middleton, who had acted Washington Irving in *Knickerbocker Holiday* ten years earlier and had had a recent success as Buffalo Bill opposite Ethel Merman in *Annie Get Your Gun*, played Sam Cooper, Elia Kazan directed and the conductor was Joseph Littau, who had *Carmen Jones* and *Carousel* among his credits. (Maurice Abravanel, whom one would have expected to see on the rostrum, had gone to Salt Lake City in 1947 as conductor of the Utah Symphony, albeit not without a certain heaviness of heart at leaving behind a friend whose life he had shared for twenty-five turbulent years.) The show notched up a run of 252 performances – considerably more than *Street Scene* – which the gratified Cheryl Crawford described as 'respectable'.

During Weill's preoccupation with the composition of *Love Life* rumblings on the American political scene had been growing louder. Thoughts that some kind of non-belligerent accommodation could be reached with the Soviet Union had revealed themselves as increasingly illusory since the end of the Second World War, and the colder the Cold War became, the more strident grew the voices clamouring for the neutralisation of alleged Communist and radical influence and the 'purification' of American public life. In the vanguard of this purifying process stood the notorious House Committee on Un-American Activities (HUAC). Founded in 1938, HUAC had 'investigated' the Federal Theatre Project out of existence in 1939 and since then, particularly since the end of the war, had used the techniques of smear and association to undermine the careers of intellectuals, performing artists and others in the culture industry suspected of left-wing tendencies.

In 1946 the Committee turned its spotlight on Hollywood, which, dominated by Jewish radicals, as it claimed, had been using the cinema to spread 'subversive' ideas. Closed hearings of evidence from producers, directors, screenwriters and actors took place in Los Angeles in spring 1947 and public hearings in Washington were announced for the fall of the same year. This raised suspicions among both conservatives and liberals that the government was looking to control the policies of the motion picture industry as the most powerful of the mass communications media. The Committee distinguished, rather predictably, between 'friendly' and 'unfriendly' witnesses, the former – men like Adolphe Menjou, Robert Taylor, Ronald Reagan, Walt Disney, Louis B. Meyer of MGM – being used to incriminate the latter – Charlie Chaplin, Clifford Odets, Hanns Eisler, Lewis Milestone, the screenwriters John Howard Lawson and Albert Maltz among them. And, of course, Bertolt Brecht.

Weill was not caught up in these unpleasant matters but he had many friends who were. And although he did not see it as his place to strike a public political stance, there was no doubt in which direction his sympathies lay, and always had. At the time of the HUAC inquisition in Washington a body of prominent New Yorkers calling themselves 'Americans for Democratic Action' published in newspapers up and down the country a defiant advertisement: 'It Doesn't Take Burning Fagots To Stage A Witch Hunt. Blazing Flash Bulbs and Klieg Lights Will Serve'. When invited to join a distinguished list of signatories to this declaration – Maxwell Anderson, Moss Hart, Richard Rodgers, Oscar Hammerstein II, the actress Helen Hayes, the violinist Isaac Stern and over sixty others – Weill had no hesitation in accepting.

Brecht, who had in any case decided to leave the United States that fall, had been subpoenaed to appear before HUAC in October. Having disposed of his house in Santa Monica, he took the train, for the last time, from Los Angeles to New York – at government expense, to his impish glee – where he spent a week discussing with friends and advisers how he should deport himself before the Committee. Given the various projects they had discussed over recent years, it would be surprising if he and Weill did not meet. He was still trying to cajole Weill into doing music for his *Schweyk* play, on which he now banked for a spectacular come-back in post-war Germany. And the issue of a new production of *The Threepenny Opera* in some shape or form, whether in America or in Germany, whether by whites or by blacks, refused to go away.

But if they did meet, there is no record of it. Brecht duly travelled to Washington towards the end of October and put on a cunningly calculated and rehearsed performance for the Committee's benefit. He had never, he said, been a member of the Communist Party, looking the chairman straight in the eye – 'the surest sign of a born liar', said George Bernard Shaw. He emerged with a clean political slate and the chairman's fulsome thanks for his cooperation. Immediately after giving his evidence, he took the train back to New York and the next day he was on an Air France flight to Paris. He and Weill never saw each other again.

It had never been a close friendship – in terms of temperament and mutual emotional commitment barely a friendship at all, rather a relationship of occasional conveniences in which, in moments of unpredictable brilliance, the one had so much to give the other. During Brecht's six years in America, Weill set just two of his poems, and they met only a handful of times. Yet when he left, Brecht took something of Weill with him, if only a shared responsibility for the good old days when they had together shocked and captivated the musical-theatrical world in the Schiffbauerdamm Theatre.

Back in East Berlin in 1948, later with the Berliner Ensemble at his disposal, Brecht was to make it his own theatre again, a stylised temple dedicated to the god of epic drama. Caspar Neher's work, too, was to be seen here from time to time. All new, striking, challenging – yes. But much less fun than when Weill was around as well.

In stark contrast, firmly set on his all-American path, Weill found himself the object of an approach from an unexpected quarter which offered him two originally distinct, then combined sources of pleasure. The one was the chance to reactivate a piece he had written earlier for an occasion that had never materialised; the other was a request to recommend a musico-dramatic work for performance by university students.

In the autumn of 1945 Olin Downes had been approached by a cultured, public-minded businessman called Charles McArthur with a proposal for a series of musical plays for radio based on American folk tunes. If a framework could be devised, said McArthur, he would seek to finance the undertaking. Among other composers Downes consulted Weill, who suggested 'a weekly dramatisation of a specific folksong', an idea that Downes found attractive. As it happened, the proposal coincided with an idea which Hans Heinsheimer had recently put to Weill of a 'non-Metropolitan-Opera-type' opera, something in the spirit of *Gebrauchsmusik* that would be within the financial and spiritual reach of the common man.

The next step was to find a poet, or poets, to supply dramatic texts. A few weeks' later the theatrical grapevine turned up one Arnold Sundgaard, a young playwright steeped in American folklore, who saw the possibility of just such a drama in the verses of the song 'Down in the Valley'. Weill found Sundgaard's text admirable and after a few weeks' work completed a score for four soloists, mixed chorus, speaking parts and orchestra, which was recorded and offered to prospective sponsors. But it found no takers. 'They were frightened by the idea,' observed Weill ironically, 'that they might be accused of submitting an opera to the public.' The Downes-McArthur plan died and Weill's score went into a drawer.

Early in 1948, over two years later, Weill was asked on behalf of the University of Indiana if he could suggest a piece of musical theatre for student performance. The impulse for the request came from Hans Busch, a member of the music faculty and the son of Fritz Busch, conductor of the first performance of Weill's *Protagonist* in 1926. 'I remembered the wonderful experience I had with a school opera which I wrote in Europe years ago,' Weill told *The New York Times*, 'and it occurred to me that the piece we had written for Mr Downes' radio program would be readily adaptable for an American school opera.' So, at an in-between moment when *Street Scene* had come off and *Love Life* was not quite finished, *Down in the Valley*, slightly extended and modified but basically still the work of 1945, had its first performance at the University of Indiana campus in Bloomington in July 1948. Weill travelled to Bloomington with Lenya to help with production matters and was present to enjoy the tumultuous applause with which the work, which lasts some forty-five minutes in performance, was received by an audience of over four thousand.

The simple little story that Sundgaard built round the folksong 'Down in the Valley' tells a familiar tale of love, jealousy and death. A young man called Brack Weaver has been condemned to death for a murder he did not commit and awaits execution in a jail in the American South. He had become involved in a fight with Thomas Bouché, his rival for the love of Jennie Parsons, during which Bouché, who has a financial hold over Jennie's father, is killed by his own knife. Brack is nevertheless found guilty of murder. Determined to spend his last hours with Jennie, Brack escapes and goes to her. The events that led up to his arrest are re-enacted as a flashback and at the end, happy to die in the knowledge that Jennie loves him, he gives himself up to his pursuers and serenely accepts his fate.

In the project that he had put to Olin Downes, Weill envisaged 'a weekly dramatisation of a specific folksong'. In effect he has pre-empted more than a month's supply, for as well as the title song, full settings of which fill the first and last of the set scenes, and fragments of which drift like a Leitmotiv through the whole piece, he has used four further folksongs as the basic substance of the remaining scenes. No doubt this accords with the spirit of the exercise but it inevitably reduces the scope for original melodic material and tends to turn the work into a string of folksong arrangements linked by narrative choruses and underscored spoken dialogue. It is sometimes difficult to keep Constant Lambert's tart observation out of one's mind: 'The whole trouble with a folk-song is that once you have played it through, there is nothing much you can do except play it over again and play it rather louder.'

Something of this kind surfaced in the minds of Weill's critics at the time. Irving Sablosky, a journalist on the *Chicago Daily News*, doubted whether the 'corny' little 'Down-in-the-Valley' tune could sustain the weight it was being made to bear. To which Weill replied: 'What you call corn ... is really a part of life in our time (and probably in other times too), and life is what I am interested in as the basis of musical expression.'

It sounds very reasonable, very humane, but it does not meet the charge implicit in Sablosky's suspicion. Life is 'the basis of musical expression' for Bach, for Mozart, for Beethoven – but where is the 'corn'? Do we want corn in our music? Does art, great art, really do no more than accept the parameters of the life of its age, however these parameters be defined, and claim merely to reflect or express what it finds within them? If it were so, art could not outlive the age in which it arose, for succeeding ages will have their own values of 'life' – and their own species of 'corn'. Art under this aegis becomes, in the strict sense, a period piece, its meaning and its appeal confined to the age that gave it birth, for later periods a curio that shows how things used to be. Fortunately art of real quality, even if the declared product of a narrow, functional view, has the innate power to transcend the limitations which its creator may have been at pains to impose upon it.

But the populist strain in Weill ran deep, and his reply to Sablosky emphasises the gulf that he had deliberately, and delightedly, opened up between himself and the 'serious music' establishment. 'Instead of worrying about the material of music,' he goes on,

> the theory behind it, the opinion of other musicians, my main concern is to find the purest expression in music for what I want to say, with enough trust in my instincts, my taste and my talent to write always 'good' music, regardless of the style I am writing in.

The 'good music' *versus* 'bad music' antithesis returns which he had postulated in a newspaper interview eight years earlier, proposing to substitute it for that of 'serious music' *versus* 'light music'. His emphasis on his instincts and talents, applied here to the tell-tale phrase 'the style I am writing in', shows how calculated, how goal-oriented his composing has become. In a way it is a re-statement of the objective philosophy of *Neue Sachlichkeit*, of the values embodied by the neo-Classical Stravinsky.

But whatever the procedural validity in literary analysis of a distinction between content and style, between what is said and how it is said, in music there can be no such distinction. The what and the how are one. If there is an inclination to say that a composer has adopted a new style, the meaning is, not that he has discovered new technical devices (though he may have) but that he has found new things to say. He cannot say one and the same thing in different 'styles'. The moment he changes his style, he changes the 'thing'. Weill's phrase 'the style I am writing in' really means 'the emotional substance I have chosen to express'. It is that substance, that musical utterance in its wholeness, to which we react, assessing its quality by reference to the utterances that surround it and charting the fluctuating intensity that a composer's *oeuvre* in its totality makes upon us. *The Rise and Fall of the City of Mahagonny* gives us more, and demands more from us, than, say, *Lady in the Dark*. But the difference lies in the substance, not in the 'style'.

As to the context of *Down in the Valley* itself, Weill took his American folklore seriously. It was not a question of a few whimsical, nostalgic backdrops and a handful of heroicised historical personages but of living roots. Among the books that have survived from what appears to have been a very modest library in Brook House are almost twenty items – sources of background information, stories, ballads, song collections – which provided him with concrete raw material and at the same time induced that sense of identification with the independent traditions of his new homeland from which he derived such pleasure. He had always resented the class distinctions of an ageing European society and its affected 'connoisseurs', and he put his faith in the freshness and vigour of the young, natural, democratic United States. Soon after finishing the first, radio version of *Down in the Valley*, he wrote to Charles McArthur:

> I have been convinced for a long time that in a deeply democratic country like ours art should belong to the people. It should come out of their thinking and their emotions, and it should become part of their lives. It should be 'popular' in the highest sense of the word.

And art not only for the people but by the people. For in its final form it was conceived for production mainly by non-professional groups. Scenery and a few lighting effects, said the composer, will heighten the dramatic effect but are not obligatory. Otherwise: 'It can be performed wherever a chorus, a few singers, and a few actors are available.'

Beyond this lies the personal context of *Down in the Valley*, that established by Weill's own reference to 'a school opera which I wrote in Europe years ago'. For although it bears no political message, *Down in the Valley* stands in direct line of musical descent from his *Jasager* of 1930, also intended for amateur musicians and actors, also given its first performance by students, and also offered as a contribution to the musical experience of the people as a whole. In its origin as in its reception, it is a piece of American *Gebrauchsmusik*. Weill would have applauded Benjamin Britten's description of the composer's responsibility as 'to be useful, and to the living'.

Back home from the University of Indiana, Weill returned to the final weeks of preparation and rehearsals of *Love Life*. Coinciding with these activities was a visit from Lenya's mother. Johanna Hainisch was now eighty. A simple, working-class woman, yet with the canny sharpness of one forced to keep her wits about her, she had had a hard life, first with Lenya's drunk and abusive father Franz Blamauer, who had deserted the family while Lenya was still a teenager, then with Ernst Hainisch, with whom she was still living in the Vienna that made up her world. Lenya had not seen her for fifteen years. Weill, with characteristic generosity, had offered to pay for the flight from Vienna to New York and for Lenya's younger sister Maria to accompany her. The old lady seems to have been anything but overwhelmed by her experience of the New World, and as unsentimentally critical of what she saw in New York as of conditions back home. She and Maria stayed in Brook House for almost two months. When they left, Lenya knew that it was the last goodbye. Johanna Hainisch died two years later.

That October also saw the release by Universal Pictures of the film of *One Touch of Venus*, in which fragments of Weill's mutilated score can be found scattered over the romantic battlefield of Hollywood's version of the story. This event, coupled with the hope that some producer might also take on *Love Life*, drew him back, for the last time, to Los Angeles. He went in the company of Alan Jay Lerner, with whom he had put together a scenario in which they thought they might interest someone. They thought wrongly. But Weill saw in Lerner a writer to be cultivated and put a number of ideas to him for films and musicals, including an adaptation of Max Beerbohm's novel *Zuleika Dobson*.

Also in Weill's mind during these weeks in Hollywood was a plan that he had been pondering since his election to the directorate of The Playwrights Company two years earlier. This was that the Company should try to arrange a Hollywood tie-up for their productions on the same basis as their stage works, namely, that the control of production matters should be vested in the Company, and not left to a studio bureaucracy. With support from Maxwell Anderson Weill discussed the prospects with Arthur S. Lyons, president of a talent-spotting agency, but, as could have been anticipated, the thought that the last word should rest with a writer rather than a producer contained a heresy that no film company could stomach, and Lyons saw no point in prolonging the discussion. Let The Playwrights, and all other playwrights, stick to their last, he said.

Weill returned home from this final unprofitable excursion to the West Coast to find the artistic community in New City eagerly anticipating the Broadway opening of Anderson's *Anne of the Thousand Days*. During the months that Anderson's mind was on *Anne*, Weill had been occupied with *Love Life* and *Down in the Valley*. This was the way it had been for the last ten years – two careers, both with their ups and downs, moving in parallel or, more accurately, diverging in response to individual stimuli, meeting only at chance, insubstantial moments. *Knickerbocker Holiday* had brought them together in 1938, when Weill was a new boy on Broadway. The following year they had launched into the negro musical *Ulysses Africanus*, to which their thoughts had affectionately returned from time to time but which never saw the light of day. Otherwise the only product of their collaboration had been the trifling, if mildly amusing *Ballad of Magna Carta*.

In no way did this meagre harvest represent the personal relationship between the two men. Their mutual respect was undiminished, the beaten track through the woods from the one house on South Mountain Road to the other was still in great demand, and the two families had their social evenings and parties together as always. But Anderson, the poetic moralist, struggling to come to terms with the loss of his Christian faith, could only on occasion accept that the message of his words might gain from the addition of music. So after the romp of *Knickerbocker Holiday* he had gone back to the investigation of moral issues and personalities in turmoil in a 'straight' dramatic form which made no concessions to a superimposed music. Then a subject was put into his mind which made him think of music again – and of Weill.

At that moment Weill was listening to a familiar, not always welcome voice from the other side of the Atlantic. Brecht, now re-established in familiar haunts in East Berlin, had sent him proposed 'modernisations' of the text of *Dreigroschenoper*, with the introduction of references to Goering, Schacht and other figures of the Nazi establishment, asking for his consent to a new production. Weill gave him a frosty answer. The objections he raised were not all that convincing but he had no desire, aesthetic or financial, to put himself at Brecht's mercy. The prospect of doing something with Anderson again was far more pleasurable.

The story of this 'something' goes back to December 1947. Anderson had been in Greece for a performance of *Joan of Lorraine* and was on board the *Mauretania* en route from Southampton back to New York. Among his fellow-passengers were the lyric writer Oscar Hammerstein II and his wife, returning from a European tour. Somewhere on their travels Dorothy Hammerstein had learned of a recent novel set in the racially divided society of South Africa. It told a tragic story of a native family whose unity had been destroyed when some of its members were tempted away from their village by the allurements of the white man's city, where they fell victim to degradation and crime.

So impressed was she by what she had heard about this novel that Dorothy Hammerstein urged Anderson to turn it into a play. Back in New City, Anderson, moved by the subject, talked about it to Weill, who also felt its social and moral significance for a highly segregation-conscious America, and the possibility of a collaboration began to emerge even before either of them had read the book. When Mrs Hammerstein met Anderson again at a party in New York the following March, she gave him a copy. The book was Alan Paton's *Cry, the Beloved Country*.

Paton's novel, published in 1948, owed its impact as much to its realistic depiction of the racial tensions in South African society as to its powerful narrative, couched in an emotional language sometimes almost Biblical in its poetic passion. Born in Natal in 1903, Paton had for thirteen years been principal of a boys' reformatory near Johannesburg, and it was largely from this experience that he drew his raw material – his very raw material. *Cry, the Beloved Country* centres on the figure of Stephen Kumalo, a black preacher who sets out from his homestead in search of his sister Gertrude and his son Absalom, who have sought to improve their lot among the bright lights of the city. In Johannesburg he finds that Gertrude has become a prostitute and that Absalom is in jail, awaiting execution for his part in the murder of the son of James Jarvis, a white farmer. Kumalo can do nothing to save them but when he returns to his village, he takes Gertrude's child and Absalom's pregnant wife with him.

On the morning of Absalom's execution Kumalo chances to meet Jarvis in the mountains (in his play Anderson, characteristically but quite implausibly, has Jarvis come to Kumalo's home). United in their grief over the loss of their sons, the two men bury for a precious moment the racial antagonisms that divide white from black, a moment that symbolises the peace that will surely come to the beloved country.

Long before he put the book down, Anderson knew that here was something for him, something that not only raised fundamental moral issues in the conduct of human affairs but also had an immediate and painful relevance to the state of race relations in contemporary America. He at once wrote to Alan Paton to tell him how deeply moving he found his novel and to ask his permission to dramatise it in cooperation with Weill. 'For years,' he told Paton, 'I've wanted to write something which would state the position and perhaps illuminate the tragedy of our own negroes. . . . Now that I've read your story, I think you have said as much as can be said both for your country and ours. . . . It would be our task to translate into stage form, without dulling its edge or losing its poetry, this extraordinarily moving tale of lost men clinging to odds and ends of faith in the darkness of our modern earth.'

This is typical Anderson language, and the drama he ultimately produced, with newly-written scenes and considerable changes of emphasis and motivation, occupied the high moral ground which was his preferred domicile. In *Cry, the Beloved Country* the moral values, the hopes for a release from fear and bondage, from the slave-driven inhumanity of *apartheid*, emerge from the totally realistic sequence of events that Paton unfolds, a realism anchored in his own experience. In *Lost in the Stars*, as Anderson's and Weill's work would be called, the action served the demonstration of abstract ideals, ideals of understanding, of tolerance and of human brotherhood.

All this took them back to the never-completed but never-forgotten *Ulysses Africanus*, story of a black man's loyalty to his white master through years of bewilderment and temptation. That work had foundered less on its authors' creative difficulties than on their inability to attract Paul Robeson or any other negro star to the main role. Now, ten years later, Anderson returned to the moral dilemmas that had affected him so deeply. At the same time a number of the songs that he and Weill had already written at that time, including the eponymous 'Lost in the Stars', spoke the same musical language as that which Weill now conceived for the new work, and so found a natural new home. The subject of Paton's 'true, moving and honest story', as Anderson called it, 'fitted exactly into the scheme for a musical tragedy which Kurt Weill and I had hoped for some years to be able to write'.

Anderson and his producers would have retained the title *Cry, the Beloved Country* but wanted Alexander Korda, who had acquired the rights of the novel for London Films, to pay them a fee for so doing, on the ground that a Broadway production would give the film advance publicity. This somewhat Byzantine argument did not impress Korda, and *Lost in the Stars* is what the musical became. London Films issued its version in 1951 with the original title, and with Sidney Poitier as Kumalo.

The musical component of the work grew organically around the dramatic action in an interesting way. From the very beginning Anderson saw the music as a unifying force. 'To keep the plot and the dialogues in the form you gave them,' he wrote to Paton, 'would only be possible if a chorus – a sort of Greek chorus – were used to tie together the great number of scenes, and to comment on the action as you comment on the philosophic and descriptive passages.' Since the two acts of the drama have no fewer than twenty scenes, the commentative musical chorus sometimes a group of white women or men, sometimes black, sometimes mixed – has a vital integrating role to play. And originally this was to be its only role. The physical action and the psychological motivation were to be carried by spoken dialogue, and if the matter had been left there, the result could have been described as a play with music.

Then things began to develop, especially after Anderson and Weill succeeded in finding themselves a producer – Rouben Mamoulian, no less, who, as well as a row of productions for the Theatre Guild, had

Porgy and Bess, Oklahoma! and *Carousel* to his name. The Playwrights Company were willing to sponsor a production – a not overly lavish one, they made clear – towards the end of the year. For the role of Stephen Kumalo, the noble black minister with a mission to preach the healing of mindless racial hatred, Mamoulian found Todd Duncan, the original Porgy, with Leslie Banks – who had played a similar part opposite Paul Robeson in the film *Sanders of the River* – as the enlightened, liberal white farmer James Jarvis.

Gradually, as the three men discussed the form of the work, the music came to acquire an ever-increasing importance. More and more space was made over for songs in what had originally been the areas of spoken dialogue, until in the end they found themselves looking at an unusual animal – a full-scale tragic musical, putting them in mind at times of *Porgy and Bess*. Weill made the situation quite clear – the situation as he saw it, that is: not everyone saw it in the same light – in a letter to Olin Downes:

> It must be somewhat surprising indeed to find a serious subject treated in a form which (in this country at least) has been used so far only for a lighter form of entertainment. But that was exactly the nature of my experiment – to do a 'musical tragedy' for the American theatre so that the typical American audience (not a specialized audience) can accept it.

The description 'musical tragedy' – the term is Anderson's – as a counterpart to 'musical comedy' may be acceptable as a characterisation of the dramatic action which culminates in Absalom's execution, although the heavy morality in which Anderson shrouds the final scene of reconciliation between black man and white man turns the work into nothing so much as a humanist sermon on a text of trust and optimism. But musically nothing has changed. Weill's talent for assuming whatever mood the moment requires is undiminished. There is some immensely effective choral writing, flavoured in parts with elements from the world of negro spirituals. 'Cry, the Beloved Country' is magnificent, so is the railroad music of 'Train to Johannesburg', while the incidental music behind the spoken dialogue and the scene changes reveals his old familiar skill in making a musical point in a mere handful of bars.

But, too many of the songs live on the same conventional, popular-song fare as those in his 'non-tragic' musicals. Some show an appealing touch; too many have an anodyne blandness which cloys all sense of drama, leave alone of tragedy. It is almost as though, after a flash of dramatic insight, his attention had wavered, leaving him to rely on familiar formulae and his indestructible professionalism to see him through the next few pages. The threat of overstatement hovers over him, a tendency to drive an idea too hard, like the pentatonic idiom of the narrative opening number 'The Hills of Ixopo', or even the passionate Leitmotiv of 'Cry, the Beloved Country' itself. He was anxious, as he told Olin Downes, for audiences to accept what he described as 'my experiment'. They did indeed accept it. There was no cause for either anxiety or surprise, for what they experienced was not an 'experiment', which might have produced novel results, but a musical of the familiar stamp, satisfying the expectations of its audience in the way its creator usually succeeded in doing.

Perhaps to a greater degree than Weill's other works for Broadway – though they were all, true to their genre, subject to such treatment – *Lost in the Stars* underwent constant changes from its inception, when the music was to be confined to the sidelines of the action, down to the day of its first performance as a fully-fledged musical. Numbers were added, dropped, rewritten, some of them new, some salvaged from *Ulysses Africanus*, one alteration often bringing others in its train, as Mamoulian kneaded the work into the shape he wanted.

Alan Paton came to New York during the final rehearsals in October 1949 and stayed for the opening night. Kind, tolerant man that he was, he tried to be as polite as he could but the changes of meaning and spiritual content that Anderson had introduced made him profoundly unhappy, and the rehearsal he saw was for him a 'terrible evening', as he confessed in his autobiography many years later. No doubt it was good musical theatre but in spirit it was not his novel. And when the première was warmly applauded, his embarrassment prevented him from sharing in the general rejoicing – although, as he conceded, Weill's choruses and the singing helped to make the experience more endurable.

Mamoulian, no stranger to the tantrums thrown by the personalities of Broadway, was greatly taken by Weill's modesty and amenability. 'I have many warm memories of Weill,' he said. 'One of my favorites is the following:

> On the first day of rehearsals of *Lost in the Stars* I suggested a few musical cuts to which Kurt willingly agreed. On the second day I came up with a couple of other possible cuts. Again he accepted them gracefully. On the third day in the theatre, before the start of rehearsal, the cast was on the stage, I sat in the front row with Maxwell Anderson, when Kurt Weill arrived. As he came down the aisle towards me, he enthusiastically rubbed his hands together and with an ecstatic smile, like a boy about to open his Christmas present, said to me: 'What do we cut today?'

But this equable, easygoing exterior protected an anxiety that he was desperate to conceal from the outside world, above all from Lenya. One day last July he had been playing tennis in the garden of Alan

Jay Lerner's house in New City. It was extremely hot. Suddenly, as Lerner describes it, Weill dropped his racket and staggered to the side of the court, complaining of the heat. Lerner and the others rushed across and put a chair under him. The right side of his face was contorted, he had turned white and the colour had drained from his lips. Lerner thought it might be a stroke, or maybe heat prostration. He shouted at him but Weill gave no answer.

They carried him out of the sun and into the house, and after a while the colour began to return to his features and he was able to speak. Lerner wanted to call an ambulance but Weill assured him it was not necessary. It had merely been a recurrence of an old stomach complaint he had contracted as a schoolboy during the First World War, he said, promising that he would go and see a doctor in the next few days. He never did. He then swore Lerner and the others to secrecy over the incident – nobody, least of all Lenya, should discover that he had had a mild stroke.

The alarming experience was a harbinger of the tragedy to come. At the time, however, he made light of it, and the effects passed quickly enough for him to be able to conceal it from all but those who had witnessed it. When George Jenkins, the Hollywood stage designer whom Mamoulian had engaged to do the sets for *Lost in the Stars*, met him at rehearsals, he observed nothing untoward – he was his usual quiet, friendly self. He made the same favourable impression on the journalist Harry Gilroy, who interviewed him for *The New York Times* and described him 'as being of a size and general air of amiable unconcern that one would associate more with a retired jockey than with one of the theatre's more sensitive composers'.

Lost in the Stars opened in the Music Box Theatre at the end of October 1949, conducted by Maurice Levine. 'It was an outstanding success,' said Alan Paton:

> People wept and shouted and clapped. At the end there were ovations,
> for the cast, the singers, the dramatist, the composer, the director, and
> for the author of *Cry, the Beloved Country*.

For the first couple of months it played to full or nearly full houses. Then, to the authors' mystification and annoyance, attendances began to drop. This not only wounded their pride; it made itself felt in their pockets. Anderson had put over 12,000 dollars of his own money into the production, and Weill 3,000 dollars.

The flagging box-office receipts reflected, cruelly put, the flagging creativity which Brooks Atkinson, in *The New York Times*, lamented in the work. Weill complained to Atkinson about his write-up but in his reply Atkinson would not take anything back. 'The main subject of my article,' he wrote to Weill, 'was the creative spirit,

> and I am very sorry to say that I was not aware of any in Mr Anderson's playwriting in this instance. It has integrity and high principle and technical knowledge of the medium, but I thought his scenario was on the pedestrian side. Also I am not aware that *Lost in the Stars* creates a new form of musical theatre. Many of the admirable and ambitious musical plays that we have had for the past few years are presented as creating a new form. But I don't see in what respect *Lost in the Stars* is a new form.

What Atkinson, a man well-disposed to Weill's music, did not see, Broadway theatregoers apparently did not see either.

The situation preyed on everybody's nerves. John F. Wharton, a lawyer who oversaw the legal affairs of The Playwrights Company and left an insider's semi-autobiographical account of the sometimes stormy relationships that developed within it, watched with embarrassment as Anderson and Weill, convinced of the quality of their product, virtually accused their business manager and press agent of not marketing it properly. 'Max became more and more irascible,' Wharton recorded, 'and Kurt more and more excitable. Bill [William Fields, the press agent] said to me, "I'm scared that Kurt is going to have a heart attack."'

Lost in the Stars closed, four weeks earlier than planned, after some 280 performances, then went on tour in an effort to at least break even on its production costs of 90,000 dollars. This was a modest enough outlay for a musical – maybe the modesty was itself partly responsible for the situation – but when the Broadway run ended still 45,000 dollars short, the target looked frighteningly out of reach. Anderson remained proud of what he and Weill had achieved convinced, as he loftily put it in a telegram to the cast at the final Broadway performance, 'that our country will be a better place in which to live because of what we were trying to do'. Art as a moral force. Art in the service of the community, of the nation. Amen to that, Weill would have said. If he had still been there to hear it.

Having found his way back to Anderson after so many years, and whatever the attractions of other projects, Weill now felt surer than ever that he had found in this dramatist, the closest friend of his American years, his ideal collaborator. Hardly had *Lost in the Stars* opened than they set about drafting a scenario for a musical based on *Huckleberry Finn*, the most American piece of Americana that Weill could have asked for. Indeed, a growing number of American titles figured in his plans for future works – *The Grapes of Wrath*, *Gone with the Wind*, Stephen Vincent Benét's *The Devil and Daniel Webster*, Anderson's *Winterset*.

Christmas 1949 came and went. For all his involvement in this project and that, he always found time to write to his parents – letters telling them of the progress of his works but also concerned to keep their spirits high. Albert Weill was now very frail, suffering from a weak heart and dropsy, and Kurt was anxious that his needs were catered for. They must not stint themselves on domestic help, labour-saving devices and the like, he tells them: he will send the money they require.

In these early weeks of 1950, friends and professional associates alike noticed an increasing irritability in him, an unusual acerbity and testiness quite unlike the gentle composure of the Kurt Weill they know. So out of character was his behaviour, indeed, that it became obvious that something fundamental was wrong. But who knew what? Since his trip to Palestine, at the latest, when Nathan had checked his state of health and told him of the history of high blood pressure in the family, he had realised what hung over him. But he said nothing. His collapse on Lerner's tennis court the previous summer had been a warning he recognised for what it was. Still he said nothing. The physical and mental stress of the rehearsals of *Lost in the Stars* had taken more out of him than many previous shows and was exacerbated by the show's drooping popularity at the box office, followed by arguments over what to do about it. The nervous tension brought on a severe attack of psoriasis which spread over his whole back. The energy drained away from him, and at the end of February, quite uncharacteristically, he was forced to spend some days in bed.

This did not prevent him from working, or attempting to work, on the songs for *Huckleberry Finn* when Anderson brought him his lyrics. He managed to sketch the music for five of them – commonplace folksy melodies, half-dance tune, half-musical comedy in manner, the struggles of a tired mind to force something out of itself.

An episode to raise his spirits was the news that *Lost in the Stars* had won the Brotherhood Award of the National Conference of Christians and Jews as a contribution to mutual understanding among the peoples of the world. But he was not well enough to attend the ceremony at the Waldorf Astoria Hotel at the beginning of February and had to content himself with Anderson's account of the occasion and with reading the acceptance speech that Anderson had made on their joint behalf. By the time of his fiftieth birthday, however, on March 3, he had recovered sufficiently to be able to go downstairs and celebrate with Lenya and the Andersons.

Over the following two weeks his condition fluctuated. There were days when he felt well enough to take a walk in the woods, then another attack of psoriasis would confine him to the house. Lenya was deeply worried but all he needed, he insisted, was a few days' rest. Hans

Curjel, then teaching at Oberlin College, and Hans Heinsheimer, who had become head of publications at Schirmer's in New York – men who had known him for twenty-five years and more – came out to visit him. According to Curjel, he was even toying with the idea of returning to Europe for some length of time. 'I felt,' said Curjel, 'that he had *Bürgschaft* and *The Seven Deadly Sins* in mind – possibly even Brecht.'

On March 16 the Andersons walked across to Brook House and found him in bed, though able to give his mind to the *Huckleberry Finn* music from time to time. Having read him a new scene and some new lyrics, Anderson left him in comparative comfort, with Lenya and Mab playing cards together. During the night he woke up with violent chest pains which persisted until a local doctor, summoned by Lenya the next morning, gave him an injection to make him sleep. The doctor suspected it was the first sign of a coronary and ordered complete rest.

The following night was equally terrible, with Weill tormented by a constant feeling of oppression round his heart. A specialist was called. He diagnosed a coronary and arranged for nurses to watch over him day and night. 'Mab and I at Kurt's all afternoon,' Anderson wrote in his diary. 'I saw him for a moment. He looked ghastly.'

'Sunday, March 19,' noted Anderson. 'A terrible day. Kurt on the verge.' The doctors decided he should be moved to hospital, and an ambulance came to take him to Flower Hospital in Manhattan; the Andersons followed with Lenya, who spent the night at the hospital with Mab. Weill was put in an oxygen tent – 'in precarious condition', Anderson wrote.

Suddenly a remarkable improvement took place. When Lenya and Mab Anderson went into his room on the 20th, he waved to them from the oxygen tent. The next day he was better still and said to Anderson: 'Finish the script. I'll be back to work on schedule.' By the end of the week he had been taken out of the oxygen tent, and the word 'recovery' was being whispered by the doctors. Visions of *Huckleberry Finn* returned and he began correcting the proofs of the vocal score of *Lost in the Stars*.

A week went by, each day seeming to bring its own ray of hope. When the Broadway conductor Lehman Engel called the Flower Hospital on the morning of Monday, April 3 to ask Lenya how Kurt was progressing, she told him he was 'recovering nicely' and looking forward to a visit from him.

Shortly before five o'clock that afternoon the Andersons received a telephone call from Lenya at the hospital. She urged Mab to come at once. The thirty-five-mile drive took the Andersons a little over an hour. When they arrived, they found Lenya waiting in the corridor outside his room.

'I think this is the end,' she said. He had suffered a cerebral embolism. At seven o'clock he died.

Although she sought solace elsewhere and married her friend George Davis a little over a year later, Lenya never lost her sense of guilt over her relationship with Kurt Weill. She even asked his brother Nathan whether she had neglected to care for him properly once it had become dramatically clear, at least three months before, that something terrible was happening. Explaining to her the consequences of hypertension and the nature of his brother's condition, Nathan quoted a leading American heart specialist: 'Most patients with coronary thrombosis recover or die without regard for what the physician does'. The cerebral embolism had resulted from the first heart attack. But, he assured her: 'You need not blame yourself in any way or think that anything was left undone.' Physically, no. Psychologically and spiritually, her self-reproachment was not so easily dispersed. 'There was always a wall around him,' she said the year before she died:

> People never really knew him. And I'm not sure *I* ever really knew him, even after twenty-four years of marriage and the two years we lived together before that. And when he died, I looked at him and asked myself, did I ever really know him?

In the end, however, whoever really knew whom, and although neither had set much store by the Seventh Commandment, Weill and Lenya, the antipodal couple, belonged in some perverse, inscrutable way to each other. And knew it. The will that he made in 1944 provided for his parents in Palestine but left everything else to her.

On the afternoon of Wednesday, April 5, 1950 Kurt Julian Weill returned to the green, wooded tranquillity of Brook House for the last time. Lenya was waiting, with Rita Weill, Hanns' widow, and Kurt's sister Ruth Sohn with her husband Leon, who had left Israel two years earlier and also settled in the United States. The Andersons, the Caniffs and others of the Rockland County artistic community were there, with Rouben Mamoulian, Elmer Rice, Marc Blitzstein and Robert E. Sherwood among those who drove out from New York City. 'At three Lenya looked at Kurt for the last time and the casket was closed and we started for the cemetery,' wrote Maxwell Anderson in his diary.

Five miles away, in the village of Haverstraw, lay Mount Repose cemetery, a steep, grassy bank sloping down from the noble forest hills that overlook the majestic Hudson River. The cortège drove along the undulating, twisting roads to the cemetery gates and up the winding track to the highest point. Here, a few yards short of the trees, a grave had been prepared. It was raining.

The mourners assembled round the coffin, and Maxwell Anderson, spokesman for liberal, humanitarian America, stepped forward and spoke a few words of farewell to his quiet friend. 'I have loved him more than any man I knew . . . He made so many beautiful things that he will be remembered and loved by many not yet born.' Then Leon Sohn, German refugee from the holocaust, a voice from the Old World, recited the mourner's Kaddish, the Jewish prayer for the departed: 'He who maketh peace in his high places, may he make peace for us and for all Israel; and say ye, Amen'. The two halves of his being, consciously kept apart in life, spiritually and aesthetically irreconcilable in his divided world, had found a union in the rites of death.

His gravestone says simply:

Kurt Weill

1900–1950

Beneath, accompanied by their hymn-like melody, are engraved four lines from the penultimate scene of *Lost in the Stars*, sung by the congregation in Stephen Kumalo's chapel:

> This is the life of men on earth;
> Out of darkness we come at birth
> Into a lamplit world, and then –
> Go forward into dark again.

In 1981 Lotte Lenya was laid to rest beside him.

Epilogue

Some three hundred pages ago we asked the real Kurt Weill to stand up. Whether he has done so – whether there is, in the simple denominational sense, one single real composer called Kurt Weill – is a question to which readers will have their own answer. On this depends the answer to the further question – who was the man laid to rest in Haverstraw in April 1950? In what historical tradition, or traditions, should his compositions be judged?

Critical judgements, if they are to have any chance of being fair and helpful, must not stray from their proper context. To talk of *Der Protagonist* and *One Touch of Venus* in one and the same critical breath will contribute little to an understanding of either. Like can only be compared with like – *Der Protagonist* with *Wozzeck*, perhaps, and *One Touch of Venus* with *Oklahoma!* But with a chameleonic character like Weill, confronting us now in this guise, now in that, making eyes-wide-open decisions to go now this way, now that, we soon find ourselves unable to avoid judging the relative merits of the contexts themselves. This then leaves us contemplating the apparent incompatibilities and paradoxes of Weill's situation which polarised critical opinion during his lifetime and cannot but continue to do so.

Virgil Thomson put the dichotomy about as bluntly as it could be put. 'His [i.e. Weill's] American work,' wrote Thomson, 'was viable but not striking, thoroughly competent but essentially conformist. His German works, on the other hand, made musical history.' With Weill's 'German works' Thomson was thinking of the *Dreigroschenoper* and the *Mahagonny* opera – 'his masterpieces', he called them – but also to be included in the German works is the earlier operatic, orchestral and vocal music which constitutes a further context of its own.

The segregation of these contexts one from the other was hardened by the combined pressures of exile and geography. Some of the artists, writers and musicians who fled from the Nazis in the 1930s already had firm international reputations; in an objective, if slightly facile sense, one might say that they could continue in their new surroundings the activities they had been forced to break off in the old. There is nothing in Thomas Mann's novel *Doktor Faustus* that tells us it was written in California, not in Munich. Beethoven is Beethoven, whether Bruno Walter conducted him in Berlin or in Boston.

But Weill, though not unknown in American musical circles when he landed in New York in 1935, had no public eagerly awaiting his arrival. The world in which he had been so sensational a success was not exportable – nor were the financial pickings of that success. He had to earn a new living, and, man of the theatre that he was, he made his deliberate decision to do so by competing in the cut-throat world of the Broadway musical, where the rewards of success were celestial but the punishment for failure diabolical. Whichever way it was to go, it was a context of his own choice.

Ironically, it was only in the decade after his death that the German Weill began to come into his own on the other side of the Atlantic. Marc Blitzstein's English *Threepenny Opera*, with Lotte Lenya in her old role of Jenny, took New York by storm in 1954, and on its return to the Theatre de Lys the following year ran for almost seven years. The 1950s also marked the beginning of Lenya's personal crusade on behalf of her husband's music, which led to German recordings, with her participation, of *Dreigroschenoper*, *Happy End*, the *Mahagonny* opera, *The Seven Deadly Sins* and smaller items.

But until recently there was no corresponding movement of the American Weill to Europe, where the mere fact that he had gone slumming on Broadway was enough to banish him to another exile – the critical exile that awaits the man who is seen as having betrayed, for whatever reason, the highest ideals of his art, his heritage and even his own artistic being. 'He got too involved in American show business and all the terrible people in it,' said Otto Klemperer. 'Weill's last pieces I find awful.' Some may jib at the last word but the sentiment is not uncommon. *Knickerbocker Holiday*, *Lady in the Dark*, *Street Scene* and the rest were shunted into a siding and left there, an embarrassing consignment the authorities would rather not acknowledge.

Over the last five or ten years things have changed. And the pace of change is accelerating. Weill is in process of being proudly and publicly 'discovered' – the whole Weill, from Berlin to Broadway, from the First Symphony and *The Seven Deadly Sins* to *Johnny Johnson* and *Lost in the Stars*. Singers from the world of opera and from the world of cabaret are recording his songs and putting them into their concert programmes. University schools of music and local music societies have found refreshing new material on which to lavish their enthusiasm. The German Weill pierces more and more deeply into the American musical consciousness, while the American Weill's *Street Scene* finds its way to Germany, and to the English National Opera. Freewheeling assemblages of items from individual works to form 'concert suites' – musical meat-balls in which most of the ingredients may be Weill's but the final concoction is certainly not

– are less unequivocally welcome but at least they testify to the existence of a market for such products.

'I write for today,' Weill once said to a New York journalist. 'I don't give a damn about writing for posterity.' But he would not be too disappointed to know that the posterity of forty years on is eager to find out what he had been writing, whenever and wherever. We do not mind how many Kurt Weills stand up.

Select Bibliography

This short bibliography makes no claim to comprehensiveness. It offers a selection of works relevant, directly or indirectly, to the study of Kurt Weill's life and career, together with source-books on the contemporary historical and cultural background, both in Europe and America.

An archive of materials – scores, correspondence, personal documents, newspaper clippings, photographs etc. – has been assembled at Yale University and catalogued, not always accurately, by Adrienne Nesnow as *The Papers of Kurt Weill and Lotte Lenya*, Yale University Library, New Haven, 1984.

Complete catalogues of Weill's musical works can be found in Mario R. Mercado, *Kurt Weill: A Guide to His Works*, Valley Forge 1989 (which also has an up-to-date discography) and, in far greater detail, in David Drew, *Kurt Weill: A Handbook*, London 1987.

Weill's Writings

Weill, Kurt, *Musik und Theater. Gesammelte Schriften* ed. S. Hinton and J. Schebera, Berlin 1990. Now the standard collection of Weill's writings in German, replacing that below. A companion volume of his English writings is planned by the same editors.
——*Ausgewählte Schriften* ed. D. Drew, Frankfurt 1975

Memoirs and Reminiscences by Contemporaries

Aufricht, Ernst Josef, *Erzähle, damit du dein Recht erweist*, Berlin 1966
Busoni, Ferruccio, *Selected Letters* ed. A. Beaumont, London 1987
Butting, Max, *Musikgeschichte, die ich miterlebte*, Berlin 1955
Clurman, Harold, *The Fervent Years*, New York 1945, 1975
Crawford, Cheryl, *One Naked Individual*, New York 1977
Engel, Lehman, *This Bright Day*, New York 1974
Gershwin, Ira, *Lyrics on Several Occasions*, New York 1959
Hecht, Ben, *A Child of the Century*, New York 1955
Heinsheimer, Hans W., *Menagerie in F sharp*, Garden City 1977
          ——*Best Regards to Aida*, New York 1968
Kessler, Harry Graf, *Tagebücher 1918–1937*, Frankfurt 1961. Transl.: *In the Twenties: The Diaries of Harry Kessler*, New York 1971
Lerner, Alan Jay, *The Street Where I Live*, New York 1978
Logan, Joshua, *Josh*, New York 1976
Rice, Elmer, *Minority Report*, New York 1963
Stuckenschmidt, Hans H., *Zum Hören Geboren*, Munich 1979
Vogel, Wladimir, *Schriften und Aufzeichnungen über Musik*, Zurich 1977
Wagner-Régeny, Rudolf, *Begegnungen*, Berlin 1968
Weisgal, Meyer W., *So Far*, New York 1971

Zuckmayer, Carl, *Als wär's ein Stück von mir*, Vienna 1966. Transl.: *A Part of Myself*, London 1970

Zweig, Stefan, *Die Welt von Gestern*, London 1945. Transl.: *The World of Yesterday*, London 1943

Biographies, Critical Studies, Secondary Literature in General

Baxter, J., *The Hollywood Exiles*, London 1976

Beaumont, A., *Busoni the Composer*, London 1985

Drew D. (ed.),*Über Kurt Weill*, Frankfurt 1975

A collection of articles and part-articles by various hands, intended for a German readership, with the non-German contributions, unfortunately, translated into German and thus deprived of their original flavour.

——*Kurt Weill: A Handbook*, London 1987.

An invaluable reference book to which all concerned with Weill's music are deeply indebted. All known works are listed and described in detail, with information on surviving sketches and autographs, dates of composition and first performances and other details. The book also contains interesting information on the many projects which Weill had in his mind at various times but never carried out.

Dümling, A., *Lasst euch nicht verführen. Brecht und die Musik*, Munich 1985

Einem, G.von and Melchinger, S. (eds), *Caspar Neher*, Velber 1966

Esslin, M., *Brecht: A Choice of Evils*, London 1959

——*Brecht: The Man and His Work*, London 1961

Fermi, L., *Illustrious Immigrants*, Chicago 1968

Hennenberg, F., *Das grosse Brecht-Liederbuch*, 3 vols, Berlin and Frankfurt 1984

A selection of 141 settings of Brecht's poems by Weill, Eisler, Dessau, Bruinier, Wagner-Régeny and Kurt Schwaen, with an exemplary commentary to each item.

Heyworth, P., *Otto Klemperer: His Life and Times*, Vol.I, Cambridge 1983

Hinton, S. (ed.), *Kurt Weill: The Threepenny Opera*, Cambridge 1990.

A range of historical, analytical and interpretative essays by various hands, providing a broad commentary on the work.

Jarman, D., *Kurt Weill. An Illustrated Biography*, London 1982

Kiaulehn, W., *Berlin: Schicksal einer Weltstadt*, Munich 1958

Kliemann, H., *Die Novembergruppe*, Berlin 1969

Kortländer, B., Meiszies, W., and Farneth, D. (eds), *Vom Kurfürstendamm zum Broadway. Kurt Weill (1900–1950)*, Düsseldorf 1990

A volume of essays (in, or translated into, German), with a good collection of accompanying photographs, playbills and other illustrations, published in connection with the exhibition which formed part of the Kurt Weill Festival in Düsseldorf in the spring of 1990.

Kowalke, K. H.,*Kurt Weill in Europe*, Ann Arbor 1979

A specialist's study concentrating on Weill's European music but packed with information of all kinds and especially noteworthy for the attention it pays to Weill's writings and for the range of its painstakingly collected material.

——(ed.), *A New Orpheus: Essays on Kurt Weill*, New Haven 1986

A collection of critical essays by various scholars, specialised in nature and providing much detailed information.

Laqueur, W., *Weimar. A Cultural History 1918–1933*, London 1974

Lucchesi, J. and Shull, R.K., *Musik bei Brecht. Mit einem Verzeichnis der Vertonungen*, Berlin 1988

Lyon, J.K., *Brecht in America*, Princeton 1980

Marx, H. (ed.), *Weill-Lenya*, New York 1976

A brochure of illustrations and short texts to accompany an exhibition mounted by the Goethe House in New York.

O'Connor, J. and Brown, L., *The Federal Theatre Project*, London 1980

Panofsky, W., *Protest in der Oper. Das provokative Musiktheater der zwanziger Jahre*, Munich 1966

Reed, R., *Do You Sleep in the Nude?*, New York 1969

Contains a journalist's interview with Lotte Lenya in which many of her often-quoted recollections of life with Weill are recorded.

Sanders, R., *The Days Grow Short: The Life and Music of Kurt Weill*, New York 1980

A very full-length 'popular' biography, in the best sense, especially informative on the works of Weill's American years. Based almost entirely on secondary sources, it still manages to be a most useful book, particularly in its accounts of circumstantial evidence.

Schebera, J., *Kurt Weill: Eine Biographie in Texten, Bildern und Dokumenten*, Leipzig 1990

The illustrations, which take up a large part of the book, are a treasure trove.

Schürer, E., *Georg Kaiser*, New York 1971

Shivers, A.S., *The Life of Maxwell Anderson*, New York 1983

Spoto, D., *Lenya: A Life*, Boston 1989

Stuckenschmidt, H.H., *Ferruccio Busoni*, transl. S. Morris, London 1970

Volker, K., *Bertolt Brecht, Eine Biographie*, Munich 1976

Wagner, G., *Brecht und Weill: Das musikalische Zeittheater*, Munich 1977

Willett, J., *The Theatre of Bertolt Brecht*, London 1959

——*The New Society 1911–1933: Art and Politics in the Weimar Period*, London 1979

Index